Alternatives for Welfare Policy

Demographic change and increasingly international markets are putting severe pressure on developed welfare states in the OECD countries. The contributors to this book assess the magnitude of these challenges and discuss in depth, and in concrete terms, what policy options are open to meet them. Looking at public service production, social insurance, tax policy and debt policy, they examine the main costs and benefits associated with an extensive welfare state and ask whether the same objectives can be reached with a welfare regime that is less costly. They also discuss whether the current organisation of the welfare state is capable of meeting future challenges facing a changing society. This rigorous analysis draws on empirical material from OECD countries with a focus on the Scandinavian countries.

TORBEN M. ANDERSEN is Professor of Economics in the Department of Economics at the University of Aarhus, Denmark.

PER MOLANDER has worked at the Swedish Ministry of Finance and is currently a Private Consultant at Mapsec. He is author of the book *Turning Sweden Around* (with A. Lindbeck et al.), 1994.

Alternatives for Welfare Policy

*Coping with internationalisation and
demographic change*

Torben M. Andersen and Per Molander (eds.)

CAMBRIDGE UNIVERSITY PRESS
Cambridge, New York, Melbourne, Madrid, Cape Town, Singapore, São Paulo

Cambridge University Press
The Edinburgh Building, Cambridge CB2 8RU, UK

Published in the United States of America by Cambridge University Press, New York

www.cambridge.org
Information on this title: www.cambridge.org/9780521814065

First published 2003
This digitally printed version 2007

A catalogue record for this publication is available from the British Library

ISBN 978-0-521-81406-5 hardback
ISBN 978-0-521-04719-7 paperback

Contents

Contributors

TORBEN M. ANDERSEN is professor of economics at the University of Aarhus, Denmark, and research fellow at the Centre for Economic Policy Research. His research interests are in international integration and the welfare state, labour markets and product market integration, and wage and price formation.

FREDRIK ANDERSSON is associate professor of economics at Lund University. His main fields of interest are in public economics and economics of organisations.

CARL EMMERSON is programme director of research on public finances and pensions at the Institute for Fiscal Studies, London.

MARTIN FLODÉN is assistant professor at the Stockholm School of Economics and research affiliate at the CEPR.

STEFAN FÖLSTER is assistant professor in economics and chief economist at the Confederation of Swedish Enterprise. His research has mainly concerned public economics and industrial economics.

ROBERT GIDEHAG is chief economist at the Swedish Research Institute of Trade. His main field of interest is public economics and the tax system.

BERND HUBER is professor of economics at the University of Munich. His main field of interest is public economics.

KAI A. KONRAD is professor of economics at the Freie Universität Berlin and director of the unit 'Market Processes and Governance' at the Social Science Research Centre at Berlin. His main field of interest is public economics.

THOMAS LINDH is professor of economics at Uppsala University and research director at the Institute for Futures Studies in Stockholm. His main research interests are structural growth models and demographic effects on the macroeconomy.

PER MOLANDER, currently adviser in developing and transitional economies, has worked for the Swedish government, responsible for reforms of agricultural policy and the central government budget process. Publications include game theory and institutional reform.

ERIK NORRMAN is doctor of economics and works at the University of Lund. His main field of interest is in public economics.

MIKE ORSZAG is head of research at Watson Wyatt. His research concerns the design of pension systems.

MÅRTEN PALME is associate professor at the Department of Economics, University of Stockholm. He has published extensively on labour economics, economics of education, income distribution and social insurance.

PEDER PEDERSEN is professor of economics at the University of Aarhus, Denmark. His research is focused on labour economics – labour demand, income distribution and mobility, and migration.

PIERRE PESTIEAU is professor of economics at the University of Liège. He is a member of CORE and Delta and a research fellow of the CEPR. His main field is public economics.

JØRN RATTSØ is professor of economics at the Norwegian University of Science and Technology, Trondheim. His main research interests include public finance and fiscal federalism.

HOWARD REED is programme director of research on work and incomes at the Institute for Fiscal Studies, London.

KLAS RIKNER has a PhD in economics from the University of Lund. His dissertation is devoted to the economics of sickness insurance.

MARIANNE RØED is researcher at the Institute of Social Research in Oslo, Norway. Her main research interest is in micro-incentives to migration.

LENA SCHRÖDER is head of the Division of Social Analysis at the Swedish Board of Integration. Her research has been in the area of labour market policy.

DENNIS J. SNOWER is professor of economics at Birkbeck College, University of London. His research has concerned macroeconomic theory and labour economics.

LARS SÖDERSTRÖM is professor at the Department of Economics at the University of Lund, Sweden. His main research interests are in the economics of the welfare state, public management and fiscal federalism.

ANN-CHARLOTTE STÅHLBERG is associate professor of economics at the Swedish Institute for Social Research, Stockholm University, Sweden. Her main research interests are the economics of social insurance, non-wage benefits differentials and income distribution.

INGEMAR SVENSSON is researcher at the Swedish National Social Insurance Board.

Preface

High levels of ambition for the public sector in combination with slow economic growth and various economic shocks have led to increasing strain on public finances in the OECD countries during the last couple of decades. Since the tax burden is already high and under both internal and external pressure, from distortions and tax base mobility respectively, the adjustment is by no means easy. Although some policy initiatives have been taken, e.g. in EU countries that have been involved in the Maastricht process, the underlying pressure on public finances remains and is expected to grow in the future. A number of independent studies from *inter alia* the OECD, the EU Commission and the World Bank have highlighted the problems associated with ageing populations. Increased mobility across borders – resulting from changes in both technological change, economic structure and policy – will make it increasingly more difficult for countries that deviate from the mainstream with respect to social benefits or tax ratio. At the same time, demand for public services and social security remains strong in the industrialised countries; there seems on the whole to be little political preparedness to alter or redefine established welfare political goals.

The project leading up to the present volume started in the international discussion on future pressures on the public sector in developed industrial countries. One aim has been to appreciate the order of magnitude of these pressures, as a basis for the policy discussion. But the central goal has been to discuss, in as concrete terms as possible, how to reconcile the pressures envisaged with established goals for welfare policy. We believe that time is ripe for this fairly down-to-earth policy discussion, given that the problems have been fairly well analysed, and that the spectrum of countermeasures is also fairly well known, at least in principle. This also implies that we have set ourselves a more difficult, and we believe also more relevant, task of finding policies that do not require drastic departures from established policies, even though none of the policy alternatives discussed is politically easy.

The problems discussed are international, and it has been our ambition to analyse them in an international perspective. Nonetheless, there is some focus on the Scandinavian countries, justified by the leading role that these countries have played in the development of welfare policy in the post-war era. Of the twenty-plus researchers engaged in the project, about half are Swedish and half non-Swedish, so as to guarantee a many-faceted analysis and cross-fertilisation of ideas and solutions.

The research group has profited from discussions with a reference group chaired by former minister of finance Kjell-Olof Feldt. Valuable comments on the manuscript were given by Robert Boije, Stefan Lundgren, Edward Palmer and Kjetil Storesletten.

The project has been financially supported by the Bank of Sweden Tercentenary Foundation, the Jan Wallander and Tom Hedelius Foundation, the Marcus and Amalia Wallenberg Memorial Foundation, and the Trygg-Hansa Research Foundation.

The SNS Centre for Business and Policy Studies assumes no responsibility for the conclusions and recommendations presented; the authors alone are to be held accountable.

Stockholm, September 2002   TORBEN M. ANDERSEN,
                                               PER MOLANDER

1 Introduction

Torben M. Andersen and Per Molander

1.1 The public sector and the welfare state

The growth in the relative size of the public sector is one of the most important facts of economic development during the second half of the twentieth century. Growing public sectors not only reflect a substantial improvement in material wellbeing, but are also in their own right considered to be a core element in the development of so-called welfare societies, purposely designed to affect the allocation and distribution of resources.

The growth of the public sector has always been controversial, since it raises fundamental questions concerning the balance between the private and the public spheres. The welfare states that have developed reflect political compromises between markets and public intervention, and the route taken differs between countries, depending on power balance, institutional heritage and other factors. At present these issues are increasing in importance. The welfare state faces a number of challenges, which lead many to question whether it can be maintained in its present form.

Traditionally, the main reason given for state intervention has been redistribution, and the choices made have been interpreted as reflecting a particular trade-off between equity and efficiency (Okun 1975). Even in the absence of market failures, an outcome may be considered unacceptable on political or ethical grounds. In such cases, public intervention can be justified, but it comes at a cost. In this perspective, the size of the welfare state is basically a political question. Cross-country comparisons of socio-economic performance would indicate the price of equalisation, as a basis for identifying the trade-off.

There are numerous studies correlating growth rates and the size of the public sector, as measured by expenditure-to-GDP ration or tax ratios. The results are mixed. Some studies have found a negative growth impact from a large public sector (e.g. Barro 1991; Engen and Skinner 1992; Hansson and Henrekson 1994; Grier 1997), whereas others have failed to find such connections (e.g. Easterly and Rebelo 1993; Mendoza, Milesi-Ferreti and Asea 1997). There are several reasons for this apparent inconsistency. First, if there is a negative impact, we should expect to find it most pronounced in developed countries with large public sectors, so the country sample is important for the possibility of establishing stable relationships. Second, the size of the public sector is a crude measure, which includes very diverse activities – consumption, transfers, interest on public debt, etc. – some of which are detrimental to growth whereas others are conducive to growth. Third, variations in the administrative handling of transfers and taxes create artificial differences. Some countries tend to tax household transfers, whereas others do not, and others still subsidise certain households via tax expenditures (see section 1.3 below). Also tax ratio comparisons are marred by statistical problems (Volkerink and de Haan 2001). Fourth, there may be substantial socio-economic effects associated with a large public sector without this necessarily affecting the growth rate or other macroeconomic key variables.

Quite apart from these technical reasons for the difficulty of finding stable relationships, there are fundamental economic reasons why no simple conclusions can be drawn. Public intervention may be justified by the presence of market failures, the aim being to make the economy work more efficiently. Such failures can take many forms, including *imperfect competition, incomplete information, incomplete market structures* and various forms of *transactions costs*. Market failures in the provision of insurance are particularly important in a discussion of the welfare state, since many public sector activities can be interpreted as social insurance. The public sector offers services and transfers if various contingencies are realised through life, and part of this insurance is offered for circumstances which cannot be handled by private insurance markets. Modern economic theory has shown that this applies not only to public services, transfers and taxation (Varian 1980; Barr 1992; Sinn 1995) but also more generally to various institutional arrangements, e.g. in the labour market (Agell 2000). The implications of the public sector are both microeconomic, in terms of coping with individual risks, and macroeconomic, by affecting exposure to aggregate risks (Andersen 2002).

The social insurance implications make it difficult to separate redistributive from efficiency-related arguments for public-sector activities. The existence of social insurance schemes may enhance efficiency. On the other hand, to the extent that insurance schemes are not fully actuarial, that is, premia do not fully reflect differences in risk, there is systematic redistribution within the insurance system. Indeed, as shown by Pestieau (chapter 10), there are efficiency arguments for such arrangements. This shows that the traditional distinction between public sector activities aiming at correcting market failures and those aiming at redistributive objectives is problematic.

Another aim of public intervention is to secure the supply of certain *basic services* irrespective of household income. A reasonable supply of such services may require resources beyond the means of many households, in which case we are back to the redistributive argument. In some cases, those affected may not be fully autonomous decision-makers; this goes for children, and parents cannot always be perfect representatives of their children. As an example, it is generally recognised that a binding, collective decision about basic education is necessary to guarantee a minimal level common to all citizens. In the case of pensions, there is a moral hazard or myopia argument for mandatory schemes; some individuals may abstain from saving in the conviction that they will be taken care of for altruistic reasons. In the area of cultural policy, paternalistic arguments are often advanced; this seems more difficult to defend on a general welfare-theoretical basis.

Whatever arguments of efficiency and/or equality can be presented for public intervention, there are several reasons for concern. First, it does not follow that any form of public intervention is justified; to the risk of market failure corresponds a risk of political failure. The proper intervention in the market mechanism often puts unrealistically high demands on the informational base of the decision-makers. Second, the need and scope for public intervention depends on the way in which the economy functions. Given that society is always changing, policies that were well justified in the past may have become obsolete. Third, although market failures may justify public intervention, a number of political questions remain concerning the scope, character and level of ambition of this intervention. Indeed, if the debate about the public sector has been intensified in recent years, it is because there is a widespread feeling that costs of current policies are not fully outweighed by the benefits. A number of challenges, new and old, now have to be faced by the decision-makers in the public sphere.

1.2   Challenges for the welfare state

Among the reasons for a renewed interest in the organisation of the welfare state, we highlight five. Two of them – the general trade-off between *costs and benefits* and the so-called *Baumol's disease* – are classical. What justifies another look at these two aspects of public-sector design is simply the fact that they are underlying tendencies, the effects of which accumulate and therefore become more pronounced over time. The next two – *internationalisation* and *demographic change* – can be considered external to the public sector (at least to the first approximation). The final

Table 1.1 *Administrative cost in social security systems in per cent of the amounts transferred for a number of OECD countries*

Australia	2.4
Canada	4.1
France	4.9
Germany	2.8
Netherlands	3.2
Norway	1.9
Sweden	2.5
Switzerland	7.0
UK	4.7
USA	4.1

Source: Mitchell et al. (1994), based on ILO material.

factor to be taken into consideration is the way public-sector arrangements affect *value formation*.

Costs and benefits of the welfare state

The benefits from the welfare state are multifarious – basic services in education and care, income security, and a basic safety net strong enough to guarantee a reasonable level of social cohesion. These benefits do not come for free, however, but have to be traded against other goods and services that have to be sacrificed. The costs of the welfare state can be sorted roughly into three different categories: administrative costs, leakage and incentive-related costs. *Administrative* costs are the easiest to measure. As shown in table 1.1, they normally account for a few per cent of the amounts transferred in social security systems, in some countries more.

Notice that costs are in per cent of amounts transferred, so in absolute terms, countries with large flows such as the Scandinavian ones fare worse in the comparison. Even in relative terms, there is no clear correlation between social insurance system design and costs. Australia, Germany and Sweden represent very different traditions but have nonetheless similar relative costs of administration.

Leakage problems (dead-weight losses) arise from the difficulty of targeting subsidies or transfers with full accuracy. Subsidies to goods or services, for instance in the health care sector, will affect price formation in that sector; as a consequence, some of subsidy will accrue to the producers. Likewise, transfers will sometimes end up among non-intended recipients. These costs are more difficult to estimate than administrative costs, but conservative estimates indicate that they are one order of magnitude larger than the latter.

Incentive-related costs are the most important, and at the same time the most difficult to estimate. Basically, they arise because subsidies, transfers and taxes affect the behaviour of citizens. A *service* that is supplied at a fraction of its cost of production or for free will exhibit excess demand – by how much will depend on the service in question, and is in practice very difficult to estimate.

Social security affects the choice between working and not working over all time horizons – day-to-day, month to year, and life cycle time spans. This is the classical moral hazard problem encountered in any insurance sector. Estimates of these effects vary. Atkinson and Mogensen (1993) report relatively limited effects. By contrast, a number of micro studies have identified significant effects. The organisation of sickness insurance, for instance, will affect everyday choices, depending on remuneration levels, number of waiting days, requirements on medical examination, etc. Johansson and Palme (1998) report a significant effect on absenteeism from rule changes, when heterogeneity of the workforce is taken into account.

At the intermediate level, unemployment insurance can be expected to affect the willingness to change employment and to commute, the intensity in job search, etc. Holmlund, in a survey of the literature on labour-market insurance (Holmlund 1998), summarises the state-of-the-art by saying that there are significant effects on the incentive to work but no consensus as to the size of these effects. More recently, a specific study of a temporary rule change in labour-market insurance (Carling et al. 1999) showed a fairly strong influence of the benefit level on the intensity of search for a new job among unemployed.

In the lifecycle perspective finally, pension benefits have been shown to affect the decision to retire. Actual retirement age has been decreasing steadily in the OECD countries, and there is a strong connection between this parameter and the incentive to continue working (Gruber and Wise 1999).

Taxes affect economic incentives directly – by reducing the interest in activities or goods that are taxed. In some cases, such as alcohol or environmental damage, this is a desired effect. More often, taxes have a purely fiscal motive – to finance public expenditure – and a large effort has gone into estimating the socio-economic cost of taxes, as well as designing tax systems that attempt to minimise these costs. Estimates of the cost associated with tax extraction – *the excess burden of taxation* – vary a lot, and depend both on the tax base, the tax level and the purpose for which the taxes levied are used. Estimates for the mid-1990s from Sweden made for the Committee on Tax Reform Evaluation (Agell et al. 1998; Aronsson and Palme 1998) indicate an excess burden of 20 to 30 per cent for the general income tax for mid-range assumptions on the labour supply elasticity (0.11). Uncertainties are large, however; an elasticity of 0.25 trebles the excess burden. Further, the non-linear character of the excess burden makes the cost rise faster than proportionally to tax rates and incomes; calculations on the basis of average incomes will therefore underestimate the true cost.

An important reason why trade-offs between costs and benefits are particularly cumbersome in the public sector is the way in which decisions are made. Households and private companies meet hard budget constraints, whereas public decisions are often marred by a certain asymmetry; benefits are visible and accrue to certain stakeholder groups, whereas costs are diffuse. The problem is that the individual decision-maker does not fully take into account the effect that her own decisions have on the common budget. This so-called *common-pool problem* calls for countermeasures in the area of institutions. A well-designed budget process can compensate for the asymmetry and induce the decision-makers in the direction of meeting a more reasonably balanced trade-off.

Baumol's disease

Baumol's disease – a steady increase in the relative prices of certain services – stems from the fact that certain activities are more difficult to rationalise than others. It is an empirical fact that a number of activities of this kind appear in the public sector. If wages followed productivity this would not be a problem, but this does not seem to be the case in the public sector. Productivity development, as far as it can be traced (Murray 1993), is sluggish and to a considerable extent determined by exogenous factors such as budget restrictions and demography. The traditional presumption of zero public-sector productivity increase seems to be not too far off the mark, but development has been uneven across sub-sectors.

Wage formation in the public sector, on the other hand, largely follows that of the private sector (Holmlund and Ohlsson 1992; Jacobson and Ohlsson 1994). If productivity in the public sector is roughly constant while wages increase, the relative prices of the service produced will also increase. If the service level is kept constant, there will be an upward pressure on the public expenditure level. When public services are financed by proportional income taxes (as is the case, for example, for local taxes in Sweden), automatic revenue increases will match this upward pressure, and a constant tax ratio will be sufficient to compensate for the Baumol effect. If, by contrast, there is a preference for maintaining a fixed relation between private and public consumption, there will be a persistent upward trend in the tax ratio.

Internationalisation

While a process of international integration is an integral part of post-war economic development, there is no doubt that the process has been intensified in recent years due to both political decisions and technological change. Political decisions have been taken to reduce various forms of barriers to trade and to promote economic integration. Trade links are developing at a more rapid pace, and information flows globally at the speed of light at very low costs. As a result the economic sphere is expanding beyond the sphere of any national state (see further chapter 2).

The international integration process affects the public sector through many channels. The most obvious effect is that tax revenues in high-tax countries are negatively affected by increased mobility of important tax bases and that the distortions from some forms of taxation increase. But the need and scope for various welfare activities may also be affected, given that increased economic integration changes both economic structures and the character and frequency of shocks to which the national economy is subject. The expenditure side may also be affected to the extent that differences between national social security systems affect migration patterns (social shopping). In short, international integration implies that welfare policies in different countries become more interdependent.

Demographic change

Health care, care for the elderly and pensions are important building blocks in the welfare state that account for a large proportion of total expenditure. These services are heavily age-dependent, and demographic change now poses challenges in most developed industrial nations (World Bank 1994; OECD 1999). In 1960 average male longevity in the OECD area was 67 years, 46 of which were spent on work. Today, average longevity has increased to 74, average time in education has increased, and the working period has shrunk to 37 years (OECD 1999). These changes have had dramatic consequences for family life and social relations, and also for public finances. Demographic projections for the twenty-first century show beyond doubt that the combined effects of varying cohort sizes, increasing educational periods, early retirement and continued increased longevity will lead to severe strain on public finances over the whole OECD area.

Old-age pensions in the agrarian society were naturally of a pay-as-you-go form within the family or local community. Given structural changes in society in the form of industrialisation and urbanisation as well as increased longevity, this model was no longer feasible, and a need for social insurance developed. An attractive solution was to introduce a collective pay-as-you-go system, since it takes time to build up a funded system. Such a system is very vulnerable to decreases in population growth, however, as the return is basically equal to population growth, and this may fall short of the desired path for pensions.

The effects of demographic changes go beyond the direct effects on public expenditures. Aggregate labour productivity, saving, and other important macro-variables are affected by variations in cohort size (see chapter 3). Consequently, the demographic impact on the way in which economies function is multi-dimensional.

Dynamics of the welfare state

Social behaviour even in the economic arena is not determined by economic incentives alone. Norms play a significant role. In many cases, norms can be considered as given, and their effect is imbedded in the behaviour observed. In a longer time perspective, it is not always possible to defend such a simplification.

A crucial factor is that norm-dependent choices are typically contingent on other people's behaviour. A common rule is to choose a particular alternative provided that sufficiently many others do likewise. Such choice rules, when universally applied, often yield multiple social equilibria (Schelling 1975).

In the area of welfare policy, important examples of norm-dependent behaviour are work supply, consumption and saving (Lindbeck 1997; Lindbeck, Nyberg and Weibull 1999). Norms against cheating are another case in point. The contingent character of the choices involved can lead to rapid deterioration of performance, such as discontinuities and hysteresis in expenditure levels and tax revenues. In order to retreat from an unsustainable combination of transfer levels and tax revenues, it may in such cases be necessary to reduce benefits and taxes simultaneously.

This sort of model is inherently difficult to test empirically, in particular when long-term value change is in focus. There is nonetheless some evidence that work norms in the younger generation can be affected by growing up with parents who are strongly dependent on transfers. A Danish study (Christoffersen 1996) reports that the probability of being unemployed as grown-up is significantly higher if one or both parents have been subject to durable unemployment while the persons in focus are in their teens, controlling for other background variables.

Given these threats and challenges to the welfare state, there are good reasons to consider reform possibilities. To this end it is necessary to start by identifying the basic problems which the welfare state faces, and from there proceed to consider possible reform avenues that can be pursued. A commonly heard proposal is to 'roll back the welfare state' – Tanzi and Schuknecht (2000) present this view – but defensive economic arguments for the welfare state have also been put forward (Atkinson 1999).

One of the basic premises of the present study is that there are strong reasons why the welfare state has been developed, and why the public sector has been growing. Much of this development is clearly based on genuine demand, and there is no need to invoke public-choice type explanations for the expansion of the state. To the extent that lobbying efforts among interest groups, bureaucratic expansion and similar factors have had an impact, this merely adds to a development that would have occurred anyway. Nonetheless, the size of the problems and the strength of the forces of change that we now see are sufficient justification to reconsider seriously policy choices made in the past. Hence, the present analysis asks the more difficult but also policy-relevant question of whether there are ways to reform the welfare state that do not jeopardise its basic objectives.

1.3   Welfare states in international comparison

Discussing the problems and challenges faced by the welfare state does not make sense unless we make precise what is understood by a welfare state. By *welfare state* is commonly understood in broad terms the institutions, norms and rules in society aiming at correcting the outcome of an unregulated market economy and in particular aiming at a more egalitarian outcome. Although parts of the public sector are an essential and large element of the welfare state, it is misleading to equalise the two, given that the objectives of the welfare state go beyond the activities of the public sector in a narrow sense. There are of course also public sector activities that have very little to do with welfare policy as we normally understand it. Therefore the term *welfare society* may be more appropriate than the welfare state.

Welfare-political strategies

Moreover, the above definition is not precise since there are different ways of organising a welfare state. Esping-Andersen (1990) made an often-used distinction between three different types of welfare states or models, namely, the liberal, the corporatist and the universal model. The different models are distinguished by the weight given to the market, the civil society (family, church, friends, private organisations, etc.) and the state in providing social services.

Some countries, mainly Anglo-Saxon, have opted for a relatively small public sector, leaving plenty of room for traditional solutions and markets. Other countries, particularly in Central Europe, have given an important role to employers, thus stressing the link between work and welfare. In Scandinavia, by contrast, the state has developed encompassing collective welfare systems, still mainly based on work-life participation, but with limited room for private alternatives or supplements.

In the liberal welfare model the state plays a limited and well-defined role in the sense of providing the ultimate floor in cases where the market and civil society do not suffice. State-provided benefits are often targeted, and concern about work incentives plays a dominant role. The corporatist or continental European model relies on the family and employers as the backbones of society and therefore also as providers of social services. In its modern form, private insurance schemes play a crucial role, and they are mostly tied to labour-market participation. The activities of the state tend to be directed towards families rather than individuals. Finally, the universal or Scandinavian model has the state in a crucial role as supplier of social services. Benefits tend to be defined at the individual level, but with differences depending on the individual's labour market history. The main financial sources are taxes and fees.

Obviously no country can be classified unambiguously as belonging to one of these prototypes of welfare models, and the relative importance of the three pillars has changed over time. Nonetheless, it is clear that this classification captures important differences between, say, the welfare model in the US, the UK, Germany and Sweden.

Comparing welfare states

Historically, the major burden of welfare state arrangements has rested on the civil society. Societal changes such as industrialisation and urbanisation have weakened many traditional networks. Further, the ability of the household to meet expectations has been further impaired by the shrinking average size of the household. In the year 2000, the share of single-person households in Sweden was 54 per cent, corresponding to 28 per cent of the population (Statistics Sweden 2002: 65).

This development also implies that many activities cannot ideally be left to the civil society. *Insurance* problems are more effectively dealt with

Table 1.2 *Public-sector size relative to GDP*

Country	1966	1976	1986	1996
Denmark	33.1	46.1	50.8	52.2
Germany[1]	33.2	40.9	37.7	38.1
France	35.7	42.7	44.0	45.7
Italy	28.8	35.3	36.1	43.2
Sweden	36.9	54.1	53.0	52.0
UK	31.5	41.0	37.6	36.0
US	25.3	33.6	28.9	28.5
Japan	18.4	23.6	28.4	28.4

[1] For 1966–86 only West Germany.
Note: Measure by total taxes relative to GDP.
Source: Statistics Denmark.

in a large collective group over which to pool risks rather than within, for example, a household. Both the market and the state can therefore offer superior solutions, the choice between the two being a matter for further deliberation. *Redistribution* will not be carried out to an extent corresponding to the public support for such activities in the absence of a state, the main reason being the collective nature of redistribution. Formally, the income distribution is a collective good (Thurow 1971). A different way of phrasing the interdependent nature of redistribution is that the support for redistributional activities is conditional on other people's support; in the absence of coordination, redistribution will therefore be under-supplied (Friedman 1962).

By consequence, the market and the state have taken over a number of tasks previously associated with the civil society. While countries differ in the roles they have assigned to the market and the public sector, it is a common phenomenon that the public sector has grown. Table 1.2 shows the development of the size of the public sector relative to GDP for selected OECD countries from 1966 to 1996. All countries have experienced substantial growth in their public sector. The EU average was 42.4 per cent in 1996, whereas it was 37.7 per cent for all OECD countries.

The increase reflects an increase in both public consumption and in transfers, although the latter have increased more in recent decades. For most countries one finds that the growth of public consumption relative to GDP levels off in the mid-1970s, whereas the growth of transfer payments drives the subsequent growth of the public sector. During the 1990s, many countries have emphasised the need to consolidate public finances, and growth has levelled off.

Table 1.3 *Social expenditure indicators, 1997 (per cent of GDP factor cost)*

Country	Gross public social expenditure	Net publicly mandated social expenditure	Net total social expenditure
Australia	18.7	18.8	21.9
Austria	28.5	23.9	24.6
Belgium	30.4	27.5	28.5
Canada	20.7	18.7	21.8
Denmark	35.9	26.9	27.5
Finland	33.3	24.8	25.6
Germany	29.2	27.9	28.8
Ireland	19.6	17.1	18.4
Italy	29.4	25.2	25.3
Japan	15.1	15.3	15.7
Netherlands	27.1	20.8	24.0
New Zealand	20.7	17.0	17.5
Norway	30.2	25.1	25.1
Sweden	35.7	28.7	30.6
UK	23.8	21.9	24.6
US	15.8	16.8	23.4

Source: Adema (2001).

In interpreting these figures two important caveats should be stressed. First, considering the gross expenditures of the public sector in a cross-country comparison may be misleading, as institutional arrangements may differ significantly. This measure depends critically on whether, for example, transfers are paid in net terms or in gross terms as taxable income. Some countries use subsidies in the form of tax deductions, which further distorts the comparison. Howard (1997) estimates that welfare-related tax deductions in the US amounted to 346 billion dollars, close to one-half of visible welfare-related expenditures over the public budget.

Correcting for these implies that the differences are much smaller than the gross figures reported in table 1.2 indicate. To see this, consider social expenditures in table 1.3. When adjustments have been made for differences in bookkeeping practices and administrative routines, not only are differences between nations substantially reduced but the ranking with respect to public-sector size is also altered. The first row gives the *gross* expenditures in the public sector to social purposes (consumption and transfers). The next row gives the *net* public mandated social expenditures, which are derived by correcting for taxes (direct and indirect) and social contributions, and by adding mandatory private social payments.

The final row adds voluntary private expenditures to arrive at the net total social expenditures. The table shows that the differences in net publicly mandated social expenditures between most European countries level out. This suggests that the public sector problems discussed in this book are, or soon will be, on the policy agenda in many countries.

Secondly, despite the growth of the public sector it would be misleading to conclude that the role of the civil society has become trivial. Notwithstanding the changes reported above, the family remains dominant if judged on the basis of working hours. In 1993, Swedish households spent 7 billion hours on household work and 5.9 billion hours on salaried work in the private and public sectors (SOU 1997: 17). The household is also an important unit for redistribution. The Gini coefficient of disposable income drops substantially in the transition from individuals to household consumption units, which testifies to the important role played by the family in redistributing material resources.

The remarks made above on the effects of welfare state activities on the economy and on the data immediately suggest that one should not expect to find significant effects on economic growth rates and other important macroeconomic variables from the choice of welfare-political regime. This suggests that it is not very interesting to address the challenges faced by the welfare state by posing the question of whether the public sector is too large. It is necessary to consider in more detail the precise structure and the mechanisms through which the welfare state works. This can only be done at the microlevel. It is the positive and negative incentives facing single households, companies and other agents that determine the dynamics of the welfare systems and ultimately of the economic system at large.

When evaluating the achievements of different welfare policies, a number of indicators are relevant. This could for instance be in terms of inequality – a central issue in the welfare state. Table 1.4 gives some standard measures of inequality for selected industrial countries. While these data might suggest that countries having strong universal elements in their welfare policies may be more successful in reducing inequality, it is obvious that unambiguous conclusions cannot be drawn. The outcome is in part determined by the inequality measure chosen. Moreover, in order to evaluate the effects of given welfare regimes, one has to control for various background variables. At the aggregate level this is a very difficult, if not impossible task.

While suggestive, the aggregate data considered in this section reveal that no simple conclusions can be drawn by simple comparisons across countries. A more disaggregated approach has to be followed to identify possible reform areas.

Table 1.4 *Indicators of inequality – selected countries*

Country	Ratio of high to low incomes	Gini coefficient	Poverty gap
Australia (1999)	4.26	0.31	1.3
Belgium (1992)	2.76	0.23	n.a.
Canada (1991)	3.86	0.30	1.4
Denmark (1992)	2.84	0.24	n.a.
Finland (1991)	2.71	0.22	n.a.
France (1994)	3.51	0.29	1.3
Germany (1984)	2.98	0.26	0.7
Norway (1991)	2.79	0.23	0.5
Netherlands (1991)	2.94	0.25	0.8
Spain (1990)	4.04	0.31	n.a.
Sweden (1992)	2.77	0.23	0.9
Switzerland (1982)	3.43	0.31	1.0
UK (1986)	3.80	0.30	1.2
USA (1991)	5.67	0.34	2.5

Note: The first column shows the ratio between the 9th decile and the 1st decile.
Sources: Smeeding (1996) (columns 1 and 2); Mitchell et al. (1994) (column 3; based on LIS statistics).

1.4   Four fundamental questions

The present study aims at analysing the role of the public sector as a crucial element of welfare societies, and at identifying possible reforms to address the challenges outlined in section 1.2. The time perspective that we have in mind is about three decades, although this varies depending on the issues analysed. In the context of demographic change, the horizon is naturally half a century or longer.

The roles of state and market

The most fundamental question to ask, before embarking upon discussions about efficiency, excess burdens etc., is of course what social activities the state should be involved in at all. The classical categories mentioned above – insurance, redistribution and basic social services – give some indications, though this is but a first step towards decisions about the scope for public action in given areas. Are problems of adverse selection large enough to justify state financing and management of social insurance? What is the justification for state subsidies in the area of cultural policy?

To complicate matters further, it is in many cases very difficult to disentangle the market from the state. If the rules under which a market operates are laid down by the state, the size of the public sector may be minuscule, although public intervention is not.

Second, the distinction between markets and public sectors is often taken to suggest a distinction between an individualised and a collective system. But market activities may also have a collective element. Most obviously this is the case for all insurance activities that rely on risk sharing among a larger group. More generally, the market is not necessarily atomised and collectively bargained arrangements may play a crucial role also with respect to provision of social services. Collectively bargained insurance and pension schemes are an important example.

Third – as noted above – it is often impossible to make a sharp distinction between insurance and redistribution. Many arrangements including taxation (Varian 1980) and labour market institutions (Agell 2000), which usually are considered redistributive, also have the role of providing implicit insurance. Conversely, insurance systems that do not adequately account for systematic differences in risk profiles between various individuals – whether for lack of information or as a deliberate choice – will contain an element of redistribution. It is thus not possible to characterise one system as more redistributive than another simply because insurance arrangements are organised by the state. To the extent that, for example, taxation also provides social insurance, conventional measures of the distortionary effects of taxation may be misleading. Equally important, it is not possible to evaluate the efficiency properties without explicitly considering the roles of social insurance.

When considering reforms of the welfare state, it is thus essential to make a distinction between the following three roles: namely, that of *organising*, *financing* and *providing* particular services or activities. In some cases the state has all three roles, while in other cases it might only have the organising role, for example, by making certain types of insurance mandatory. In the latter case the state relies on the market for financing and provision, but still the market is not left on its own. In some cases the state may use only the financing instrument to achieve its goals, for example, by providing subsidies for certain activities or by levying special taxes on specific services or commodities. Thus the extent of public involvement cannot be judged simply from considering the relative size of the public sector. To this end it is essential to consider the organising role of the state which can be in the form of either public provision or mandatory provision via the market. Financing can have a universal element via general taxation or social security contributions, or be related to use through user payments of various forms. In the provision of services the public sector may rely on its own production or use private suppliers. The multiplicity of combinations along these three dimensions shows that the welfare state cannot be measured by the relative size of the public sector as measured in national accounts. This also points to a variety of reform possibilities, and in particular to that of reforming the public sector without necessarily jeopardising the overall objectives of the welfare state.

Organisation: centralised versus decentralised models

What are the pros and cons of a universal or centralised model relative to a model which is more decentralised (across groups or sectors), as is often the case for the corporatist welfare model, and definitely for the liberal model? Comparing a universal system to a decentralised system basically involves two fundamental issues: namely, the properties of the two systems with respect to risk diversification, and the distortions arising from the mode of financing social security broadly interpreted.

Consider, first, risk diversification. If various groups are affected differently by shocks, there is clearly a gain in terms of better risk diversification by organising social insurance at a centralised rather than at a decentralised level. This follows from basic principles of risk pooling. At what level economies of scale are exhausted depends on the risk under discussion. Health care insurance according to the Health Maintenance Organisation model requires about half a million individuals to be efficient. Unemployment, by contrast, is often driven by aggregate shocks, which implies that there is a case for pooling at the national level.

On the other hand, financing of social insurance involves – as does the financing of any insurance scheme – a 'common pool' problem or a tax externality. This is because all contribute to the system, but the link between contributions and benefits is not apparent to the single decision-maker. This creates a distortion – the single individual does not in her decision-making take fully into account the effects that contributions made in terms of, for example, tax or social security payments have for the common resources of the system. For private insurance this is known as the moral hazard problem. This distortion is clearly stronger in larger systems, given that the relation between contributions and benefits perceived by the single decision-maker is reduced, the larger the number of participants in the risk sharing arrangement. It follows that the distortions arising in a centralised system are potentially larger than those arising in a decentralised system.

Evaluating the pros and cons of the universal model relative to a more decentralised model from an efficiency point of view therefore becomes a question of weighting the relation between risk diversification achieved via the social insurance provided and the distortions arising from the financing of these activities. The universal model has the attraction that it achieves the most in terms of risk diversification – all are part of the risk sharing arrangement. On the other hand the distortions are larger under this system as the link between payments and benefits is weaker. Evaluating the universal model relative to a decentralised model thus involves a trade-off between risk sharing and tax distortions.

Related to this issue is the degree of centralisation within the public sector – the fiscal federalism design problem. The relation between the different layers in the public sector – municipalities, counties and state – reflects many concerns. Decentralisation allows municipalities to tailor their activities to the preferences of their constituency, whereas centralised solutions tend to be standardised and less flexible. A decentralised system allows less risk diversification and more heterogeneity among otherwise similar groups in society, something running counter to basic objectives in the welfare state. Further, a centralised system may be more cost effective to the extent that there are substantial fixed costs or economies of scale involved in public sector activities. A decentralised system may give rise to inefficiencies to the extent that there are substantial externalities involved among municipalities. Finally, the decentralised solution may allow for more institutional competition, which can be important for flexibility and adaptation in the public sector.

The process of international integration has raised a new question in this debate, to wit, that the expansion of the economic sphere may imply that the existing structure is too decentralised, that is, the relative size between the political and economic sphere is being affected. If so, it may be necessary to centralise fiscal policy, and perhaps even move some competence to a supra-national level. The latter applies in particular to issues in relation to taxation where increased mobility of certain tax bases increases the externalities between tax jurisdictions. Obviously, such changes raise deep questions of authority beside the economic ones.

Another argument suggests that, at least for certain tasks, it might be possible to allow for more decentralised or flexible solutions. Advances in information and communication technologies change some of the constraints that have supported more standardised solution which have tended to characterise centralised solutions in the past. Hence, more flexible and individualised systems are becoming possible.

Financing

The standard mode of financing public sector activities is by general taxation. Taxation affects economic incentives, which distorts decision-making, and the distortions tend to increase more than linearly in the tax rate (see above). Financial reforms are consequently an integral part of any consideration of possible avenues for welfare state reforms.

For public provision of services there are two main alternatives for financing. One is user payments in various forms, which on top of the revenue effect have the advantage that it strengthens the relationship between benefits and costs and thereby improves the allocation of economic resources. The disadvantage is that the distributional objectives pursued via general taxation are less easy to fulfil.

Another possibility is to extend the use of means testing to target public activities more directly to those who need them the most. Most welfare states transfer large gross amounts between individuals relative to the net amounts redistributed, implying that the distortions necessary in order to reach the distributional objectives might be excessive. On the other hand, means-tested benefits may raise administrative issues as well as the problem that composite marginal tax rates can be rather high. It has also been suggested that more targeting has political implications – to the effect that it would be more difficult to maintain such a system compared to a system with larger gross redistribution (see e.g. Korpi and Palme 1998). Both theoretical and empirical arguments can be advanced against this hypothesis, however; we will return to the choice of welfare-political strategy in the concluding chapter.

For public transfers one possibility is to make more use of explicit insurance and funding, that is, to decentralise the financing of (social) insurance. This does not mean that one necessarily has to privatise transfers. Welfare objectives can justify that such arrangements be made mandatory, and that they are associated with redistribution and risk sharing arrangements that will not necessarily arise in an unregulated market. Moreover, such systems can be market based or publicly administered. On top of reducing tax distortions this step may have the advantage of increasing visibility, that is, it is clearer to individuals how costs and benefits are related.

A more radical proposal is the introduction of so-called welfare accounts. The basic idea here is that many welfare arrangements perform a capital market function in the sense that the amounts transferred at a given point during a lifetime are unnecessarily large relative to the transfer over the life cycle needed to achieve a certain redistributional objective. By defining an account for each single individual it would be possible to 'internalise' these payments, and thereby reduce tax rates and the excess burden of the present system at the same time as the individual incentives are created to economise on transfers. An open question is whether one in such a system can attain the same risk diversification as in the current systems. Proposals have been made to introduce welfare accounts for specific areas or more generally for most of the activities currently financed via general taxation in the universal welfare model. Chapter 11 looks into the pros and cons of welfare accounts in more detail.

Provision

Even with public organisation and financing there is *a priori* no reason why the provision should also be public. Public organisations tend to be run on non-market principles, and while there are reasons for this in a few exceptional cases, there is no pertinent conflict between private provision and the objectives of the welfare state. Private provision implies that the advantages of the market mechanism can be exploited. On the other hand, contracting of any kind leads to principal/agent problems that have to be analysed in concrete terms in any given situation. There are consequently reasons to discuss the pros and cons of contracting out, in order to establish limits without ideologically predetermined positions.

1.5   Plan of the book

This book starts out by discussing some of the main challenges faced by the welfare state – internationalisation and demographic change. Chapter 2 examines the current process of internationalisation, with special reference to the problem of risk management. In the following chapter, Thomas Lindh examines the implications of demographic change for public finances. The main message is that aging has both a direct effect but also indirect effects on macroeconomic performance, due to shifts in the relative sizes of various age groups. Chapter 4, by Peder Pedersen, Marianne Røed and Lena Schröder, is devoted to a problem in the intersection of the preceding two – migration. Facing the argument that increased mobility also of human capital calls for substantial changes in fiscal policy, it seems necessary to establish the facts about current migration patterns, in particular with reference to highly educated groups.

The following two chapters are devoted to public service production. In chapter 5, Jørn Rattsø surveys the literature on efficiency of public service production and poses the question whether it can be improved by institutional reform, such as strengthening the budget process or switching to other tax bases for the financing of public services. Chapter 6, by Carl Emmerson and Howard Reed, analyses the consequences of increasing user fees in the financing of public services, that is, publicly produced private services that form the bulk of public consumption.

Given the importance of social insurance in public budgets, it should come as no surprise that no less than five chapters are devoted to this complex. Chapter 7, by Lars Söderström and Klas Rikner, tries to determine the scope for privatisation of social insurance, whereas Ann-Charlotte Ståhlberg in chapter 8 asks similar questions for collectively negotiated but privately produced social insurance. In chapter 9, Mårten Palme and Ingemar Svensson analyse the incentive problems of pension systems, with particular reference to the recent Swedish pension reform. The following chapter, written by Pierre Pestieau, asks what are the arguments for redistribution within a social insurance system. Textbooks normally declare that insurance systems should be actuarial and that redistribution is a matter for the tax-cum-transfer systems, but in a second-best world, things may turn out differently. The social insurance block is concluded by a chapter on welfare accounts by Stefan Fölster, Robert Gidehag, Mike Orszag and Dennis Snower.

Increased mobility of tax bases is perceived as one of the main threats to high-tax welfare states. This is the problem addressed by Bernd Huber and Erik Norrman in chapter 12. Mobility is not the only problem, however, and the authors discuss a range of problems in their contribution. Chapter 13 discusses a particular aspect of taxation, namely taxation of human capital. Fredrik Andersson and Kai Konrad focus on the problems of education investment from the perspective of human capital being the main source of finance for the public sector in developed countries, and also address issues related to the international mobility of labour.

Public debt policy has been a contentious issue against the background of soaring debts during the 1970s and 1980s. Fiscal discipline has improved during the last decade, in particular among the countries involved in the Maastricht process, but fairly little has been written on the choice of policy parameters. Should high taxes be used to reduce the public debt, or should tax rates be reduced in order to foster economic growth, assuming there is a positive connection? This is the problem analysed in chapter 14 by Martin Flodén, against the background of demographic changes envisaged.

The concluding chapter draws together the contributions from the various chapters in order to form a consistent set of alternatives for welfare policy discussion. We offer an indication of the effects on the public budget of the main factors of change, and provide building blocks for reform packages to meet these strains. As stated earlier, our time horizon is about three decades. Given that time-lags can be substantial for certain types of policy change – pensions system reform is a case in point – a thorough policy discussion is urgent.

References

Adema, W., 2001, *Net social expenditure* (2nd edition), DEELSA/ELSA/WD (2001) 5, Paris: OECD.

Agell, J., 2000, 'On the determinants of labour market institutions: rent-sharing vs. social insurance', Working Paper, Department of Economics, Uppsala University.

Agell, J., Englund, P. and Södersten, J., 1998, *Incentives and redistribution in the welfare state*, London: Macmillan Press.

Andersen, T. M., 2002, 'International integration, risk and the welfare state', *Scandinavian Journal of Economics*, 104, 343–64.

Aronsson, T. and Palme, M., 1998, 'A decade of tax and benefit reforms in Sweden: effects on labour supply, welfare and inequality', *Economica*, 65, 39–67.

Atkinson, A., 1999, *The economic consequences of rolling back the welfare state*, Cambridge, Mass.: MIT Press.

Atkinson, A. and Mogensen, G. V., 1993, *Welfare and work incentives: a north European perspective*, Oxford: Oxford University Press.

Barr, N., 1992, 'Economic theory and the welfare state: a survey and interpretation', *Journal of Economic Literature*, 30, 741–803.

Barro, R., 1991, 'Economic growth in a cross section of countries', *Quarterly Journal of Economics*, 106, 407–43.

Carling, K., Holmlund, B. and Vejsiu, A., 1999, *Do benefit cuts boost job findings?* IFAU Working Paper 1999: 8, Institute for Labour Market Policy Evaluation, Uppsala (accepted for publication in the *Economic Journal*).

Christoffersen, M. N., 1996, *Opvaekst med arbejdsloeshed* (Growing up with unemployment; with an English summary), Report 96: 14, Copenhagen: Institute of Social Research.

Easterly, W. and Rebelo, S., 1993, 'Fiscal policy and economic growth: an empirical investigation', *Journal of Monetary Economics*, 32, 417–58.

Engen, E. M. and Skinner, J., 1992, 'Fiscal policy and economic growth', NBER Working Paper No. 4223.

Esping-Andersen, G., 1990, *The three worlds of welfare capitalism*, Princeton: Princeton University Press.

Friedman, M., 1962, *Capitalism and freedom*, Chicago: University of Chicago Press.

Grier, K. B., 1997, 'Governments, unions and economic growth', in V. Bergström (ed.), *Government and growth*, Oxford: Clarendon Press.

Gruber, J. and Wise, D. A. (eds.), 1999, 'Introduction and summary', in *Social security and retirement around the world*, Chicago: University of Chicago Press.

Hansen, H., 2000, *Elements of social security*, The Danish National Institute of Social Research, Report 00: 07.

Hansson, P. and Henrekson, M., 1994, 'A new framework for testing the effect of government spending on growth and productivity', *Public Choice*, 81, 381–401.

Holmlund, B., 'Unemployment insurance in theory and practice', *Scandinavian Journal of Economics*, 100: 1, 113–41.

Holmlund, B. and Ohlsson, H., 1992, 'Wage linkages between private and public sectors in Sweden', *Labour* 6: 2, 3–17.

Howard, C., 1997, *The hidden welfare state: tax expenditures and social policy in the United States*, Princeton: Princeton University Press.

Jacobson, T. and Ohlsson, H., 'Long-run relations between private and public sector wages in Sweden', *Empirical Economics*, 19, 343–60.

Johansson, P. and Palme, M., 1998, *Assessing the effect of compulsory sickness insurance on worker absenteeism*, SSE/EFI Working Paper series on Economics and Finance No. 287, Stockholm School of Economics, Stockholm (to appear in the *Journal of Human Resources*).

Korpi, W. and Palme, J., 1998, 'The paradox of redistribution and strategies of equality...', *American Sociological Review*, 63, 661–87.

Lindbeck, A., 1997, 'Incentives and social norms in household behavior', *American Economic Review*, 87: 2, 370–7.

Lindbeck, A., Nyberg, S. and Weibull, J. W., 1999, 'Social norms and economic incentives in the welfare state', *Quarterly Journal of Economics*, 114: 1, 1–35.

Mendoza, E. G., Milesi-Ferretti, G. M. and Asea, P., 1997, 'On the ineffectiveness of tax policy in altering long-run growth...', *Journal of Public Economics*, 66: 1, 99–126.

Mitchell, D., Harding, A. and Gruen, F., 1994, 'Targeting welfare', *Economic Record*, 70: 210, 315–40.

Murray, R., 1993, *Productivity trends in the public sector in Sweden*. Report to the Expert Group on Public Finance, Ministry of Finance, Stockholm.

OECD, 1999, *Maintaining prosperity in an ageing society*, Paris: OECD.

Okun, A. M., 1975, *Equality and efficiency: the big trade-off*, Washington, DC: Brookings Institution.

Sandmo, A., 1998, 'The welfare state: a theoretical framework for justification and criticism', *Swedish Economic Policy Review*, 5: 1, 11–33.

Schelling, T., 1975, *Micromotives and macrobehavior*, New York: Norton.

Sinn, H.-W., 1995, 'A theory of the welfare state', *Scandinavian Journal of Economics*, 97, 495–526.

Smeeding, T., 1996, 'America's income inequality: where do we stand?', *Challenge*, Sept–Oct, 45–53.

SOU, 1997, *Skatter, tjänster, sysselsättning* (Taxes, services, employment), Stockholm: Fritzes.

Statistics Sweden, 2002, *Statistical Yearbook of Sweden*, Stockholm.

Tanzi, V. and Schuknecht, L., 2000, *Public spending in the 20th century: a global perspective*, Cambridge: Cambridge University Press.

Thurow, L., 1971, 'The income distribution as a pure collective good', *Quarterly Journal of Economics*, 85, 327–36.

Varian, H., 1980, 'Redistributive taxation as social insurance', *Journal of Public Economics*, 14, 49–68.

Volkerink, B., De Haan, J., 2001, *Tax ratios: a critical survey*, OECD Tax Policy Studies No. 5, Paris: OECD.

World Bank, 1994, *Averting the old age crisis*, Oxford: Oxford University Press.

2 International integration and the welfare state*

Torben M. Andersen

2.1 Introduction

International integration is a frequently highlighted challenge facing welfare states, not least the extended models developed in Northern European countries. The process of tighter international integration is by some taken to imply that welfare states have to be rolled back, while others point to this as strengthening the need for welfare state activities. These issues are increasingly brought to the forefront in policy debates on the welfare state, but also in many cases shaping views on the pros and cons of international integration.

It is indisputable that international integration is proceeding at a rapid pace and that it changes economic structures, and therefore in turn both the scope and need for welfare state activities. In the increasing amount of literature on these issues it is possible to identify three different lines of reasoning. One view is that the welfare state will have to be rolled back since it will become increasingly difficult to finance welfare state arrangements through general taxation (see e.g. Sinn 1998; Tanzi 2000; Wildasin 2000a). A contesting view is that the welfare state has developed in response to various changes in society including different family structures and gender equalisation, but also risks induced by, among other things, international integration (see e.g. Rodrik 1997, 1998; Kautto et al. 2000). Countries may differ in how far they have proceeded in this development, but they will eventually all encounter these factors, which necessitate an expansion of welfare state activities. Finally, the development of welfare arrangements are by some seen as primarily reflecting political processes and institutions which in turn exhibit strong forces to preserve existing arrangements and therefore equally strong opposition to changes, and this tends to make differences between countries persist (Boix 1999; Esping-Andersen 1999; Swank 2002). Hence, according to

* Comments and suggestions made by participants and in particular Martin Flodén at the Krusenberg workshop and an anonymous referee are gratefully acknowledged.

this view few changes in welfare state arrangements are to be expected in a comparative perspective.

This chapter addresses the main mechanisms through which international integration affects welfare state activities. The starting point is that changes in the costs and benefits of the activities of the welfare state eventually will affect policies. Hence, even though political processes may influence the particular form and structure of welfare states, it is assumed that it eventually will have to respond to changes in market fundamentals. Accordingly, the chapter focuses on identifying the effects international integration may have on the marginal costs and benefits of welfare state activities. The outset is a welfare model of the Scandinavian or universal type where an extensive supply of services and social security arrangements are provided by the public sector and financed by general taxation (see chapter 1).

The remainder of this chapter is organised in four parts. To set the scene for the following discussion, section 2.2 starts out by reviewing a few basic facts on the international integration process. Section 2.3 offers a brief review of the literature on welfare states and international integration. Section 2.4 turns to a more detailed analysis of effects arising via the labour market, and the consequences they may have for both the costs and benefits of welfare state activities. Finally, section 2.5 considers some policy implications.

2.2   Basic facts about international integration

European countries are becoming increasingly integrated as a result of both political decisions and technological changes reducing trade costs and enhancing information dissemination among countries. This is a continuous process, which in recent years has been accelerated by free trade agreements in the context of GATT and WTO as well as technical advances. The European Union has implied tighter integration among European countries, and steps like the internal market (1987–92) and the third phase of the Economic and Monetary Union (1999–2001) are meant to strengthen this process even further. This process is extending the market, not only in size but also in scope, allowing for more division of production and therefore exploitation of gains from specialisation. It is also changing both preferences and the production possibility set. Changing travel patterns and the instantaneous flow of information at a global level is enhancing knowledge concerning norms and habits in foreign countries, which in turn shape new demands. Equally, a speedy transfer of information also affects production possibilities by allowing a swifter and less costly flow of knowledge on new production possibilities. Last but not least these changes also affect market interdependencies and thus market forms, and the possibilities of exerting market power. The most visible effects of the process of international integration are found in the areas where transactions across countries can be observed, such as in financial markets and international trade, but it affects society through a variety of more or less visible channels.

Like most countries in the world, European countries have experienced a steep increase in international trade with growth rates for trade volumes that far exceed growth rates in economic activity. While this process has gone on since trade liberalisation was initiated after the Second World War, there is no doubt that this process is continuing at a rapid pace. The trade share of the manufacturing sector in EU countries was about 55 per cent in 1970 and towards the end of the 1990s it had increased to about 120 per cent.

There are a number of important facts concerning the increase in international trade, which are of importance to the current discussion. First, while the growth of international trade is tremendous it tends to be concentrated within Europe. European countries seen as a whole remain more or less as closed today as they were thirty years ago, with an aggregate trade share being steady at a level slightly above 10 per cent of GDP. Hence, the European integration is proceeding rapidly while the global element in product markets is less strong. In a global context we thus see a concentration in regions, which is reflected in measures of openness for Europe, North America and Asia being remarkably constant over recent decades despite the increase in international trade (see OECD 1999).[1] This implies that to a first approximation it makes sense to concentrate on European integration as the main factor influencing welfare state activities. Another implication is that the globalisation threat which is asserted to arise from a large net-import from emerging low-wage (and social standard) countries into Europe is not well founded. This might, however, change with tighter integration of Eastern European countries.

Another important fact is that the increase in international trade tends to be concentrated within so-called intra-industrial trade, that is, trade in basically similar or related products, which are differentiated along one or more dimensions, and where producers located in a single or few countries supply several markets with their specific product. Simply put,

---

[1] While trade with emerging economies has been increasing absolutely, it has not been increasing faster than trade between industrialised countries. Hence, the market share of low- and middle-income countries in trade with OECD countries has remained at a level of about 20 per cent of total imports (OECD 1999).

trade is changing from the traditional (Heckscher–Ohlin) type based on differences in factor endowments to trade being driven by product differentiation, the exploitation of scale economies etc., i.e. the new trade theory (see Krugman 1995). At the start of the twentieth century, trade in primary products accounted for about two-thirds of world trade, and by the end of the century the fraction had dropped to one-quarter (Crafts 2000). This changes the nature of interrelations between European countries since more and more trade is in commodities that in principle could be produced anywhere in Europe. That is, competitiveness and comparative advantages come to play a larger and larger role in where production, and thus employment, is placed.

Another increasingly important factor is the enhanced mobility of firms, that is, the incentive of firms to set up foreign production units, to acquire foreign firms or to merge with foreign firms. This is reflected in an increasing number of multinational firms, and increasing levels of foreign direct investments. Although starting out at a very low level, globally foreign direct investments were about twenty-five times larger in 1996 than in 1970 (OECD 1999).

The internal market has also aimed at removing all obstacles to the mobility of labour within the EU, but the fact is that mobility is fairly low.[2] Labour mobility among EU countries is not at present a major issue. For further discussion of this issue see chapter 4 in this volume.

Finally, the liberalizations and subsequent integration of international capital markets is well documented (see, e.g., IMF 1999). Among EU countries participating in the third phase of the EMU there is effectively one capital market in which exchange rate risk has been removed as an impediment to trade, although, of course, it remains a factor influencing financial transactions with outside areas.

To sum up we can conclude that the European situation today is characterised by strong globalisation of financial markets, strong Europeanisation of product markets, and national labour markets.

2.3   International integration and the welfare state

The literature on welfare states and international integration is fairly modest but rapidly growing as a reflection of the political importance of these issues. This section considers three basic mechanisms which have been stressed in the literature, namely, tax base mobility, risk and race to the bottom.

---

[2] This is so, despite the fact that labour market developments in European countries have been fairly asynchronised.

Before turning to the details of this discussion it is useful to point to a basic – though often overlooked – implication of international integration. In general, international integration makes room for aggregate welfare improvements; although the costs and benefits may not be equally distributed, the net benefits are positive (the gains from free trade argument). The expanded opportunity set created in this way will also induce an increase in the demand for public sector services.[3] With a high income elasticity for welfare state activities (usually taken to be close to or above one), it follows that welfare state activities will grow by the same as or a higher growth rate than, for example, private consumption. Accordingly, international integration has basic effects tending to expand welfare state activities. However, other effects may be at stake, which may change the costs and benefits of welfare state activities, and we will turn to these next.

Tax base mobility

Most of the debate on international integration and the welfare state has centred on the possibilities of financing welfare state activities collectively when economies integrate. Mobility is a key issue since it is facilitated by international integration, which therefore also makes the tax base more mobile. Accordingly, there will be a tendency for the tax base to move to the areas that offer the most favourable tax treatment.[4] The mobility of various sources of taxation varies substantially. Obviously, financial capital is highly mobile (to which may be added intensified control problems) and the same applies to goods, although explicit or implicit trade costs make an important distinction between tradable and non-tradable commodities. Firms are also increasingly mobile – in principle it is possible to supply the European market from any place in Europe. While labour in principle could be equally mobile, there is – at least at present – not much labour mobility within Europe and cultural and linguistic barriers are likely to preserve this situation for the foreseeable future (except

---

[3] This can easily be seen by turning to the so-called Samuelson rule for the optimal level of public consumption. Let aggregate welfare be $U(b) + V(g)$ where the first term denotes utility from private consumption (b) and the last term utility from public consumption (g). The structure of the economy determines how private consumption depends on the policy variable public consumption $(b = f(g))$. The optimal level of public consumption is determined by the condition $V'(g) = U'(b)(\frac{\partial b}{\partial g})$ where the LHS gives the marginal benefits and the RHS the marginal costs of public consumption. Clearly, increases in b will, other things being equal, lower the marginal utility of private consumption and thus the marginal costs of public consumption, implying that the optimal level of public consumption increases. See Andersen 2002.

[4] Items on the expenditure side can also affect the mobility of firms, for example, infrastructure investments.

for specialized groups such as highly educated people).[5] Finally, natural resources and real estate are obviously immobile tax bases.

Accordingly, countries with high tax levels will have a choice between either accepting that economic activity moves out of the country, which erodes the tax base and thus revenue, or reducing the tax rate to maintain the tax base, but still the loss of revenue cannot be escaped. This is a losers' game seen relative to the need to finance welfare state activities to which the policy-maker can react by trying to shift the tax burden to other tax bases, or to cut welfare state activities. The former strategy raises the issue of shifting taxes from mobile to less immobile tax bases (Christensen, Hagen and Sandmo 1994). The immobile tax bases include natural resources, real estate, but also possibly labour, since labour is relatively less mobile across countries (see, however, section 4.2. below). For further discussion see chapter 12 in this volume.

The policy dilemma arising from mobility of tax bases is considered in Rodrik (1997) in a context where increasingly mobile real capital is taxed to finance transfers to immobile labour. Immobile labour is exposed to risk via terms of trade variations (exogenous) and the issue is whether via taxation of mobile real capital it is possible to compensate immobile workers for this risk effect. Improved mobility for real capital may increase the exposure of immobile labour to terms of trade risk, but also make it more difficult to tax the mobile capital, the net result being that for sufficiently mobile real capital immobile workers are unambiguously worse off. While the need for welfare state activities increases, the constraint set by tax mobility implies that welfare state arrangements will have to be rolled back.

Wildasin (1995) also considers the issue of taxing mobile factors of production (capital, or highly skilled) to finance transfers to immobile factors of production, but adds that mobility is not only a response to differences in taxes but also to variations in the return to the mobile factors of production. Increased mobility for the mobile factors of production is therefore not unambiguously bad for the immobile factors of production, since the return to the latter tends to be stabilised by the mobility of the former. The basic point is thus that there is a social insurance mechanism involved, and increased mobility may reduce the need for social insurance since mobility works as a buffer. Accordingly, integration may reduce the possibility for taxing mobile factors of production, but the need may also be reduced.

---

[5] A separate question is that of social shopping or mobility, that is, the extent to which individuals and households relocate across European countries to take advantage of differences in taxation systems and social security arrangements. For evidence for the US see Brueckner 2000.

Wildasin (2000b) endogenises skill acquisition and finds that when capital markets are complete increased mobility implies efficiency gains for both skilled and unskilled labour. However, if capital markets are incomplete and education is financed via taxation the situation is different, since the tax burden is shifted on to immobile (unskilled) workers and the level of human capital investment tends to be too low. Andersson and Konrad (this volume, chapter 13) point to the fact that mobility may reduce a time-inconsistency problem in taxation leading to excessive taxation of the return to human capital. With complete private insurance markets improved mobility is welfare improving, whereas with incomplete insurance markets they find that it is ambiguous how subsidies to education are affected, although education effort increases. These issues are further analysed in chapter 13.

The quantitative importance of tax base mobility is open for discussion. It is indisputable that tax base mobility is increasing, but the strength of the mechanism is unclear. The knowledge on how tax base mobility can be affected by taxation is scant, but Gorter (2000) finds that a typical EU country increases its Foreign Direct Investment (FDI) position in another country by about 4 per cent if the latter decreases its effective corporate tax rate by one percentage point. For labour the mobility has not so far seemed to be very sensitive to variations in taxation. For a further discussion see chapter 4 in this volume.

Even if the mobility of certain tax bases like capital income or corporate taxation is going to be substantial the consequences should be seen in perspective of the importance of these forms of taxation for overall public sector revenue. For most countries the revenue raised via corporate taxation is contributing only a minor fraction of overall public sector revenue (cf. table 2.1), and the primary burden rests on taxes levied directly or indirectly on labour income. This may reflect the fact that the tax structure from the outset is already fairly robust to integration, or that other issues are more important for taxation of corporations and capital income.

Risk

Modern economic theory has shown (see chapters 1 and 10) that it is useful to think about welfare state activities as mechanisms to achieve various forms of implicit or social insurance. To evaluate how international integration affects the need for welfare state activities it is therefore natural to start by turning to the relation between international integration and various forms of risk calling for insurance mechanisms.

A key assumption is that the capital market is incomplete, leaving market failures in risk diversification, and that these market failures are not

Table 2.1 *Public sector revenue and distribution on sources – EU countries 1996*

| Country | Total taxes % of GDP | Of which in % | | | | |
		Personal taxes	Social security	Corporate taxes	Indirect taxes	Other
SWE	62.7	35.3	29.4	5.6	22.8	6.9
DNK	57.5	53.2	3.2	4.6	32.7	6.3
FIN	55.3	35.0	24.7	6.7	30.1	3.5
FRA	50.2	14.1	39.6	3.8	27.3	15.2
NLD	49.7	17.5	31.8	9.5	28.6	12.6
BEL	49.6	31.0	29.5	6.8	27.0	5.8
LUX	47.5	22.0	23.0	16.0	27.7	11.2
AUT	47.0	20.9	31.8	4.7	28.6	14.1
DEU	45.2	24.7	38.1	3.8	27.9	5.5
ITA	44.9	25.1	30.5	9.2	25.9	9.3
PRT	41.7	18.9	24.0	9.5	42.6	5.1
ESP	39.9	23.0	31.1	5.9	29.2	10.8
GRC	35.7	12.4	30.6	6.3	42.8	7.9
IRL	33.9	31.3	12.7	9.6	39.7	6.6
GBR	38.4	25.9	16.8	10.5	35.2	11.6
EU	46.6	26.0	26.4	7.5	31.2	8.8

Source: OECD (2000).

significantly reduced as a consequence of capital market integration. It is well established that risk diversification achieved via international capital markets falls short of the implications of complete capital markets (see Lewis 1999). Moreover, basic market failures relate to human capital, and it is not obvious through which routes international integration should reduce these market failures caused by basic information and incentive problems for individual decision-making.

The basic question is whether more openness and tighter international integration leads to a more risky environment, which in turn can be countered by social insurance provided by public sector activities. If so, one would expect that more open economies also have larger public sectors.

The relationship between openness and public sector size has been extensively discussed in the political science literature starting with Cameron (1978) pointing to the positive correlation between the two for a sample of OECD countries. In the political science literature this is explained from a power structure perspective according to which political support for further integration can only be ensured if proponents of more international integration are willing to offer compensation to groups suffering from this, and the latter tend to require an expansion of the public sector (see also Pierson 1998; Boix 1999). In the economics literature Rodrik (1997, 1998) has introduced the risk aspect as a possible explanation, and he presents empirical evidence to support the claim that more open economies (measured by the trade share) tend to have larger public sectors (measured relative to GDP), and that risk related to trade (terms-of-trade risk) is causing this relationship. If correct, this hypothesis has important policy implications since it implies that the need and demand for welfare activities will increase along with international integration.

The hypothesis has two links: first, that international integration enhances the exposure to risk, and second, that various welfare state activities can diversify or mitigate the consequences hereof. Rodrik (1998) presents an illustrative model in which integration is assumed to imply more terms-of-trade variability, and where an expansion of the public sector can be used to mitigate the consequences of this risk, because resources are moved from the private sector exposed to market risk to the public sector, which by definition is insulated from these risks.

The two links are considered jointly in Andersen (2002) where risk is related explicitly to product market interaction, and international integration is modelled as reduction of trade frictions in product markets. The basic source of risk is shocks to both domestic and foreign markets, and trade is driven by product specialisation. Lower trade frictions are shown to imply more risk in private consumption. While more exposure to foreign shocks is straightforward, it might be conjectured that the exposure to domestic shocks is reduced when markets get more integrated, and therefore the net effect on risk should be ambiguous. This is not the case, and the reason is that the trade friction works as a buffer between income and consumption, and the less the friction the more income can be transferred to final consumption, and accordingly private consumption becomes more exposed to risk when markets integrate. However, the mean level of consumption also goes up, capturing the welfare gains from integration. The enlarged exposure to risk can be mitigated by state contingencies in public consumption, transfers and taxes (automatic stabilisers), and it can be shown that product market integration makes the optimal contingencies larger, that is, the optimal policy response to increased integration is to expand social insurance mechanisms. A possible outcome is thus that product market integration implies a reduction in the optimal level of public sector activities, at the same time as there is a need for stronger contingencies in public sector activities.

A long list of authors (see, e.g., Cameron 1978; Rodrik 1997, 1998; Boix 1999; and Fatas and Mihov 1999) have tried to explain country differences in public sector sizes by including variables such as country size, political power structure, institutions, income per capita, geographical position, etc. Within this list, openness (defined as the average of import and exports to GDP) has been included, and usually this variable is found to have a positive effect on public sector size. Rodrik (1997, 1998) includes a variable[6] capturing terms-of-trade risk and finds that this has a positive effect on public sector size. This has been taken as support for the hypothesis that openness creates a need for a larger public sector.

There are several problems related to interpreting this as evidence supporting the risk-hypothesis (see also Alesina and Wacziarg 1997 and Iversen and Gusach 2000). Firstly, openness may be correlated with other variables (country size), and the correlation found in the studies referred to above may be spurious. Secondly, openness is a poor measure of the degree to which international integration affects economies – increasing international integration may have large effects without equally large effects on the trade share. Thirdly, when considering the timing of increasing international integration and public sector expansion, it is not obvious that the hypothesis can be supported for many countries since a large part of public sector growth is concentrated in a period from some time in the 1960s to the late 1970s, while international integration has been an ongoing process before and after the major expansion in public sector activity. This is concealed by studies based on average values over long sample periods. Fourthly, the results may depend critically on the included set of countries. Among EU countries there is hardly any relation (Andersen 2001d). Finally, and most importantly, these studies do not test whether more open economies actually have more volatility in key macro variables such as production, consumption and employment.

The latter issue has been considered in the open macroeconomics literature. Smaller countries tend to have more volatility in various measures for aggregate activity (Lumsdaine and Prasad 1997 and Zimmerman 1997). This may reflect the fact that they have a less diversified production structure than larger countries. If international integration reinforces specialisation then one may expect more volatility. However, empirical studies have also found a significant 'international component' in business cycle fluctuations reflecting that shocks are transmitted between countries through various linkages highlighted in the open macroeconomics literature. This may suggest that with more international integration the 'domestic component' comes to matter less. In an attempt to assess the

[6] This variable is defined as the trade share multiplied by the standard deviations of the terms of trade. It is not obvious that this is the theoretically correct measure since it disregards the sensitivity of exports and imports to relative prices.

strength of the 'specialisation effect' relative to the 'transmission effect' Frankel and Rose (1998) in an important study find a positive relation between international trade and the co-movements in business cycles among countries. The 'transmission effect' seems to dominate, and this indicates that more international integration will lead to more similar business cycle developments.[7] This result is contested by Kalemi-Ozcan, Sørensen and Yosha (2000) who find a positive relation between industrial specialisation and asymmetry in fluctuations. Since capital market integration seems to explain specialisation, this suggests that more integration leads to more specialisation and more dissimilar business cycle developments.

However, none of these results indicates whether risk will increase or decrease, but only that business cycles will become more similar across countries. Empirical studies (see Andersen 2003) do find a weak negative correlation between openness and macroeconomic volatility (measured by the standard deviation of some measure of business cycle variations in aggregate activity). However, comparisons over longer time periods do not make it possible to conclude whether international integration leads to more or less aggregate volatility (Romer 1999). It is therefore an open question how quantitatively important the aggregate risk link is.

Race to the bottom

There is a widespread fear that international integration releases competitive forces causing a race to the bottom in which social standards and welfare state arrangements are rolled back. This arises through interdependencies between countries, causing a process whereby successive undercutting countries perceive that they can improve their relative position. However, if all act in this fashion the end result is an unchanged relative position and lower social and welfare standards. From the outset it is worth pointing out that the term 'race to the bottom' is not used here in the narrow sense of implying a drastic reduction in social and welfare standards, but in the more broad sense of a downward trend which can lead to inefficiently low levels.

The primary example of a potential race to the bottom process is tax competition induced by the mobility of tax bases. Given this mobility, a country may perceive that if it sets its tax rate on mobile source of income below that of other countries it may gain, since the direct revenue loss is compensated by an inflow, which will have beneficial effects not only for tax revenues but also for economic activity and employment in general.

---

[7] This may reduce the scope for risk diversification within the EU.

Taxation of corporate income is a primary example of this, since a low tax may induce companies to locate in the country. The importance of this is reflected in a tendency towards lower taxation of corporations,[8] and the case of Ireland is often highlighted as an example of a country that has exploited this mechanism with some success.[9] However, other countries cannot passively accept an outflow of companies, and will have to react by eliminating the tax motive for mobility, that is, effective taxation will have to be lowered. In the end this may lead to inefficiently low levels of taxation (as pointed out by, for example, Zodrow and Miekovsky 1986 and many others – see references in Sørensen 2000). If tax rates are inefficiently low (seen relative to the cooperative case) it follows that tax revenues (from this source of taxation) are inefficiently low, and therefore potentially that welfare state activities are inefficiently low. In an interesting quantitative evaluation, Sørensen (2000) finds in an analysis of capital and corporate income taxation that tax rates in the non-cooperative case tend to be about fifteen percentage points below the cooperative level. The aggregate welfare consequences are, however, modest partly because these taxes are not important sources of revenue (see table 2.1 above). However, there may be important adverse distributional consequences since the position of low-income groups might be worsened because they tend to bear more of the burden of adjustment when tax revenues are reduced.

Baldwin and Krugman (2000) have contested the argument that tax competition causes a race to the bottom, arguing that agglomeration effects do not make core and periphery countries symmetrical, and therefore the scope for periphery countries to compete via low taxes (and other measures) for the location of firms supplying the core market is modest.

Another argument for a race to the bottom effect runs via the activity effects of public sector activities, e.g. in relation to employment policies. It is a widespread view that public sector activities in open economies are inefficiently low due to the import leakage implied by such activities, that is, expanding public activity will, via imports, benefit trading partners and this makes policy-makers choose too low a level of public activity. This line of reasoning often motivates calls for coordinated fiscal expansions among the major economies. However, this view does not have unequivocal support in economic theory, and it turns out that the opposite situation has support in a wide range of circumstances. The reason is the following: an expansion of public sector activity tends to improve the

---

[8] This has, however, been accompanied by an expansion of the tax base; hence tax reductions are not proportional to reductions in the rates.

[9] The Primarolo-group (2000) considered 271 arrangements for the taxation of corporations in EU and associated areas, and found 66 cases in which the principle of non-tax competition was broken.

terms of trade, that is, foreign goods become cheaper relative to domestic goods, and this has a positive real income effect for domestic residents. Hence, in planning public sector activities each country perceives that it can change the terms of trade to its advantage, and this adds to the benefits of expanding public sector activities. However, if all countries act in this way the terms-of-trade effect will be eliminated, and the end result is an inefficiently (seen relative to the cooperative case) large level of public activity, i.e. a risk of 'a race to the top'. This result has been demonstrated for public activities in the case of full employment (see, e.g., Ploeg 1987; Turnovsky 1988; Chari and Kehoe 1990; and Devereux 1991), imperfect competition and individual involuntary unemployment (Andersen, Rasmussen and Sørensen 1996), and in relation to the tax structure (Holmlund and Kolm 2002).

Another source of the race-to-the-bottom effect is through social standards (unemployment benefits, work rules etc.), which can be lowered either to improve competitiveness or prevent inward mobility of people wanting to benefit from more generous welfare arrangements. Brueckner (2000) considers the latter issue and shows that if mobility is sensitive to social standards, there is a tendency for countries to choose inoptimally low levels of social standards to prevent inward mobility. Evidence is presented for the US, which indicates that this mechanism is shaping welfare policies, if only because policy-makers act under the perception that this is an important mechanism. However, the relevance for Europe is less obvious, both because mobility is low (although mobility of a few groups heavily dependent on social welfare can be a burden to any potential host country), and because EU rules have been designed to prevent this form of 'social mobility' by making free mobility contingent on employment: that is, it is not possible to move to take advantage of differences in social standards for the unemployed, for example. This does not preclude concerns for 'competitiveness' causing a downward bias in employment and social policies in an attempt to safeguard domestic employment (see discussion on job mobility below).

2.4   Integration, labour markets and the welfare state

This section turns to labour market implications of international integration for two reasons. First, labour market issues are essential to the welfare state, and it is therefore essential to consider the labour market implications of international integration. Second, it is sometimes wrongly asserted that the labour market consequences are minor since labour mobility across countries is very small. As shall be argued below there are important consequences even if labour mobility remains modest. To develop this idea the following discussion completely disregards mobility of workers.

Job mobility

The way in which labour markets function depends critically on product market structures, for the simple reason that the latter shape labour demand. It is a basic insight of international trade theory that trade in products can be a substitute for factor mobility between countries. According to the factor price equalisation theorem, trade may even be a perfect substitute for factor mobility under idealised conditions including perfect competition in product and factor markets, and identical technologies. In the current European situation the factor price equalisation theorem is not directly applicable, but still it points to important effects.

International integration is likely to have two major effects on product markets (see Andersen, Haldrup and Sørensen 2000). The first is more intensive competition because various forms of frictions are reduced and this improves the terms at which foreign producers can compete for market shares in the domestic market and vice versa. Second, more integrated markets also enhance the mobility of firms, since it becomes easier to service a given national market from a production unit placed where the most profitable production conditions are available. This applies in particular to goods that underlie intra-industrial trade, which has become the dominant source of international trade (cf. section 2.2). This mobility may show up in terms of foreign direct investments and outsourcing.

Both of these effects have one basic consequence for labour markets, namely, that they tend to make labour demand more sensitive to the wage rate (the numerical value of the labour demand elasticity increases). This is potentially important since this elasticity is critical for the distortions arising from taxation of labour income: that is, the costs of financing welfare state arrangements can be critically affected even though labour is not mobile across countries.

The effect on the employment level is in general ambiguous since although more integrated markets offer opportunities for export which tend to improve labour market conditions, they also face a threat from imports with the opposite effects. This is not, however, a zero-sum game between countries since product market integration also affects market power both in product and labour markets, and under wide circumstances the net effect is an overall increase in employment. However, equally important is the fact that the opportunities and threats are not necessarily equally distributed across countries and different groups in the labour market, and this may be critical for the need for welfare state activities.

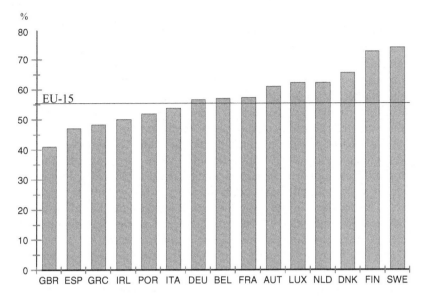

Figure 2.1 Implicit tax rate on labour
Note: Measure includes direct taxes, social security contributions and indirect taxes. Calculated on the basis of implicit tax rate on employed labour and implicit tax rate on consumption.
Source: Own calculation based on EU (2000).

Tax distortions

Despite the differences in the specific organisation of the welfare state in various EU countries it is a fact that the larger part of welfare state activities is financed by taxes or social security contributions levied on labour (cf. table 2.1). As a consequence, all EU countries have a rather high tax burden on labour measured by the tax-wedge (cf. figure 2.1). However, there are also substantial variations, which suggest that labour tax issues may become an important competitive parameter. With more integration it follows that the competition for jobs becomes more intensive due to the effects discussed above, and therefore the effects of labour taxation change.

The basic channel runs from higher labour taxation via wages to a deterioration of the competitive position of the country. There are two basic insights from the labour market literature on taxation of relevance for the present discussion. First, most models for imperfectly competitive labour markets predict that an increase in the average tax burden on labour will increase wages (for a survey see Pissarides 1998). The reason is that an increase in the average tax lowers the compensation to workers, which under very general conditions would lead to an upward wage pressure. The degree to which wages respond to a tax change depends on the specific labour market model. Second, the effects are stronger the more decentralised the wage negotiations (see Summers, Gruber and Vegara 1993; Andersen 2001a). The reason is an externality running via the public budget. A tax levied on labour is going to finance expenditures, which are beneficial to workers as a group, but a collective financing method creates the problem that to the individual or small sub-group there is no direct relation between the tax paid and the services offered by the public sector. With fully centralised wage bargaining the public sector budget would be internalised, and there is no distortion. However, the more decentralised the wage formation process the less the budget effect is internalised in the wage formation process and the more taxes are shifted over into wages, that is, tax distortions are increasing in the degree of decentralisation in the wage formation process.

There is a fairly voluminous empirical literature on wage formation and the responsiveness of wages to taxes (summaries have been provided by OECD 1994 and Sørensen 1997). The general finding is a positive spillover from average taxes to wages, but with substantial variations in the elasticities across countries. This could be explained by the fact that the studies do not control for the institutional structure of the labour market. This is done in Alesina and Perotti (1997) and Daveri and Tabellini (2000) and both studies find that the elasticity of wages with respect to average taxes is smaller in countries with centralised wage formation relative to countries with a more decentralised wage setting.

These results indicate that the costs of financing welfare state activities through general taxation can be significantly affected by international integration. However, assessing the quantitative importance of this is complicated not only by the fact that knowledge of how elasticities are affected by international integration is very scant, but also by the fact that the wage formation process will not be unaffected. A change in the labour demand elasticity will in general affect wage setting, and a more elastic labour demand will moderate wage demands.

A simple framework makes it possible to assess how the costs of financing welfare state activities through labour income taxation are affected by international integration (see appendix available upon request). The costs are measured by the marginal costs of public funds, which are a monetary metric of the total costs of raising revenue to the public sector, that is, it includes both the direct resource use and the distortions. In the special case where expenditures can be financed by lump-sum taxes, the marginal costs of public funds are equal to one, but with distortionary taxes the marginal costs of public funds are larger than one.

Table 2.2 *Marginal costs of public funds and product market integration*

	Marginal cost of public funds		
Demand elasticity	Base case	Increased tax spillover	Larger labour market distortions
1.2	1.05	1.10	1.05
1.4	1.10	1.15	1.11
1.6	1.14	1.19	1.15
1.8	1.16	1.21	1.17
2.0	1.18	1.23	1.19

Source: Own calculations, see appendix available upon request.

The model has international integration affecting product markets via a reduction in trade frictions, which makes product demand, and therefore in turn labour demand, more price elastic, and a wage relation which can capture the effect of both taxation and integration.

Table 2.2 summarises the results of numerical evaluations of the sensitivity of the marginal costs of public funds to variations in the product demand elasticity. The first column displays the base case and it shows that the marginal costs of public funds are quite sensitive to demand elasticity. Larger demand elasticities increase the distortions (though at a decreasing rate). An increase in the demand elasticity from 1.4 to 1.6 would thus increase the marginal costs of public funds from 1.10 to 1.14 or increase the distortion from 10 per cent to 14 per cent of the amount of revenue raised via taxation. Moving rightwards in the table, the second column shows the marginal costs of public funds if wages are slightly more sensitive (sensitivity increased by 10 per cent) to taxes. This is seen to increase the distortions, but the sensitivity to demand elasticity is relatively unchanged. The final column shows a deviation from the base case where the underlying labour market distortion is increased, causing an increase in structural unemployment (also by 10 per cent). This increases the marginal costs of public funds, but not quite as much as for a larger tax sensitivity of the wage. This suggests that labour market imperfections and the institutional structure may play a crucial role for how international integration affects tax distortions, that is, the effects may be smaller in high-tax countries with centralised wage setting than in low-tax countries with more decentralised wage setting.

The net result of further product market integration is likely to involve all three effects. Tighter product market integration is going to increase the demand elasticity; this suggests that the marginal costs of public funds are going to increase, and the sensitivity seems to be large, since moderate increases in demand elasticity can double the distortions. However, labour market behaviour will not remain unchanged for a number of reasons. More elastic product demands will reduce labour market power, which in turn under general conditions will lower both labour market distortions and the spillover from taxes into wages. This will work to moderate the increase in the marginal costs of public funds, but never to overturn the direct effect (Andersen 2001a). However, integration may be a separate reason for more decentralisation of wage formation (Flanagan 1999) and this tends to increase the spillover from taxes into wages. Since the available empirical knowledge on the latter mechanisms is very scant it is difficult to make precise estimates of the net effects, but non-trivial effects cannot be ruled out. Hence, even without any consideration of tax base mobility it can be concluded that the costs of financing welfare state activities through general taxation can be significantly increased as a result of product market integration.

Heterogeneity[10]

One important question in the debate on international integration is whether it leads to more inequality in labour markets. Product market integration has two immediate effects on labour markets: one is the threat of imports, that is, foreign firms capture the domestic market; the other is the possibility of entering the foreign market via exports, which will give new opportunities and be good news for wages and employment.[11] Hence, there are positive and negative effects from product market integration. Are there any compelling reasons why the gains and losses should be unequally distributed in the labour market such that low-wage groups tend to bear the threat of imports, while the high-wage groups enjoy the opportunities created by exports? Simple intuition suggests that there might be, since low-wage groups are more directly affected by the import threat, while the export opportunity tends to accrue to high productive and thus high-wage groups. Empirical evidence indicates that there is such a systematic pattern (cf. figure 2.2).

---

[10] This section is based on Andersen 2001b.

[11] There is a large literature addressing the relation between international integration and inequality based on the Heckscher–Ohlin model. However, since the relative importance of trade with non-European countries has not risen over the last decades, the channel running from an increase in the global supply of unskilled labour to the labour market situation for unskilled in Europe seems to be weak. Slaugther and Swagel (1997) provide an overview of this literature and conclude that the empirical evidence does not yield clear support for this link between international integration and inequality.

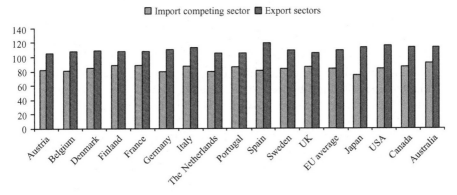

Figure 2.2 Wages and international trade
Source: OECD (1997).

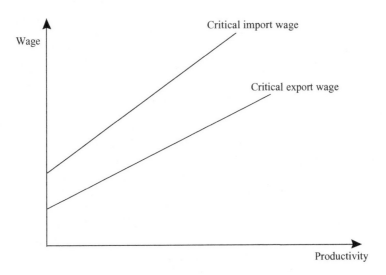

Figure 2.3 Critical import and export wages

To consider more closely how product market integration may cause more inequality, consider figure 2.3, which brings out some very basic mechanisms. For any given level of productivity in a particular sector or for a given group of workers there is a critical wage – the critical import wage – above which the wage cannot be set since that would make domestic production unprofitable, and the goods would be imported.

Similarly, there is a wage – the critical export wage – at which domestic production would also be competitive at the export market. Clearly, the critical export wage is lower than the critical import wage. Moreover, the larger the trade frictions in product markets the larger the difference between the two. With low trade frictions and tightly integrated product markets the difference between being in a position threatened by import and one of having an export possibility is very small. With large frictions and little integration the margin is of course wider.

Figure 2.3 shows how the critical export and import wage depends on productivity – the more productive the workers the higher the wages they can claim. The difference between the two critical wage levels creates a corridor within which the domestic labour market is protected from international competition in the sense that for wages in this interval there would neither be imports nor exports – the sector is a so-called non-tradables.

Consider now two basic issues related to wage formation: first, social objectives in the form of a lower wage limit set by either an explicit minimum wage or indirectly via unemployment benefits or social security arrangements. Term this the reservation wage. For some groups with low productivity (in general low comparative advantage) it would be impossible to find employment at the reservation wage. The reason is that the potential jobs for this group are lost through imports, that is, domestic production is not profitable. Second, trade frictions make it possible for workers to exert market power; or put differently, they can appropriate rents created by the trade frictions. Assume for the sake of argument that there is a desired wage, which workers or unions are striving for: call this the 'union monopoly wage', cf. fig. 2.4. The corridor implied by trade frictions makes it possible for a group with intermediary productivity to protect themselves from trade and claim the union monopoly wage. Not all can demand this wage; some are under severe threat from imports, and therefore forced to accept a lower wage, that is, the critical import wage. For very high productive workers it is possible to demand a higher wage and still maintain their jobs since they can make it on export markets (see figure 2.4). An interesting implication is that low productive workers are those facing low wages because they face the threat of imports, while high productive workers have the possibility of claiming a high wage because they have an export opportunity, in accordance with the facts reported in figure 2.2.

Turn next to the effects of a reduction in trade frictions due to international integration. Consider first the social objectives captured by the minimum wage. Lower trade frictions will make this wage a more binding constraint since the import threat becomes stronger. This implies that

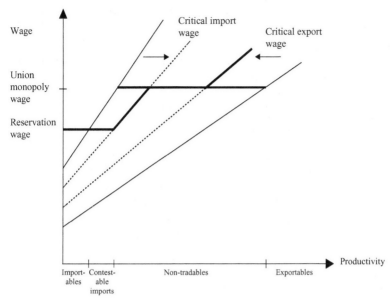

Figure 2.4 Wage functions – symmetric equilibrium

unemployment problems for low productivity groups will increase, and that the financial burden of maintaining social objectives through wage floors increases. Note that the effects discussed here do not imply that all low-wage jobs will disappear, since some can be protected by relatively high trade frictions, e.g. for a number of service activities. Lower trade frictions have the implication of reducing the possibilities of exerting market power, that is, the non-tradables sector shrinks. This is like an implicit structural reform since it forces wages to move closer with productivity.

Finally, the distribution of wages for employed workers becomes more unequal. The reason is that those facing the import threat will have to accept lower wages to maintain their jobs, while those having an export possibility face an improvement in their terms of trade. Since there is a systematic tendency between the position in the wage distribution and trade, with the import threat tending to be concentrated in low-wage jobs, and the export possibility for high-wage jobs, it follows that wage dispersion increases. The intuition is basic: those claiming a high wage must have a high productivity (comparative advantage), otherwise the wage would have to be lower, and vice versa. It is thus a straightforward implication that more integration strengthens the import threat for low-wage groups and enforces the export possibility for high productive groups, and this tends to make the wage distribution more unequal.

This raises an obvious policy dilemma. The need for a wage floor to achieve social objectives increases, because a larger proportion of the labour force is facing the import threat more fiercely, and the wage dispersion increases. This increases the financing burden, which it can be increasingly difficult (mobility argument) or costly (the distortion argument) to finance via taxation.

Another implication is that it points to an important difference between the short-run and long-run strategy to achieve social objectives in the labour market. The short run is that it will be more costly to maintain social standards as a consequence of international integration, and this has to be financed somehow. The long-run perspective is that since it becomes increasingly costly to maintain a qualification structure which does not match social ambitions with respect to the wage structure, it becomes important through labour market and education policy to affect the qualification structure in the direction matching the political objectives with respect to the distribution of pay and employment.

2.5   Policy implications

International integration is a gradual process, not a regime shift. Hence, the development will not display abrupt changes calling for sudden and drastic changes in welfare policies. However, the costs and benefits of welfare state activities will gradually be affected and this will eventually have to affect both the size and structure of the welfare society.

On the cost side an important effect is the increase in the distortionary consequences of labour taxation – the primary source of revenue in most countries. This effect arises via product market integration, implying that job location across countries becomes more sensitive to wages, and therefore in turn taxes. These effects will be stronger if labour markets are or become more decentralised due to international integration or for other reasons. The financing problems can be further strengthened by increased labour mobility.

This raises the question whether tax distortions can be reduced while still maintaining basic welfare state arrangements. An immediate solution would be to decentralise the financing of welfare arrangements to reduce tax distortions. This can be done either by linking arrangements more closely to the structure in the labour market (decentralised unemployment insurance, etc.) or by choosing more individualised solutions. In either case basic welfare state objectives can be maintained by making the arrangements mandatory, but they imply that pensions are more dependent on labour market performance and less risk diversification is ensured compared to more universal arrangements. This creates a difficult policy dilemma since international integration may increase the need for such risk diversification because the exposure to shocks becomes larger and because further specialisation increases the vulnerability to shocks.

Related to this is the question of whether the financial burdens of the welfare state can be reduced in other ways. Since large gross amounts are transferred, back and forth between individuals relative to the net amounts effectively transferred, one important issue is whether more targeting of welfare state activities can be implemented in the form of, for example, user payments. If so, the objective of the welfare state can be achieved with less distortions. This may involve more use of means testing and (mandatory) private insurance arrangements.

One conclusion from the preceding is that it may be difficult to avoid more heterogeneity and inequality as a consequence of both the direct consequences of international integration and the indirect effects on welfare arrangements. Passive measures in the form of transfers and minimum wages, etc. will have increasing difficulties in meeting basic distributional objectives. A major challenge for future welfare policies is therefore to create incentives and design labour market and social policies so that they result in a qualification level and structure that is in accordance with the objectives in relation to the level and distribution of material wellbeing.

The universal model also has the problem that it is less robust towards mobility since it is based on a collective arrangement over a lifetime – by in- and outward mobility this link can be broken. At present this is not a major problem, but the tensions may increase in not too distant a future, not only because labour becomes more mobile, but also because recipients of transfer may take advantage of the mobility (for example, as is currently happening for pensioners). This may in particular be an important problem for universal elements defined as citizens' rights.

Finally, it is worth pointing out that the challenges faced by the welfare state due to international integration do not arise from outside political pressure, but are caused by changes in the way in which economies work. Or to put it differently, fundamentals are changing and this calls for adjustment in policies.

References

Alesina, A. and Perotti, P., 1997, 'The welfare state and competitiveness', *American Economic Review*, 87, 921–39.

Alesina, A. and Wacziarg, R., 1997, 'Openness, country size and the government', NBER working paper 6024.

Andersen, T. M., 2001a, 'Welfare policies, labour markets and international integration'. *International Tax and Public Finance* (forthcoming).

—2001b, 'Product market integration, wage dispersion and unemployment', IZA working paper.

—2002, 'International integration, risk and the welfare state', *Scandinavian Journal of Economics*, 2002, 104, 343–64.

—2003, 'European integration and the welfare state'. *Journal of Population Economics*, 16, 1–19.

Andersen, T. M., Haldrup, N. and Sørensen, J. R., 2000, 'Labour market implications of EU product market integration', *Economic Policy*, 30, 105–33.

Andersen, T. M., Rasmussen, B. S., and Sørensen, J. R., 1996, 'Optimal fiscal policies in open economies with labour market distortions', *Journal of Public Economics*, 63, 103–17.

Atkinson, A. B., 1999, *The economic consequences of rolling back the welfare state*, Munich Lectures in Economics, Cambridge, Mass.: MIT Press.

Baldwin, R. E. and Krugman, P., 2000, 'Agglomeration, integration and tax harmonization', CEPR discussion paper 2630.

Boix, C., 1999, 'Why does the public sector grow? The role of economic development, trade and democracy?' Els Pucles del CREI, Universitat Pompeu Fabra.

Brueckner, Jan K., 2000, 'Welfare reform and the race to the bottom: theory and evidence', *Southern Economic Journal*, 66, 505–25.

Cameron, D. R., 1978, 'The expansion of the public economy', *American Political Science Review*, 72, 1243–61.

Chari, V. V. and Kehoe, P. J., 1990, 'International coordination of fiscal policy in limiting economies', *Journal of Political Economy*, 98, 617–36.

Christiansen, V., Hagen, K. P. and Sandmo, A., 1994, 'The scope for taxation and public expenditure in an open economy', *Scandinavian Journal of Economics*, 96, 289–309.

Crafts, N., 2000, 'Globalization and growth in the twentieth century', IMF working paper WP/00/44.

Daveri, F. and Tabellini, G., 2000, 'Unemployment, growth and taxation in industrial countries', *Economic Policy*, 30, 47–104.

Devereux, M. B., 1991, 'The terms of trade and the international coordination of fiscal policy', *Economic Inquiry*, 29, 720–36.

Dowrick, S., 1989, 'Union-oligopoly bargaining', *Economic Journal*, 99, 1123–42.

Esping-Andersen, G., 1999, *Social foundations of postindustrial economies*, Oxford: Oxford University Press.

European Commission, 2000, *Structures of the taxation systems in the European Union, 1970–1997*, EUROSTAT.

Fatas, A. and Mihov, I., 1999, 'Government size and automatic stabilizers, international and intranational evidence', CEPR discussion paper 2259.

Flanagan, R. J., 1999, 'Macroeconomic performance and collective bargaining: an international perspective', *Journal of Economic Literature*, 37, 1150–75.

Frankel, J. A. and Rose, A. K., 1998, 'The endogeneity of the optimal currency area criteria', *Economic Journal*, 108, 1008–25.

Gorter, J., 2000, 'How mobile is capital within the European Union?' Central Planning Bureau, 00/4.

Holmlund, B., and Kolm, A.-S., 2002, *Economic integration, imperfect competition, and international policy coordination*, Oxford Economic Papers.

IMF, 1999, *International capital markets: developments, prospects and key policy issues*.

Iversen, T. and Cusack, T. E., 2000, 'The causes of welfare state expansion, deindustrialization and globalization', *World Politics*, 52, 313–49.

Kalemi-Ozcan, S., Sørensen, B. and Yosha, O., 2000, 'Economic integration, industrial specialization, and the asymmetry of macroeconomic fluctuations', working paper.

Kautto, M., Bjørn Hvinden, J. F., Kvist, J. and Uusitalo, H., 2000, *Nordic welfare states in a European context*, London: Routledge.

Krugman, 1995, 'Increasing returns, imperfect competition and the possible theory of international trade', in *Handbook of International Economics*, Vol. III.

Lewis, K. K., 1999, 'Trying to explain home bias in equities and consumption', *Journal of Economic Literature*, 37, 571–608.

Lumsdaine, R. L. and Prasad, E. S., 1997, 'Identifying the common component in international economic fluctuations', NBER working paper 5984.

OECD, 1994, *The Job Study*.

—1997, *Employment Outlook*, July.

—1999, '*Policy briefs – open markets matter: the benefits of trade and investment liberalisation*', October.

OECD, 2000, *OECD in Figures*, Paris: OECD.

Pierson, C., 1998, *Beyond the welfare state: the new political economy of welfare*, London: Polity Press (2nd edn).

Pissarides, C., 1998, 'The impact of employment tax cuts on unemployment and wages: the role of unemployment benefits and tax structure', *European Economic Review*, 42, 155–84.

Ploeg, R. van der, 1987, 'Coordination of optimal taxation in a two-country equilibrium model', *Economics Letters*, 24, 279–85.

Primarolo group, 1999, 'Code of conduct (business taxation), European Commission', www.ue.eu.int/newsroom.

Rodrik, D., 1997, *Has globalization gone too far?* Washington: Institute for International Studies.

—1998, 'Why do more open economies have bigger governments?' *Journal of Political Economy*, 106, 997–1032.

Romer, D., 1999, 'Changes in business cycles: evidence and explanations', *Journal of Economic Perspectives*, 13, 23–44.

Sinn, H.-W., 1998, 'European integration and the future of the welfare state', *Swedish Economic Policy Review*, 5, 113–32.

Slaugther, M. J. and Swagel, P., 1997, 'The effects of globalization on wages in advanced economies', IMP working paper, 97–43.

Sørensen, P. B., 1997, 'Public finance solutions to the European unemployment problem?' *Economic Policy*, 25, 223–64.

—2000, 'The case for international tax co-ordination reconsidered', *Economic Policy*, 31, 429–72.

Summers, L., Gruber, J. and Vegara, R., 1993, 'Taxation and the structure of labor markets', *Quarterly Journal of Economics*, 94, 385–411.

Swank, D. H., 2002, *Global capital, political institutions and policy change in developed welfare states*, Cambridge: Cambridge University Press.

Tanzi, V., 2000, 'Globalization and the future of social protection', IMF working paper, WP/00/12.

Turnovsky, S. J., 1988, 'The gains from fiscal cooperation in the two-commodity real trade model', *Journal of International Economics*, 25, 111–27.

Wildasin, D. E., 1995, 'Factor mobility, risk and redistribution in the welfare state', *Scandinavian Journal of Economics*, 97, 527–46.

—2000a, 'Factor mobility and fiscal policy in the EU: policy issues and analytical approaches', *Economic Policy*, 31, 337–78.

—2000b, 'Market integration, investment in risky human capital, and fiscal competition', *American Economic Review*, 90, 73–95.

Zodrow, G. R. and Miekovsky, P., 1986, 'Pigou, property taxation and the underprovision of local public goods', *Journal of Urban Economics*, 19, 356–70.

Zimmerman, C., 1997, 'International real business cycles among heterogenous countries', *European Economic Review*, 41, 319–56.

3   The changing age structure and
     the public sector

Thomas Lindh

3.1   Introduction

Over the next fifty years developed countries will be ageing to such an
extent that net population growth – when positive – will mostly take place
in age groups that are retired. This is a new historical experience. It is
obvious that a number of problems will arise in economies that have a
much higher proportion of elderly. Many of these problems will have a
direct impact on public finance and public services. As argued in Flodén's
chapter in this book (chapter 14), such ageing can be expected to lead
to a financial debt problem. That applies particularly to Sweden, where
the average tax rate is already somewhere around 60 per cent and, as
Huber and Norrman point out in chapter 12, it will be difficult even to
maintain the current rate of taxation – much less raise it – in view of the
tax competition within the EU.

Although Sweden has an exceptionally high ratio of public expenditure
to GDP, it is by no means exceptional in terms of its ageing process. Other
countries are ageing much faster and will end up with a much higher
proportion of persons above 65 (see figure 3.1 for estimates according to
UN 1998). As argued in the introduction to this book, this fact provides
incentives to discuss whether there are more efficient ways to organise a
welfare state.

In three senses Sweden leads the way into this ageing society. Firstly,
Sweden's population started to age at a relatively early stage due to the
dramatic decline in birth rates that took place during the 1920s and 1930s.
When the large cohorts born at the beginning of the twentieth century
started retiring in the late 1960s the Swedish population share above the
age of 65 expanded rapidly. Sweden became the oldest country in the
world in the 1980s with around 18 per cent of the population above
the age of 65. This provided one important impetus to the expansion of
the public sector in Sweden in the 1970s and 1980s and helps to explain
why Sweden has a large public sector in the first place. In the 1990s the
Swedish population share aged above 65 stagnated and actually decreased

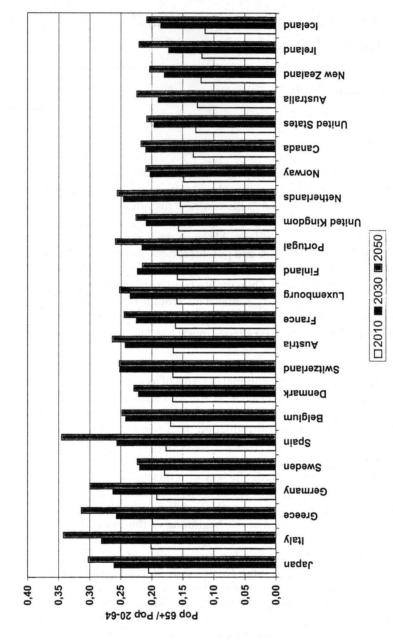

Figure 3.1 The projected age shares above 65 in a number of OECD countries
Source: UN (1998).

for a while. Nevertheless, as seen in figure 3.1, only Japan, Italy, Greece and Germany are projected to be somewhat older than Sweden in 2010. However, in the longer run, nearly all OECD countries shown will age faster than Sweden during the next fifty years.

Secondly, at a comparatively early stage, ageing in Sweden induced a comprehensive reform of the earlier defined benefit pension system into a defined contribution system complemented with an individual pension fund. This reform was undertaken in order to ensure as far as possible the autonomous financial stability of the pension system. It represents one of the earliest responses to the ageing challenge in the industrialised world (see chapter 9).

Thirdly, while most industrialised countries experienced baby booms *after* the Second World War the Swedish war baby boom was contemporaneous with the war and peaked in 1945. Sweden was therefore destined to encounter the problems associated with an acceleration of retirement *before* other countries.

Thus an analysis of the Swedish situation constitutes a pilot study of problems that will occur somewhat later in most European nations and in Japan in a more serious form. It is apparent from figure 3.1 that Anglo-Saxon countries will not have an equally dramatic ageing process although the problems studied here will also have some impact in these countries.

The retirement of the baby boom cohorts born in the 1940s has already started as some people in those cohorts have begun to take early retirement and will continue up to around 2015 when the last of the birth cohorts from the 1940s reach mandatory retirement age. The issue of how the Swedish economy will be affected by ageing has therefore come into political focus during the last few years. The Swedish Long Term Survey 1999/2000 focused on the issue of diminishing labour supply. However, it also discussed public sector expenditure. The SNS Welfare Council has discussed social insurance issues in Söderström et al. (1999) and fertility in Björklund et al. (2001). Several new pressure groups have formed to lobby for the rights of the elderly. The Ministry of Social and Health Affairs has started a major investigation into the conditions affecting the future ageing population as well as a committee on low fertility. A number of recent reports have dealt with the ageing problem, for example Malmberg and Lindh (2000), and Nordén and Olsson (2000). The appendix to the government's spring budget proposition 2001 considered the debt issue. The problem has for a long time been appreciated internationally and the OECD (1998) argued that ageing will radically alter the macroeconomic foundations for financing the welfare state.

It is obvious that health, education, fertility, earnings and experience vary in a systematic way over the life cycle. It is less obvious that

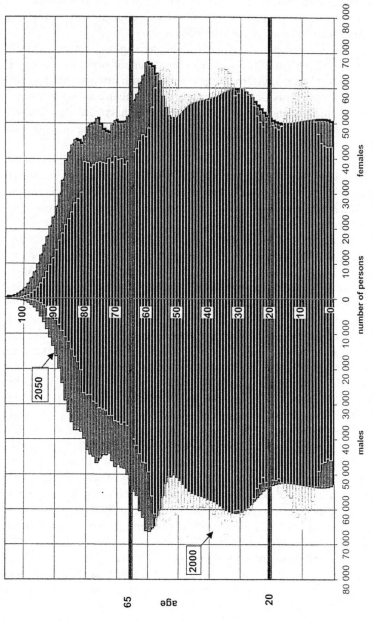

Figure 3.2 The Swedish age pyramid in 2000 superimposed on the projected age pyramid of 2050

preferences and risk behaviour have a fairly predictable life-cycle pattern, resulting in age patterns of behaviour in areas as diverse as criminality, migratory behaviour and investment choices; as well as radically different consumption choices. There are systematic multi-dimensional economic effects of changes in the age distribution which will interact to shape the future conditions for the welfare state.

One important prerequisite for this assertion is that age distributions in industrialised countries are not stable. In the Swedish case it is a kind of roller coaster (see figure 3.2). The representative agent in the Swedish population will be a rather shifting personality as the various baby booms roll through the distribution, confronting highly variable economic environments.

The long run is unusually long when discussing demography. The most serious ageing problems are liable to arise some thirty years from now. At that horizon not much can be known with reasonable certainty except for the demographic projections.

Within the bounds of this chapter, only a quick sketch of the ageing issues can be given. Below I will:

1. *describe* the age structure that has developed over the last century in Sweden and discuss the official projections during the next half century;
2. *survey* briefly some empirical results on how age structure correlates with macroeconomic development;
3. *discuss* how the public sector in particular may be affected both by the age structure of the population and in particular the age structure of those employed in that sector;
4. *present* a reduced form estimate of the total budget effect to be expected from the age structure in the next half-century given the historical experience of the last half-century.

3.2   What are the demographic facts in Sweden?

First, it is important to appreciate the dramatic nature of the demographic changes in Sweden, even though they appear rather moderate in comparison to OECD countries like Italy, Spain, Germany and Japan. Population ageing has been a clearly discernible trend over most of the last century. What is new in the twenty-first century is that population ageing is reaching a stage where the only growing part of the population is the dependent retired population.

The share of the population above 65 years of age has been growing for most of the twentieth century. However, the increase in the dependent part of the population has been offset by the decrease in the share of those aged 0–19. The dependency ratio (those aged 0–19 and those aged 65 and above divided by those aged 20–64) was around 1.0 at the end of the nineteenth century and subsequently decreased to a low of about 0.6 persons around 1945. The dependency ratio then increased again to a high of 0.75 around 1980. Today the ratio is just above 0.7 and is expected to stay at that level for another ten years. The projections imply that it will rise to nearly 0.9 in the 2030s, i.e. we are back to the levels prevailing at the beginning of the twentieth century. The dependency ratio is a rough but simple measure that overestimates dependency at the end of the nineteenth century while most probably underestimating it in the future, since active economic life has tended to begin ever later.

That is the picture we obtain when we assume children and elderly dependants to be the same. If we instead treat the elderly separately, the dependency ratio at the beginning of the twentieth century was around 0.15 elderly persons to be supported by each potentially economically active individual between the ages of 20 and 64. It took half a century from 1900 before the elderly dependency ratio began to rise, because the growth in the elderly was matched by the growth in the active population. When the elderly dependency ratio started to increase in the 1950s it reached 0.3 in the mid-1980s and then flattened out and will not start increasing again until around 2010. Then it is expected to make a rapid spurt up to above 0.45 in the 2030s and then flatten out again.

By then many of those aged 20–29 will in fact need support from the active population. Accordingly at the end of the period we tend to overestimate those who will actually be potential suppliers of support. The actual ratio of dependent retirees to active workers may quadruple, rather than increase threefold over the period from 1900. Taking account of the secular decline in the numbers of working hours, the actual hours worked to support each dependant may be decreasing even faster.

The forecasts from Statistics Sweden are based on an increase in the total fertility rate (TFR, that is the fertility we would have if current birth rates for women in each age group were to continue) to 1.8 children per woman from the current rate of 1.5. However, 1.8 is still well below the balanced reproduction rate of around 2.1. The projection also assumes a slowly subsiding growth trend in life expectancy and a moderate net immigration.

There are, of course, uncertainties in the demographic projections. These uncertainties derive from changes in the out- and in-flow of population, i.e. fertility, migration and mortality. The TFR assumption has the character of an educated guess mostly based on surveys of planned fertility. What we do know is that European and other developed countries exhibit a secular trend towards decreased fertility. Sweden differs from other countries by having a substantially higher variation in the TFR and an amazingly stable cohort fertility of around two children per woman over the twentieth century. That is as far as we can tell up to the cohorts born around 1955. Whether women born in the latter half of the last century will reach the same completed fertility remains to be seen. The Swedish birth rate fluctuations mainly reflect changes in the timing of births rather than any radical change in the average number of children born to each woman. It is hard to doubt that this has something to do with the Swedish welfare state even if it is hard to prove (Björklund et al. 2001)

One reason for the large variation in Swedish births is that fertility is pro-cyclical rather than counter-cyclical as in many other countries. This is partly explained by the fact that parental benefits are rather tightly linked to active work. As with most other welfare benefits in Sweden, qualification for parental leave benefits are conditional on previous employment in the labour market. This 'workfare' policy has resulted in both a comparatively high female labour participation rate and in incentives to plan births to occur when labour market conditions are favourable. The benefits are fairly generous, with up to 450 days' paid leave with a replacement ratio of currently 80 per cent. Fertility should follow a pro-cyclical course in the future as well, rather than the flat trajectory assumed in the Statistics Sweden projections. The effect of a constant TFR assumption is clearly seen in figure 3.2 where the age pyramid of 2000 has been superimposed on the projected age pyramid of 2050. The smoothness of the lower half of the projection is unlikely to materialise.

When it comes to mortality, previous Statistics Sweden projections based on constant expected life length have been notorious for underestimating the elderly part of the population. The current projections take account of further lengthening of life expectancy. However, much uncertainty remains. There are claims that medicine has now advanced to such an extent that it should be possible to keep a majority of people living up to over 100 years. Historical changes in adult mortality have been much slower than would be necessary to fulfil that promise within a fifty-year horizon. Nevertheless technological change in medicine is so rapid that it perhaps cannot be ruled out. In that case the future elderly dependency ratio is grossly underestimated in all developed countries.

The third uncertainty in the demographic projections is migration. Statistics Sweden bases its projections on a more or less unchanged pattern of a net immigration of 15,000 a year (actually a little more up to 2010). This may easily change due to economic conditions and incentives as well as major wars around the world. Gross immigration has been particularly volatile over the post-war period. There is also an increasing trend in emigration from Sweden which makes predictions on net migration highly uncertain (see also chapter 4, below). However, migration is concentrated among adults between 20 and 40 years old. Hence it would seem a fair guess that migration may compensate somewhat for the pro-cyclical fertility pattern by increasing when a small birth cohort reaches maturity and enters the labour market and vice versa. It is, however, a fairly limited influence. Net migration rates at the projected magnitudes will only have small effects on the age distribution. At the ages below 30 where migration is maximal a specific age cohort only increases around one percentage point. As migrants also become older this is hardly discernible in the age distribution projections.

Taking all this into account, it is still a fact that even substantial uncertainty regarding demographic projections cannot change the general picture of an ageing Sweden over the next fifty years. The severity of the ageing trend is somewhat uncertain although the general direction will be very robust.

A simple formal analysis clarifies the robustness of this trend. Assume that we have a two-generation model where in any discrete period there are a_t economically active persons. The retired persons are $b_t = a_{t-1}e^{-m}$ where a positive m denotes the mortality parameter. Assume domestic fertility to be high enough to reproduce the active population in each period.

The support ratio is $k = a_t/b_t = a_t/(a_{t-1}e^{-m}) = e^m$ for this stationary population. Now suppose m decreases to m_0 so the support ratio decreases. To keep the support ratio, given fertility, immigration has to increase so $a_t = e^g a_{t-1}$ where g satisfies $g + m_0 = m$. Then

$$k = \frac{e^g a_{t-1}}{a_{t-1}e^{-m_0}} = e^m$$

If the immigrants have the same fertility and mortality rates as the indigenous population, the retired population in the next period will be $a_t e^{-m_0}$ and the economically active only $a_{t+1} = a_t$ leading to the uncomfortable conclusion that the same proportion of immigrants must be imported again to keep the support ratio constant. In other words, net migration must continually increase in absolute numbers due to a once and for all permanent decrease in mortality. If mortality decreases in each period, immigration also needs to accelerate relatively in each period to sustain the support ratios when mortality decreases. The same effect can be achieved by increasing fertility above reproduction level in the previous period. We need *faster* than exponential population growth.

It is interesting to note that Kremer (1993) demonstrates that this has actually been the case up to the 1960s on a world scale. Since then the world population growth rate has started to fall and demographers like Lutz et al. (2001) attach a high probability to a stationary population scenario towards the end of this century.

The conclusion is that with a fixed period of economic activity neither immigration nor fertility can keep the support ratio fixed in the long run. Either the supply of immigrants dries up at some point or the world population bomb resurfaces. A fixed support ratio and a fixed period of economic activity cannot be sustained when mortality decreases. In the short run – which in this context is on the scale of the current century – some combination of fertility increase and increased net immigration could be sufficient for a small country like Sweden, but it would require quite unrealistic increases in fertility and net immigration to preserve the support ratio in Sweden. Annual net immigration into Sweden would then have to be about half a million in 2050. In the EU up to 700 million people would be needed for that purpose (see UN 2000 for further numerical examples).

However, by increasing the span of economically active years support ratios can also be increased. Current trends are, however, in the opposite direction. It would seem to be fairly optimistic to believe that even the age span 20–64 could be maintained as the economically active years for the average citizen within any near future.

3.3   Demographic effects on the economy

Demographic effects on the economy are multi-faceted since ageing has an impact on nearly every kind of human behaviour and resource. Life-cycle saving is, to economists at least, the most obvious case. However, empirically the importance of life-cycle saving is far from uncontroversial. Microeconomic evidence indicates that saving propensities are far from stable with age (Bosworth et al. 1991). Macroeconomic evidence, however, shows that national saving rates do vary with cohort size in roughly the pattern expected from life-cycle hypothesis, i.e. increasing when a large proportion of the population is middle-aged and decreasing when this proportion falls (Kelley and Schmidt 1996).

This may seem puzzling at first. However, a closer examination reveals several reasons why there is no direct link between measures of microeconomic household saving and national accounts saving. Firstly, there is a substantial bookkeeping problem since account is seldom taken of accumulated pension claims (see Miles 1999). Micro behaviour becomes more compatible with life-cycle behaviour when adjustments are made for this variable. There is also a problem in distinguishing between cohort, period and age effects in the cross-section data (Attanasio and Weber 1995).

A problem at another level is that some of the period and cohort effects arise because there is feedback through the economic equilibrium, which tends to reinforce even weak tendencies of the middle-aged to save relatively more. Although growth may theoretically affect savings either way, it generally has a positive effect on macro savings (Mason 1987 and Fry and Mason 1982). However, a large number of middle-aged persons in the population may also boost growth (Lindh 1999) independently. If we believe that higher wages indicate higher marginal productivity, this is obvious. Otherwise there is also some direct empirical evidence from cost function studies in Swedish manufacturing to rely on (Mellander 1999). Higher savings are associated with higher investment (Feldstein and Horioka 1980), which has a positive correlation with growth (Levine and Renelt 1992). This relationship may be explained by technical change being embodied in new capital equipment (Wolff 1996).

Thus a large share of middle-aged people in the population creates a positive feedback loop in the economy. Cross-section micro evidence accordingly becomes fairly irrelevant for judging the total demographic effect on aggregate savings.

Finally, household savings do not exclusively determine national saving rates. Retained firm earnings and the budget deficit are other important components in national saving. The former are positively connected to growth and, as will be argued in greater detail below, the budget balance will tend to show surpluses when the middle-aged are numerous.

In the present context the implication of this argument is not comforting. One way to disarm the decrease in the support ratio would, of course, be to increase the size of the cake we are all living off. But these empirical results indicate that the decrease in the support ratio will be accompanied by decreasing economic growth rates thus making it even harder to satisfy the redistribution equation between dependants and economically active. Theoretical results indicate that even if people choose schooling and retirement age optimally the current increase in survival rates will have negative growth consequences (Boucekkine et al. 2001). Even if retirement schemes are entirely free of distortions – such as disincentives for labour supply – the decline in mortality among the elderly still presents a redistribution problem. In Sweden we have unusually high participation rates in the older part of the labour force. However, there are still substantial distortions due to institutional regulation (Palme and Svensson 1999). Although substantial increases in labour supply may be achieved by relaxing, for example, mandatory retirement age, simulated responses suggest that the absolute numbers are still insufficient to prevent decreasing support ratios.

During the last decade, empirical evidence has accumulated on correlations between age structure and a host of macroeconomic variables. There are now both time series and cross-country panel evidence from many different samples, periods and contexts showing that:

- *GDP growth* is boosted by the active population and depressed by the dependent population. In world cross-country regressions, age effects have been verified by Bloom and Sachs (1998), Bloom and Williamson (1998), Bloom et al. (2000). They have also been found in OECD panel regressions by Lindh (1999) and Lindh and Malmberg (1999a). In country time series they have been found by McMillan and Baesel (1990) for the United States, Malmberg (1994) for Sweden (also measured as TFP growth in manufacturing) and in Australia by Lenehan (1996). Further evidence for the Nordic countries is available in Andersson (2001). It can even be discerned in panel regressions over state data in the USA over the twentieth century (Persson and Malmberg 1996).

- *Inflation* is boosted by high numbers of young retirees, see Lindh and Malmberg (1998, 2000), for OECD panels, and Lindh (2003) in Swedish time series data. The latter paper shows that age structure has potential for improving inflation forecasts for the medium term. The previously cited papers by McMillan and Baesel (1990) and Lenehan (1996) also find inflation effects. Fair and Dominguez (1991) find a money demand effect. In a textbook IS-LM framework, life-cycle saving and variation in relative cohort sizes will quite obviously have an impact on inflation unless sterilised by variations in money supply.

- *Savings* have a positive relationship with the middle-aged population. Although early results by Leff (1969) were much criticised (see, e.g., Ram 1982), the basic life-cycle story has received increasing support from more sophisticated econometric techniques, e.g. Horioka (1991), Kelley and Schmidt (1996).

- *Investment* has a similar correlation pattern to age structure but is more positively related to young adults as well as possibly young retirees (Higgins and Williamson 1997; Higgins 1998; Herbertsson and Zoega 1999 on world samples; and Lindh and Malmberg 1999b on OECD samples). These differences create current account effects (savings less investment is the current account) that carry over to real exchange rates (Andersson and Österholm 2001 on Swedish time series).

- *Budget deficits* grow with the dependent population. This is discussed in a world sample by, e.g., Herbertsson and Zoega (1999), and will be further discussed in Swedish time series below.

• *The demand for consumer durables* increases with young adults; see Fair and Dominguez (1991) on US data.

There are also more controversial assertions about the relationship between age structure and house prices (Mankiw and Weil 1989) and asset prices (Bakshi and Chen 1994; for a critical assessment see Poterba 2000). Criminality, suicide and drug abuse as well as traffic accidents are well known to be highly concentrated among young adults. At least in the US, unemployment rises when the number of young adults increases (Shimer 1998).

Theoretically OLG models with unbalanced age distributions show that general macroeconomic assumptions about, for example, the interest rate sensitivity of consumption may become invalid. In fact most of our theoretical results from OLG models are derived in steady state assuming a balanced age distribution. When we allow variations in age structure of the magnitude that we can observe in the Swedish data, conclusions from these models may well be invalid. Blomquist and Wijkander (1994) simulate an OLG model allowing for a baby boom shock calibrated to the Swedish war boom. One conclusion is that there should not exist any stable relationship between savings and interest rates at the aggregate level.

Although space does not allow us to carry out a full discussion of the indirect effects of changing cohort sizes, this background should be borne in mind when analysing public sector effects.

3.4   The public sector and its age dependence

The first and most important fact concerning the relation between the public sector and the age distribution is that the demand for public services and transfer payments derive mostly from those age groups who contemporaneously pay the least for it. In other words, the public budget involves a great deal of inter-temporal redistribution, as is further discussed in the chapter by Fölster et al. (chapter 11, below). In Nordén and Olsson (2000) public consumption and transfer payments in Sweden in 1998 have been decomposed by age groups. (Similar data in more detail are also available in Bilaga 9 LU1999/2000). In figure 3.3 these data have been used to re-compute – at 2000 prices – an estimate for the age profile of public expenditure on transfers and consumption. Public consumption is around 80,000 SEK per person in age groups up to 20, then recedes to around 25,000 SEK between the ages of 30 and 60. For these groups, public consumption consists of defence, police and other public services, which cannot be directly attributed to any specific age group and accordingly have been evenly divided over the population. Age-dependent public consumption starts to rise after the age of 60, accelerating up to around the age of 80 to finally reach about 200,000 SEK per person for the age groups above 90.

The transfer pattern is similar, starting at 50,000 SEK for youngsters under the age of 5 to a level around 25,000–30,000 SEK, fluctuating with peaks in the 20s and 50s and then increasing rapidly to a maximum of more than 120,000 SEK between the ages of 60 and 64. It then declines to around 80,000 SEK for the oldest age groups. The downturn for the oldest is almost certainly a cohort effect due to their lower lifetime income. Increasing dependency rates will for given levels of services and transfer payments tend to increase total expenditure fairly substantially even when relative prices remain stationary. We know, however, that this is not the case. The implicit relative price of public consumption has increased steadily over time. (The National Accounts in Sweden assume productivity growth in the public sector to be equal to zero.) Thus even for a stationary population the GDP share of public consumption will increase for the same level of services.

Figure 3.3 also provides data for personal taxes (including capital and property taxes, social insurance charges and most payroll taxes) paid by each age group in 1997. Mats Johansson, who generously provided me with this data, has computed these figures from the Swedish Income Panel. Here it is evident that the age pattern of personal taxes reflects the life-cycle pattern in income. It is important to note that in Sweden most transfer payments – including pensions – are taxed, which accounts for most of the taxes paid by the retired. Indirect taxes and payroll taxes are not included, although the pattern of these will be similar to that of the income taxes. The main contributors to the state income tax which starts at incomes above a threshold of around 230,000 SEK, are the high-income middle-aged groups.

Extrapolating these patterns forward using demographic projections, tax revenue will start declining around 2020, transfer payments will increase at a much more rapid rate than revenue between 2005 and 2035, while the same applies to government consumption between 2020 and 2035. Hence after 2035, the budgetary pressure will stabilise, whereas up to that date it will steadily increase. The Swedish government's spring budget for 2001 contains a similar but more sophisticated computational exercise based on a stationary demographic expenditure pattern and the current surpluses in the budget. It implies decreasing expenditure up to around 2010 followed by a rapid increase. Thus the pressure on the budget balance would start to increase again in the next decade, although a serious deficit situation would not develop until the 2020s. This general pattern seems to agree well with Flodén's computations in this book of the direct demographic debt impact.

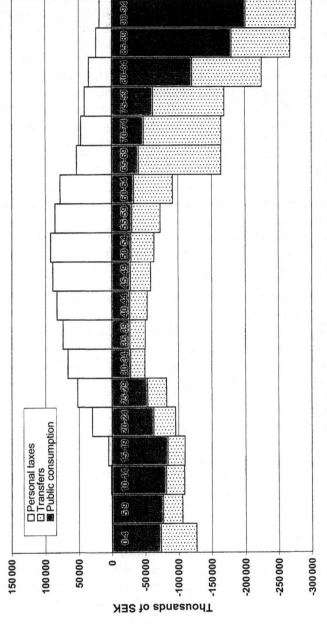

Figure 3.3 Public consumption and transfer expenditure per capita in age groups 1998
Source Nordén and Olsson (2000). Personal taxes per capita in 1997 from the Swedish Income Panel. Recomputed to prices in 2000 by Mats Johansson.

3.5   Modifying factors

It would be possible to create a great diversity of different scenarios based on more or less realistic assumptions. The format of this chapter does not allow any more detailed study of the many possible modifying factors. Faster productivity growth, immigration, increased labour participation rates and better health of the elderly etc. would, for example, contribute to improving budget balances. Poorer health, lower pension incomes, lower taxes and the secular trend of rising relative public service prices would work in the other direction. International factors such as raw material prices, interest rates and financial markets could affect the budget balance in any direction.

However, macroeconomic development is not wholly unpredictable, since demographic pressures will affect most macroeconomic variables in one direction or another. In Malmberg and Lindh (2000) the age patterns in growth and a number of macroeconomic variables have been extrapolated. Taking growth as the most important variable here, Swedish growth over the post-war period is positively correlated to the share of the population in the active age groups. Within the active age groups it is the middle-aged 50–64 age group who have the most positive effect. Extrapolating that growth pattern, Sweden will be in a high growth regime until the cohorts from the 1940s start to retire. Growth rates then will recede and may even become negative around 2030. In Lindh and Malmberg (1999a) these patterns have been verified in an OECD panel of countries using an extensive battery of tests to exclude a large number of potential statistical problems.

Looking at the uncertainty in the demographic dimension, we do not today know whether the fertility assumption of a TFR of 1.8 children per woman will be achieved or exceeded. If fertility rises, it will worsen the budget situation. If it decreases, it will improve the budget situation at least over the following twenty years. Concerning mortality the fairly moderate increases in life expectancy assumed in the demographic projections may be exceeded. The budget effect is, however, extremely uncertain. The pension system is in principle rigged to take care of this eventuality by decreasing pension replacement rates. However, if levels become too low, the government has to step in to uphold guarantee levels. To the extent that this increase in expected longevity is coupled to better health for a longer period, it may decrease expenditure pressures, especially if it leads to an increase in the length of the average working life. However, an increasing part of the electorate being retired may exert a strong political economy force that contributes to increased public expenditure. Even if that does not happen, the wage indexation of the pension system carries a certain financial risk in a situation where labour supply may tighten and increase wages and public expenditure at a rate that outstrips GDP growth.

Immigration can obviously alleviate some of the budgetary pressures since incoming migrants will mostly be in their early active years and will accordingly contribute to revenue, provided of course that they find work. Storesletten (2000) examines whether there is a feasible immigration policy for the United States to offset the fiscal problems of ageing. He finds, for example, that admitting 1.6 million 40–44-year-old high-skilled immigrants annually would do the trick. This is, however, an unlikely group to attract to Sweden. The countries within the European labour market area will all start to experience declines in their active populations. Accordingly the rest of the Union can hardly be a source for large-scale migration.

It is likely that increased investments in human capital may be very worthwhile in order to improve our long-run ability to pay the bill for our ageing population. However, it has to be remembered that the pay-off from such investments will be forthcoming only with a lag of several decades and may be quite costly. Moreover, increased higher education will conflict with policies aimed at inducing higher labour participation.

There is also a specific demographic problem in the employment structure of the public sector. Although the workforce as a whole has been ageing in the 1990s, this ageing has been highly concentrated to the public sector (see figure 3.4: this data is an update of a material presented by Henry Ohlsson to the Labour Market Committee of the Swedish parliament in 1993). In a situation where there is a general downturn in the labour supply, it is probable that the strong outflow from the public sector will result in increasing upward wage pressure unless it is possible to recruit sufficient numbers of immigrants to the public sector (see Broomé et al. 2001 for a fairly pessimistic view). In order to maintain the service level, an increase in the relative wage level of the public sector seems almost unavoidable.

However, it should also be noted that replacement needs on such a scale may also provide a window of opportunity to introduce efficiency improving reforms without any strong union resistance.

The replacement problem is troubling in relation to health care and the elderly care sector. However, it is even worse within the education sector where 47 per cent of the current personnel are born between 1939 and 1955. This may prove to be a serious stumbling block for one of the strategies available to increase general productivity growth. The domestic production of human capital may turn out to be too expensive to be a feasible option.

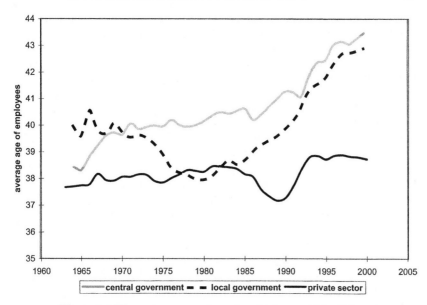

Figure 3.4 The average age of employed labour within different sectors of the economy
Source: Computed from the Labour Force Surveys by Henry Ohlsson.

This problem gets even worse if easy labour markets for small birth cohorts discourage private incentives for education, while education costs rise due to a scarcity of educated and in particular experienced teachers.

3.6   A reduced form approach

In the background material (Bilaga 9) of the Swedish Long Term Survey 1999/2000 the experiment is made to 'back-cast' current expenditure per age group using the demographic structure in order to check the reliability of the forward extrapolations of expenditure. These 'back-casts' miss a good deal of the actual development, casting some doubt on the method employed. It seems that any good forecast must also take into account developments in the rest of the economy.

Extrapolation of current expenditure and revenue patterns contains important information on what will happen *ceteris paribus*. However, the actual growth of expenditure and revenue is subject to both brakes and accelerators that arise from the overall balance of the economy. Extrapolations cannot take such factors into account. Actual budget deficits are influenced by all of these processes. If we want to gain some appreciation of how deficits in the economy vary with the age structure, a simple approach may be adopted. If we regress the budget deficit on age shares, this will not yield structural parameters since we only have a reduced form where all kinds of indirect mechanisms are present. Thus, it is hard to predict how policy changes will affect the age-related mechanisms.

The reduced form has the advantage, however, that a host of indirect mechanisms will be taken into account. Of course, the forecast will be conditional on the future stability of these mechanisms. There is no guarantee that the forecast will be accurate under a different policy regime. However, experiments with this approach have turned out to work quite well. One reason is that the in-data are demographic projections which are a lot more reliable further into the future than any purely economic projections. Consequently they will introduce much less uncertainty when used as forecasting variables. Another reason is that the basic correlations between demographics and economics build on quite inert life-cycle processes, which do not easily change their course.

Now, keeping these caveats in mind, let us see what a simple regression model indicates. I use annual National Accounts data on the financial savings of the consolidated government sector, i.e., including transfer payments and pensions from 1950 to 1998 from Statistics Sweden. (Lennart Berg has generously allowed me use of his linked series.) Using this measure of budget deficit divided by GDP as dependent variable and population age shares as the independent variables we obtain

$$\frac{S^{Gov}}{GDP} = \beta_1 \frac{n_{0-19}}{Pop} + \beta_2 \frac{n_{20-49}}{Pop} + \beta_3 \frac{n_{50-64}}{Pop} + \beta_4 \frac{n_{65+}}{Pop} + u$$

as the basic specification with the results reported in table 3.1 with two variants to account for serial correlation in the residuals. The autoregressive model is estimated under the assumption that the error term $u_t = \rho u_{t-1} + \epsilon_t$ where the ϵ_t is assumed to be i.i.d. The lag model simply includes three lags of the dependent variable.

In figure 3.5 we can see the implied forecast using Statistics Sweden demographic projections and the estimates for the age shares-only model. The forecast, somewhat surprisingly, agrees quite well with the previous informal reasoning and extrapolations. However, it is also apparent that the model has a very poor fit over the post-1975 period. This, of course, lowers the precision of the estimates and causes serial correlation among the residuals. Dependants have the expected negative effects while working-age groups and especially the middle-aged groups have positive effects. From an economic point of view, the coefficients make quite good sense, as does the forecast. We know that the period after 1975 in Sweden has been characterised by numerous regime shifts in economic policy. It

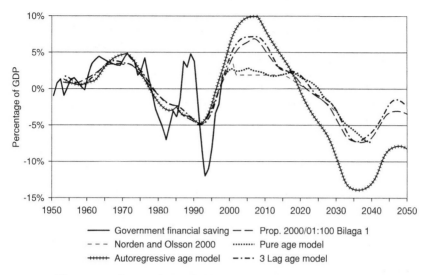

Figure 3.5 Comparison of different forecast models for the budget deficit in terms of Swedish financial savings of the consolidated government sector

is not very hard to argue that these shifts should be independent of the age structure. Thus it would be a much worse sign if the demographic structure actually correlated with these shifts in policy since that would surely indicate a nonsense correlation. The recursive coefficient estimates obtained by successively shortening the estimation sample turn out to be quite stable even as far back as to 1970 in spite of the turbulence of the 1970s and 1990s. We have also only twenty years of data to estimate the coefficients from the last regression.

It is evident from table 3.1 that the relative coefficient pattern is fairly insensitive to changes in specification. The alternatives reported here are an autoregressive error model and a lag model. The coefficient magnitudes fall in the lag model, as we would expect them to: diminishing to about one-third since the lag coefficients sum to 0.64. The corresponding magnification in the autoregressive model is explained by the strong autocorrelation in the age share series themselves. This model transforms the series by quasi differencing; $x_t - \rho x_{t-1}$. This tends to reduce variation in this case and increase collinearity among the age shares leading to magnified coefficient estimates.

In figure 3.5 it is evident that the model for autoregressive errors in the age model exaggerates the coefficients and the impact of the age distribution changes, while the lag model and the pure age model essentially

Table 3.1 *Least squares estimates 1950 to 1998 of the impact of age group shares on government financial savings as a share of GDP*

Dependent variable	Government financial saving/GDP		
Children 0–19/Pop	−1.32	−2.68	−0.47
	(2.06)	(1.76)	(1.64)
Adults 20–49/Pop	0.30	1.11	0.10
	(0.85)	(1.06)	(0.56)
Middle age 50–64/Pop	2.41	3.48	0.85
	(3.05)	(2.50)	(2.99)
Retirees 65+/Pop	−1.21	−2.20	−0.41
	(2.40)	(1.67)	(1.79)
ρ (col 2) First lag (col. 3)		0.80	1.15
		(8.64)	(13.33)
Second lag of dep var			−0.33
			(2.34)
Third lag of dep var			−0.18
			(2.09)
$\overline{R}^2$	0.35	0.76	0.84
Durbin-Watson	0.40		

Bold numbers are coefficient estimates indicating the percentage impact of a one percentage change in the variable except for ρ which is the autoregressive error coefficient. Absolute t-statistics in parentheses below the coefficient estimates.

produce the same forecast. Even more, the models also appear to satisfactorily track the forecasts from quite different simulation models. A deficit forecast from the Swedish government's spring budget Proposition Bilaga 1 and the estimate by Nordén and Olsson 2000, are also inserted in figure 3.5. The latter two estimates are generated by simulation from (different) macro-models. The budget estimate is based on the assumption that surpluses above 2 per cent will be used to lower taxes or increase expenditure up to 2015. Although based on a completely different idea, the general trend is quite similar to the age model-generated forecasts, with the exception of the autoregressive variant which tends to have larger swings but essentially the same timing.

The forecast models could be refined in different ways. There is a possibility that spurious regression results may make inference invalid. Controls for regime shifts, trade conditions etc. may certainly improve the fairly poor fit of the model, etc. However, the aim here is not to find a model that snugly fits the data. It is only a demonstration that age variables can produce a fairly good long-range forecast in a simple way. If there were a spurious regression problem, we would detect this by obtaining completely unreasonable forecasts. Since the forecasts look perfectly reasonable when compared to other types of forecasts, the probability of a spurious regression problem must be exceedingly small.

Feedback loops like the growth slump that age structure would predict have been allowed to influence the forecast. Whatever the reason, the prediction conditional on the post-war experience of Sweden is a continuous and large budget deficit after 2020 that eventually (after 2030 when the 1940s baby boom reaches the more care-demanding age groups) varies around a level of 5 per cent of GDP. Obviously this is not a feasible trajectory. Our government debt would quickly outgrow our creditors' confidence. However, in trying to foresee the problems we are not assuming that they will actually occur. Instead we are trying to find ways to avoid them.

Although a deficit of 5 per cent of GDP is serious, we have over the course of the 1990s moved between a surplus of around 5 per cent to a deficit that exceeded 10 per cent and then back again. Clearly it is not the size of the deficit *per se* but rather its permanence that gives cause for worry.

Demographic projections incorporate uncertainty about fertility, mortality and migration. Statistics Sweden have a number of different alternatives to their main projection which have been used with the pure age model to examine the sensitivity of the forecast to different assumptions about fertility, mortality and migration. The different scenarios do not affect the timing of trend breaks in the forecasts but rather rotate the direction of the curve. This reflects that the alternatives are constructed by more or less constant differences in parameters.

High migration (net immigration 30,000 persons annually) and high mortality (i.e. remaining at today's level) contribute to smaller deficits while low migration (7,000 net immigrants) and low mortality (continuing along the current trend of mortality decrease) will in the long run increase deficits. However, the differences for these variants are fairly small and do not affect the previous conclusions to any great extent. In figure 3.6, the migration scenarios, which produce very similar forecasts have been excluded for clarity.

Much more radical differences in the forecasts are caused by changing the fertility assumptions. In the low fertility (TFR 1.35) scenario at common European levels, no budget deficit will materialise even when the surpluses decrease to zero in the 2030s while the high fertility (TFR 2.0) scenario worsens the situation considerably up to 2050. However, the low fertility alternative means that in 2050 we would have 800,000 fewer persons in Sweden compared with today, 600,000 of them between 20 and 39 and almost 200,000 between 40 and 64. Referring back to figure 3.2 we see that the latest baby boom will in 2050 be at the age

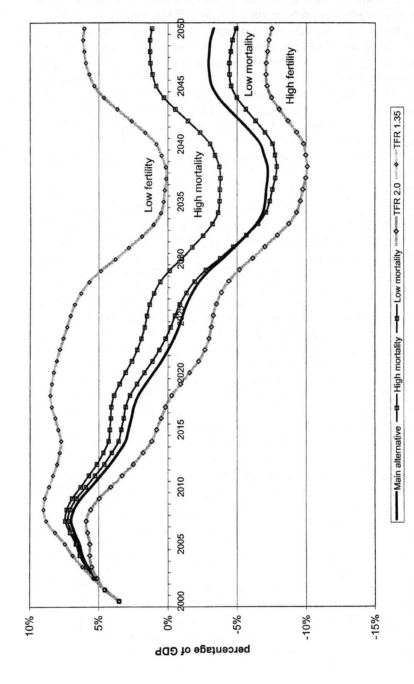

Figure 3.6 Demographic sensitivity of the age share only forecast of the deficit using alternative population projections from Statistics Sweden

when they contribute most to the tax base. Accordingly, a decade later the budget problem will reappear. The negative initial budget effect of fertility reflects the simple fact that children cost a lot of money and time. In Sweden about as much is invested in children as in buildings and machinery (Klevmarken and Stafford 1999).

3.7   Discussion

The ageing of the Swedish population gives no cause to pronounce any impending catastrophe. Other countries will face much harsher conditions, both because they are less prepared with regard to pension systems, as in the case of Spain, Italy and Greece, and because fertility has been considerably lower for a long time, as is the case in Germany. The Anglo-Saxon countries will do better since fertility has dropped less and immigration has been at a higher level. However, there are still serious problems that require adaptation.

The most obvious way to adapt to the situation is to reverse the trend of a shorter economically active life. A higher average retirement age would help at one end. At the other end, we must perhaps ask whether the production of human capital is optimised by keeping children and young adults in school as long as possible. Greater differentiation in primary and secondary education could make tertiary education more efficient and less time consuming.

Increasing human capital investment could also help. To preserve human capital, a health and social insurance policy that contributes to longer work lives and healthier retirement is a worthwhile complement to reforms of working life that would allow a more gradual retirement process than the present restrictive regime.

The main distributional issue to face is the generational redistribution from the old to children. Since children have no votes, this may pose a democratic problem when the elderly dependants increasingly approach a majority. There are reasons to worry about a situation where the median voter is primarily concerned about his or her retirement years.

Increasing migration to maintain a smooth inflow to the labour force would also help. Current migration policies and xenophobic trends in Europe may well prevent this, however, further compounding the problems. From a Swedish perspective it may be especially hard to compete for labour within the European labour market. Swedish is not an internationally very useful language and the climate is not overly attractive.

Cutting down on investments in children is not a long-run sustainable solution although as a temporary budget solution it might appear tempting for short-sighted politicians. It is difficult, however, to see how welfare could be improved by abstaining from children. Personally I find it hard to take such a remedy seriously.

In this book, there is a general discussion about how globalisation will affect the conditions for the welfare state and suggestions on how the welfare state can be more efficiently organised. This chapter as well as a number of other estimates indicate that efficiency gains need to be of the order of 5 per cent of GDP to meet the demographic challenge.

References

Andersson, Andreas and Österholm, Pär, 2001, 'The impact of demography on the real exchange rate', working paper 2001: 11, Dept of Economics, Uppsala University.

Andersson, Björn, 2001, 'Scandinavian evidence on growth and age structure', *Regional Studies*, 35, 377–90.

Attanasio, Orazio P. and Weber, Guglielmo, 1995, 'Is consumption growth consistent with intertemporal optimization? Evidence from the Consumer Expenditure Survey', *Journal of Political Economy*, 103, 1121–57.

Bakshi, Gurdip S. and Chen, Zhiwu, 1994, 'Baby boom, population aging, and capital markets', *Journal of Business*, 67, 165–202.

Björklund, Anders, Aronsson, Thomas, Edin, Lena and Palme, Mårten, 2001, *Ny kris i befolkningsfrågan?*, Stockholm: SNS Förlag.

Blomquist, N. Sören and Wijkander, Hans, 1994, 'Fertility waves, aggregate savings and the rate of interest', *Journal of Population Economics*, 7, 27–48.

Bloom, David E., Canning, David and Malaney, Pia N., 2000, 'Population dynamics and economic growth in Asia', *Population and Development Review*, April supplement, 26, 257–90.

Bloom, David E. and Sachs, Jeffrey D., 1998, 'Geography, demography, and economic growth in Africa', *Brookings Papers on Economic Activity*, 1998: 2, 207–73.

Bloom, David E. and Williamson, Jeffrey G., 1998, 'Demographic transitions and economic miracles in emerging Asia', *World Bank Economic Review*, 12, 419–55.

Bosworth, Barry, Burtless, Gary and Sabelhaus, John, 1991, 'The decline in saving: evidence from household surveys', *Brookings Papers on Economic Activity*, 1991: 1, 183–241.

Boucekkine, Raouf, de la Croix, David and Licandro, Omar, 2001, 'Vintage human capital, demographic trends and endogenous growth', *Journal of Economic Theory*, June, 104, 2, 340–75.

Broomé, Per, Carlsson, Benny and Ohlsson, Rolf, 2001, *Bäddat för mångfald*, Stockholm: SNS Förlag.

Easterlin, Richard A., 1961, 'The American baby boom in historical perspective', *American Economic Review*, 51, 869–911.

Fair, Ray C. and Dominguez, Kathryn M., 1991, 'Effects of the changing US age distribution on macroeconomic equations', *American Economic Review*, 81, 1276–94.

Feldstein, Martin S. and Horioka, Charles Y., 1980, 'Domestic saving and international capital flows', *Economic Journal*, 90, 314–29.

Fry, Maxwell J. and Mason, Andrew, 1982, 'The variable rate-of-growth effect in the life-cycle saving model', *Economic Inquiry*, 20, 426–42.

Herbertsson, Tryggvi Thor and Zoega, Gylfi, 1999, 'Trade surpluses and life-cycle saving behaviour', *Economics Letters*, 65, 227–37.

Higgins, Matthew, 1998, 'Demography, national savings, and international capital flows', *International Economic Review*, 39, 343–69.

Higgins, Matthew and Williamson, Jeffrey G., 1997, 'Asian demography and foreign capital dependence', *Population and Development Review*, 23, 261–93.

—1999, 'Explaining inequality the world round: cohort size, Kuznets curves, and openness', Staff Report No. 79, Federal Reserve Bank of New York.

Horioka, Charles Yuji, 1991, 'The determinants of Japan's saving rate: the impact of the age structure of the population and other factors', *The Economic Studies Quarterly*, 42, 237–53.

Kelley, Allen C. and Schmidt, Robert M., 1996, 'Saving, dependency and development', *Journal of Population Economics*, 9, 365–86.

Klevmarken, Anders N. and Stafford, Frank P., 1999, 'Measuring investment in young children with time diaries', in J. P. Smith and R. J. Willis (eds.), *Wealth, work and health: innovations in measurement in social sciences*, University of Michigan Press.

Kremer, Michael, 1993, 'Population growth and technological change: one million B.C. to 1990', *Quarterly Journal of Economics*, 108, 681–716.

Leff, Nathaniel H., 1969, 'Dependency rates and saving rates', *American Economic Review*, 59, 886–96.

Lenehan, A. J., 1996, 'The macroeconomic effects of the postwar baby boom: evidence from Australia', *Journal of Macroeconomics*, 18, 155–69.

Levine, Ross and Renelt, David, 1992, 'A sensitivity analysis of cross-country growth regressions', *American Economic Review*, 82, 942–63.

Lindh, Thomas, 1999, 'Age structure and economic policy – the case of saving and growth', *Population Research and Policy Review*, 18, 261–77.

—2003, 'Medium-term forecasts of potential GDP and inflation using age structure information', forthcoming in *Journal of Forecasting*.

Lindh, Thomas and Malmberg, Bo, 1998, 'Age structure and inflation – a Wicksellian interpretation of the OECD data', *Journal of Economic Behavior and Organization*, 36, 17–35.

—1999a, 'Age structure effects and growth in the OECD, 1950–90', *Journal of Population Economics*, 12, 431–49.

—1999b, 'Age structure and the current account – a changing relation?', working paper 1999: 21, Dept of Economics, Uppsala University.

—1999c, 'Demography and housing demand – what can we learn from residential construction data?', manuscript presented at European Network of Housing Research, June 2000, Gävle.

—2000, 'Can age structure forecast inflation trends?', *Journal of Economics and Business*, 52, 31–49.

Lutz, Wolfgang, Sanderson, Warren and Scherbov, Sergei, 2001, 'The end of world population growth', *Nature*, 412, 543–5.

74   Alternatives for welfare policy

Malmberg, Bo, 1994, 'Age structure effects on economic growth: Swedish evidence', *Scandinavian Economic History Review*, 42 (3), 279–95.

Malmberg, Bo and Lindh, Thomas, 2000, *40-talisternas uttåg – en ESO-rapport om 2000-talets demografiska utmaningar*, Rapport till expertgruppen för studier i offentlig ekonomi, Ds 2000: 13, Stockholm: Ministry of Finance.

Mankiw, N. Gregory and Weil, David N., 1989, 'The baby boom, the baby bust, and the housing market', *Regional Science and Urban Economics*, 19, 235–58.

Mason, Andrew, 1987, 'National saving rates and population growth: a new model and new evidence', in D. Gale Johnson and Ronald D. Lee (eds.), *Population growth and economic development: issues and evidence*, chapter 13, University of Wisconsin Press.

McMillan, Henry M. and Baesel, Jerome B., 1988, 'The role of demographic factors in interest rate forecasting', *Managerial and Decision Economics*, 9, 187–95.

—1990, 'The macroeconomic impact of the baby boom generation', *Journal of Macroeconomics*, 12, 167–95.

Mellander, Erik, 1999, 'The multi-dimensional nature of labor demand and skill-biased technical change', working paper 1999: 9, Institute for Labour Market Policy Evaluation, Uppsala.

Miles, David, 1999, 'Modelling the impact of demographic change upon the economy', *Economic Journal*, 109, 1–36.

Nordén, Carl J. and Olsson, Hans, 2000, *Befolkningsutvecklingen och framtida välfärden. De demografiska förändringarnas inverkan på de offentliga utgifterna och deras finansiering*, En rapport på uppdrag av TCO från Konjunkturinstitutet och Riksförsäkringsverket, Stockholm.

OECD 1998, *Maintaining prosperity in an ageing society*, Paris: OECD Publications.

Ohlsson, Rolf, 1986, *Högre utbildning och demografisk förändring*, Lund: Ekonomisk-historiska föreningen.

Palme, Mårten and Svensson, Ingemar, 1999, 'Social security, occupational pensions, and retirement in Sweden', in Jonathan Gruber and David A. Wise (eds.), *Social security and retirement around the world*. NBER Conference Report series. Chicago and London: University of Chicago Press, 355–402.

Persson, Joakim and Malmberg, Bo, 1996, 'Human capital, demographics and growth across the US states 1920–1990', seminar paper No. 619, Institute for International Economic Studies, Stockholm University.

Poterba, James M., 2000, 'Demographic structure and asset returns', *Review of Economics and Statistics*, lecture at Harvard University, March, Cambridge, Massachusetts.

Ram, Rati, 1982, 'Dependency rates and aggregate savings: a new international cross-section study', *American Economic Review*, 72, 537–44.

Shimer, Robert, 1998, 'Why is the US unemployment rate so much lower?', *NBER Macroeconomics Annual*, 13–61.

Söderström, L., Björklund, A., Edebalk, P. G. and Kruse, A., *Från dagis till servicehus – välfärdspolitik i livets olika skeden – 1999 års rapport*, Stockholm: SNS Förlag, 1999.

Spring Budget proposition 2001, *Svensk ekonomi, Bilaga 1*, Prop. 2000/01: 100, Stockholm: Ministry of Finance. SCB 2000, *Sveriges framtida befolkning –*

befolkningsframskrivning för åren 2000–2050, Demografiska rapporter 2000: 1, Stockholm: Statistics Sweden.

Storesletten, Kjetil, 2000, 'Sustaining fiscal policy through immigration', *Journal of Political Economy*, 108, 300–23.

Swedish Long-term Survey 2000, *Långtidsutredningen 1999/2000*, SOU 2000: 7, Ministry of Finance, Stockholm.

UN (1998) Sex and age annual, 1950–2050, Revision 1998, New York: United Nations: Department of Economic and Social Affairs, Population Division.

—(2000) *Replacement migration: is it a solution to declining and ageing populations?*, New York: United Nations Population Division.

Wolff, Edward N., 1996, 'The productivity slowdown: the culprit at last? Follow-up on Hulten and Wolff', *American Economic Review*, 86, 1239–52.

4 Emigration from the Scandinavian welfare states*

Peder J. Pedersen, Marianne Røed and Lena Schröder

4.1 Introduction

The topic of this chapter is the challenge international mobility, both emigration and immigration, poses to the Scandinavian welfare states. Earlier contributions have mainly discussed issues related to immigration from low-income countries. We turn the focus mainly on to the emigration and return migration of Scandinavians from a 'brain gain or drain' point of view. Thus, a specific object of interest is the selection pattern, that is, the distribution of human capital and (earning) abilities in the emigrant and return migrant groups compared to the distribution of these variables in the populations of the Scandinavian countries.

Labour market institutions and welfare systems vary among countries, including within the Scandinavian region. There are, however, a number of similarities in the Scandinavian systems that may have some relevance regarding international mobility. Compared to other countries, the Scandinavian labour markets are characterised by high participation rates (for both women and men), high employment rates, low variance and high mean values in the wage distribution and strong emphasis on active labour market policies. Especially in the lower part of the wage distribution unemployment insurance benefits are generous. Further, the labour markets are highly organised and the minimum wage is high, i.e., fairly close to the average wage. The Scandinavian welfare state model is characterised by very comprehensive eligibility for most benefits. Some benefit programmes depend on domestic labour market experience, but all residents are eligible for welfare benefits should they be unable to provide for themselves. Health and education services are supplied by the public sector at low or no cost. The financing of these welfare programmes and the broad range of collective consumption goods depend

* Financial support from SNS, Stockholm and from NOS-S is gratefully acknowledged. We are grateful for comments from participants at two project meetings at Krusenberg Manor and from the two editors, T. M. Andersen and P. Molander. We have had competent research assistance from Anne-Sofie Reng Rasmussen. The micro data sets have been supplied by Statistics Denmark, Statistics Norway and Statistics Sweden.

more heavily than in most other countries on income taxes and social contributions. Accordingly, the Scandinavian countries have among the highest tax/GNP ratio within the OECD area (cf. Joumard 2001).

This is the background on which we focus discussions and analyses of emigration from the Scandinavian countries, placing special emphasis on the human capital composition of the annual outflow and return flows. In relation to discussions about the long-run viability of the Scandinavian welfare model, an important question concerns the current and future impact of increased international mobility on the domestic stock of human capital.[1] The Scandinavian educational systems, with low or no tuition fees and fairly generous stipends or subsidised loans, combined with the much higher post-tax returns on skills offered by many other Western countries, lead to the expectation that the emigration propensity is increasing with the level of human capital. On the other hand, high minimum wages and a generous welfare system may stimulate immigration of individuals with relatively low earning abilities. The gross flows may thus represent a net loss of human capital, a 'brain drain', like the phenomenon discussed in the Canadian–US case (cf. DeVoretz and Iturralde 2000).

In the empirical analysis we investigate the migration patterns of Scandinavian citizens from the early 1980s to the late 1990s. We focus on differences between countries and on changes that have occurred over time. In 1994, Norway and Sweden joined the common labour market within the EEA. All Norwegian and Swedish citizens thereby gained formal access to the labour markets in other Western European countries, which Danes had enjoyed since the early 1970s.

The data set available for the analysis is register-based and provides both panel information and cross-sectional data on the migration histories, income, human capital variables and personal characteristics of all individuals who moved away from Scandinavian countries in three selected years between 1981 and 1998. With the exception of the migration histories, the same type of information is available for control groups of non-migrants.

In the following, section 4.2 relates our topic to some relevant contributions within the economic literature on labour migration. Section 4.3 presents the specific Nordic setting, where free labour mobility has existed for a long time. These five European countries, which have shared a free labour market for several decades, offer an interesting testing ground

---

[1] The Scandinavian welfare model differs from that of other European countries with respect to the taxes/GNP ratio and the variance in the wage distribution. Problems related to skill mobility, however, are not isolated Scandinavian phenomena, but are more broadly relevant for many countries; cf. the discussion of the Canadian/US case below.

for the functioning of a broader European labour market.[2] Section 4.4 describes 'the Scandinavian micro data set on migration'. Section 4.5 presents summary statistics which briefly describe developments in the Scandinavian migration flows from 1980 with regard to level, geographical direction and educational composition. Section 4.6 presents results from logit estimations of emigration probability and return probability. Section 4.7 concludes the chapter.

4.2   Migration and the welfare state: the background

We say that a group is positively selected if their average labour market quality is higher than that of the total labour force. In the opposite case, a group is negatively selected. What determines the selection of emigrants with regard to labour market quality, or, in other words, human capital and abilities? Applying the 'self-selection model' developed by Roy (1951) to the migration field, Borjas (1987) suggests an answer to this question. He maintains that, if potential emigrants are income maximisers, two conditions must be satisfied in order for positive selection to take place: (a) there must be a strong positive correlation between the earnings a worker may expect in the home country and the earnings the same worker may expect in the destination country, and (b) the destination country must have a more unequal income distribution than the sending country. In the case where (a) is fulfilled but (b) is not, negative selection will take place. Borjas (1987) also shows that when (a) is fulfilled and income distributions in the sending and receiving countries are normal, the level of net migration between two countries is determined by the inter-country differences in mean income, while the selection bias in the immigration groups is determined by the variance of the income distributions.

According to this theory, the compressed income structure and the high level of income redistribution makes the welfare states attractive destinations, especially for low-skilled immigrants. And even if highly skilled workers, attracted by the high average income levels in the Scandinavian countries, are willing to move here from other parts of the world, they are negatively selected compared to the average earnings ability of corresponding skill groups in the sending countries. So, for example, in this view the less able Indian civil engineers would be the ones more likely to choose Scandinavia as a destination region. If we accept this theory, the same arguments apply in the opposite direction with regard to emigration from the Scandinavian welfare states. That is, the high

---

[2] Besides Denmark, Norway and Sweden, Finland and Iceland participate in the free Nordic labour market.

level of income redistribution could expose the welfare state to increased emigration among high-skilled, high-ability residents. And by the same argument, it would be the most able Scandinavian civil engineers who would choose to emigrate to the United States.

Also assuming income maximisation, Borjas and Bratsberg (1996) analyse the selectivity of return migration. Among those who remain in the host country, return migration intensifies the type of initial selectivity which took place when the emigrants left their home country. In other words, if emigrants were positively selected in the first place, the return migrants will be the least skilled among them. In the opposite case, the return migrants will be the most skilled among the emigrants. Again the implications of the theory are worrying from the point of view of the welfare states. The most desirable workers, in terms of labour market quality, are leaving the home country, and only the weaker among them come back. With regard to immigration to the welfare state, this theory predicts the opposite pattern: those who are least desirable in labour market terms are coming in, and it is the strongest among these who choose to leave again.

If we accept that the Scandinavian countries have some of the most equal income distributions in the world, and that the human capital and ability components of earnings are strongly correlated among countries, this theory predicts a positive relationship between the Scandinavian emigration probability and the income level in the home country. Further, the theory predicts a negative relationship between the return migration probability and the income level in the home country.

In a static model of a national economy, the welfare loss from a given net outflow of emigrants increases with the level of human capital and earning abilities comprised in this flow. This statement is clearly true if labour markets function perfectly; migrants settle permanently in the destination countries and do not remit any money to their home countries. However, within a more complicated framework that includes dynamics, return migration or market imperfections, the relationship between welfare effects and the level and composition of migration flows is far more complex. In the remaining part of this section we review some recent contributions to this discussion in the economics literature with particular relevance to the welfare state setting.

The main approach in analyses of the economic impact of international mobility on the welfare states has so far been directed towards immigration. A central aspect here has been the integration of immigrants into the labour market, measured by indicators such as participation rates, employment and unemployment rates, and the ratio between immigrants and native wages for given background variables. Typically, the concern in empirical analyses has been about how immigrants overcome the entry barriers in labour markets, which – at least in a Scandinavian setting – are highly organised and include relatively high effective minimum wages (see Bevelander and Nielsen 1999; Husted et al. 2000; and Longva and Raaum 2003). If these entry barriers are not overcome within a reasonable period, even fairly low annual net immigration flows would result in increasing pressure on the financial situation in a welfare state. Friedberg and Hunt (1995), writing on a US background of fairly quick labour market integration of immigrants, point to the risk of long-term unemployment in other institutional settings with wage rigidities. Razin and Sadka (1995) analyse a situation where the resistance towards immigration found in many countries is based on wage rigidities and income redistribution aspects. All immigrants are assumed to be unskilled. Resistance to immigration in this model is the combined effect of rigid wages creating higher unemployment among native unskilled workers and higher taxes due to expensive welfare programmes. Wellisch and Walz (1998) raise the question of why rich welfare states support free trade but oppose free immigration. Even though their model includes full factor price equalisation, their conclusion is that, for countries pursuing income redistribution policies, free immigration results in a lower social welfare than free trade. This is due to the net fiscal costs associated with unskilled immigrants in a comprehensive welfare state. Razin and Sadka (2000) assume implicitly that unskilled immigrants to the welfare state become employed – either without or with an impact on domestic relative factor prices – and they analyse the positive dynamic implications for a setting with a pension system confronted with an ageing population. Epstein and Hillman (2000) analyse a scenario opposite to the one used by Razin and Sadka (2000), i.e., a situation where immigrants to a large extent are unemployed and net recipients relative to the welfare state. Their point is, however, that this could be interpreted as a situation of social harmony, as some segment of the resident population has to shoulder the burden of unemployment, either in an efficiency wage or an insider–outsider setting. This segment could then consist disproportionately of immigrants who could be seen as rendering a (short-term) advantage to natives.

Razin et al. (1998) analyse the interaction between the tax burden and migration in a public-choice setting. The counter-intuitive main point in their model is that low-skill immigration can result in a lower tax burden on labour and in less redistribution than in a no-immigration setting. This is the outcome, even though the low-skill immigrants are supposed to join the native pro-tax and pro-transfers coalition. The mechanism behind this result is an assumption that immigrants do not take part in the domestic political process and that a greater share of natives in the middle part of the income distribution, due to fear of future higher taxes as a consequence of low-skilled immigration, shifts to support the domestic high-income anti-tax coalition. A statistical analysis of macro data for eleven European countries gives supporting evidence to the theoretical model. Razin et al. (2002) analyse only immigration. An interesting extension of the model would be to include selective emigration when highly skilled people have the highest emigration propensities, as found in most empirical studies. As they tend also to have the highest lifetime earnings, their emigration would imply a weakening of the anti-tax coalition in the economy, which would potentially jeopardise the counter-intuitive conclusion in Razin et al. (2002).

Changing the focus to emigration, Stark et al. (1997, 1998) show that the eventuality of applying for work in a bigger international labour market increases the return to human capital, and thus, the incentives to invest in it. In Stark et al. (1997) this is reinforced by return migrants who originally invested more in human capital due to the emigration option and who, by returning, increase the average level of human capital in the home country. In Stark et al. (1998) the emigration option has a positive impact on human capital investment without recourse to the return migration element. Haque and Kim (1995) use a model of endogenous growth in a two-country setting where the countries pursue different tax policies. Emigration from the high-tax country tends to truncate the skill distribution at a critical level, and the model results in a permanent reduction in the growth *rate* in the high-tax economy.

DeVoretz and Iturralde (2000) analyse the emigration behaviour of highly educated workers within a setting which is quite applicable to the Scandinavian context. The empirical part of the paper analyses the propensity to move from Canada to the USA using a small sample of highly educated people who were trained in a public-sector-subsidised Canadian university system and subsequently had the option of moving to the neighbouring US labour market, with its significantly higher post-tax private returns on human capital investments. DeVoretz and Iturralde open their paper by turning the question around, asking why the great majority of highly educated Canadians stay in Canada. A paradoxical answer is found in a quotation from the Canadian prime minister Jean Chrétien, who refers specifically to the Canadian welfare state – topping the international Human Development Index – as the main motive for not leaving Canada. From a narrow, individual, private-returns-based calculation, it would be expected that there should be an exodus from Canada to the US. A broader, family and life-cycle-based calculation will instead highlight the advantages of a more elaborate welfare state, making the majority – also among the highly educated – stayers (and return migrants).

Another recent Canadian study, by Iqbal (2000), presents results from a statistical analysis of the number of professionals emigrating from Canada to the USA as a function of the cross-country gaps regarding incomes, taxes and unemployment. Iqbal concludes that out-migration of highly skilled people is an increasing problem relative to the Canadian economy. Kesselman (2001) discusses eventual policy implications of the Canada–USA case and concludes than an 'Americanisation' of Canada would not be an appropriate policy response. If Canadian policy-makers were to react in this way, Kesselman argues, the response could be a faster out-migration because the welfare state attractions that keep most people in Canada would no longer exist.

Return migration is another important factor to be included in analyses of the overall impact of international mobility in the Scandinavian welfare states. Longva (2001) studies the annual flows of foreign-born individuals into and out of Norway in the period 1961 to 1999. He finds that the outflow as a share of inflow has a mean of 0.79 for the period, which then is a crude measure of the probability of return migration. The propensity to return to one's country of origin differs among migration groups. Borjas and Bratsberg (1996) analyse out-migration from the USA of immigrants from seventy different countries of origin. They conclude that immigrants tend to return to countries that are not distant and that are not poor. Their empirical analysis confirms the theoretical prediction, referred to above, that the skill composition of the return migration flows depends on the type of selection that generated the immigrant flow in the first place.

Earlier studies show that a large proportion of Scandinavian emigrants in the early 1980s had returned within a decade (Pedersen 1996). Among immigrants to the Scandinavian countries from other Western countries the same pattern is found, i.e., most of the migration is temporary (Larsen 1998; Longva 2001). In the Danish case this is illustrated by the fact that the stock of immigrants from other Western countries has been roughly constant during the most recent twenty years (cf. DEC 2001). But looking instead at the flow of immigrants from low-income countries to the Scandinavian countries, we see that return migration is at a low level.

The high incidence of temporary migration may indicate that Scandinavian emigration is motivated to some extent by home country career considerations. This can be the case if working or studying abroad improves the income prospects in the home country more than working or studying for the same period at home. Knowledge about other national markets, cultures, languages, technologies and organisations may be particularly productive in the international sector, which is relatively big in the small open Scandinavian economies. The range of sectoral and firm variations regarding training and jobs is probably narrower in small countries than it is in bigger ones. Thus, compared to residents in bigger countries, individuals in small countries may be more constrained by national borders when planning their careers.

If a person undertaking a period of work in another national labour market acquires new skills, resulting in a higher level of human capital on return to the home country, this should be entered into the human capital account. However, it is usually not possible to obtain direct measures of human capital investments for those staying abroad. Instead, alternative approaches are used, typically analysing whether post-return earnings are significantly affected by the time spent in the labour market of another country; the question is whether there is a positive return to returning (cf. Barrett and O'Connell 2000; Co, Gang and Yun 2000; and Røed 2002). If the answer is affirmative, this should be included on the human capital gain side of the accounts. Another important aspect regarding temporary migration is the impact on the overall fiscal balance. If individuals typically emigrate for a period after graduation from a heavily subsidised educational system, their tax payments to the home country would drop out during some of their most productive working years. At the same time, temporary immigrants from high-income countries would be taxed by the host country during their stay. The net fiscal impact would depend, among other things, on the net human capital balance.[3]

4.3   The Nordic countries: an early case of free mobility

Free labour mobility among the Nordic countries has a long history. It became formalised in an agreement between the Nordic countries in 1954, but, before that, Sweden had a liberal policy towards workers from the other Nordic countries. Denmark entered the EEC, now the EU, in 1973, and Finland and Sweden followed in 1995. Norway stays outside the EU but joined the European Economic Area (EEA). This last international agreement extends the free labour mobility inside the EU to members of the former EFTA area who stay outside the EU.

The Nordic countries thus have a long and comprehensive experience regarding labour mobility among them. In the 1960s and 1970s net migration from Finland to Sweden was at a fairly high level. Apart from that period, which was followed by an equally big wave of return migration

---

[3] High-tax countries like those in Scandinavia will typically have favourable tax programmes for highly skilled foreigners who are temporary residents. This is another factor to be included in an overall calculation of fiscal costs and benefits from temporary migration flows.

to Finland, the inter-Nordic flows have been fairly small, reflecting to a certain extent cyclical and group-specific differences in employment and income prospects. In quantitative terms, the inflow in the most recent decades from low-income countries has far outnumbered the inter-Nordic flows. In qualitative terms these flows are also very different from the inter-Nordic flows and the flows between the Nordic countries and other Western countries. The migration from high-income countries to Norway, Sweden or Denmark is typically related to reasons of work or education, while a large majority of the people entering from low-income countries are tied movers and refugees.

In a Nordic setting, Pedersen (1996) presents an analysis of emigration by skill from the Scandinavian countries in the 1980s. One of the purposes in the following is to update this analysis to include the subsequent decade, placing more emphasis on the potential problems of the Scandinavian-type welfare state in an even more competitive global environment. The level of emigration from the Scandinavian countries (by citizens of these countries) in the 1980s was at a fairly low level, showing some sensitivity to cross-country cyclical differences. The aggregate return migration was high and independent of the cyclical situation in the home countries. About 70 per cent of a cohort of emigrants at the beginning of the decade had returned ten years later. Skill migration was analysed in two dimensions; we related it to the length of education for all, and, more specifically, we looked into the emigration pattern for seven specific educational groups. Especially for Denmark, we found big differences in the emigration propensities by level of education, with the most highly educated group having an emigration propensity about three times higher than that of the group with only basic education. This very big differential in the Danish case could, however, be related to the much higher level of unemployment in Denmark than in Norway and Sweden in the 1980s. In estimations of the inter-Scandinavian mobility pattern it was possible to include group-specific average earnings and unemployment rates among the variables explaining the emigration propensities. In general, we found significant contributions from these group-specific average earnings and unemployment differentials. The relative impact of these two variables, however, differed systematically between skill groups. The impact of unemployment differentials was decreasing in the level of education, while the impact of cross-country income differentials was insignificant for those with basic education only, but was found to have a significant impact for more highly educated people. An increasing share with high education in the subsequent decade should thus increase the sensitivity of migration flows to income differentials.

The return pattern by skill in the 1980s was characterised by fairly small group differences but with the highest share returning among the highest educated group. However, ten years after emigration, the differences in accumulated return migration by skill groups was in no case higher than ten percentage points.

4.4   'The Scandinavian micro data set on migration'

The econometric analyses presented in this chapter build on three sets of micro data constructed from administrative registers in Denmark, Norway and Sweden. For each of the countries we have full samples of all emigrants 20 years and older for the three years 1981, 1989 (1991 for Norway) and 1998. Furthermore, we have 5 per cent random samples of the adult population in each of the years prior to the three emigration years. For all persons, emigrants and those in the population samples, we have an array of background variables. The demographic variables are age, gender, marital status, children, country of birth and citizenship, and the highest level of education completed. In addition, we have data on industry of work, unemployment, accumulated work experience and yearly income. All these variables are measured in the year before the relevant (potential) emigration year.[4]

For the emigrants, we know the reported country of destination. Furthermore, we have some knowledge of return migration. For the 1981 emigrants, we know whether they have returned by 1988 and/or by 1997 (Sweden and Denmark). For the 1989 (1991) emigrants we know if they have returned by 1997. We have attempted to ensure that the three national data sets are as comparable across countries as possible, but certain differences have been unavoidable.

4.5   Trends in Scandinavian emigration and return migration flows

In this section we present summary statistics to describe some main trends in the level, geographical directions and skill composition of Scandinavian emigration and return migration from the early 1980s to the late 1990s. In addition to the micro data set described in the former section, providing information about the three emigration years, we use available official statistics to give a general outline of the migratory behaviour of Scandinavian citizens during the two decades.

The aggregate annual emigration flows of all citizens from the Scandinavian countries are shown in figure 4.1.[5] As is evident from table 4.2

---

[4] Not all variables are available for all three countries.
[5] The somewhat higher flows of residents emigrating from the three countries have the same profile.

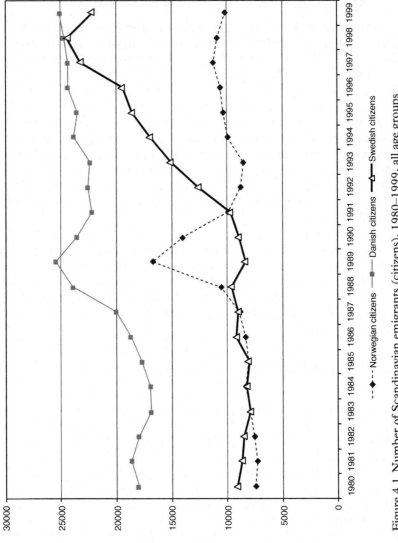

Figure 4.1 Number of Scandinavian emigrants (citizens), 1980–1999, all age groups
Source: The population statistics in Central Bureau of Statistics of Norway (SSB), Denmark (DS) and Sweden (SCB)

Table 4.1 *Percentage change in the Scandinavian migration flows to different regions between two years. Citizens, 21–65 years of age*

	Norway		Sweden		Denmark	
	1981–91	1991–98	1981–88	1988–97	1981–89	1989–98
Other Nordic countries	100	1	14	200	109	−48
EU countries outside the Nordic region	34	48	11	160	87	16
Other rich OECD countries	14	15	−12	150	23	1
Rest of the world	11	35	−9	266	12	41
Total	42	22	2	195	61	−2

Source: 'The Scandinavian micro data set on migration'.

below, the absolute numbers shown in figure 4.1 correspond to emigration propensities well below 1 per cent in all three countries. During the entire period, Danish residents have clearly had the highest propensity to move abroad.

Looking at the absolute numbers, we see that emigration shows cyclical movements around an increasing trend. The Danish and Norwegian 'hump' shapes around 1990 reflect cyclical downturns, as in the strong increase in Swedish emigration during the early 1990s when the Swedish economy went through a deep recession. In all three countries there is a marked increase in emigration propensity from the early (and late) 1980s to the late 1990s. Even though the increasing trend in out-migration did not become apparent until the late 1980s, the change is most pronounced in Sweden. In the 1980s, Swedish citizens had the lowest emigration propensity in the region. From 1988 to 1998 the total number of adult Swedish emigrants (citizens) increased, however, by no less than 200 per cent, and in the late 1990s the Swedes have clearly surpassed the Norwegians with regard to their tendency to move abroad. In Norway and Denmark the increase in number of emigrants is relatively smaller and more evenly distributed between the two decades.

Table 4.1 describes the changing geographical direction of the Scandinavian emigration flows with regard to their composition on four main destination regions. It summarises the shifts by presenting the relative change during the 1980s and 1990s. The two decades are obviously quite different. Looking, for example, at Sweden, we see that the number of emigrants to other Nordic countries increases by 200 per cent during the

Table 4.2 *Emigration propensities – percentage of emigrants among citizens, 21–65 years of age, in different educational groups*

	Norway			Sweden		Denmark		
	1981	1991	1998	1988	1997	1981	1989	1998
Compulsory	0.10	0.13	0.13	0.05	0.13	0.08	0.08	0.13
High-school level	0.30	0.33	0.29	0.11	0.27	0.40	0.58	1.00
University, low level	0.59	0.44	0.28	0.15	0.43	0.64	0.73	0.35
University, medium level	0.44	0.44	0.48	0.21	0.61	0.34	0.48	0.52
University, high level	0.85	0.67	0.80	0.34	0.77	1.18	1.45	1.06
Total	0.20	0.26	0.29	0.12	0.35	0.23	0.36	0.35
Engineers	0.48	0.45	0.45	0.12	0.51	0.52	0.56	0.68
Civil engineers	1.11	0.78	0.97	0.32	1.08	1.56	1.81	1.31

Source: 'The Scandinavian micro data set on migration'.

1990s, while the number of Danes emigrating to other Nordic countries declines by 48 per cent, and the number of Norwegians is constant. A possible 'escape' from the Scandinavian high-tax welfare states to realise higher private returns on investments in public-sector-subsidised human capital is not clearly visible. Between the late 1980s and the late 1990s the growth in emigration flows from Sweden to all the destination regions is much higher than in the two other Scandinavian countries. However, the growth in the number of Swedish citizens going to other Nordic countries and to low-income countries – 'The rest of the world' group – is clearly higher than the growth in the number going to high-income OECD countries.

Table 4.2 shows the emigration propensity in the adult population by level of education. In addition, the migration propensities of two well-defined occupational groups, engineers and civil engineers, are shown. Engineers and civil engineers in this context represent professions with a relatively internationally transferable human capital which demand relatively high basic investment costs.

Looking at the emigration propensities, we can see that they are strongly increasing with the length of education. However, from the summary statistics in table 4.2, there is no clear indication that this pattern was reinforced during the 1980s and 1990s. In Denmark, rather the opposite seems to have happened from the early 1980s to the late 1990s. In Norway, the emigration propensity within each educational group has changed very little between the selected years. Thus, in these two countries, the aggregate emigration propensity in the population increased

Table 4.3 *Propensity to return by education – percentage of emigrants within each educational group, citizens, 21–65 years of age, who returned within eight years*

	Norway		Sweden	Denmark	
Emigrated in	1981	1991	1988	1981	1989
Compulsory	43	64	54	33	48
High school level	44	63	47	30	31
University, low level	43	65	52	32	35
University, medium level	52	71	50	46	48
University, high level	52	79	48	48	51
Total	46	66	48	49	58
Engineers	52	74	49	52	55
Civil engineers	56	82	47	56	44

Source: 'The Scandinavian micro data set on migration'.

during an educational boom, i.e., as the composition of the population shifted towards higher, and more mobile, levels of education. In Sweden the picture is different; emigration propensities have increased strongly within all educational groups from 1988 to 1997. In all the Scandinavian countries and in all the selected years, civil engineers have a higher emigration propensity than the high-level university-educated group as a whole. With the exception of Sweden from 1988 to 1997, the development over time does not indicate an increasing trend in the relative number of civil engineers moving abroad. However, since the absolute number of Scandinavians educated within this profession has increased significantly, the absolute number of civil engineers emigrating from Norway, Sweden and Denmark increased sharply during the two decades. Of course, this is also the case with regard to the highly educated group in general.

Table 4.3 illustrates differences in the propensity to return migrate among the same educational groups as in table 4.2. In Sweden, the return pattern seems to differ very little from one educational group to another. In Norway, and to some extent also in Denmark, the return migration propensity rises with level of education, that is, those who seem most eager to migrate out also seem most eager to return to the home country. In the Norwegian data this pattern is particularly pronounced. In Norway, the return migration propensity also increases strongly for all educational groups from the 1981 cohort to the 1991 cohort of emigrants. In Denmark, the return pattern seems to be more stable over time.

Table 4.4 *Share of emigrating Scandinavian citizens with destination EU countries outside the Nordic region or other high income OECD countries, by education*

	Norway			Sweden		Denmark		
Emigrated in	1981	1991	1998	1988	1997	1981	1989	1998
Compulsory	46.7	33.4	43.8	52.8	38.1	48.5	43.9	58.7
High-school level	53.7	48.5	44.2	57.1	45.5	49.2	47.5	54.5
University, low level	60.9	50.6	53.0	54.4	47.4	40.6	41.9	46.1
University, medium level	50.4	51.4	54.6	68.3	55.6	38.9	54.6	49.9
University, high level	62.5	58.6	64.3	56.0	67.7	38.2	55.0	57.2
Engineers	53.3	49.2	61.8	65.8	45.7	24.6	49.6	43.7
Civil engineers	66.0	63.1	65.3	75.6	65.2	33.0	59.1	57.3

Source: 'The Scandinavian micro data set on migration'.

Exceptions in this regard are the strong increase in the return migration propensity among Danes with only a compulsory level of education and the marked decrease in the Danish civil engineers' tendency to return.

Schröder (1996) shows that, during the 1980s, relatively low-educated Scandinavians mainly emigrated to other Nordic countries, while the relatively highly educated emigrated to destinations within the EEA or other high-income OECD countries. This pattern was less pronounced in Denmark, since low-educated Danes to a greater extent than low-educated Swedes and Norwegians explored the common labour market within the EU. In general, Schröder (1996) and Røed (1996) both indicate that the migratory behaviour of low-educated Danes was more affected by the EU membership than were their more highly educated fellow citizens.

Table 4.4 shows the share of emigrating Scandinavian citizens, by level of education, who moved to a destination country within the EEA outside the Nordic region or another high-income OECD country. In Norway this share increased somewhat during the 1990s, while the opposite development took place in Sweden. However, these shifts in composition may have less to do with Norway and Sweden joining the common labour market in the EEA than with the fact that, compared to the emigration flows out of Scandinavia, the intra-Nordic migration flows are more sensitive to fluctuations in the Nordic economies. Finally, for Denmark, there has been a strong upward trend in the shares going to high-income countries outside the Nordic area throughout the 1990s. The only exception is the group with medium-level university training, but

Table 4.5 *Sweden. Accumulated net immigration 1987–1999 and population 31 December 1998, number of individuals*

	Net immigration 1987–1999	Population 1998	Net migration in % of population
Non-university	99,845	4,068,984	2.5
University	30,974	1,401,986	2.2
Physicians	−284	23,189	−1.2
Nurses	−1,639	105,936	−1.5
Civil engineers	−2,875	64071	−4.5
Economists	−2,811	57,102	−4.9

Source: Swedish Ministry of Education.

we find for this group as well a significantly higher share going to non-Nordic high-income countries in the late 1990s than in the early 1980s.

For Sweden, education-specific annual migration data are available from the Swedish Ministry of Education (2000) for the period 1987–99.[6] Some central accumulated group differences are illustrated in table 4.5. Overall, the Swedish population has increased by slightly more than 2 per cent due to migration. This is true both with regard to the university-educated and the non-university-educated segment of the population. However, the picture is different when we look at specific educational groups with a relatively high level of education and a type of education which (probably) is relatively internationally transferable, i.e., physicians, nurses, civil engineers and economists. For these groups, and especially for civil engineers and economists, there is a significant net loss throughout the period.

4.6   Estimation results

In this section we present some logit estimations of the individual emigration probabilities for each of the countries, for each of the three emigration years.[7] Since we do not have data on employment prospects and incomes in the destination countries, the analysis does not explain migratory behaviour. The results presented in table 4.6 are primarily a descriptive analysis of the distinctions between movers and stayers, emphasising the impact of variations in human capital and earning ability variables.

[6] We are grateful to Dan Andersson at the Swedish Ministry of Education for giving us the data for 1987–99.

[7] The specifications in this and the next section follow fairly closely a recent Danish study of emigration in the 1990s; cf. Danish Economic Council (2001), where emigration logits are estimated on micro data for 1993 and 1999.

Table 4.6 *Logit estimation of the Scandinavian emigration probability, Denmark, Norway and Sweden, 1981, 1988, 1989, 1991 and 1998*

	Denmark			Norway			Sweden		
	1981	1989	1998	1981	1991	1998	1981	1988	1998
Constant	-3.25	-3.34	-2.80	-3.50	-3.25	-3.52	-3.86	-4.85	-3.37
Level of education, preceding year (1):									
High school	0.89	1.48	0.83	0.91	0.68	0.63	0.86	0.78	0.57
University low	1.92	2.34	1.28	1.50	1.15	0.76	1.47	1.30	0.83
University medium	1.42	1.97	1.60	1.33	1.19	1.28	1.59	1.77	1.70
University high	2.42	2.79	1.81	2.18	1.81	1.90	1.91	2.31	2.03
Education missing	2.35	2.16	1.08	2.05	2.14	1.93	1.62	1.93	2.15
Student (in education)	-0.72	-0.89	-0.31	na	na	na	na	na	na
Single, children (2)	-0.11	-0.30	-0.29	-0.02 z	-0.28	-0.17	na	na	na
Married, or cohab.	-0.79	-0.74	-0.74	-0.69	-0.53	-0.33	-0.60	-0.43	-0.27
Female	-0.09	-0.12	-0.09	-0.02 z	-0.03 z	0.02 z	-0.11	-0.02	-0.03 z
21–24 years	0.50	0.44	0.73	-0.43	-0.21	-0.08	-0.22	-0.14	-0.19
30–39 years	-0.43	-0.52	-0.65	-0.17	-0.32	-0.25	-0.66	-0.48	-0.52
40–49 years	-0.99	-0.84	-1.28	-0.76	-0.82	-0.72	-1.25	-0.75	-1.38
50–65 years	-2.51	-1.55	-1.76	-1.79	-1.56	-1.08	-2.58	-1.84	-2.21

Level of yearly gross income (in 1,000s national currency, 1996 prices), preceding year:

Between 0 and 50	0.78	0.95	1.12	0.78	0.97	0.94	1.53	1.75	1.25
From 50 to 150	0.21	0.24	0.30	0.72	0.59	0.54	0.70	0.65	0.54
From 250 to 400	0.13	0.17	0.55	0.51	0.37	0.26	0.39	0.77	0.66
More than 400	0.86	0.92	1.37	1.08	1.09	1.11	1.59	1.59	1.58
Income = 0 or missing	1.05	1.30	1.84	1.40	1.57	1.69	2.45	2.88	2.23
Self-employed	−0.11	−0.4	−0.65	−0.70	−0.34	−0.32	−0.34	0.11	−0.39
Number of years of work experience, preceding year:									
0–5	na	0.23	0.75	na	na	na	na	na	na
10–14	na	−0.25	−0.35	na	na	na	na	na	na
15 or more	na	−0.53	−0.69	na	na	na	na	na	na
Experience missing	na	−0.76	−1.19	na	na	na	na	na	na
−2 Log-Likelihood	42401	58948	57449	29482	40782	48918	38811	37848	87916

(1) Level of education is defined in relation to the stipulated number of years necessary to complete the individual's highest level of education. The reference, Compulsory: 10 years or less, High school: 11–12 years, University low: 13–14 years, University medium: 15–16, University high: more than 16. The exception to this rule is Sweden, University medium: more than 14 years, excluding the PhD level, Sweden, University, high: PhD level. For 1981 the educational variable must be interpreted with caution since it was measured in 1971. This is also the reason Swedish 1981 data are excluded from tables 4.2–4.4, where education is the only criterion.

(2) Demographic variables are measured in the same year (the year of emigration or non-emigration).

(3) z indicates that the coefficient is not significantly different from zero on a 1 per cent level (Wald-chi-square test).

The first group of explanatory background factors in table 4.6 are five levels of education, with compulsory school as the excluded category. The universal result is that the emigration propensity is increasing in education. Looking at the profile over time in the educational coefficients, we can find no evidence of the profile becoming steeper, i.e., of highly educated people showing an increasing relative emigration propensity. Especially for Denmark, there seems to be a clear trend towards more equal education-specific emigration propensities.[8] The profile of the educational coefficients implies that emigration from the welfare state will tend to be on an increasing trend as even bigger shares in the population will be in the more highly educated categories.

Not surprisingly, it turns out that being single with one or more dependent children implies a reduction in the propensity to emigrate, which is significant in the two last years of observation in Denmark and Norway. This variable is not available for Sweden. Being married or cohabitating also has a negative impact on emigration propensity in each country. For Denmark, the level of the coefficient is nearly the same at all three points of time. In both Norway and Sweden, there is a clear trend towards marital status having less importance towards the end of the period. The gender variable shows that women have a significantly lower emigration propensity than men in Denmark and Sweden. The absolute level of the coefficient, however, is small, and in Norway gender has no significant impact.

Looking next at the profiles of the age coefficients where the excluded category is the age group 25–29 years, for Denmark we find the same profile in each of the three years, i.e., the propensity to emigrate is declining with age. For Norway and Sweden, the coefficient profiles show a maximum regarding the emigration propensity for the excluded group, with the youngest group, 20–24 years old, having emigration propensities slightly below the group in their late twenties. The fact that the age profile peaks later for Norway and Sweden could indicate that job-related mobility might be more important here than in Denmark.

Turning to the profile of the coefficients to the income interval variables, the excluded category here will encompass most blue-collar workers. The profiles for all three countries in all of the years are consistently U-shaped, with the minimum located at the excluded group. Looking

---

[8] The coefficient to the variable for 'education missing' shows that individuals in this group tend to have significantly higher emigration propensities than individuals with elementary schooling only. In general this may have something to do with problems related to registering information about people who are relatively internationally mobile. It may, for example, be the case that the proportion of people with education from abroad is higher in the migrant group.

only at individuals with positive incomes, we see that the highest value of the coefficient is found for the highest income interval. However, the coefficients related to the group with zero (or missing) income in the year prior to migration are even higher. The lowest income intervals are dominated by people outside or only marginally in the labour force. Thus, the profiles of the income dummy coefficients in table 4.6 clearly indicate that the Scandinavian emigration probability increases with income for those who are well established in the labour market. If we assume that the income distributions in the Scandinavian countries are among the most compressed in the world, this result is in accordance with the prediction of the 'Borjas model' described above.

In the Scandinavian welfare states very few adults would be without an individual income, either from work or from an income transfer programme. Thus, the high values of the income dummy coefficients for the individuals with no income or with income information missing presumably reflects a special composition of this group. They are mostly young and in school or university. However, the high emigration probability in the lowest income groups may also to some extent reflect that their (alternative) emigration costs are relatively small. Being self-employed implies a significantly lower emigration propensity in nearly all cases. The Danish data set contains information on aggregated individual work experience which is entered among the explanatory variables from 1989.[9] In both years, emigration propensities are clearly declining with work experience.

As is evident in table 4.6, the emigration propensities are determined in a complex interaction between many individual background factors. To give an indication of the net effect for a number of 'typical' male individuals, we show in table 4.7 the probability of emigration calculated from the estimated coefficients in table 4.6. As expected, education has a big impact. Looking at the changes in the propensities over time, we see emigration propensities peak in Denmark and Norway around 1990, while Sweden experiences a very strong increase for all the selected groups in the 1990s.

For one of the groups shown in table 4.7 we illustrate the interaction with prior income in figure 4.2. The general U-shape of the income effect is very clear as is the different development during the 1990s between Denmark and Norway on the one hand and Sweden on the other. Observe that the weights in the income distributions differ between the groups in the same way as the levels of the emigration propensities do.

---

[9] Collection of information for this variable began in 1964 based on a supplementary labour market pension scheme where contributions are determined as a step function of the number of working hours.

Table 4.7 *The percentage probability of emigration from a Scandinavian country, male citizens with different characteristics*

	Norway			Sweden		Denmark		
	1981	1991	1998	1988	1997	1981	1989	1998
Single, 25–29 years of age, compulsory education, income 50–150,000	0.31	0.35	0.25	0.07	0.29	0.24	0.21	0.22
Single, 25–29 years of age, high level university education, income 250–400,000	2.18	1.68	1.26	0.84	2.46	2.42	3.23	3.11
Married, 25–29 years of age, high-level university education, income 250–400,000	1.12	1.01	0.92	0.55	1.89	1.11	1.57	1.51
Single, 40–49 years of age, high-level university education, income 400,000 or more	1.77	1.52	1.50	0.85	1.57	1.88	2.99	2.00
Married, 40–49 years of age, high level university education, income 400,000 or more	0.91	0.90	1.05	0.55	1.20	0.86	1.45	0.97
Single, 40–49 years of age, compulsory education, income 250–400,000	0.12	0.12	0.60	0.03	0.08	0.08	0.08	0.15

Note: The probability examples are calculated from the estimated logit-coefficients in table 4.6.

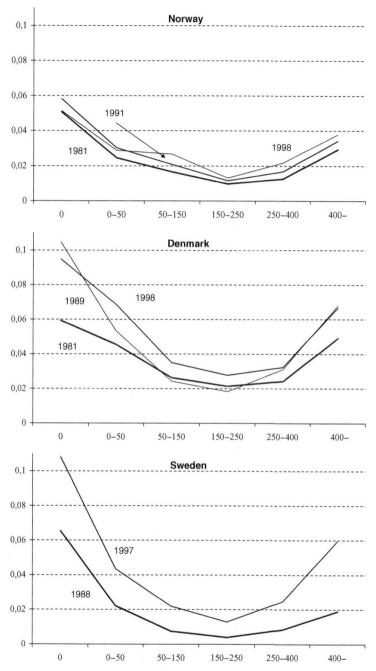

Figure 4.2 Scandinavian emigration probabilities, by level of income (in 1,000, national currency 1996 value). Single male citizens, 25–30 years of age, with a high-level university education

Table 4.8 *Return of 1981 and 1989/91 emigrants in 1988 and in 1997*

	Denmark			Norway		Sweden		
	1981/88	1981/97	1989/97	1981/90	1991/97	1981/88	1981/97	1989/97
Constant	-1.15	0.18	0.53	-0.04 z	0.50	0.29	0.67	0.54
Level of education, preceding year:								
High school	0.03	002 z	0.09 z	0.00 z	-0.17	-0.28	-0.26	-0.34
University low	0.19	0.16 z	0.03 z	-0.04	-0.04 z	-0.17 z	-0.04 z	-0.12 z
University medium	0.26	0.16 z	-0.04 z	0.22 z	0.20	-0.39	-0.37	-0.28
University high	0.21	0.13 z	0.16	0.12 z	0.50	-1.48	-1.46	-0.37 z
Education missing	-0.39	-0.51	-0.32	-0.07 z	-0.32	-0.47	-0.56	-0.68
Student (in education)	-0.13 z	-0.26 z	0.04 z	na	na	na	na	na
Single, children (2)	-0.07	-0.02 z	0.13 z	-0.14 z	0.22 z	na	na	na
Married, or cohab.	0.19	0.27	0.24	0.24 z	0.65	0.21	0.31	-0.07 z
Female	-0.12	-0.08 z	-0.09	-0.09 z	-0.11	-0.15	-0.24	-0.29
21–24 years	0.30	0.28	0.25	0.04 z	0.43	0.28	0.28	0.03 z
30–39 years	-0.03 z	-0.05 z	-0.13	-0.13 z	0.01 z	0.03 z	0.03 z	-0.10 z
40–49 years	-0.12 z	-0.05 z	-0.20	-0.26	-0.10 z	0.09 z	0.28	-0.08 z
50–65 years	-0.43	-0.24	-0.61	-0.35	-0.42	-0.28	0.15 z	-0.25

Level of yearly gross income (in 1,000 national currency, 1996 prices), preceding year:

Between 0 and 50	0.86	−0.24	−0.44	0.05 z	0.03 z	−0.27	−0.09 z	−0.12 z
From 50 to 150	1.18	0.08 z	−0.01 z	−0.09 z	0.05 z	−0.16	0.08 z	0.09 z
From 250 to 400	0.00 z	0.07 z	−0.10 z	0.15 z	0.17 z	0.09 z	0.19 z	0.16 z
More than 400	−0.17	−0.25	−0.34	0.01 z	0.03 z	−0.24 z	−0.21 z	0.12 z
Income = 0 or missing	0.99	−0.01 z	−0.45	−0.40	−0.70	−0.80	−0.69	−0.45
Self-employed	−0.40	−0.50	−0.28	−0.32	−0.33	−0.24 z	−0.01 z	0.48

Number of years work experience, preceding year:

0–5	na	na	−0.20	na	na	na	na	na
10–14	na	na	0.01 z	na	na	na	na	na
15 or more	na	na	−0.04 z	na	na	na	na	na
Experience missing	na	na	0.19	na	na	na	na	na
−2 Log-Likelihood	8155	8095	12822	5511	7046	6298	6113	6193

For Norway, data are not available for 1981 emigrants who are back in the country in 1997. For 1981, the Swedish educational variable must be interpreted with caution since it was measured in 1971, cf. the note to table 4.6. Explanatory variables: see notes to table 4.6.

Return migration

In table 4.8, return migration is analysed with respect to the same set of variables used to explain emigration.[10] In general, the relationship between human capital and ability characteristics and return migration behaviour seems to be weak, and the pattern of estimated coefficients varies between the countries and over time.

For the emigrants who left Denmark in 1981, the probability of return migration is significantly higher in the university-educated group. However, this pattern is not traceable in the 1989 cohort of Danish emigrants. For Sweden, a more or less opposite pattern is found for the 1981 cohort, i.e., return migration is decreasing with education. For Norway, no significant educational pattern is traceable in the 1981 cohort. However, with regard to the 1991 Norwegian emigrants, the university-educated groups have significantly higher return probabilities than the lower-educated categories. According to the results in table 4.8, the association between home country earning ability and return migration behaviour seems to be even weaker than the educational relationship. That is, fairly few significant coefficients to the income-level dummy variables are found. However, in the Danish case, the highest income group has a significantly lower return probability in both emigration cohorts. For Norway and Sweden, the observed return migration behaviour seems to be independent of the pre-emigration income interval. The only exception is that in both countries emigrants with zero (or missing) income in the year preceding emigration have a significantly lower return probability than the other income groups. The prediction in the 'Borjas and Bratsberg' model, referred to above, is that, when emigrants are positively selected, the relationship between the return migration probability and pre-emigration income is negative. This prediction is not supported by the results in table 4.8.

No consistent pattern is found for those who had their own business at the time of emigration. Finally, for Denmark, people with little experience have a significantly lower return propensity. The pattern of the estimated coefficients related to the demographic variables is neither very strong nor stable between countries or over time. Being married or cohabiting at the time of emigration means a higher return probability in Denmark in

[10] For Denmark and Sweden the data sets contain information on the emigrants from 1981 and 1989 who have returned to their respective countries in 1988 and in 1997 (for the 1981 emigrants) and in 1997 (for the 1989 emigrants). For Norway, we do not have information on who among the 1981 emigrants are back in the country by 1997, while the other Norwegian data on return migration are similar to what we have for Denmark and Sweden.

both decades, while in Norway the variable gains significance in contrast to Sweden, where it is insignificant in the 1990s. Overall, women tend to have a smaller probability of return than men, most significantly in the Swedish case.

Overall, the profiles of the age coefficients show return migration to be declining monotonously with age. In Denmark and Norway, the profiles become steeper, i.e., age differences regarding return propensities become bigger from the 1980s to the 1990s, while the opposite occurs in Sweden. In all three countries in both decades, we find the lowest return propensities for the group 50 years or older at the time of emigration.

4.7   Conclusions and perspectives

International migration flows are among the challenges facing the Scandinavian welfare states. Discussions of this challenge have moved on two different tracks. One has been a fear that their provision of generous universal benefits would expose countries to the risk of becoming 'welfare magnets', attracting low-skilled immigrants. Another track has been a somewhat parallel worry, i.e., that the high taxes necessary to finance very high levels of welfare spending and public consumption would create incentives for highly skilled people to emigrate to get higher pre- and post-tax returns on their human capital abroad. Even though part of this emigration is temporary, it would still have public finance consequences. The empirical results in the present chapter are mixed with regard to the development in skill migration from the Scandinavian countries since 1980. In Denmark and Norway, the overall emigration propensities peak around 1990, at the time of a cyclical downturn. For the whole period from the beginning of the 1980s to the end of the 1990s, the migration propensity among citizens in both countries follows an increasing trend. The Swedish experience is somewhat different, showing a stable level during the 1980s followed by a strong increase in the emigration propensity during the 1990s.

In all the Scandinavian countries the emigration propensity clearly rises with the level of education. There are no clear indications that this pattern has been reinforced or weakened from the early 1980s to the late 1990s. However, as the level of education has increased, the distribution of the Scandinavian population has shifted towards more mobile educational categories. Thus, the absolute number of highly educated people moving abroad has increased strongly.

In Sweden, information is available on the education among immigrants as well, making it possible to calculate that Sweden has had net losses in specific highly skilled groups in the years since the late 1980s.

Differences also appear among the Scandinavian countries regarding the composition on emigrant destinations. Danish and Norwegian emigrants have increasingly moved to EEA countries, while the strongly increasing number of emigrants from Sweden have shown a preference for the 'rest of the world' group and the other Nordic countries over the EEA countries.

The econometric analyses with micro data reveal that emigration probabilities vary positively with the level of education and negatively with age. Thus, with regard to total human capital, the emigrants have invested more than the population average with regard to education, but less with regard to labour market experience.

Relative to income in the year before emigration we find a strong U-shape in the coefficients. Emigrants who are well established in the labour market before going abroad seem to be positively selected with regard to earning abilities. In Sweden and Denmark, the strongest increases in the emigration probability from the early (and late) 1980s to the late 1990s appeared at the bottom and at the top of the income distribution.

With respect to return migration, we find a strong age dependence and only a few significant differences in the 1990s in the return pattern among the different educational groups. In Norway especially, the propensity to return is increasing with education in the 1990s.

References

Barrett, A. and O'Connell, P. J., 2000, *Is there a wage premium for returning Irish migrants?* IZA discussion paper, No. 135.
Bevelander, P. and Nielsen, H. S., 1999, *Declining employment assimilation of immigrants in Sweden: observed or unobserved characteristics?* CEPR discussion paper, No. 2132, London.
Borjas, G. J., 1987, 'Self-selection and the earnings of immigrants', *American Economic Review*, 77, 531–51.
Borjas, G. J. and Bratsberg, B., 1996, 'Who leaves? The out-migration of the foreign born', *Review of Economics and Statistics*, 78, 165–76.
Co, C. Y., Gang, I. N. and Yun, M.-S., 2000, 'Returns to returning', *Journal of Population Economics*, 13, 57–79.
Danish Economic Council, 2001, *The Danish Economy. Spring 2001*, Copenhagen.
DEC, 2001, Danish Employers Confederation. *Integration & arbejdssmarkedet (integration and the labour market)*, Copenhagen.
DeVoretz, D. and Iturralde, C., 2000, *Probability of staying in Canada*, Vancouver Centre of Excellence, RIIM, working paper, No. 00–06.
Epstein, G.S. and Hillman, A. L., 2000, *Social harmony at the boundaries of the welfare state: immigrants and social transfers*, IZA discussion paper, No. 168.

Friedberg, R. M. and Hunt, J., 1995, 'The impact of immigrants on host country wages, employment and growth', *Journal of Economic Perspectives*, 9, 23–44.

Haque, N. U. and Kim, S.-J., 1995, ' "Human capital flight": impact of migration on income and growth', *IMF Staff Papers*, 42, 577–707.

Husted, L., Nielsen H. S., Rosholm, M. and Smith, N., 2000, 'Employment and wage assimilation of male first generation immigrants in Denmark', *International Journal of Manpower*, 22, 1/2, 39–68.

Iqbal, M., 2000, 'Brain drain: empirical evidence of emigration of Canadian professionals to the United States', *Canadian Tax Journal*, 48, 674–88.

Joumard, I., 2001, *Tax systems in European Union member countries*, OECD Economics Department, working paper, No. 301, Paris.

Kesselman, J. R., 2001, 'Policies to stem the brain drain – without Americanizing Canada', *Canadian Public Policy*, 27, 77–94.

Larsen, K. A., 1998, *Migration between Norway and the EEA region 1989–1996*, Memorandum, ECON, Oslo.

Longva, P., 2001, 'Out-migration of immigrants: implications for assimilation analysis', unpublished PhD dissertation. Department of Economics, University of Oslo.

Longva, P. and Raaum, O., 2003, 'Earnings assimilation of immigrants in Norway: a reappraisal', Memorandum, Department of Economics, University of Oslo.

Ministry of Education, 2000, *International mobility among the highly skilled. Description of emigration and immigration in Sweden during the 1990s* (in Swedish), Stockholm.

Pedersen, P. J. (ed.), 1996, 'Scandinavians without borders – skill migration and the European integration process', in E. Wadensjö (ed.), *The Nordic labour markets in the 1990s. Vol. II*, North-Holland, Amsterdam.

Razin, A. and Sadka, E., 1995, 'Resisting migration: wage rigidity and income distribution', *American Economic Review*, 85 (2), 312–16.

—2000, 'Unskilled migration: a burden or a boon for the welfare state?' *Scandinavian Journal of Economics*, 102, 463–79.

Razin, A., Sadka, E. and Swaigel, P., 2002, 'Tax burden and migration: political economy theory and evidence', *Journal of Public Economics*, 85, 167–90.

Røed, M., 1996, 'Educational background and migratory behaviour in the Scandinavian labour market', ch. 6 in P. J. Pedersen (ed.), *Scandinavians without borders – skill migration and the European integration process*. Also in E. Wadensjö (ed.), *The Nordic labour markets in the 1990s. Vol. II*, North-Holland, Amsterdam.

—2002, 'The return to return migration', paper presented at the 17th Annual Congress of the European Economic Association, Venice, 22–24 August.

Roy, A. D., 1951, 'Some thoughts on the distribution of earnings', *Oxford Economic Papers*, 3, 135–46.

Schröder, L., 1996, 'Scandinavian skill migration in the 1980s', ch. 5 in P. J. Pedersen (ed.), *Scandinavians without borders – skill migration and the European integration process*. Also in E. Wadensjö (ed.), *The Nordic labour markets in the 1990s. Vol. II*, North-Holland, Amsterdam.

Stark, O., Helmenstein, C. and Prskawetz, A., 1997, 'A brain gain with a brain drain', *Economic Letters*, 55, 227–34.

—1998, 'Human capital depletion, human capital formation, and migration: a blessing or a "curse"?' *Economic Letters*, 60, 363–7.

Wellisch, D. and Walz, U., 1998, 'Why do rich countries prefer free trade over free migration? The role of the modern welfare state', *European Economic Review*, 42, 1595–1612.

5 Productivity and costs in public production of services*

Jørn Rattsø

5.1 Introduction

During the last two decades there has been a global trend of management reforms in the public sector and of attempting to scale down the public sector with privatisation and contracting out of public service production. Most countries have experienced fiscal pressure and imbalance, and have had the additional motivation for reform that public sector production is assumed inefficient. Government failure has substituted for market failure as the main concern. The reforms aim at overcoming the monopoly producer model and the associated agency problems in public institutions.

The analysis of productivity and costs in public service production must be based on an understanding of the decision problems of governments. We will use the principal-agent model as a framework and two aspects are important. The first concerns the principal, basically the electorate, but represented in various forms in political institutions. Collective decisions represent a challenge of preference aggregation, and characteristics of the political structure have been shown to influence the outcome. The problem is worsened in situations when public spending is separated from financing, the typical case with free or subsidised public services. The 'common pool' problem is discussed in the introduction by Torben Andersen and Per Molander, and the challenges of political decision-making are left out here.

This chapter addresses the second aspect: incentives for the agency, the actual provider of the services. When production is delegated to government agencies, well-known agency problems arise because of conflicting interests and limited information. They are expected to show up as slack,

* This chapter reports on joint research with Lars-Erik Borge, and I have received input to the evaluation of education and health care by Hans Bonesrønning and Rune Sørensen, respectively. I am grateful to SNS and the Norwegian Research Council for financing, for comments and suggestions from the editors, and for discussion with all project participants at Krusenberg Manor in May 2001.

that is, low productivity and high costs. When services are produced under government monopoly, consumer interests are weak and producer interests are strong. Attempts to control costs and stimulate productivity must overcome the agency problems created in this environment. The role of financing of the services is addressed in chapter 6 by Emmerson and Reed.

Government activities and organisation vary across space and time. There exists no well-defined set of goods and services produced in the public sector. Some key areas of government activity can be identified in most countries, such as national defence, legal system and infrastructure. They are basically collective goods and hard to arrange at private markets. In addition to the collective goods, governments produce individualistic welfare services, including schooling, health care and social services such as care for the elderly. The rationale for public provision is not as clear cut as for the collective goods, but social insurance, income distribution concerns and information problems are the main arguments for government control. Production is often arranged in a mix of public and private production, although some countries still mainly apply a government monopoly model. Welfare services are often decentralised to local governments, and with primary and secondary schooling as the dominating activity. Decentralisation allows taking account of heterogeneity of preferences, and also reduces the overload of the central government administration. When public service production is delegated to local governments, another dimension is added to the decision problem – the financing and control of local governments. Market-oriented consumer services produced by public institutions are a third type of services, but are assumed away in this chapter. These are old natural monopolies and many countries have undertaken privatisations in areas such as electricity and telecommunications.

A comprehensive literature exists on the productivity and costs of public sector service production, comparison of public and private production, and the consequences of reform, notably contracting out and privatisation. This chapter presents a short overview of the empirical results of this literature. The chapter offers new empirical analysis of two institutions that can control costs: budget processes and property taxation. The variation in budget institutions and property taxation among local governments in Norway allows an econometric analysis of the effects. A broad evaluation of public sector performance is offered in section 5.2, while education and health care are addressed in more detail in sections 5.3 and 5.4. The evaluations indicate that incentives are important beyond ownership. Incentive mechanisms in public institutions are addressed in section 5.5, and empirical analysis of incentives and costs are presented in sections 5.6 and 5.7, testing for the effects of budget processes and property taxation respectively. Section 5.8 summarises the main findings and challenges.

5.2   Broad evaluation of productivity and costs

The evaluation of any public project in principle must balance benefits and costs. Since cost-benefit analyses are not generally available, characterisations are based on simpler measures of performance. This section summarises studies of productivity and costs compared across similar public institutions and investigated as consequences of reform. The reforms typically imply some kind of introduction of competition in public service production, and the studies offer information about the potential to improve productivity and reduce costs in existing public activities. The chapter also addresses comparison of private and public production of similar services. This is the main approach in the literature on schools and hospitals discussed in sections 5.3 and 5.4

Efficiency variation among public institutions

Public sector service provision is organised in many institutions supplying the same services, such as universities, hospitals and courts. The main conclusion from many comparisons of the resource use in these institutions is that productivity varies significantly. Studies of the efficiency variation show potential for improvements in the service production.

The methodological approach to technical efficiency analysis is based on production functions. The production functions show the relationship between resource inputs and service outputs. The frontier production function represents the 'best practice' institutions in the sector and serves as a reference point to rank all institutions of the sector. The frontier is usually established with Data Envelopment Analysis (DEA), a programming technique. Charnes et al. (1978) generalised the method to multiple inputs and outputs, which is of particular interest in describing multi-dimensional government services. More recent studies analyse productivity growth in this framework. The strength of the method is that the productivity ranking of all institutions allows a measure of the total efficiency potential. The main weakness is sensitivity of extreme observations, and obviously the quality of data on inputs and outputs. Pestieau and Tulkens (1993) offer a survey.

Published DEA analyses are now in the hundreds, and they cover most aspects of public service production including kindergartens, schools and universities, hospitals and care for the elderly, police departments and prisons, courts, employment agencies, social security agencies, administrative services, etc. Examples of studies are Ozcan et al. (1992) on hospitals, Ray (1991) on schools, Kalseth and Rattsø (1995) on local government administration, and Kittelsen and Førsund (1992) on courts. As long as there are differences in technical efficiency among the institutions studied, there is an efficiency potential. Inefficient institutions can be brought up to the best practice frontier. The studies consequently always show a potential for improvement. If all institutions are brought to best practice, the productivity typically can be increased in the range of 10–20 per cent. The estimates may overstate the potential for improvement since the variables included do not capture all relevant factors affecting the performance. On the other hand, the observed frontier reflects existing institutions and even the best probably can improve.

While the efficiency studies suggest a potential for more efficient resource use within the public sector, they do not offer much information about how the potential can be realised. While some attention has been given to management reforms in the public sector ('new public management'), most of the literature has been oriented towards efficiency gains that can be achieved by opening up the public sector monopolies to outside competition. Efficiency studies have served as input to evaluations of competition and privatisation, as addressed below.

Consequences of reform: cost savings of contracting out

While full-scale privatisations basically have been made for old natural monopolies (telecommunications, electricity, etc.), introduction of competition for existing public institutions has been the dominating reform for welfare services and many linked support services. The public sector continues to control the service provision and the financing, but private and public institutions compete for the contract. The many studies available investigate services such as household waste collection, road maintenance and law enforcement, and also support services such as cleaning and catering. The evidence about contracting of government services is concentrated to a few countries – the United States, the United Kingdom and Australia, although some evidence is available from Canada, New Zealand, Switzerland and the Scandinavian countries.

Three methodological approaches are taken to throw light on cost savings with competition. The simplest method is to compare costs before and after reform based on a sample of episodes. Econometric cost analyses attempt to control for background factors that may influence the outcome and that may change over time (or with the reform). Case studies are more process-oriented and are used to demonstrate the sources of success or failure. There are hundreds of studies, and meta-analyses summing up the evidence are available by Domberger and Jensen (1997) and the Australian Industry Commission (1996). Lopez-de-Silanes et al. (1997) offer a broad analysis based on local governments in the USA. Needless to say, the cost effects of contracting out vary over time and space. And the costs can go up with competition reform. But the majority of the studies report positive cost savings. In the 203 studies evaluated by the Australian Industry Commission, only 10 per cent of the cases report cost increases, and more than half of them indicate cost savings between 10 and 30 per cent. The extremes imply cost reductions of 68 per cent and cost increases of 28 per cent. It is important to notice that the cost reductions are also observed when public institutions win the contracts in competition with private. Competition is the important factor, not ownership.

The criticism of the studies has concentrated on the inclusiveness of the cost concept and the quality aspect of the services. The studies typically compare the operating costs of internal government provision with the payments made to outside contractors. It follows that costs associated with the decision process and the design of the competitive tendering are not included. Transaction costs and transition costs must be added. On the other hand, the costs of organising and controlling services within the public sector are often neglected. Also many authors emphasise the costs associated with competitive tendering have benefits anyway, by raising the information level of politicians and bureaucrats and by focusing the policies towards service outputs. The other criticism concerns the incentive of private suppliers to gain profits by reducing quality. Many studies have attempted to control for quality, and analysis of the consequences of reform for quality offers a mix of results, from significant deterioration to substantial improvement. While criticism of cost coverage and quality in the empirical studies is relevant, the broad conclusion seems to be that cost reductions are achieved with competition.

The sources of cost reductions with competition are hard to identify and have not been subject to systematic analysis. The general understanding is that institutions subject to competition experience a pressure for more focus on service output and efficient resource use. The subsequent improvements in planning, coordination and management of the service provision will raise the productivity. Cost savings are not related to reduced wage levels, but to different use of labour. Institutions subject to competition seems to be less labour-intensive, that is, they make more use of technology, they apply more flexible work practices, and they make better use of unskilled labour (see Domberger and Jensen 1997).

5.3   Evaluation of productivity and costs in schools

Education is the core of the publicly provided welfare services. All countries have a basic public education system, although they allow private alternatives to a varying degree. Primary and secondary education is dominated by public schools everywhere and is basically tax-financed. Public institutions also exist in tertiary education, but competition between private and public institutions is more important, and of course the importance of individual choice by students is much larger. The primary school system is often closed and protected from the rest of the society and dominated by producer interests, that is, teachers and their teacher unions. Competition is limited since school choice is restricted and to a large extent determined by where the parents live.

Racial issues in the USA stimulated the interest for analysis of the relationship between resource use and student attainment. The famous Coleman report investigated how more school resources could improve the achievements of black students. The conclusion of this evaluation of the US primary and secondary school system has been summarised as 'it's all in the family'. Family background characteristics are the major determinants of student achievement. This finding is consistent with the welfare state occupation with the effects of social inheritance in schooling. In our context of productivity, the Coleman study was the beginning of the 'educational production functions', and Hanushek (1986) is the classic reference and overview of studies. The literature generally concludes that school resources have limited impact on student achievement. Student achievement is measured by test scores, continued education, or labour market performance. On the other hand, there are large differences in performance between schools. Bonesrønning and Rattsø (1994) address the systematic differences in student achievement between upper secondary schools in Norway. Consistent with the literature on educational production functions, they find that the differences are accounted for by scale effects and variation in student composition, while school resources are unimportant. Their welfare state paradox is that the centralised and standardised system designed for equalisation creates such systematic differences.

A particular aspect of the school comparisons has been the separation between private and public schools relating to the significance of the Catholic schools in the USA. The broad conclusion is that Catholic schools perform better than public schools, but the literature is large and full of methodological controversy. The main problem is control for self-selection. Catholic schools seem to be most advantageous for minority students. More recent analysis (Neal 1997) indicates that the better student achievement first and foremost is obtained in inner cities. The differences are generally understood as a result of more autonomy in Catholic schools.

Vouchers and charter schools

Competition exists also without local school choice (as with Catholic schools), since the parents can migrate to their favourite school. Size of school district is used as a measure of such competition in an empirical literature again concentrated on the USA. Hoxby (2000) and Zansig (1997) conclude that this type of competition reduces costs and improves student achievement, and their results are supported by other studies. More efficient competition is obtained when parents can choose schools independent of residence, as with voucher schemes and charter schools. Reforms of this kind to encourage competition in the school system imply that the allocation of students across schools is affected and that the incentives of each school are changed. Competition in schools influences performance both through allocation and productivity. Allocation efficiency is promoted by allocation of students to exploit peer group effects. The mirror image of this reallocation is sorting according to characteristics of the students. Productivity in each school is improved if students and teachers observe more rewards for effort at the margin. If private schools are allowed, public schools will only survive if they perform as well as the private. Public schools will have strong incentives to improve their quality.

Hoxby (2001) analyses the experiments in Milwaukee (vouchers) and Michigan (charter schools). She concludes that vouchers improve the productivity growth (measured by improved achievement divided by spending) and that charter schools contribute to student achievement. Self-selection problems are a great challenge in these studies, since parents changing school for their child and the establishment of new charter schools will reflect the dissatisfaction with a (bad) public school. The good news is that public schools experiencing these types of competition have also improved student achievement.

Resource use and student performance in education illustrate the complexities of organisation and reform. It seems clear that more competition, by the use of vouchers and/or charter schools, raises the productivity of schools. They produce better students given the resources they have. Talented students from low-income families may gain most from this competition, since they get away from bad public schools. But there is a downside of competition reform. The sorting that results may lock students with low abilities and from low-income families into public schools with unproductive student composition. These schools must show significant productivity improvement to compensate for the worsening of student allocation. It seems hard to avoid a trade-off between productivity and sorting, and even if all students gain from competition, new differences between students may result. The sorting of students clearly is a challenge for the design of school reform.

Universities

The competition in tertiary education seems to be increasing, since geographic mobility and information flows are on the increase. The individual choice aspects of tertiary education are addressed in chapter 13 by Andersson and Konrad. Here we will have a short look at the institutions involved. Public sector reforms in this area address organisation of ownership and financing and with some attention to economies of scale and scope. Empirical analyses are few and it is hard to single out background factors explaining the differences. The cost structure of 147 US universities offering doctoral degrees, 33 of them private, is investigated by de Groot et al. (1991). The universities are described by lower and higher level student production and research publishing. They find no clear difference in unit costs between private and public universities, but economies of scale and scope are important. This is confirmed in a more recent study by Koshal and Koshal (1999). The scale effect reflects specialisation, while scope effects are linked to the use of higher level students teaching lower level and the use of good researchers in teaching. Private universities tend to be too small to exploit in full these advantages of scale and scope. The analysis of Brown (2001) indicates that the quality of teaching (as evaluated by students) increases with the share of donations in the financing, but goes down with the share of public financing. Characterisations of both costs and teaching in private universities must be corrected for their selective recruiting of students, and generalisations about private–public differences on this basis are hard to make.

5.4   Evaluation of productivity and costs in hospitals

The market imperfections involved in schooling are discussed in chapter 13 by Andersson and Konrad, and the main arguments are relevant for health care, although health care in most countries makes more use of market mechanisms than schooling. Two market imperfection arguments stand out in health care. First, consumers have limited information about the services provided and the treatment needed, and the producers may exploit their information advantage. Quality may be 'too high' to bring in extra revenue or 'too low' to minimise costs and raise profits. Second, consumers pay only a small part of the costs involved, and they consequently have limited interest in holding down quality and costs. The demand side of the market is complex, with public and private insurance companies in the background.

These market deficiencies explain the structure of the production. Private for-profit hospitals are in a minority everywhere, and governments have set up public hospitals or encouraged not-for-profit hospitals (typically through tax incentives). Public hospitals dominate in the Scandinavian countries and the UK and are important all over Europe (60 per cent in France). Not-for-profit hospitals dominate in the USA (70 per cent) and are important in the European continent (about 30 per cent in Germany and Switzerland). For-profit hospitals are on the rise in the USA, but from a low of about 10 per cent, and are more widespread in Germany (about 30 per cent) and Switzerland (20 per cent).

Not-for-profit hospitals often are considered a politically acceptable alternative to government institutions. They take away some of the overload of the public sector and offer more flexibility. On the other hand, not-for-profit hospitals produce services that are harder to arrange in for-profit hospitals, often called 'uncompensated care' (Thorpe et al. 2000). Uncompensated care includes treatment of people without health insurance, long-term care, and non-patient activities such as teaching and research. There is a general concern that for-profit hospitals will exploit the information advantage. But more for-profit hospitals are entering the market, in particular in the USA. This may be understood as a result of reduced information problems due to increased public (media) interest and increased outside control.

Given the arguments above, it is not surprising that cost studies do not come up with clear cost differences according to ownership. Since for-profit hospitals may end up with 'too high' quality due to the information problem, it is not *a priori* clear that they have lower costs. The meta-study of Sloan (2000) concludes that 'overall, the empirical evidence demonstrates no systematic differences in efficiency between for-profit and not-for-profit hospitals'. The general result is that different studies reach different conclusions. Needless to say, cost comparisons are hard to do. Costs are measured per patient-units that are imperfectly standardised, the costs reflect accounts with different handling of capital costs and indirect and direct taxes, and in particular the quality aspects are hard to isolate. There is no perfect way of discriminating between slack and quality. Selection of patients to hospitals is another challenge to cost comparisons.

High costs may reflect advanced technology and high-quality service rather than slack. This was certainly the understanding of the 'medical arms race' in the USA under the cost-plus financing of Medicare up to 1984. Competition, often understood as a disciplining device, may have fostered growth of costs under this financial system. Again the empirical evidence is controversial. Dranove et al. (1992) offer a re-examination and analysis of the 'medical arms race'. They acknowledge that cost-plus contracts stimulate competition for patients and then competition in advanced technology, but do not find strong cost-increasing effects. Medicare switched to fixed-price contracts in 1984, and costs were reduced (Feder et al. 1987). At the same time insurance companies turned to more active control of costs with the growth of so-called 'managed care' organisations.

The broad conclusion of the literature on productivity in hospitals is that ownership has no clear effect. This seems to be a fairly general conclusion in evaluation of welfare state services (see Gouyette and Pestieau 1999). Attention should rather be directed towards competition and incentives of the producers.

5.5   Incentive mechanisms in the public sector

Given the overwhelming evidence that the productivity in public institutions varies, the next step is to identify the sources of low productivity and evaluate mechanisms that can improve efficiency. The sources of low productivity and high costs in the public sector are complex, and the extensive theoretical literature on incentives is matched by only a few empirical studies. The theoretical literature on the control of bureaucrats originates in the innovative contribution of Niskanen (1971). Unfortunately the empirical evidence concerning bureaucratic slack is limited, probably because statistical descriptions of institutional environment and bureaucratic performance are hard to get.

Kalseth and Rattsø (1998) show two steps needed for the empirical analysis. First, a best-practice frontier of administrative costs in local governments is established. Since administration is an input into service production, the trick is to relate administrative spending to the demand and composition of public services in the local government. Overspending is defined as spending above the minimum needed at best practice given a set of local characteristics. In step two the overspending is related to characteristics of political controls in the local governments. Overspending is calculated to about 20 per cent of administrative costs, and party fragmentation is identified as an important source of cost excesses. Frontier production functions form the basis of the evaluations of Duncombe and Miner (1997), Hagen (1997) and Hayes et al. (1998). While Hagen integrates the efficiency measure in a model of the budgetary process, the others relate efficiency measures to a broad set of institutional and socio-economic variables. Hassapis (1996) estimates a generalised cost function and studies conditions for cost minimisation. They all show political and institutional factors that can reduce the inefficiencies concerned.

The linking of productivity analysis and incentive mechanisms is a promising area of future research. The comprehensive literature on productivity analysis and cost studies documenting performance variation within the public sector offers a solid database for the analysis of incentive mechanisms. But the empirical descriptions of incentive mechanisms are scarce, and the productivity and cost measures at this stage are only related to broad measures of the control system. The methodological challenge is to handle the endogeneity of the incentive mechanisms established. The empirical analysis of sections 5.6 and 5.7 is an attempt to investigate relations between costs and incentives more closely.

5.6   Empirical analysis: budget process as incentive mechanism

As mentioned in the introduction, cost problems within the public sector can be understood as agency problems. The production is delegated to an agency and creates challenges for control. When the bureau has preference for slack, a conflict of interest exists between politicians and bureaucrats in standard fashion. When the politicians have limited information about costs, slack may be hard to control. This decision-making situation can be described as a game between the political leadership and the agency, and the outcome of the game depends on the structure of the interaction. The political leadership of the local government typically designs the interaction by determining the financing of the bureau and how the bureau budget is decided.

The theoretical literature suggests various incentive mechanisms to hold costs down. In this section we investigate the empirical relevance of organisation of budget processes. The background motivation of this emphasis is the broader literature on the role of budgetary institutions (Von Hagen and Harden 1994). Borge and Rattsø (2001a) provide a full documentation of the analysis. The setting is public services provided by a bureau reporting to a political institution. Local governments in Norway allow an analysis of comparable institutions. Production of utility services is delegated to a bureau, and control of slack is related to alternative ways of organising the financing of the agency. The key hypothesis is that organisation of the budget process affects the local government demand responsiveness to higher costs reported from the bureau, and thereby the cost setting of the bureau. The political institution is a local government and the highest political authority is an elected local council based on proportional representation and party lists. The preferences of the (majority of) elected politicians are worked into an annual budget including a bureau producing utility services The access to a detailed panel data set of most Norwegian local governments over five years allows an investigation of how the relationship is spelt out.

Understanding of the cost problem

When the bureau supplying the public services enjoys slack, the services may be produced above cost-minimisation. The slack may take the form of reduced effort or having extra rewards beyond salary. The bureau can only achieve slack when the political leadership has limited information about the true production costs of the bureau. The decision problem studied assumes strategic behaviour of a bureau when the local government determines the demand of the service. Migue and Belanger (1974) constructed the workhorse model of political–bureaucratic interaction in the case of slack. Boadway et al. (1999) have recently designed an integrated model of government-funded decentralised agencies emphasising how the structuring of financing creates incentives to reveal costs and induce effort. Their model motivates the empirical study reported below, with a clear separation between production and financing. However, their analysis is richer in addressing several agencies and handling incentive problems, and they are oriented towards the study of the marginal costs of public funds.

The conventional way of analysing local government decision-making is a demand model of local public services. Individuals demand public services depending on private incomes and tax prices of the services. The individual demands enter a political process whereby the local council makes a collective decision about financing and provision. Since the focus is set on control with a bureau, we will avoid entering the political decision problems here. The economic mechanisms described can be understood in an economy without residential mobility and with regulated taxes. It is reasonable to expect that increased mobility will reduce the problems of cost control, as in the analysis with and without mobility by Wilson and Gordon (2000).

The key decision concerns a local service produced by a bureau. The local utility service is private in character and is rationed to households in the community. The utility service competes with welfare services within the local government budget. The local government sets the priority between the utility service and the welfare service, and demographic factors affecting the demand for welfare services are important in the background. The budget constraint assumes grants and a regulated property tax, with revenue determined by the regulated tax rate and the housing volume (tax base of the property tax).

The local government demand for the utility service is essential for the interaction with the bureau. The demand for the services (utilities) depends on the unit cost asked by the bureau, the housing price, the property tax rate, private income, grants and the size of the welfare service client groups. Higher grants give room for provision of new services including the utility service. The shift of demand towards welfare services following an increase in the size of the welfare client groups is expected to reduce the demand for utility services. The local government demand responsiveness to the reported cost from the bureau is the key parameter of cost control. A higher cost asked for the utility service induces a substitution towards other services. The shifting allocation is described by the (absolute value) price elasticity. This demand elasticity certainly is affected by the design of the financing of local government. Empirical studies of demand functions under various systems of tax financing typically conclude that local government services are highly price-inelastic and in the order of 0.2 to 0.4 (in absolute value, see Oates 1996). Although the tax price concept used in these studies is not directly comparable with the local governments investigated here, it will be assumed that the price elasticity in absolute value is less than one (when the unit cost is taken as given).

The bureau producing utilities is assumed to enjoy high output and slack. The slack represents bureau revenue in excess of the true unit costs. The bureau now will trade off the increased slack resulting from higher revenue and the reduced output depending on the actual demand elasticity. The price elasticity perceived by the bureau depends on the budget process, and the analysis addresses both a Stackelberg game where the bureau acts as a leader and a Nash game where the local government is able to commit to a fixed budget. In the Stackelberg game the perceived elasticity is equal to the elasticity of local government demand and in the Nash game the perceived elasticity equals unity. A rise in the absolute value of the perceived price elasticity shifts the desired allocation to less reported costs and more output. More demand responsiveness to reported cost motivates the bureau to reduce cost and slack and increase output. This is the essential aspect of our understanding of bureaucratic interaction. In a top-down (centralised) budget process the local government is able to fix a budget for the bureau. When the budget is fixed, a rise in the reported cost must be compensated by a proportional reduction in the service volume. It follows that a top-down budget process will reduce the reported cost and slack compared to a bottom-up (decentralised) budget process where the bureau can take advantage of the limited demand response of the local government.

Design of empirical analysis

The empirical analysis covers a broad measure of unit costs (including capital costs and administrative costs) of a utility service (discharge of sewage). Unit costs are measured as total costs divided by the number of standard users (household with three persons). Unit costs on average (1993–96) are NOK 2,800, and with substantial variation across local governments (standard deviation of NOK 1,800). In 1997 the unit cost varied from NOK 500 to 15,000 (US$ 55 to 1,600). The main topic of this analysis is to investigate how the unit cost level is affected by mechanisms of political control, notably the local organisation of the budgetary process.

The budgetary process is described by data from a questionnaire, and separates between bottom-up process (decentralised), top-down administrative process and top-down political process (led by politicians). During the period under study, more and more local governments have switched from a bottom-up to a top-down political budgetary process, and the latter is now most widespread. The bottom-up budgetary process where the service departments prepare their own budgets at an early stage, resembles the model where the bureau acts as a Stackelberg leader. The 174 observations (about one-third) of local governments in this group for the whole period have the highest average unit costs, NOK 2,661. The two top-down processes resemble the Nash game as an overall budget is put forward to the service departments and the political committees, and they have average unit costs of NOK 2,579 (administrative) and NOK 2,272 (political). Local governments with a top-down political budgetary process have substantially lower cost than the two other groups (12–15 per cent).

The econometric formulation analyses unit costs depending on the variables describing demand for utility services (notably grants, private income, age composition of the population, local cost factors). Investigation of incentive effects splits the local governments in groups according to budgetary process. Two dummy variables describing the budgetary process are included. The main hypothesis is that a top-down budgetary process will reduce unit costs. It can be shown also that with a top-down budgetary process, the unit cost is expected to be less responsive to the fiscal condition of the local government. In a discussion of the empirical evidence concerning the effects of budget institutions in the US states, Poterba (1995) questions the interpretations of the estimated correlations between budget rules and fiscal policy. They may reflect correlations between fiscal institutions, fiscal performance and background preference variables. Our analysis can be criticised on the same grounds – budget process may be the result of political characteristics also important for the control of costs. This criticism is taken into account by including two variables representing the political leadership of the local government, the share of socialist members of the council and a Herfindahl index of party fragmentation of the local council.

Results: top-down budget process reduces slack

The econometric estimation is documented in Borge and Rattsø (2001a) and key results are shown in the appendix. The analysis shows that the variation in unit costs certainly reflects the economic conditions of the local governments. Grants dominate local government revenues and the cost level varies with grants. Bureaux are able to exploit revenues distributed from the central government. The elasticity is 0.3 and has economic importance when the grant level varies strongly (standard deviation of NOK 5,000 per capita around an average of NOK 19,000). The other economic factor highlighted is the demand pressure from the client groups (age groups) of the welfare services produced. The fiscal pressure resulting from high shares of young and old in the population has consequences for the cost level, and one percentage point increase in the share of young or elderly will reduce the unit cost by around 4 per cent. Background cost factors are included as controls. They show that a more decentralised settlement pattern leads to higher costs and that an economies of scale effect is present. To be expected, local cost conditions are the major determinants of local costs.

A political top-down budget process reduces unit costs by about 6 per cent compared to a bottom-up budgetary process. The sign effect for the administrative top-down group is correct, and smaller than for political top-down, but never statistically significant. The possible bias due to endogenous budgetary process will not necessarily weaken our results. If cost problems associated with a bureau have motivated a top-down budget process, our analysis may underestimate the effects of the two control systems. When the local governments with different budget processes are analysed separately, we can study whether the effects of economic variables are different under different budget institutions. Since a top-down budget process reduces the price elasticity of the utility service in question, we expect less cost-sensitivity to exogenous revenue, fiscal pressure/interest payments, demand pressure from demographic shift, and private income. The estimates show that these variables all affect costs under fragmentation and have no effect on costs under political top-down.

Political characteristics are included to account for background preference factors possibly influencing the choice of budgetary process. Socialist orientation of the local council contributes to higher cost level. Less party fragmentation of the local council is associated with lower cost level. A ten percentage point increase in the share of socialists will increase costs by roughly 3 per cent, whereas an increase in the Herfindahl-index by one standard deviation will reduce costs by 4 per cent. The results are consistent with another study of political characteristics and administrative costs by Kalseth and Rattsø (1998). They show that administrative costs go up with socialist orientation and weak (fragmented) political leadership. They understand political strength in an agenda setter model where the bureaucrats attempt to raise administrative costs. Falch and Rattsø (1999) relate socialist orientation and weak leadership to high spending per student in high schools. They see political strength as an important factor in determining the outcome of bargaining between the government and the teacher union about cost factors in schools. Political organisation seems to be important for costs independent of the role of budget processes.

5.7   Empirical analysis: property tax financing as incentive mechanism

Recent theoretical contributions on taxation are concerned with incentive effects. In particular, property taxes are discussed as a mechanism to hold costs down. Brennan and Buchanan (1977) introduce the incentive effects of taxation in a discussion of designing a tax constitution to constrain revenue-maximising governments. Glaeser (1996) develops the understanding of property taxes as a disciplining device for revenue-maximising governments. In a situation of regulated taxes, he shows that property taxation creates incentives for local service provision, since the services raise housing values and thereby the property tax base. Wilson and Gordon (2000) and Gordon and Wilson (1999) analyse similar relationships between voters and officials emphasising government waste (or slack) and in the context of tax competition. Property taxation may reduce waste since the officials will take into account the feedback via property values. Hoxby (1999) relates property tax finance to costs and efforts in schools. In her model, property taxation links school quality to school financing and helps control costs and efforts in schools. Local governments in Norway allow an empirical evaluation of this proposition. Full documentation of the analysis is given in Borge and Rattsø (2001b). The analysis addresses the same unit costs investigated in section 5.6 for the budget processes.

Understanding the incentive effects of taxation

Property taxation as a mechanism of cost control must be investigated in the context of a political institution financing service production. The key element is that housing prices respond to local government services and costs and have feedback to local government accounts. In practice, property taxes produce this link, with the associated system of house value assessment. Their cost challenge is the control of lower-level bureaux organising the service production. Property tax incentives in this analysis concern the financial constraints of the bureau, as analysed above with information advantage and utility of budgetary slack. It is shown how property tax financing affects the economic incentives of the bureau and thereby the costs of services.

Again the standard demand model of local services is the starting point of the analysis. To understand the property tax, the individual demand functions must include housing, as well as private consumption, utility services and welfare services. The link between supply of utility services and housing demand is of importance for the incentive effects here, and it allows for complementarity between housing and utility services. In this case the incentive effect will work even with no mobility. The main linkage at work is that bureau costs affect housing values and thereby the tax base of the local government. Mobility is expected to strengthen the effects on housing values.

The individual voter allocates exogenous private income to private consumption and housing, and the rest of the decision-making is taken at the local government level. The demand for housing and thereby the tax base of the property tax responds to the supply of local utility services given the assumption of complementarity. The migration equilibrium includes two types of capitalisation effects of utility services. First, more utility services raise the individual household demand for housing when they are complementary. Second, more utility services make the community more attractive for in-migration. Both factors drive up the gross housing price, and this property tax base feeds into the extended budget constraint (compared to section 5.6) of the local government. Property tax revenue is determined by the regulated tax rate, the net price of housing and the available housing.

The cost setting of the bureau will depend on the budget trade-off between service output and slack. Higher unit cost raises slack per unit by the same amount, but also reduces service supply given the budget constraint. In the case of no property taxation, the elasticity of service output with respect to unit costs is -1. In this case the bureau is financed by a fixed budget determined by grants in excess of welfare service spending. Property taxation changes the budget responsiveness to unit costs, and the utility services are more responsive when housing demand is inelastic. Empirical studies of housing demand typically support inelasticity. It follows that property taxation then has a negative effect on costs.

Design of empirical analysis

Norway is an interesting case because of the centralised tax regulation whereby property taxation is an option only for a part of the local governments. Our database concentrates on property tax for residential property in 1996 and includes about 120 municipalities (out of 435). We have access to data about actual property tax revenue for a standardised house. In the local governments with residential property tax, the property tax on average is about NOK 1,300 (US$150) per standard house per year. The cost data are the same as those analysed in section 5.6. When the municipalities are divided with respect to property tax, the average unit cost in those with a property tax is about 20 per cent lower than in those without. The raw data are consistent with our hypothesis about incentive effect.

The econometric formulation is similar to the analysis of budget processes. In particular we have taken into account that the residential property tax is voluntary and may reflect the result of political characteristics also important for the control of costs. In addition to including variables representing the political leadership of the local government (socialist share in local council and index of party fragmentation), we have estimated the model using an instrument for the property tax dummy. The instrument is a similar dummy capturing whether the local government had residential property tax in 1991.

Results: property taxation reduces slack

The economic determinants of costs are in accordance with the budget process model, as discussed above and shown in some detail in the appendix. It is important to control for local cost factors, and grants and demographic factors explain a significant part of the cost variation. Bureaux in rich municipalities and with little fiscal pressure can take out more slack. When property taxation is in place, the unit costs are lower. In the instrument variable model, the cost level is 14 per cent lower with property taxation. OLS estimates seem to underestimate the taxation effect, possibly reflecting that high-cost communities introduce property taxation to avoid lower service standards. The cost effect of property taxation is robust to inclusion of the political variables. We conclude that the Norwegian data provide evidence that design of tax financing matters to overcoming agency problems and thereby reducing costs. This is the first analysis known to document such a link between tax financing and costs.

5.8   Concluding remarks

Concern about low productivity and high costs in public service production has motivated management reform, competition and privatisation. The evidence about public sector service production and the consequences of reform are addressed in this chapter. Productivity and costs in government service production vary across producing institutions and depend on the economic environment. This chapter addresses three types of studies to give a broad evaluation of public service production: productivity and costs are compared across similar public institutions based on estimated production functions; private and public production of similar services are compared (in particular for schools and hospitals); and the cost consequences of reforms introducing competition in public service production are discussed.

The focus of the overview is set on collective goods and welfare services produced in public administration, while market-oriented consumer services typically produced in public or privatised enterprises (such as electricity and telecommunications) are left out. The welfare services are often delegated to the local public sector and raise issues of control and financing of decentralised government.

Productivity analyses and studies of contracting out indicate that technical inefficiencies are often in the range of 10–30 per cent. It should be noticed that quality aspects are hard to evaluate, and that public production is often burdened with complex goals. Schooling represents the core of the welfare services and competition reforms in this area seem to face a trade-off between productivity and sorting. Analyses of health care confirm the general understanding that cost and productivity differences are not primarily related to public versus private ownership. When competition is introduced, costs are reduced even when the production continues in public institutions.

We conclude that future research must address the effects of various incentive mechanisms for production efficiency. The theoretical literature of the principal-agent model is well developed, but empirical evaluations are few. The chapter offers new empirical analysis of two fiscal institutions that can control costs, budget processes and property taxation. The variation in budget institutions and property taxation among local governments in Norway allows an econometric analysis of the effects. The background understanding is that agency problems explain high costs as a result of slack from conflicting interests and asymmetric information. The analyses indicate that centralised budget processes and property taxation may contribute to reduction of cost levels in the range of 5–15 per cent. Other incentive mechanisms should be studied. Many countries experiment with new ways of financing public services, like vouchers or incentive pricing.

It should be noticed that our evaluation has concentrated on the performance of existing public institutions like schools and hospitals. There are potentials for cost reductions above the level of each institution, but these are played out in the political system. The structure and location of public institutions (such as colleges or hospitals) are controversial, but may have major cost consequences. The size structure of local governments also has large economic consequences in the many countries where public welfare service production is decentralised. While the costs of inefficient structures and locations can be large, they are also very hard to change. There seems to be a status quo bias in public institutions.

Appendix: econometric formulation of the incentive models

The appendix offers a short documentation of the econometric analyses discussed in sections 5.6 and 5.7, while a full documentation can be found in Borge and Rattsø (2001a and b). The empirical analysis of budget institutions is based on the following econometric model:

$$
\begin{aligned}
\log c_{it} = {} & \beta_t + \beta_1 \log y_{it} + \beta_2 \log r_{it} + \beta_3 i p_{it} + \beta_4 rural_{it} \\
& + \beta_5 \log pop_{it} + \beta_6 ch_{it} + \beta_7 yo_{it} + \beta_8 el_{it} + \beta_9 SOC_{it} \\
& + \beta_{10} HERF_{it} + \beta_{11} CADM_{it} + \beta_{12} CPOL_{it} \\
& + \Sigma_j \gamma_j CD(\mathcal{J})_{it} + v_{it}
\end{aligned}
$$

where c_{it} is the unit cost in community i in year t. The key economic demand variables are private income (y) and grants (r). Three variables describe the age composition of the population: the share of children 0–6 years of age (ch), youths 7–15 years (yo) and elderly 80 years and above (el). An increase in the relative size of these age groups is expected to increase welfare spending and reduce the amount of resources available to the bureau. The bureau responds by reducing slack, and consequently, we expect β_5, β_6 and β_7 to come out with negative signs. The share of the population living in rural areas (rural) and the population size (pop) are included to capture cost disadvantages in sparsely populated communities and possible economies of scale. The interest payment as share of revenue (ip) is included as an additional variable describing the economic situation of the local government, and is expected to have the opposite effect of local government revenue. Two variables represent the political leadership of the local government, the share of socialist members of the council (SOC) and a Herfindahl index of party fragmentation of the local council (HERF). Two dummy variables describe two budgetary systems, CADM is the centralised administrative type and CPOL is the centralised political budget process, while the decentralised budget process serves as a reference category.

The time series variation of many of the variables is limited, whereas the cross-section variation is substantial. Consequently, we do not rely on estimation methods that only make use of the time series variation in the data. The analysis first and foremost takes benefit of the cross-section variation. Common trend is captured by time-specific constant terms (β_t), and a set of county dummies (CD) to represent regional fixed effects. v is an error term. The empirical analysis is based on an unbalanced panel data set for the years 1993–98. Budgetary process data are only available for 80 per cent of the local governments for which we have cost data. With budgetary variables included, the total number of observations is 1,872.

The empirical analysis of property taxation is based on the following econometric model:

$$\log c_{it} = \beta_t + \beta_1 \log y_{it} + \beta_2 \log r_{it} + \beta_3 ip_{it} + \beta_4 rural_i$$
$$+ \beta_5 \log pop_{it} + \beta_6 ch_{it} + \beta_7 yo_{it} + \beta_8 el_{it} + \beta_9 SOC_{it}$$
$$+ \beta_{10} HERF_{it} + \beta_{11} PRTAX_i + \Sigma_j \gamma_j CD(\mathcal{J}) + u_{it} \qquad (13)$$

where c_{it} is the unit cost in community i in year t, etc. The economic and control variables are the same for the two analyses. The local governments

Appendix table 1 *Estimated cost effects of incentive mechanisms*

	Cost control of budget process	Cost control of property taxation
Centralised administrative budget process	−0.011 (−0.35)	
Centralised political budget process	−0.063 (−2.26)	
Property tax		−0.141 (−2.56)
Log of private income	−0.531 (−2.76)	−0.552 (−3.24)
Log of grants	0.282 (2.84)	0.349 (3.18)
Decentralised settlement pattern	0.617 (9.11)	0.493 (7.75)
Share of youth	−3.892 (−3.02)	−1.099 (−0.84)
Share of elderly	−4.477 (−3.11)	−3.240 (−2.11)
Share of socialists	0.267 (2.35)	0.458 (4.39)
Herfindahl index of party fragmentation	−0.511 (−2.34)	−0.162 (−0.73)
Method	OLS	IV
# obs	1872	1994
R^2_{adj}	0.445	0.455

Dependent variable: log of unit cost per standard user T-values in parentheses.
Note: Time and county dummies (not reported) are included in all equations estimated, other control variables are population size, share of children and interest payments, data for the period 1993–96.

with property taxation have value 1 for the dummy variable PRTAX. To address the endogeneity of property taxation, the variable is instrumented (for 1996) using observations about property taxation in 1991.

The estimates of the models are shown in the appendix table 1, while appendix table 2 documents the data set. In the first column, centralised political budget process is shown to give 6.3 per cent lower costs, while property taxation reduces costs by 14 per cent according to the second column. The interpretation of the other coefficients is addressed in the text.

Appendix table 2 *Data description and descriptive statistics*

Variable	Description	Mean (st. dev.)
Unit cost (c)	Total costs per standard user for discharge of sewage, Norwegian kroner (NOK)	2874 (1762)
Private disposable income (y)	Taxable income minus income and wealth taxes to local, county and central government, NOK per capita	64468 (9619)
Exogenous local government revenue (r)	The sum of lump-sum grants from the central government and regulated income and wealth taxes, NOK per capita NOK	19125 (5167)
Net interest payment (ip)	Net interest payment as fraction of exogenous local government revenue	0.023 (0.052)
Settlement pattern (rural)	The share of the population living in rural areas (1990)	0.533 (0.286)
Population size (pop)	Total population, 1 January	10145 (18442)
The share of children (ch)	The share of the population 0–6 years, 1 January	0.093 (0.012)
The share of youths (yo)	The share of the population 7–15 years, 1 January	0.117 (0.015)
The share of elderly (el)	The share of the population 80 years and above, 1 January	0.047 (0.015)
The share of socialists (SOC)	The share of socialist representatives in the local council	0.397 (0.149)
Party fragmentation (HERF)	Herfindahl index measuring the party fragmentation of the local council	0.268 (0.081)
Property tax (PRTAX)	A dummy variable that equals 1 if more than 50% of residential property is subject to property tax	0.305 (0.461)
Centralised administrative (CADM)	Dummy variable that equals 1 if the local government has a centralised administrative budgetary process	0.275 (0.446)
Centralised political (CPOL)	Dummy variable that equals 1 if the local government has a centralised political budgetary process	0.380 (0.485)

References

Australian Industry Commission, 1996, *Competitive Tendering and Contracting Out by Public Sector Agencies*, report No. 48, Melbourne.

Boadway. R., Horiba, I. and Jha, R., 1999, 'The provision of public services by government funded decentralization agencies', *Public Choice*, 100, 185–201.

Bonesrønning, H. and Rattsø, J. 1994, 'Efficiency variation among the Norwegian high schools: consequences of equalization policy', *Economics of Education Review*, 13 (4), 289–304.

Borge, L.-E. and Rattsø, J., 2001a, 'Design of budgetary processes for cost control: an empirical analysis', mimeo, Department of Economics, Norwegian University of Science and Technology.

—2001b, 'Property taxation as incentive for cost control: empirical analysis of utility services in Norway', mimeo, Department of Economics, Norwegian University of Science and Technology.

Brennan, G. and Buchanan, J., 1977, 'Towards a tax constitution for Leviathan', *Journal of Public Economics*, 8, 255–73.

Brown, W. O. 2001, 'Sources of funds and quality effects in higher education', *Economics of Education Review*, 20 (3), 289–95.

Charnes, A., Cooper, W. and Rhodes, E., 1978, 'Measuring the efficiency of decision making units', *European Journal of Operational Research*, 2, 429–44.

De Groot, H., McMahon, M. and Volkwein, H., 1991, 'The cost structure of American research universities', *Review of Economics and Statistics*, 73 (3), 424–31.

Domberger, S. and Jensen, P., 1997, 'Contracting out by the public sector: theory, evidence, prospects', *Oxford Review of Economic Policy*, 13, 67–77.

Dranove, D., Shanley, M. and Simon, C., 1992, 'Is hospital competition wasteful?', *Rand Journal of Economics*, 23, 247–62.

Duncombe, W. and Miner, J., 1997, 'Empirical evaluation of bureaucratic models of inefficiency', *Public Choice*, 93, 1–18.

Falch, T. and Rattsø, J., 1999, 'Local public choice of school spending: disaggregating the demand function for educational services', *Economic of Education Review*, 18, 361–73.

Feder, J., Hadley, J. and Zuckerman, S., 1987, 'How did Medicare's prospective payments system affect hospitals?', *New England Journal of Medicine*, 317, 867–73.

Glaeser, E. 1996, 'The incentive effects of property taxes on local government', *Public Choice*, 89, 93–111.

Gordon, R. and Wilson, J., 1999, 'Tax structure and government behavior: implications for tax policy', mimeo, University of Michigan and Michigan State University.

Gouyette, C. and Pestieau, P., 1999, 'Efficiency of the welfare state', *Kyklos*, 52, 537–53.

Hagen, T. P. 1997, 'Agenda setting power and moral hazard in principal-agent relationships: evidence from hospital-budgeting in Norway', *European Journal of Political Research*, 31, 287–314, also in J. Rattsø (ed.), *Fiscal federalism and state–local finance: the Scandinavian approach*, Cheltenham: Edward Elgar, 1998.

Hanushek, E., 1986, 'The economics of schooling: production and efficiency in public schools', *Journal of Economic Literature*, 24, 1141–77.

Hassapis, C. 1996, 'Are bureaucrats efficient? An application to the provision of AFDC', *Public Choice*, 86, 1–18.

Hayes, K., Razzolini, L. and Ross, L., 1998, 'Bureaucratic choice and nonoptimal provision of public goods: theory and evidence', *Public Choice*, 94, 1–20.

Hoxby, C., 1999, 'The productivity of schools and other local public goods producers', *Journal of Public Economics*, 74, 1–30.

—2000, 'Does competition between private and public schools benefit students and taxpayers?', *American Economic Review*, 90 (5), 1209–38.

—2001, 'School choice and school productivity', paper presented at conference on school choice, Islamorada, Florida, February.

Kalseth, J. and Rattsø, J., 1995, 'Spending and overspending in local government administration: a minimum requirement approach applied to Norway', *European Journal of Political Economy*, 11, 239–51, also in J. Rattsø (ed.), *Fiscal federalism and state–local finance: the Scandinavian approach*, Cheltenham: Edward Elgar, 1998.

—1998, 'Political control of administrative spending: the case of local governments in Norway', *Economics and Politics* 10 (1), 63–83, also in J. Rattsø (ed.), *Fiscal federalism and state–local finance: the Scandinavian approach*, Cheltenham: Edward Elgar, 1998.

Kittelsen, S. and Førsund, F., 1992, 'Efficiency analysis of Norwegian district courts', *Journal of Productivity Analysis*, 3, 277–306.

Koshal, R. and Koshal, M., 1999, 'Economies of scale and scope in higher education: a case of comprehensive universities', *Economics of Education Review*, 18 (2), 267–77.

Lopez-de-Silanes F., Shleifer, A. and Vishny, R., 1997, 'Privatization in the United States', *Rand Journal of Economics*, 28 (3), 447–71.

Migue, J. and Belanger, G., 1974, 'Towards a general theory of managerial discretion', *Public Choice*, 17, 27–43.

Neal, D., 1997, 'The effects of Catholic secondary schooling on educational achievement', *Journal of Labor Economics*, 15, 98–123.

Niskanen, W., 1971, *Bureaucracy and representative government*, Chicago: Aldine Pub. Co.

Oates, W., 1996, 'Estimation the demand for public goods: the collective choice and contingent valuation approaches', in D. Bjornstad and J. Khan (eds.), *The contingent valuation of environmental resources*, Aldershot: Edward Elgar.

Ozcan, Y., Luke, R. and Hagsever, C., 1992, 'Ownership and organizational performance: a comparison of technical efficiency across hospital types', *Medical Care*, 30, 781–94.

Pestieau, P. and Tulkens, H., 1993, 'Assessing and explaining the performance of public enterprises', *Finanzarchiv*, 50, 293–323.

Poterba, J., 1995, 'Balanced budget rules and fiscal policy: evidence from the states', *National Tax Journal*, 48, 329–36.

Ray, S., 1991, 'Resource-use efficiency in public schools: a study of Connecticut data', *Management Science*, 37 (12), 1620–8.

Sloan, F., 2000, 'Not-for-profit ownership and hospital behaviour', in A. Culyer and J. Newhouse (eds.), *Handbook of health economics*, Oxford: Elsevier, 1141–74.

Thorpe, K., Florence, C. and Seiber, C., 2000, 'Hospital conversions, margins, and the provision of uncompensated care', *Health Affairs*, 19, 187–94.

Von Hagen, J. and Harden, I., 1994, 'National budget processes and fiscal performance', *European Economy*, 3, 311–418.

Wilson, J. and Gordon, R., 2000, 'Expenditure competition', mimeo, Michigan State University and University of Michigan.

Zansig, B. 1997, 'Measuring the impact of competition in local government education markets on the cognitive achievement of students', *Economics of Education Review*, 16 (4), 431–41.

6   Use of fees in the provision of public services in OECD countries

Carl Emmerson and Howard Reed

6.1   Introduction

Reform of public services is never far from the agenda in any OECD country with debates often focusing on the level of spending that should be done publicly. This has led to different countries varying widely in the degree to which they rely on private spending through charges and insurance for many services.

A first indication of the variation across countries is demonstrated in figure 6.1, which gives the percentage of GDP spent on items such as fees and charges. This varies from negligible amounts in countries such as Turkey, Japan, Belgium and Spain to around 3.7 per cent in Norway and Poland and 5.3 per cent in Switzerland. In fact this figure only tells part of the story since the organisation of the delivery of public services in many countries is arranged in such a way that any private payment is not received by the state, but instead by a private sector institution delivering the service.

This chapter focuses on the methods of funding four services – higher education, health care, long-term care and child care – across OECD countries. We ask, are there stark differences between countries? Is it the case that countries that rely on a relatively high level of tax-based financing in one service also rely on high levels of tax-based financing on other services? How is the allocation of resources affected from both an efficiency and an equity perspective if there is an increase in private financing of a service? What consequences result from a greater reliance on the use of charges for a service?

The chapter is arranged as follows. In section 6.2 we describe the funding arrangements for the provision of higher education in a range of OECD countries. We then go on to analyse the recent trend in policy seen in the UK and its likely effects both in terms of efficiency and also any distributional effects. Section 6.3 looks at differences between countries in the provision of health care and any relationship

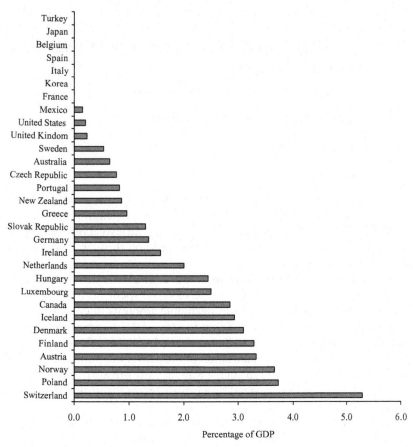

Figure 6.1 Government income from charges, fees and sales in OECD countries, % of GDP
Note: Figures for income from fee, charges and sales for the most recent year available which is 1997, 1998 or 1999 with the exception of Japan (1990).
Source: OECD, *Revenue Statistics 1965–2000*, 2001 Edition.

between greater reliance on private insurance and fees on the distribution of access to health care. Section 6.4 looks at spending on long-term care while section 6.5 turns to issues arising from state subsidies to child care and support for families with children. Section 6.6 concludes.

6.2   Higher education

The composition of expenditure on higher education in OECD countries

Every OECD country uses at least some public sector funding for higher education (HE) institutions, although the proportions of public and private sector funding vary widely, from around 85 per cent private funding in Korea to less than 5 per cent in the Czech Republic, Denmark and Austria (OECD 2001a).[1] Here we are particularly concerned with the breakdown of public sector funding into that from taxation and that from user charges (i.e. fees). There are different ways in which countries provide support to students. Some provide grants or other forms of subsidy to students or their families to assist with living costs whilst studying (known hereafter as 'maintenance grants'). Others offer such assistance in the form of loans; clearly, whereas a grant represents additional funding from taxation, a loan only does so in the short run.[2] Also, some countries impose graduate taxes, which can be viewed as a deferred user charge for HE. In the discussion below we limit ourselves in the main to looking at tuition fees, maintenance grants and loans.

Figure 6.2 shows public expenditure on higher education as a percentage of GDP. The definition of 'spending on higher education' used here is a wide one, and includes payments for living costs such as maintenance grants and student loans as well as direct expenditure on higher education teaching, research and buildings and equipment. The countries are ranked left to right by the percentage of GDP spent on HE in the public sector, which is split into loan payments to students, scholarship and/or grant payments, transfers to other private HE institutions and remaining expenditure (which includes research spending, teacher resources and capital expenditure). Countries where government spending on HE makes up a relatively large proportion of GDP include the Scandanavian countries, Canada and the Netherlands. Relatively low public spenders include Mexico, Italy and Korea. There appears to be no obvious link

[1] For a more detailed look at the extent of and composition of education spending in a wider selection of OECD countries, the reader is referred to chapter 13 in this volume.

[2] This is of course true only to the extent that the loan is eventually repaid. In the United Kingdom (for example), loan repayments are income-contingent, so that if annual income is less than £10,000, repayment is deferred until such time as income rises above the threshold. Also, in some countries (such as the UK) student loans are available at rates of interest below market levels. This represents an implicit subsidy to living costs compared with a laissez-faire policy where loans are provided by private financial institutions under normal market conditions.

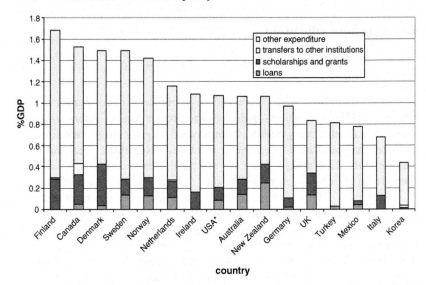

Figure 6.2 Public expenditure on higher education as percentage of GDP and its composition, 1998

between the proportion of loan funding in public expenditure and overall expenditure on higher education.

Figure 6.3 shows what happens to the ranking of countries when we add private sector funding for higher education to the picture. Korea and the United States stand out as countries that invest very large amounts of private sector funding into HE. Denmark, the Netherlands and Turkey are particularly low private spenders. With the exception of Korea and the USA, who top the league table of OECD higher education spenders (as a proportion of GDP) when public and private spending are added together, the ranking of countries does not change greatly when private spending is added.

A priori one might feel that a higher degree of public funding for higher education might encourage greater participation in HE, but as we show in the next section there are many factors to consider before making this judgement. The raw statistics, as presented in chapter 13 by Andersson and Konrad, show a rough correlation between total expenditure on higher education as a proportion of GDP and the expected years in tertiary education for the population in a number of OECD countries. However, the correlation between entry rates[3] into higher education of

---

[3] The entry rate is the proportion of young people in a country who enter higher education after leaving secondary school.

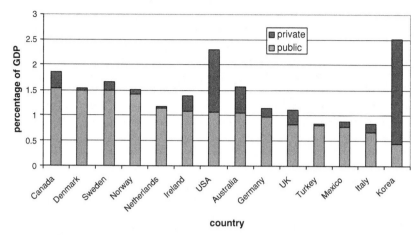

Figure 6.3 Public and private expenditure on higher education in OECD countries, 1998
Source: OECD (2001a).

Type 'A' as defined by the OECD,[4] shown in figure 6.4, is weak, and there are many outliers.[5] In order to get a better handle on the issues involved it is useful to consider one OECD country in greater detail. With this in mind we now examine the experience of the UK in the 1990s.

Recent UK experience

Higher education policy in the UK has undergone rapid changes to the structure of funding and government support for students' maintenance and tuition costs. Three distinct policy phases can be identified:

- Pre-1990: research and teaching in universities was funded by centrally determined block grants. Polytechnics and higher education colleges, which existed in parallel with universities whilst offering courses that were generally more vocationally orientated, were funded by local education authorities. Tuition fees for home domiciled students were funded 100 per cent by central government. Means-tested grants to cover maintenance costs were available to students with low parental

---

[4] Type A programmes are 'largely theoretically based and are designed to provide sufficient qualifications for entry to advanced research programmes and professions with high skill requirements ... [they] have a minimum cumulative theoretical duration of three years' full-time equivalent' (OECD, 2001a: 149).

[5] One problem with figure 6.4 is that it is difficult to compare data across countries with different educational systems and institutions; for example, Denmark and Germany have a low type 'A' entry rate, but a relatively high entry rate into type 'B' tertiary courses (vocational courses).

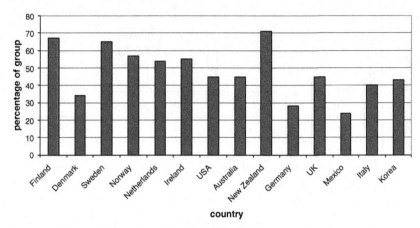

Figure 6.4 Tertiary education OECD Type 'A': entry rates, 1999
Source: OECD (2001a).

income; students from higher income families were expected to cover some or all of the maintenance costs through a parental contribution.

- 1990–97: in response to concerns about the affordability of the grant system, the Conservative government introduced a loan element to maintenance support from 1990 onwards. Initially, the value of maintenance grants was frozen in nominal terms and 'top-up' loans were introduced to make up the shortfall arising due to inflation. However, between 1993 and 1996 the value of grants was cut by an additional 10 per cent each year so that by 1997 the value of grants and loans was roughly equal. Research and teaching funding for higher education was also unified through the introduction of the Higher Education Funding Council (HEFC). This period also saw a massive expansion in the numbers of students entering HE (as shown in figure 6.6 below).
- 1997 to present: in the mid-1990s the government commissioned an inquiry into the future of higher education funding chaired by Sir Ron Dearing. The Dearing Commission reported in 1997, by which time the Conservatives had been replaced in office by the Labour Party. However, the Labour government continued the thrust towards less state subsidy for students. The new student support package, phased in between 1998 and 2000, comprised two elements:

1. maintenance grants were entirely replaced by loans for new students entering higher education;
2. for the first time in the UK, a tuition fee contribution (currently £1,075 per year) was imposed. This is financed from parental contributions for students whose families are too wealthy to qualify for exemption

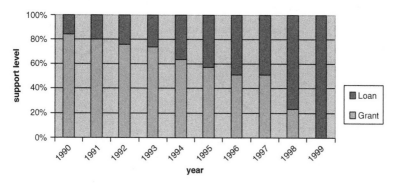

Figure 6.5 Relative contributions of grant and loan support, student on full maintenance grant, Great Britain, 1999–2000
Source: UK Department for Education and Employment Student Support Statistics, various years.

on low-income grounds. For students who depend financially on their parents, if parental income is less than £20,000 (just below male median full-time earnings in the UK), no tuition fee is payable. Between £20,000 and around £30,000, a partial contribution is payable on a sliding scale; above £30,000, the full £1,075 is payable. (For students from Scotland, the tuition fee payments were subsequently abolished by the Scottish Parliament).

In the UK total government support for students remained roughly constant over the period 1990 to 2000 at about £3,800 per year in current prices. Figure 6.5 shows how the balance between grants and loans (for students whose family income was low enough to meet the means-test for a full grant) changed over this period. It shows that the proportion made up by the grant fell every year with the exception of 1996–97. After 1997 grants were phased out completely over a two-year period. Clearly then, there has been a shift in UK funding arrangements away from tax-based funding and towards deferred user charges in the form of loans. This shift provides an ideal opportunity to assess the economic impact of switching from tax- to fee-based funding for this service, which we focus on in the remainder of this chapter.

Have maintenance loans and tuition fees deterred students from entering HE?

One of the main criticisms of the shift away from funding via general taxation and towards fees and loans is that increasing the proportion of HE costs which have to be met by the student or his or her family is likely

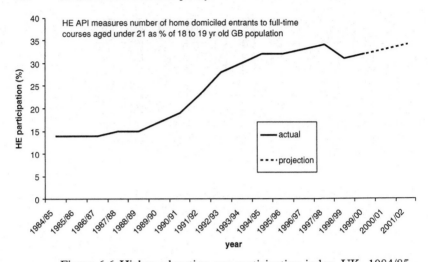

Figure 6.6 Higher education age participation index, UK, 1984/85–2001/2
Source: UK Department for Education and Employment, *Annual Report*, various years.

to deter students from participating in HE. In the UK, the Scottish Parliament's 1999 Committee of Enquiry into Student Finance (Scottish Executive 1999) argued that tuition fees should be abolished because of their deterrent effect, citing a variety of evidence from case studies and student interviews. However, quantitative estimates for the extent of deterrence are hard to come by in the UK, although the quantitative evidence available from other OECD countries suggests that deterrence may be a problem. For example, Kane (1994) finds that rises in tuition costs in the USA played an important role in depressing university enrolment rates for young black Americans during the early 1980s.

A plot of the British HE age participation index[6] over the last twelve years (figure 6.6) shows a large increase in the proportion of young people entering HE despite the funding shift. Of course this is by no means conclusive evidence of no deterrent effect. The increase in participation resulted from a large expansion in student capacity as universities, the former polytechnics and HE colleges were all encouraged to take many more students on in the early to mid-1990s. Certainly the demand for HE had to (and did) exist to fill the extra places, but this was a period of rapid change for the HE sector and it can be argued that HE would

---

[6] The age participation index is defined as the number of home domiciled entrants to full-time courses aged under 21 as a percentage of the 18–19-year-old population in Great Britain (UK Department for Education and Employment, 2001).

have expanded *even more* if loans had not been imposed in 1990. Perhaps more interesting is the slight drop in the participation index for 1998/9 in the wake of tuition fees being imposed; this provides some (very cursory) evidence of a deterrent effect.

However, arguing purely from an efficiency perspective, we might say that if students are being faced with the true cost of their education and choose not to undertake it because the expected benefits of the course do not outweigh the cost, then that is actually a good thing. From a human capital standpoint, investment in HE is like any other investment; it should only be undertaken if the benefits outweigh the costs. Whilst there may be externalities from some forms of HE which provide support for tax-based funding, these are hard to estimate accurately.[7] The private gross returns to HE are easier to measure,[8] and seem to be large. For example, Blundell et al. (2000a) show that for a cohort of people born in 1958, the average hourly earnings premium for university graduates compared with non-graduates who left school just before the point at which they could have gone on into HE was around 17 per cent for men. For women it was around 35 per cent. Many other studies of the returns to higher education produce returns of similar magnitude. In addition, we should remember that both the tuition fee component and the maintenance loan are only payable by the student if he or she, or his or her family in the case of fees, are wealthy enough to afford the payment. Thus for people on the lowest incomes, funding remains fully tax-based. In light of this, perhaps the most pressing concern is that potential students from poor backgrounds do not go into HE because of worries about its affordability. These could be based on misunderstanding of the way the system works or mistrust of the government as it may change the repayment rules at a later date. Alternatively they may face pressure from parents and their peer group to get out into the labour market as quickly as possible and start 'earning a living'.

What are the distributional consequences of the funding shift?

Clearly a change from tax-based funding to fee-based funding will have an impact on the distribution of income. In the UK, as in most other countries, the direct tax burden is broadly progressive, that is, richer people

---

[7] For recent reviews of the literature on externalities to HE, see Gemmell (1997) and Temple (2001). The reader is referred to chapter 13 in this volume for a more general discussion of externalities in the context of higher education policy in OECD countries.

[8] For a rational agent the *net* return to higher education will be reduced by additional costs such as the income forgone during study for a degree. There may also be non-financial returns to HE such as the possibility of access to more interesting forms of employment and so on; these are harder to measure.

pay a higher proportion of their incomes in tax than do poorer people. So if HE is financed through general taxation we would expect the distributional effect to be broadly progressive. What about the distributional impact of a funding shift to fees or loans? We used the IFS's tax and benefit microsimulation model (TAXBEN)[9] to consider the effect of student loan repayments on the distribution of post-tax income compared with a situation where the maintenance costs were still paid with grants financed from general direct tax receipts. The UK Department for Education and Skill's statistics show that in the 2000/1 academic year loan payments to students totalled around £1.8 billion. We used TAXBEN combined with the 1998/99 Family Resources Survey (FRS) for the UK[10] (updated to take account of price and earnings changes) to estimate the distributional impact of the loan repayments. This assumes a 'steady state' whereby the sum of the loan repayments by graduates in a year roughly equals the sum of the loans paid to new students.[11] Under current rules, a graduate only has to make a loan repayment if his or her gross income exceeds £10,000 per year in a given year; if this is the case, the graduate pays back 9 per cent of all gross income above £10,000. Using the gross income information in the FRS, we allocated £1.8 billion for the loan repayments to graduates in the sample based on the 9 per cent rule above £10,000, starting with the youngest (the 21-year-olds) and extending up to 35-year-olds. Collecting loan repayments from graduates aged between 21 and 35 raised around £1.8 billion, thus fulfilling our steady state criterion. The effects of this loan repayment on the overall distribution of income by decile are shown in figure 6.7 compared with the effects of raising the same amount by an increase in general taxation the distributional effect of which was in proportion to the existing (direct) tax burden.[12] We see

[9] TAXBEN is the Institute for Fiscal Studies' tax and benefit micro-simulation model. It uses micro-data on income, benefit receipt, labour market status and expenditure for cross-sections of households in the UK Family Expenditure Survey and Family Resources Survey (q.v.) to model the distributional effects of changes to the tax and benefit system on individual and household disposable incomes. It can also be used to estimate the aggregate cost to the public finances of tax and benefit reforms.

[10] The British Family Resources Survey is an annual cross-sectional sample of around 25,000 households. Detailed information is collected from each household on their income (broken down into different income sources in great detail), as well as ancillary information on labour market status, educational attainment and other useful characteristics.

[11] In fact, since 1990 when loans were first introduced in the UK, the increasing reliance on loan-based funding over time means that new loan payments have so far been much larger than loan repayments in any given year, However, we thought it was more instructive to examine a putative 'steady state' on the assumption that the loan payments for 2000/1 are of the kind of magnitude that the current government sees as an equilibrium position.

[12] We restrict the analysis to direct taxes because whilst TAXBEN can produce distributional effects for expenditure taxes, the FRS data contain no information on expenditure. Other taxes such as corporate taxes are much harder to allocate to individuals and so we do not discuss them here.

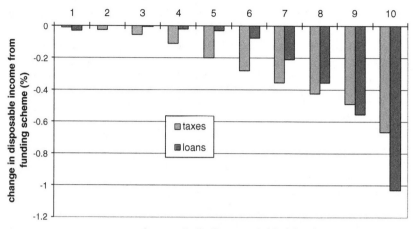

Figure 6.7 Taxes or loans to fund student maintenance? The distributional effects
Source: Authors' calculations using IFS tax-benefit microsimulation model (TAXBEN).

that loan finance is more progressive than finance out of general taxation; this is mainly due to the fact that graduates are concentrated at the top of the income distribution – in the ninth and tenth deciles in particular. It is also due to the income-contingent nature of the loan repayments we have modelled; most graduates in the bottom four deciles of equivalised income do not earn enough to cross the repayment threshold.

Taxes, fees, human capital formation and the returns to skill

So far we have only considered the 'first-round' distributional effects of a switch from taxes to loan-based funding – we have not considered how participation in higher education might respond to a change in the funding mix. There are two additional effects that need to be considered:

- **The impact of the tax structure on the return to higher education.** If taxes are progressive, individuals who undertake HE are likely to be drawn into higher tax brackets than similar individuals who do not undertake HE because there are returns to HE in the form of higher earnings. This means that the net return to HE is lower than the gross return to HE because of the tax structure. Other things being equal, we may expect a progressive income tax structure to reduce the incentive to participate in HE.[13]

- **General equilibrium effects on wages.** In a closed economy, an expansion of higher education increases the supply of skilled workers, which should reduce wages for skilled workers if demand for them remains constant. Conversely, the supply of unskilled workers should reduce and their wages increase. This is why expansion of HE is often suggested as a means of reducing earnings inequality given the increase in demand for skilled workers vis-à-vis unskilled workers which has occurred in many OECD countries in the last twenty-five years. In an open economy setting these effects may be weaker as the expansion of supply of skilled workers in one country may have little (or no) effect on equilibrium wage levels. This will be true if the country's workforce is small relative to the international workforce size and the labour and product markets are competitive.[14] Nonetheless, to the extent that market frictions allow divergence of wages for similar skill groups across different countries even in the open economy setting, the general equilibrium effects on wages may be seen.

Recent empirical work by Heckman, Lochner and Taber (1999) combines both of these additional effects into a general equilibrium model of the impact of the mix between tuition fees and taxes on university enrolment in the United States. In the model, agents differ in age, ability to learn, initial endowments and the economic histories experienced by different date-of-birth cohorts. The model allows for multiple skills, incorporating education and on-the-job training. The US tax schedule is approximated by a progressive tax on earnings and a proportional tax on capital. The economy is assumed to be perfectly competitive so that the prices of skills and capital services are determined as the marginal products of an aggregate production function exhibiting constant returns to scale. Human capital accumulation functions are estimated using microdata for the US, while the model is calibrated on aggregate data. The results show that in the partial equilibrium – holding wages for graduates

---

[13] In a labour supply context, if the disincentives to human capital formation arising from the effect of taxes on graduates are large, this may mean that the income tax has a far greater cost in terms of forgone output than is predicted by labour supply models based on a static single-period framework. This argument is developed by, among others, King and Rebelo (1990). But conversely, it has been argued that the income tax can *increase* economic efficiency if the returns to human capital are uncertain and in the absence of a full set of insurance markets against the risk associated with a costly investment in education, by allowing the government to bear some of the risk. See, for example, Eaton and Rosen (1980). The exact magnitude of either of these effects remains a subject for further research.

[14] An example of a model where this is the case is Minford (1997).

and non-graduates fixed – a $500 per year subsidy to tuition fees financed by a graduate tax increases university attendance by 5.3 per cent. In the general equilibrium setting, the subsidy increases attendance by only 0.5 per cent – as a direct result of the decrease in the returns to education brought about by the increase in the supply of graduates, which reduces the incentive to enter HE.

The Heckman et al. study illustrates that the general equilibrium effects of changing the supply of skilled workers may be very important for a proper evaluation of the merits of tax- versus fee-based funding. However, calibrated GE models of the funding of and returns to higher education are still a relatively young area of economic research. There is much work still to be done in many areas. These include examining graduate taxes versus taxes on the population as a whole, fees versus loans, the effect of different assumptions about the degree of competition in the labour and product markets, the openness of the economy, externalities to HE and endogenous growth models.

6.3   Health care

Cross-country comparisons of spending on and delivery of health care

As with higher education there is considerable variation across countries in the amount of resources dedicated to health care. The variation currently seen across OECD countries is shown in table 6.1, with Korea spending just 5.0 per cent of GDP on health care compared to 13.6 per cent being spent by the United States. Among G7 countries the table shows that Germany, France and Canada spend relatively large proportions of GDP on health care (10.6, 9.6 and 9.5 per cent respectively) while Japan and the United Kingdom spend relatively small amounts (7.6 and 6.7 per cent respectively).

Variations in levels of spending are likely to occur for at least three reasons[15]:

1. The underlying health of the population will vary between countries. This could be due to various reasons such as differences in diets, exercise or smoking habits. The age structure of the population also varies between countries – for example, in 1990 24.0 per cent of the United Kingdom population were aged 65 and over compared to 19.1 per cent in the United States and 17.1 per cent in Japan (Bos, Vu, Massiah and Bulatao, 1994).

[15] For a fuller discussion of these differences and the resulting differences across countries in potential indicators of quality of health care see Emmerson, Frayne and Goodman (2000).

Table 6.1 *Total expenditure on health care and share that is public: OECD countries, 1998*

Country	Total health care expenditure per capita (US$ PPP)	Total health care expenditure as a share of GDP (%)	Public finance as a share of total (%)
Korea	730	5.0	45.8
Luxembourg	2,215	5.9	92.3
Poland	496	6.4	73.3
Ireland	1,436	6.4	75.8
United Kingdom	1,461	6.7	83.7
Hungary	705	6.8	76.5
Finland	1,502	6.9	76.3
Spain	1,218	7.1	76.9
Czech Republic	930	7.2	91.9
Japan	1,822	7.6	78.3
Portugal	1,237	7.8	66.9
New Zealand	1,424	8.1	77.1
Austria	1,968	8.2	70.5
Greece	1,167	8.3	56.8
Denmark	2,133	8.3	81.9
Iceland	2,103	8.3	84.3
Italy	1,783	8.4	68.0
Sweden	1,746	8.4	83.8
Australia	2,043	8.5	69.3
Netherlands	2,070	8.6	70.4
Belgium	2,081	8.8	89.7
Norway	2,425	8.9	82.8
Canada	2,312	9.5	69.6
France	2,077	9.6	76.4
Switzerland	2,794	10.4	73.4
Germany	2,424	10.6	74.6
USA	4,178	13.6	44.7

Note: Countries ranked according to the proportion of GDP spent on health care.
Source: Propper (2001) using data from OECD health database 2000.

2. Different countries are likely to have difference preferences for health care.
3. Countries also differ in the institutional structure of their health care system and hence are likely to operate with different levels of efficiency.

Differences in the structure of different health care systems are, in part, demonstrated in table 6.1, which shows the percentage of health spending that is financed publicly. On average three-quarters of spending is funded publicly[16] but once again there is considerable variation between

---

[16] This corresponds to the unweighted mean share of spending financed publicly.

countries. The United States and Korea have less than 50 per cent of their health care expenditure financed publicly (44.7 and 45.8 per cent respectively) compared to over 90 per cent in the Czech Republic and Luxembourg. It is interesting to note that as shown in section 6.2, Korea also relies heavily on private funding for higher education. Across the G7 the highest public share is found in the United Kingdom (83.7 per cent). Despite this large public share it is of interest to note the United States still spends a larger proportion of its GDP on publicly funded health care than the United Kingdom and in total spends twice as big a share of GDP on health care than the UK. Some have argued that this is at least in part due to the fact that in the United Kingdom the one dominant public provider of health care (the National Health Service (NHS)) is extremely effective at providing good value for money (Commonwealth Fund, 1998). Others have pointed out that the United States health system does deliver extremely high levels of care to at least some – for example the US achieves significantly better survival rates among those diagnosed with certain forms of cancer than the United Kingdom (Coleman, 1999).

Not only do different countries fund different proportions of their health care privately and publicly, but also these proportions have varied over time. This is shown for the G7 countries from 1970 to 1997 in figure 6.8. There is no clear trend for an increasing or shrinking role for private funding in health care. In the United States, Germany, Japan and France the proportion funded privately has fallen, with the reduction in the United States from 76 per cent in 1960 to 56 per cent in 1999 being particularly noticeable. In contrast, there has been an increase in Italy from 17 per cent in 1960 to 28 per cent in 1999. In both Canada and the United Kingdom there has been relatively little change over the period.

The figures presented so far show only the proportion of health care expenditure that is funded privately; they do not provide any indication on the importance of the private sector in terms of the delivery of health care which may be funded publicly. Alternatively the public sector may be involved in delivering health care that is paid, at least in part, privately either through fees or private insurance. An attempt by the OECD to classify a range of countries health care systems is shown in table 6.2. This again highlights a range of systems used by different countries. Those countries that have a high public share in the funding of health care vary by whether this is done through general taxation, such as the United Kingdom, Norway and Sweden or through social insurance such as in France, Germany and the Netherlands. Of those countries relying mainly on public funding Canada is rather unusual in relying mainly on private providers of health care.[17]

---

[17] For a more detailed cross-country analysis of health systems see Morgan (1999).

Table 6.2 *A simple classification of OECD countries' health systems*

Broad category of health system	Country
Financed mainly by taxation with mainly public providers	United Kingdom, Ireland, Spain, Denmark, Finland, Greece, Iceland, Portugal, Norway, Sweden
Financed mainly by taxation with mainly private providers	Canada
Financed mainly by social insurance with mixed public and private providers	Belgium, France, Germany, Austria, Japan, Luxembourg, Italy, Australia, New Zealand
Financed by a mixture of social and private insurance with mainly private providers	Netherlands
Financed mainly by voluntary insurance with mainly private providers	USA, Switzerland
No dominant source of finance; mixed public and private providers	Turkey

Source: OECD (1994).

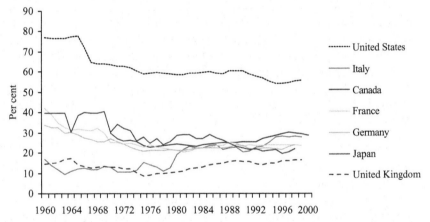

Figure 6.8 Private health spending as a percentage of total health spending in G7 countries, 1960–2000.
Note: Data on Canada only available on an annual basis from 1970 onwards.
Source: OECD Health Database (2001).

Private charges for health care

Private expenditure on health care can take many forms. Across EU countries the majority of private expenditure is on user charges or direct payments for health care with the exception of the Netherlands where

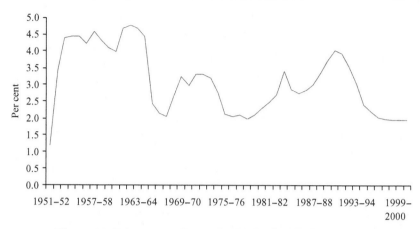

Figure 6.9 Private spending on health in the NHS as a percentage of total net NHS spending, 1951–2 to 1999–2000
Source: Office of Health Economics (1999).

17.7 per cent of total health expenditure is on private health insurance (Dixon and Mossialos, 2001). In the United Kingdom the National Health Service receives some of its income from charges for items such as prescriptions and dental and optical care. The amount of resources that the NHS has received from these sources has varied considerably over the last fifty years. Figure 6.9 shows the amount of income from private sources as a percentage of net public spending on the NHS. The contribution made from these sources was cut during the period 1966 to 1968 as prescription charges were abolished, before larger growth in charges between 1969 and 1973 and 1979 and 1992.

The imposition of fees for the health services can be expected to have a number of effects. One argument is that if goods and services are provided free at the point of use then this will lead to costly over-consumption. The extent to which this applies will vary across different types of health care, depending on the price elasticity of demand. Charging for items such as prescriptions is one possible way of reducing this problem without having a large degree of government regulation. This is one objective of the co-payment system used in France. However, if items are charged at less than marginal cost the problem of over-consumption will not go away. There are also concerns that charges will only lead to a more efficient allocation of resources if patients (consumers) have sufficient information to make an appropriate decision. Many health care products are complex, individuals may not have the experience of repeat purchases and the costs of making an inappropriate decision could be extremely large. This may make increased reliance on co-payment systems less attractive.

It is also important to note that the imposition of fees for certain items of health care may also have undesirable effects on the eventual distribution of health care that different groups receive. For this reason many groups are often exempted from such charges. For example, in the United Kingdom many groups are entitled to free prescriptions – for example, children, those in receipt of means-tested benefits and those over the state pension age. Estimates suggest that around 85 per cent of all prescriptions in the United Kingdom are dispensed free of charge although only 20 per cent of the population aged between 18 and 60 receive free prescriptions.[18] While exempting such a large proportion of the population may ensure that any unwanted distributional effects from prescription charges are reduced, it may also remove most benefits from using price rationing. It should also be noted that those who do pay for their prescriptions in the United Kingdom pay a flat rate amount per item received. This may be greater or smaller than the marginal cost of the drug. Hence the problem of over-consumption of more expensive treatments is likely only to be reduced rather than eliminated and it is possible to have under-consumption of those treatments that are actually cheaper to provide than the cost of the prescription.

The advantage of receiving income from charges for health services needs to be at least partially mitigated by the fact that individuals may subsequently need more expensive treatment due to the fact that they initially delayed receiving any care. Survey evidence from the United Kingdom suggests that 12 per cent of prescriptions are not cashed at all with a further 16 per cent only being cashed in part. In particular, those with long-term health problems are more likely to only cash in their prescription in part (National Association of Citizens Advice Bureaux, 2001). There is evidence that these figures may overstate the percentage of people getting no treatment since a study of prescriptions that were presented, but not cashed, at community pharmacies reveals that 90 per cent were substituted for over-the-counter drugs (Schafheutle et al., 2001). Further research is necessary to determine the number of people who decide not to cash in their prescription and who do not go to a pharmacy to investigate the possible availability of cheaper over-the-counter drugs. There is also evidence that the presence of prescription charges in the United Kingdom has led to GPs trying to reduce the cost to patients. Some of these incentives may be beneficial; for example, GPs may consider whether a cheaper over-the-counter drug could be better

---

[18] Figures from Hansard, written answer, column 571W, 7 February 2001.

value for money. However, other ways of reducing the burden of prescription charges on patients are potentially wasteful, such as prescribing larger quantities of drugs or trying more expensive treatments first. GPs may also try to reduce the number of items prescribed, which could potentially have a detrimental effect on the health of the patient (Weiss et al., 2001).

Distributional effects of health care systems

The distribution of the costs of health care within a tax-financed health system will depend not only on the presence of fees and whether low-income groups are exempted but also on the progressiveness of the tax system. Whether private medical insurance (PMI) receives any state subsidies, as is the case in the Republic of Ireland, the proportion of people who decide to take it out is also likely to be extremely important. Evidence from the UK shows that while, on average, 12.7 per cent of the population have PMI, 41.2 per cent of those in the richest income decile are covered (Emmerson, Frayne and Goodman, 2001). Moreover, the proportion of health care expenditures that are financed privately is not only likely to affect how the costs of the system are shared but also how the benefits from that expenditure are distributed.

The progressivity of health care systems is presented in table 6.3, from a study by Wagstaff et al. (1999). The United States, with its relatively large shares of private finance in the delivery of health care, is found to have a relatively regressive structure of finance. This is because the private medical insurance purchased in the USA tends to be the sole form of cover as opposed to the situation in UK, Portugal, Italy and Spain where individuals taking out PMI in part pay twice through the tax system and through their private premiums (Propper, 2001). The relatively high progressivity of the UK system is also achieved through the large degree of funding for the NHS that comes from direct taxation as opposed to indirect or local taxes. Of course, the distribution of the financing of health care may be of little importance since it is possible that countries with relatively regressive systems of finance could choose to compensate individuals through other reforms to the overall tax and benefit system. Potentially of greater importance is the progressivity of the delivery of health care. Estimates from some research by van Doorslaer et al. (2000) which uses individual level data to control for health need are also presented in table 6.3. Here positive numbers show when those on relatively higher incomes get more health care then would be expected given their health status, while negative numbers show when the reverse is true. Those on lower incomes are found to place greater demands on

Table 6.3 *Progressivity of financing and delivery of health care*

Country	Financing	Delivery	% of health care expenditure financed publicly
Switzerland	−0.1402	0.040	73.4
United States	−0.1303	0.009	44.7
Netherlands	−0.0703	−0.038	70.4
Germany	−0.0452	n/a	74.6
Portugal	−0.0445	n/a	66.9
Sweden	−0.0158	−0.014	83.8
Denmark	−0.0047	−0.060	81.9
Spain	0.0004	n/a	76.9
France	0.0012	n/a	76.4
Finland	0.0181	−0.029	76.3
Italy	0.0413	n/a	68.0
United Kingdom	0.0510	−0.016	83.7

Notes: A negative value of progressivity implies a regressive structure while a positive value implies a progressive structure.
Sources: For a more detailed discussion of these findings see Propper and Green (1999) and Propper (2001). Progressivity of financing from Wagstaff et al. (1999). Progressivity of delivery from van Doorslaer et al. (2000). Percentage of health care funded publicly as table 6.1.

health systems but also to have, on average, greater health needs. Once health status is controlled for there is no statistically significant variation in the receipt of health care by income.

Public attitudes to health care systems

Evidence on the levels of satisfaction in health care systems across the EU is presented in figure 6.10. Perhaps the most obvious finding from the figures is evidence of greater levels of satisfaction in Northern European and Scandinavian countries than those found in Southern European countries (Mossialos, 1997). Care should be taken in interpreting these results as necessarily reflecting actual satisfaction with the health care system, rather than general levels of satisfaction with, for example, current government policy-making in general.

In the UK evidence suggests that dissatisfaction with the NHS has fallen in recent years. In 1989 46 per cent of people reported that they were very or quite dissatisfied with the NHS. This increased to 50 per cent by 1996, but by 1998 had fallen back to just 36 per cent (Mulligan, 2000). On the specific issue of increases in private charges, evidence from the

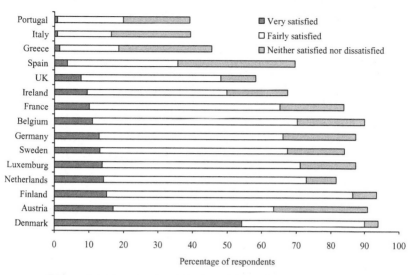

Figure 6.10 Levels of satisfaction with health care systems in EU countries, 1996
Source: Mossialos (1997).

UK suggests that there is little support for increased charges within the NHS – for example, only 8 per cent say that they would support charging for visits to a GP (Bryson and New, 2001). There is also evidence of an important interaction between the quality of public sector health care and take-up of private medical insurance (PMI). Those with PMI tend to be more dissatisfied with the NHS (Calnon, Cant and Gabe, 1996), and lower NHS quality, as measured by long-term waiting lists is also found to increase the demand for health care (Besley, Hall and Preston, 1996, 1999). This is likely to have implications for future demands on the NHS should the UK government succeed in its desire to ensure that it delivers world-class health care. There is also evidence that those who do take out private insurance are less likely to support further increases in NHS spending (Brook, Hall and Preston, 1997) which could potentially affect the long-term support for tax-based financing should the proportion of people covered by PMI continue to grow.

6.4   Care for the elderly

The percentage of GDP spent on long-term care in a range of OECD countries is shown in table 6.4. This shows that spending is highest in Norway, the Netherlands and Sweden (2.8, 2.7 and 2.7 per cent of GDP

Table 6.4 *OECD estimates of expenditure on long-term care,*
1992–5

Country	Total spending on long-term care, % of GDP	Public spending on long-term care, % of GDP	% of population aged 65+ in institutions
Norway	2.80	2.80	6.60
Netherlands	2.70	1.80	8.80
Sweden	2.70	2.70	8.70
Austria	1.40	n/a	4.90
United States	1.32	0.70	5.70
United Kingdom	1.30	1.00	5.10
Belgium	1.21	0.66	6.40
Finland	1.12	0.89	5.30 to 7.60
Canada	1.08	0.76	6.20 to 7.50
Australia	0.90	0.73	6.80
Ireland	0.86	n/a	3.50
Switzerland	0.75	n/a	n/a
Italy	0.58	n/a	3.00
Spain	0.56	n/a	2.00
Portugal	0.39	n/a	n/a
Greece	0.17	n/a	n/a
Denmark	n/a	2.24	7.00
France	n/a	0.50	6.50
Germany	n/a	0.82	6.80
Japan	n/a	0.15/0.62	6.00

Source: OECD (1998) cited in Jacobzone et al. (1999).

respectively) and lower in Southern European countries such as Greece, Portugal and Spain (0.2, 0.4 and 0.6 per cent of GDP respectively). While information on direct payments is extremely difficult to get hold of, there is some evidence that countries that have a higher proportion of publicly funded health care also tend to have a higher proportion of publicly funded long-term care (Jacobzone et al., 1999).

Care must be taken when considering these figures due to a number of difficulties in constructing cross-country comparative data in this context. First, the organisation of delivery of long-term care will vary across countries and often it may be difficult to separate long-term care expenditure from general medical expenditure. It is also the case that in many countries informal long-term care is likely to be extremely important and could easily explain the large differences in spending levels seen in table 6.4 – for example, in Spain there is an extremely low proportion of those aged 65+ in institutions.

Any change in the role of the state in funding long-term care, as with higher education and health care, would be likely to have a range of secondary effects. Any increase in public spending would lead to a partially offsetting reduction in private spending and in turn any reduction (increase) in private spending would be likely to increase (reduce) the level of bequests left to younger generations. Over a long-term horizon any increase in means-tested state support for long-term care would reduce the incentive that the working-age population has to save for their own retirement. Given that the potential costs of long-term care are considerable, this disincentive to save could be substantial. This is particularly true given that there are at least two reasons to believe that the cost of purchasing private insurance may be higher than the 'fair' price. First, adverse selection may be important – for example, it may be that individuals who have observed their parents needing a large amount of long-term care are more likely to want to purchase it themselves. These individuals will presumably have a greater than average likelihood of needing long-term care themselves. Second, it may be the case that at least part of the risks of long-term care may be uninsurable within cohorts – for example, it is possible that entire cohorts will experience large increases in unhealthy life expectancy.

Another important factor to consider is that any increased state provision of long-term care would be likely to lead to reductions in the amount of informal care provided. This is potentially extremely important; for example, in the United Kingdom there are currently around 5.7 million carers, with 880,000 providing fifty hours or more of care each week (King's Fund, 2001).[19]

In the United Kingdom the debate on long-term care has focused mainly on whether the state should play a means-tested residual role or a more universal role in the provision of long-term care. Concerns have been expressed at the disincentives to save among those who expect to be in receipt of long-term care in their retirement and the unfairness that many who have saved for their retirement are subsequently forced to sell their home to finance long-term care. This points to the importance of considering reforms to the system of long-term care alongside pension reform, so as 'to enable individuals to plan for retirement in a comprehensive and affordable manner' (IPPR, 2001). There are also important interactions between long-term care and health care.

In 1997 the UK government set up a royal commission to look at the funding arrangements of long-term care. Its report (Royal Commission

---

[19] For further information on informal care in the UK see, for example, Office for National Statistics (1998).

on Long-Term Care, 1999) proposed that while support for living costs should continue to be means-tested, both nursing and personal care should be funded from general taxation. This package was costed at around £1bn a year (0.1 per cent of GDP). In response, in England and Wales the government has only promised that, from October 2001, the provision of *nursing* care in nursing homes will be provided free at the point of use in the NHS (Department of Health, 2000). It argued that providing personal care free at the point of use to all would lead to an increase in demand, benefit the better off more than the poor and weaken incentives for private provision. However, as with higher education the situation in Scotland is different, with the Scottish parliament deciding that personal care should also be provided free at the point of use.

As with pensions and health care, the effect of cost of long-term care is set to grow in future as the population ages. Forecasting the required increase in expenditure is likely to be more difficult in the case of long-term care since any projection will be extremely sensitive to assumptions made about the degree to which future improvements in life expectancies are due to healthy or unhealthy years of life. The role of informal care is also potentially a very important determinant of future costs of long-term care. For example, if there is an increase in unhealthy ageing then this might not increase demand for long-term care if there is sufficient availability of informal care. This will depend (in part) on future marriage rates and also whether spouses' ageing is healthy or unhealthy (Lakdawalla and Philipson, 1999).

Regardless of the lack of firm forecasts for the future costs of provision it may well be the case that in the UK the current settlement proves to be politically unsustainable – in particular, given the anomaly between the level of support in Scotland compared to the rest of the country.

6.5   Child care

Most, if not all, OECD countries use child care subsidies or other forms of state support for child care such as state-provided nursery education, and in many countries such support for child care has increased over the last decade (OECD, 2001b). For example, in the USA Blau (2000) reports that expenditure on child care subsidies was approximately $17 bn, or just under 0.2 per cent of US GDP. In this section we focus on the choice governments make between relying on user charges for publicly or privately provided child care, or in subsidising child care through taxation. We review recent evidence on the impact of child care policies in the United States, Sweden and the United Kingdom, focusing on the labour supply effects.

Fees versus taxes in the provision of child care services

In the absence of any government subsidy for child care costs, the child care system would be based entirely on user charges (fees). However, even in the case of no explicit subsidy, it should be noted that government intervention might still be important for two reasons. Firstly, there may be some provision of child care by the public sector. This is important in the UK, where many local authorities provide subsidised nursery and/or crèche facilities, and even more so in Sweden, where such provision is compulsory. Secondly, to the extent that welfare benefits and/or tax credits redistribute income towards low-income families with children, this provides an extra resource to families which may be spent, at least in part, on child care. For example, in the UK in February 2001, expenditure on the child care subsidy element of Working Families Tax Credit (WFTC) (the main UK in-work benefit for families with children) was just under £20 million per month. But this was dwarfed by expenditure of almost £400 million on the other components of WFTC (UK Inland Revenue, 2001). So it is important to bear in mind that explicit child care subsidies may be only one part of a particular government's child care support package.

Why might the government want to subsidise child care? As explained in detail by Duncan and Giles (1996) and Duncan, Paull and Taylor (2002) there are three main sets of reasons. Firstly, there may be market failures arising from private provision of child care. To the extent that non-parental child care provides a positive social externality in terms of promoting social cohesion, enhancing citizenship and reducing crime in later life (for example),[20] *in addition* to conveying a private benefit on the children themselves, there are efficiency grounds for a subsidy. Secondly, there may be distributional considerations relating to the children involved. For example, if pre-school education is good for the development of children, but only richer families can afford it, we may wish to subsidise child care for poorer families to promote equality of opportunity. Thirdly, there is another set of distributional concerns relating to labour market opportunities for mothers. Child care subsidies which enable women to return to the labour market quickly after childbirth should minimise the loss of human capital (and hence earnings and prestige) which women experience on average if they take a number of years out of the labour market to have children. Hence subsidies can help to improve the position of women vis-à-vis men in the labour market.

---

[20] Recent studies of the relationship between childhood experiences and outcomes in later life include Gregg and Machin (2001) for the UK, and Karoly et al. (1998) for the USA.

The effects of tax-financed child care subsidies

A shift from a system financed by user charges to a system of subsidised child care can be expected to have three main effects:

- **Expansion of the demand for child care.** As the price of child care has been reduced, we would almost certainly expect consumers to demand more of it. Estimates of the price elasticity of child care are discussed below.

- **Labour supply effects.** Child care subsidies are often viewed as leading to an unambiguous increase in labour supply for mothers (indeed wanting to increase employment amongst families with children is often cited as a reason for making child care subsidies more generous, as in UK Department for Education and Employment, 1998). However, in a simple static labour supply model (e.g. Pencavel, 1986) there are two effects to consider, which may operate against each other. On the one hand, a child care subsidy increases the effective wage rate (by reducing per hour costs of employment) and for somebody not currently in work, this provides an unambiguous incentive to move into work – the *substitution effect*. On the other hand, for those already in work, the reduction in costs provides an *income effect* – an increase in net income – which may have positive or negative effects depending on whether leisure is a normal or inferior good. So the overall effects of a child care subsidy on work hours for those already in work are theoretically ambiguous. Below we report on studies which have attempted to quantify the distributional effects for the UK, Sweden and the USA.

- **Distributional effects across households.** As was the case with the subsidies for higher education considered earlier, when considering the distributional effects of child care subsidies it is necessary to consider the distributional impact of the increase in taxes required to pay for them.[21] If the tax increases fell disproportionately on families with children, then the overall distributional outcome of the introduction (or extension) of a child care subsidy is unclear.[22] In other cases, the

[21] Sometimes it is argued that in the long run, child care subsidies will 'pay for themselves' by encouraging an increase in labour supply for families with children which leads to a large enough increase in tax receipts and/or decrease in welfare benefit payments by the government to offset the initial cost of the subsidy. However, the estimated elasticity of labour supply with respect to child care price found in most of the recent empirical studies (discussed in the next section) does not appear to be large enough to allow child care subsidies to pay for themselves. This point is addressed explicitly by Duncan and Giles (1996).

[22] In fact in the UK and the USA the tax system and the benefit system offer more generous allowances and benefit rates to families with children. Of course, if we use an equivalised income measure to take account of the fact that households with children have higher living costs, it is still not clear *a priori* whether either of these tax systems treats families

net effect of a child care subsidy that was not means-tested with income would be to redistribute income towards families with children. In fact, most of the child care subsidies in the UK, US and Swedish tax-benefit systems are means-tested; payments decline as household income rises. This means that in addition to favouring families with children, the subsidy will also have a progressive effect on the income distribution. However, there is a third issue to consider: many child care subsidies (such as the child care credit in the UK's Working Families Tax Credit) are only available to families where at least one of the parents is *in employment*. Families in employment tend on average to be above those non-working households who rely solely on benefits in the income distribution. Thus, increasing child care subsidies for low-income working families will tend to reduce income inequality amongst the working population but exacerbate inequality between working and non-working households. This is an aspect of the trade-off faced by all governments in designing a welfare system, between providing an acceptable 'safety net' level of income for families who are unable to find work, and preserving work incentives by making sure that work does pay financially.

- **Distributional effects within households.** Child care subsidies may also have effects on the distribution of working time (and therefore of income) *within* two-parent families. To the extent that the mother is the primary carer for the children, one would expect a child care subsidy to have a positive impact on female labour supply as more resources become available to substitute paid child care for maternal care. Empirical studies of the distributional impact of child care subsidies within couples require good quality time-use data, which is rare. Most of the available literature uses bargaining models to analyse how housework (including parental child care) is divided between the husband and wife in a couple.[23] Dominique, Flood and Kocoglu (2001) analyse the determinants of the gender division of home production and use this to examine how child care provision affects the distribution of market and non-market time. Dominique et al. find that in France and Sweden, where more than 85 per cent of children over three years old are covered by subsidised child care, children have no impact on female labour supply for children over three years old. This is consistent with a positive impact of child care subsidy on female labour supply.

---

with children more leniently than those without. However, Brewer et al. (2001) show that even after equivalisation, the UK tax and benefit system is more generous to families with children than without.

[23] Recently published papers in this field include Hersch and Stratton (1994) looking at the USA.

Empirical work on the employment effects of child care subsidies

In the evaluation of the effectiveness of child care subsidies, much hinges on the magnitude of their labour supply effects. In all three of the countries we are focusing on in this section, empirical work has been carried out recently to assess the effects of subsidies. The studies we will focus on use microeconomic survey data to evaluate the impact of variations in the price of child care on the labour supply of mothers – either lone parents, or female partners in married or cohabiting relationships.[24] They are normally econometrically identified by cross-sectional (and in some cases time series) variation in child care prices and the extent of available child care subsidies across regions and across different groups of the population. Table 6.5 summarises the data, the population group to which the results referred and the estimated elasticity of employment with respect to child care costs which each study found.[25]

The studies listed in table 6.5 all use some kind of binary or multinomial model to predict changes in employment for the sample arising from changes in child care price. In the Fronstin and Wissoker study this is a binary logit. In the others, multinomial models are used, corresponding to non-employment, and employment at one of several different hourly rates. The hours choice is therefore approximated by a choice from a set of discrete 'hours points'; individuals are assumed to choose their desired hours subject to utility maximisation. In most cases, child care price is measured by the fitted value from a child care expenditure equation estimated by linear regression on the sub-sample of mothers who pay for care. A selectivity adjusted wage equation as outlined by Heckman (1979) is used to generate fitted values for wages earned whilst in work, which are included in the employment equation.

A point that should be made regarding the estimated elasticities is that the US studies listed are concerned with labour supply responses to the price of child care in general rather than in response to any specific subsidy. In contrast, the Flood study for Sweden simulates the effects of an increase in subsidy which would cap the cost of child care per child for each family. The Blundell et al. study for the UK also relates to a specific subsidy, in this case the UK Working Families Tax Credit (WFTC), an in-work benefit which provides a subsidy of 70 per cent of child care costs

---

[24] In theory, there could of course be a knock-on effect on the labour supply of fathers from the child care subsidy. However, a fully developed and empirically estimable structural model of joint labour supply by mother and father in a household context is still a long way from being feasibly estimated (see Blundell et al., 2001 for a recent review of collective labour supply literature).

[25] Note that Flood et al. (2001) only provide an hour's elasticity.

Table 6.5 *Recent studies of the labour supply effects of changes in child care price*

Study	Country	Data	Population	Employment	Child care price measure	Method	Participation elasticity
Flood et al. (2001)	Sweden	LINDA panel 1996	Lone mothers, child aged 1–12	All employees	Location-specific child care subsidy level	Simultaneous discrete choice model for labour supply and welfare participation.	≈–.05
Blau and Hagy (1998)	USA	NCCS 1990	Mothers, child aged < 6	All employees	Quality adjusted location-specific price from provider survey	Multinomial logit	–.20
Fronstin and Wissoker (1995)	USA	NCCS 1990	Mothers, child aged < 6	All employees	Average location-specific price from provider survey	Binary logit	–.45 (low income), –.06 (high income)
Ribar (1995)	USA	SIPP 1984	Married mothers, child aged < 15	Employed FT/PT	Total child care expenses per hour of care	Structural multinomial choice model for labour supply and child care take-up	Child < 15: –.09, Child < 6: –.09
Blundell et al. (2000b)	UK	FRS 1994–6	Mothers, child aged < 16	All employees	Reported child care price from FRS, adjusted for hours worked	Structural model of discrete choice over a number of hours points; allows for fixed costs of work and non-take-up of benefits.	≈–.06*

*Elasticity based on change in total WFTC payment, not change in child care subsidy in isolation (elasticity was not separately computed for child care subsidy).

Key: LINDA: Longitudinal Individual Data for Sweden; NCCS: National Child Care Survey, USA; SIPP: Survey of Income and Program Participation, USA; FRS: Family Resources Survey, UK.

up to £150 (about $240) per week for low-income working families. It is important to realise that linear elasticity estimates can be misleading for at least two reasons. First, because many actual subsidy programmes are highly non-linear with respect to household income. Second, because of the extent that there is a fixed cost of receiving the subsidy (either because of 'hassle costs' of applying or because there is a stigma attached to receipt of the subsidy) since assuming a linear labour supply response will be inappropriate.

With this in mind, the results in table 6.5 appear to show a range of elasticities between −0.05 and −0.2 (with the exception of the Fronstin result for low-income families).

What is the relationship between the elasticity estimates and the actual numbers of mothers moving into employment as a result of child care subsidies? Blundell and Reed (2000) provide some recent evidence, summarised in table 6.6, of the employment impact of the introduction of the Working Families Tax Credit (WFTC) in the UK. One of the main features of the WFTC is a subsidy of 70 per cent of child care costs up to a value of £100 per week for low-income working families with one child, and £150 for families with two or more children. The results in table 6.6 give the expected change in the numbers of people in employment as a result of the WFTC and also give the changes in terms of the percentage point increase in the employment rate for that group. Thus, the Blundell et al. (2000b) study predicts an increase in the employment rate among single mothers from 39.8 per cent to 42.0 per cent. The predicted effects for married women with working partners are *negative*; this occurs because the increase in the husband's take-home pay arising from the extra generosity of the WFTC acts as an income effect which reduces the incentive for the wife to enter the labour market as a second earner. This occurs despite the fact that in two-parent families, the WFTC child care subsidy is only claimable if *both* partners are in work.[26]

Unfortunately these studies of the impact of WFTC do not distinguish between the employment impact of the child care subsidy component of the WFTC and the other increases in generosity of the new benefit compared with its predecessor, Family Credit.[27] In terms of aggregate expenditure, the child care subsidy only accounted for a fraction – certainly less

---

[26] This is why we do not report results here for married women with non-working husbands; these groups would not be eligible for the child care subsidy unless both partners moved into work, a scenario which is not considered by the studies presented here.

[27] The other changes comprised an increase in the generosity of the benefit payment, and a reduction in the 'taper' – i.e. the rate at which benefit income is withdrawn once net income rises above a certain threshold level (£92.90 per week in April 2001). For further details on the structural changes see Dilnot and McCrae (1999).

Table 6.6 *Predicted employment effect of the WFTC: recent UK studies on groups eligible for the child care credit*

Group	Gregg et al. (1999)		Blundell et al. (2000b)		Paull et al. (2000)	
	Number	%	Number	%	Number	%
Single mothers	+28,600	+1.85	+34,000	+2.20	+24,700	+1.60
Married women with working partners	−29,050	−0.83	−20,000	−0.57	N/A	N/A

than 20 per cent – of the total increase in spending on in-work benefits arising from the introduction of WFTC. Given that the total increase in expenditure arising from WFTC was around £1.3bn during its first year of operation (UK Inland Revenue, 2001),[28] these results indicate that in the UK at least, the resultant employment effects are fairly small.

Focusing on the child care subsidy element of in-work benefit programmes, Duncan and Giles (1996) point out that one reason why subsidies might be an expensive way of encouraging labour supply amongst the target group is because there is often a large 'dead-weight loss' effect to subsidies. Families who move into work because of the reduction in child care costs produced by the subsidy will benefit, but so will families who are already in work, provided they are eligible. If the subsidy provides lower child care prices across the board, then *non-working* households may also benefit. To some extent the subsidy can be better targeted so as to minimise the dead-weight loss, for example, by restricting it to working families, or even to families who have recently entered work. However, this makes operation of the subsidy more complex and can encourage perverse labour market responses, for example, leaving work temporarily to return to another job to take advantage of the subsidy. There remains a lot of empirical work to be done on evaluating the effectiveness of child care subsidies versus alternative policies, such as higher welfare benefits for low-income families in general.

6.6   Conclusions

This survey has looked at the mix between tax-funded delivery of free at the point of use or subsidised public services on one hand, and funding by user charges and fees on the other. It has shown that across OECD

---

[28] Estimate based on a comparison of total (annualised) WFTC expenditure in May 2000 with total Family Credit expenditure in August 1999 (before WFTC was phased in).

countries, the mix varies widely, as does the public and private sectors' roles in provision. Certainly there does not at the time of writing appear to be a single unanimously accepted approach to funding or delivering any of the services looked at. At the same time, there is a clear correlation between the extent of tax-based funding for health and for higher education. At one end, the USA and Korea rely more heavily on private sector, fee-based funding, whereas at the other end, the Netherlands and the Scandanavian countries have a greater extent of tax-based funding and public provision.

Our economic analysis of the various public services has shown that trade-offs arise between distributional arguments and efficiency reasons. The former are often used to justify fully tax-funded system at little or zero cost to consumers, while the latter may be promoted better by fee-based systems where the cost to the consumer of using a public service corresponds to the benefit received from the service. However, there are exceptions to these very general rules. Possible externalities exist in the consumption of child care, education and health. There are also other potential market failures – for example adverse selection and uninsurable risks being potentially associated with private insurance for long-term care. Our empirical work illustrates that funding higher education maintenance costs through income-contingent loans is likely to be more distributionally progressive than tax-funded maintenance grants. In the case of health care, the method of financing often appears to bear little relation to how progressive the effects of health care services are. And in child care, careful design of subsidies and in-work benefits in particular can help improve work incentives rather than diminishing them, by boosting net incomes for low-paid workers and combining this with support for child care whilst parents are at work.

In all the cases we have studied, econometric modelling and micro-simulation have a role to play in quantifying the effects of taxes and subsidies on the important economic outcomes: for example, the number of people helped into employment by child care subsidies, and the effects on human capital formation of the increase in higher education participation rates resulting from subsidised tuition and maintenance. As well as measuring the magnitude of economic responses to subsidies, micro-simulation can often give us some idea of their distributional effects. However, subsidies are of course costly to the public purse, and measures of their effects are only the first step towards a cost-benefit analysis of whether it is best to use taxation to fund public services or levy charges on users. Although substantial and very useful bodies of empirical research exist for all of the areas we have studied, we are a long way from resolving the question of what the 'correct' mix between fees and taxes should be, given our distributional objectives. There is a great need in particular to integrate the insights from partial equilibrium evaluations of specific policies into full-scale general equilibrium models. These could then show how a shift from taxes to user charges or vice versa affects the distribution of income and key quantitative variables such as wages, employment and economic growth under a variety of different assumptions about the way the labour market and the economy work in general.

References

Besley, T., Hall, J. and Preston, I., 1996, *Private Health Insurance and the State of the NHS*, Commentary no. 52, London: Institute for Fiscal Studies.

—1999, 'The demand for private health insurance: do waiting lists matter?', *Journal of Public Economics*, 72, 155–81.

Blau, David, 2000, 'Child care subsidy programs', US National Bureau of Economic Research working paper 7806, July.

Blau, D. and Hagy, A., 1998, 'The demand for quality in child care', *Journal of Political Economy*, 106, 1, 104–46.

Blundell, R., Dearden, L., Goodman, A. and Reed, H., 2000a, 'The returns to higher education in Britain: evidence from a British cohort', *Economic Journal*, 110 (February), F82–F99.

Blundell, R., Duncan, A., McCrae, J. and Meghir, C., 2000b, 'The labour market impact of the Working Families Tax Credit', *Fiscal Studies*, 21, 1, 75–104.

Blundell, R., Chiappori, P.-A., Magnac, T. and Meghir, C., 2001, 'Collective labor supply: heterogeneity and nonparticipation', IFS working paper W01/19.

Blundell, R. and Reed, H., 2000, 'The employment effects of the Working Families Tax Credit', IFS briefing note no. 6, London: Institute for Fiscal Studies.

Bos, E., Vu, M. T., Massiah, E. and Bulatao, R. A., 1994, *World Population Projections, 1994–95 Edition: Estimates and Projections with Related Demographic Statistics*, Washington, DC: World Bank / Baltimore, Md: Johns Hopkins University Press.

Brewer, M., Myck, M. and Reed, H., 2001, 'Financial support for families with children: options for the new integrated child credit', Institute for Fiscal Studies Commentary 82.

Brook, L., Hall, J. and Preston, I., 1997, 'What drives support for higher public spending?', IFS working paper W97/16.

Bryson, C. and New, B., 2001, 'Health care rationing: a cut too far?' in R. Jowell, J. Curtice, A. Park, K. Thomson, L. Jarvis, C. Bromley and N. Stratford (eds.), *British Social Attitudes: Focusing on Diversity, the 17th report: 2000–01 Edition*, London: Sage.

Burchardt, T. and Propper, C., 1999, 'Does the UK have a private welfare class?', *Journal of Social Policy*, 29, 643–65.

Calnan, M., Cant, S. and Gabe, J., 1996, *Going Private: Why People Pay for their Healthcare*, Oxford: Oxford University Press.

Coleman, M. P., 1999, *Cancer Survival Trends in England and Wales 1971–1995: Deprivation and NHS Region*, Series SNPS no. 61, London: The Stationery Office.

Commonwealth Fund, 1998, *Common Concerns: International Issues in Health Care System Reform*, New York: Commonwealth Fund.

Department of Health, 2000, *The NHS Plan: A Plan for Investment, a Plan for Reform*, Cm 4818-I, London: The Stationery Office.

—2001, *The Government's Expenditure Plans 2001–02 to 2003–04 and Main Estimates 2001–02*, London: The Stationery Office.

Dilnot, A. and McCrae, J., 1999, 'Family Credit and the Working Families Tax Credit', IFS Briefing Note No. 3, London: Institute for Fiscal Studies.

Dixon, A. and Mossialos, E., 2001, 'Funding health care in Europe: recent experiences', *Health Care UK*, Spring, 66–77.

Dominique, A., Flood, L. and Kocoglu, Y., 2001, 'Intra-household time allocation in France and Sweden', School of Economics and Commercial Law, Göteborg University, Sweden: mimeo.

Duncan, A. and Giles, C., 1996, 'Should we subsidise pre-school childcare, and if so, how?', *Fiscal Studies*, 17, 3, 39–61.

Duncan, A., Paull, G. and Taylor, J., 2002, *Mothers' Employment and Childcare Use in Britain*, London: Institute for Fiscal Studies.

Eaton, J. and Rosen, H., 1980, 'Taxation, human capital and uncertainty', *American Economic Review*, 70, 705–15.

Emmerson, C., Frayne, C. and Goodman, A., 2000, *Pressures in UK Healthcare: Challenges for the NHS*, Commentary No. 81, London: Institute for Fiscal Studies.

—2001, 'Should private medical insurance be subsidised?', *Health Care UK*, Spring, 49–65.

Flood, L., Pylkkänen, E. and Wahlberg, R., 2001, 'Labor supply and welfare participation of single mothers in Sweden', Göteburg University Working Paper.

Fronstin, P. and Wissoker, D., 1995, 'The effects of the availability of low-cost child care on the labor supply of low income women', Working Paper, Urban Institute, Washington DC.

Gemmell, N., 1997, 'Externalities to higher education: a review of the new growth literature', in National Committee of Enquiry into Higher Education (Dearing Committee), *Higher Education in the Learning Society*, Norwich: HMSO.

Gregg, Paul, Johnson, Paul and Reed, Howard, 1999, *Entering Work and the British Tax and Benefit System*, London: Institute for Fiscal Studies.

Gregg, Paul and Machin, Stephen, 2001, 'The relationship between childhood experiences, subsequent educational attainment and labour market performance' in K. Vlemincx and T. Smeedling (eds.), *Child Well Being in Modern Nations: What do we Know?*, Bristol: Policy Press.

Hall, J. and Preston, I., 1998, 'Public and private choice in UK health insurance', IFS working paper W98/19.

Heckman, J., 1979, 'Sample selection bias as a specification error', *Econometrica*, 47, 1 (January), 153–62.

Heckman, J., Lochner, L. and Taber, C., 1999, 'Human capital formation and general equilibrium treatment effects: a study of tax and tuition policy', *Fiscal Studies*, 20, 1, 25–40.

Hersch, Joni and Stratton, Leslie, 1994, 'Housework, wages and the division of housework time for employed spouses', *American Economic Review*, 84, 2,

Papers and Proceedings of the 106th meeting of the American Economic Association, 120–5.

Institute for Public Policy Research, 2001, *A New Contract for Retirement: An Interim Report*, London: IPPR.

Jacobzone, S., Cambois, E., Chaplain, E. and Robine, J. M., 1999, *The Health of Older Persons in OECD Countries: Is it Improving Fast Enough to Compensate for Population Ageing?*, Labour Market and Social Policy, Occasional Papers no. 37, Paris: OECD.

Kane, Thomas J., 1994, 'College entry by blacks since 1970: the role of college costs, family background, and the returns to education', *Journal of Political Economy*, 102, 5, 878–991.

Karoly, Lynn, Greenwood, Peter W., Everingham, Susan S., Houbé, Jill, Kilburn, Rebecca, Rydell, Peter, Sanders, Matthew and Chiesa, James, 1998, 'Investing in our children: what we know and don't know about the costs and benefits of early childhood interventions', Santa Monica, USA: RAND Report MR-898-TCWF.

King, Robert G. and Rebelo, Sergio, 1990, 'Public policy and economic growth: developing neoclassical implications', *Journal of Political Economy*, 98, 5, S126–S150.

King's Fund, 2001, *Paying for Long-term Care*, Briefing no. 5, London: The King's Fund.

Lakdawalla, D. and Philipson, T., 1999, *Aging and the Growth of Long-term Care*, National Bureau of Economic Research working paper no. 6980.

Minford, P., 1997, 'The OECD problem of low wages and unemployment: the role of welfare support', in G. de la Dehesa and D. Snower (eds.), *Unemployment Policy: Government Options for the Labour Market*, London: CEPR.

Morgan, O., 1999, *A Cue for Change: Global Comparisons in Healthcare*, Social Market Foundation, discussion paper no. 41.

Mossialos, E., 1997, 'Citizens' view on the health care systems in the fifteen member states of the European Union', *Health Economics*, 6, 109–16.

Mulligan, J., 2000, 'What do the public think?', *Health Care UK*, Winter, 12–17.

National Association of Citizens Advice Bureaux, 2001, *Unhealthy Charges: CAB Evidence on the Impact of Health Charges*. Evidence Report, 3 July.

OECD, 1994, *The Reform of Health Care Systems: A Review of Seventeen OECD Countries*, Paris: OECD.

—1998, *Maintaining Prosperity in an Ageing Society*, Paris: OECD.

—2001a, *Education at a Glance: OECD Indicators*, Paris: OECD.

—2001b, *Starting Strong: Early Childhood Education and Care*, Paris: OECD.

Office of Health Economics, 1999, *Compendium of Health Statistics*, 11th edition, London: OHE.

Office for National Statistics, 1998, *Informal Carers: Results of an Independent Study Carried Out on Behalf of the Department of Health as Part of the 1995 General Household Survey*, London: The Stationery Office Ltd.

Paull, Gillian and Taylor, Jayne, 2002, *Mothers' Employment and Childcare Use in Britain*, London: IFS.

Paull, Gillian, Walker, Ian and Zu, Yhu, 2000, 'Child support reform: some analysis of the 1999 White Paper', *Fiscal Studies*, 21, 1, 105–40.

Pencavel, John, 1986, 'Labor supply of men: a survey', in O. Ashenfelter and R. Layard (eds.), *Handbook of Labor Economics*, Vol. I, Amsterdam: Elsevier Science B.V.

Propper, C., 2001, 'Expenditure on health care in the UK: a review of the issues', *Fiscal Studies*, 22, 2, June, 151–83.

Propper, C. and Green, K., 1999, 'A larger role for the private sector in health care?: a review of the arguments', Centre for Market and Public Organisation working paper no. 99/009.

Propper, C., Rees, H. and Green, K., 2001, 'The demand for private insurance in the UK: a cohort analysis', *Economic Journal*, 111, C180–C200.

Ribar, David, 1995, 'A structural model of child care and the labor supply of married women', *Journal of Labor Economics*, 13, 3, 558–97.

Royal Commission on Long-Term Care, 1999, *With Respect to Old Age: Long-Term Care – Rights and Responsibilities*, Cm 4192-I, March, London: The Stationery Office.

Schafheutle, E. I., Hassell, K., Seston, E. M., Nicolson, M. and Noyce, P. R., 2001, *Non-dispensing of NHS Prescriptions in Community Pharmacies*, 7th Health Services Research and Pharmacy Practice Conference Abstracts, University of Nottingham.

Scottish Executive, 1999, *Student Finance: Fairness for the Future*, Edinburgh: Independent Committee of Enquiry into Student Finance.

Temple, J., 2001, 'Growth effects of education and social capital in the OECD countries', University of Bristol, mimeo.

UK Department for Education and Employment, 1998, *Meeting the Childcare Challenge*, London: HMSO.

—2001, *Annual Report*, London: HMSO.

UK Inland Revenue, 2001, *Working Families' Tax Credit Statistics: Quarterly Enquiry*, February, London: HMSO.

van Doorslaer, E., Wagstaff, A., et al. 2000, 'Equity in the delivery of health care in Europe and the US', *Journal of Health Economics*, 19, 553–83.

Wagstaff, A., van Doorslaer, E., et al., 1999, 'Equity in the finance of health care: some further international comparisons', *Journal of Health Economics*, 18, 263–90.

Weiss, M. Hassell, K., Schafheutle, E. I. and Noyce, P. R., 2001, 'Strategies used by general practitioners to minimise the impact of the prescription charge', *European Journal of General Practice*, 7, 23–6.

7   Privatisation of social insurance with reference to Sweden

*Lars Söderström and Klas Rikner**

7.1   Introduction

Welfare state provisions have grown considerably during the last half-century. Public expenditures for social security now amount to 25 per cent or more of the GDP in several OECD countries. The highest figure is reported for Sweden: 33.3 per cent. Table 7.1 provides information on the structure of public expenditures for social protection in Sweden in 1998. In accordance with Eurostat guidelines, expenditures have been classified into four categories: general/cash, general/in kind, selective/cash and selective/in kind.

In the Swedish case, sickness, disability and old age accounted for over 70 per cent of the social security budget. Selective benefits play a relatively minor role: only 6 per cent. Most benefits are therefore granted according to fairly simple criteria. From table 7.1 one can get the impression that cash benefits dominate over benefits in kind, but one must bear in mind that, in Sweden, most cash benefits are taxed; hence, net benefits are considerably smaller.

Increasing expenditures over time do not mean that the welfare state is becoming more 'advanced'. The growth in public expenditures for social security is to a large extent a mere reflection of the fact that existing welfare state provisions gradually become more expensive, due to demographic and other 'exogenous' forces, such as an ageing population and new technologies in health care. There is also a growing awareness of the risk that the welfare state will become a 'black hole' in the public budget, gradually absorbing resources for other, perhaps more urgent needs. Various measures to cut public expenditures for social security were implemented in the 1990s. In Sweden, these expenditures fell over five percentage points in just six years, from 38.6 per cent relative to the GDP in 1993 to 33.3 per cent in 1998.

Social insurance schemes make up the major part of public expenditures for social security. With respect to cash benefits these schemes

* We are grateful to the editors and Dr Ed Palmer for helpful comments.

Table 7.1 *Public expenditures for social protection in Sweden relative to GDP in 1998 (%)*

	General		Selective		
	Cash	In kind	Cash	In kind	Total
Sickness (1)	1.8	5.8	–	–	7.7
Disability (2)	2.3	1.3	0.1	0.0	3.8
Old age (3)	9.3	2.7	0.2	–	12.2
Survivors (4)	0.7	–	0.0	–	0.7
Families, children (5)	1.6	1.9	0.0	–	3.5
Unemployment (6)	2.7	0.4	–	–	3.1
Housing (7)	–	–	–	0.8	0.8
Other (8)	0.0	0.3	0.6	0.0	1.0
Administration	–	–	–	–	0.5
Total	18.5	12.5	1.0	0.9	33.3

Note: Expenditures classified according to the European system of integrated social protection statistics (ESSPROS). Key: (1) Sick pay, negotiated sickness benefit, temporary parental allowance, care of closely related persons, in-patient health care, out-patient health care, dental care, out-patient medicine, other. (2) Disability pensions, pension supplement, annuity, disability allowance, attendance allowance, personal assistant, transportation and car allowance. (3) Old age pension, pension supplement, wife's supplements, elderly care, transportation. (4) Survivor's pensions, pension supplement. (5) Parental insurance, child allowance, maintenance support, child care, youth centres. (6) Unemployment insurance, severance pay and cash benefits, labour market training and other support in kind. (7) Housing allowance for retired persons, housing allowance for families. (8) Support of refugees, social assistance, care of drug addicts, judicial support. *Source*: Ministry of Social Affairs (2001).

include old age pensions, disability pensions, sickness insurance, parental insurance, workers' compensation and unemployment insurance. In addition there are benefits in kind, such as health care. The purpose of this chapter is to discuss how these schemes may be privatised, informally as well as formally. We limit our discussion to cash benefits. We assume that privatisation in other areas will be dealt with by other authors.

It is important to point out that a public insurance scheme does not have to be put under *formal* private administration in order to be privatised. An alternative is to keep a scheme public, but change its character into a more private-like scheme, either by introducing flexibility and consumer choice or by replacing taxes with insurance premiums, thereby achieving an *informal* privatisation. From an individual citizen's point of view, informal and formal privatisation may in many cases serve the same purpose.

Privatisation does not have to be a matter of either-or. In many cases it would be an advantage to have a *combination* of private and public provisions. For example, one can have a public scheme for big damages and extreme cases – such as an expensive illness like AIDS or a permanent loss of income – and at the same time private insurance schemes for normal, everyday damages, such as income losses up to, say, four weeks. A particular advantage with this type of combination is that private insurance companies do not have to worry about the long tail of the risk distribution. This would encourage the supply of private insurance. For a discussion of private–public combinations along this line, see Haslinger and Horgby (1997).

In our view, old age pensions (including survivor's pensions) and sickness insurance, including workers' compensation, are the main candidates for privatisation.[1] As we saw in table 7.1, these schemes account for about two-thirds of public expenditures for cash benefits in the Swedish welfare state (an amount equal to 11–12 per cent of the GDP). Before having a closer look at these two schemes we shall look more generally at the prerequisites for private insurance and point out why the other schemes included in table 7.1 are less suitable for privatisation.

7.2   Market imperfections

Unless otherwise stated we now look at a single *uniform* insurance scheme, characterised by:

$$(\pi, L, C, p)$$

where π is the probability of loss, L is the size of the loss, C is the compensation offered to the insured in case of a loss, and p is the insurance premium.[2] Such a scheme may be under public or private administration. In the latter case we assume – unless otherwise stated – that there are several competing firms in the insurance market. The insurance premium is understood to have two parts: $p = \pi C + \lambda$, where πC is the expected compensation in accordance with the scheme and λ is some 'loading' required by the insurance company to cover administration costs etc.

Insurance is straightforward in cases where the probability of loss is fairly well known and an insurance scheme can attract enough customers for the law of large numbers to apply. But these conditions are by no means necessary for the operating of private insurance schemes. For

[1] In countries where the unemployment insurance is public, this insurance might also be a good candidate for privatisation. The Swedish unemployment insurance scheme is under the administration of confederations of labour unions (see below).

[2] With this limitation we cannot discuss 'economics of scope', that is, gains from having a portfolio of different types of risks covered by the insurance. For a discussion of portfolio diversification as a solution to the problem of collective risk, see Horgby and Söderström (1998).

example, as pointed out by Borch (1990), in the areas of commercial telecommunication satellites and jet airlines, insurance has for a long time been offered in spite of the fact that, in the beginning, there were very few customers and practically no statistical information about the risks involved. Karl Borch suggests that one should take a pragmatic view on the issue of insurability: 'the risk covered is by definition insurable'.

There are a few reasons why a risk cannot be insured at all or at best be just partially covered by private insurance: moral hazard, collective risk, adverse selection and political regulation. We now look at these in turn.

Moral hazard

Many risks are affected by the behaviour of the insured individuals. This must be taken into account in the contracts offered by the insurer. If the insurer can observe the behaviour of insured individuals he can make the compensation (or premium) directly conditional on behaviour, typically the amount of precautions taken to prevent damage. If the insurer cannot observe the behaviour, a second-best strategy is to use some form of *co-insurance*, i.e. to offer insurance with less than full compensation for losses, $C < L$. As a result there will be a private cost for damages that do occur.

In the extreme case when individuals can shift the probability of loss towards one, the insurer has to reduce the compensation level towards zero or raise the premium close to or up to the level of compensation. In this case there might be no demand for insurance at all; the compensation will be too low relative to the premium.

The moral hazard problem is the same whether a private company or the government provides insurance. In both cases one should try to find an efficient form of co-insurance. It is hard to say whether public or private administration is better to handle issues of co-insurance. To the extent that moral hazard has an unethical element, certain legal sanctions may be called for. For a discussion of moral hazard as an ethical problem, see Söderström (1997).

The moral hazard aspect is particularly severe in the case of benefits for families with children (accounting for nearly 9 per cent of the budget in table 7.1), consisting of a package of benefits received by parents as compensation for the birth of a child. Among other things, this package includes a so-called parental insurance, i.e. a right to compensation for loss of income to a parent who stays home and takes care of a child (up to 450 days), subsidised child care, and a monthly child allowance for at least sixteen years per child.

It is doubtful, in spite of its name, whether parental insurance should be viewed as a proper insurance. The probability of having a child is almost entirely under the control of the individuals concerned. A proper insurance plan would therefore either have a very large co-insurance rate, approaching 100 per cent, or a very high insurance premium, also approaching 100 per cent of a typical compensation. Such a scheme would hardly attract any customers.

That parental insurance is not an insurance policy *per se* does not mean that subsidies to parents must be ruled out as a viable policy. For example, such subsidies might be motivated as a means to strengthen the pension system.

Collective risk

Risks for insured individuals may be anything from non-correlated to strongly positively correlated. The term 'collective risk' refers to the latter case. From the insurer's point of view a collective risk poses a problem in that he must be able to pay a huge amount of compensation at the same time. Unless he can buy reinsurance, there is no alternative to raise the loading factor. As a consequence, the insurance contract offered would be less attractive to customers and the market will be thinner. To some extent making the insurance mandatory could compensate for this.

Unemployment insurance is an example of an insurance against typical collective risks. Since private reinsurance is hard to organise, it seems, and funds to cover benefits during a severe recession would have to be excessively large, some sort of government support is needed. One possibility is that unemployment spells exceeding, for example, two months are provided out of general taxation. Another possibility would be that a substantial part of current expenditures are covered by a subsidy.

The present Swedish unemployment insurance is under private management. There is a benefit society for each federation of labour unions handling cash benefits according to rules stated by law. Swedish unemployment insurance is not mandatory. Law only requires that benefit societies should allow everyone to become a member. In particular, membership cannot be restricted to members of a labour union. The benefit societies are in return entitled to a substantial subsidy in proportion to claims. In fact, in recent years the subsidy has been of the same size as the amount of benefits claimed. This is a way to 'internalise' the political risk of becoming unemployed. Premiums paid by the insured individuals are merely symbolic. Hence, these societies are rather different from an ordinary insurance company. *They are formally private, but in essence public.* Law sets all rules of the game. Only the administration itself is left for private initiative.

In the language used above, privatisation of the Swedish unemployment insurance scheme must be informal rather than formal. An obvious step would be to lower the rate of subsidisation, thereby increasing the proportion of compensation covered by membership fees (premiums). Fees would increase more where the risk of becoming unemployed is relatively high. This would discourage industries with a high rate of unemployment and, perhaps, lower the overall rate of unemployment in the country. However, in the short run, the effect might be to increase the rate of unemployment in areas dominated by traditional industries.

To the extent that premiums are experience rated, that is, differentiated according to each person's unemployment history, some people may be inclined to seek compensation from other sources. For example, some people may report sick instead of unemployed.

Adverse selection

The adverse selection problem is a matter of asymmetric information. If individuals differ with respect to the probability of loss and the insurer cannot separate low-risk individuals from high-risk individuals, he must offer the same contract to everyone. This is a problem when the individuals themselves know to which risk category they belong, since the uniform contract will be unattractive to individuals faced with a relatively low risk. Some of them will be better off without insurance. As these individuals leave the market, the average risk will become higher and the uniform contract adjusted accordingly until, in the end, all customers but one leave the market.

Mandating insurance might solve the problem of adverse selection. The Swedish motor third party insurance illustrates how independent private insurance companies can handle a mandatory, uniform insurance with risk differences among customers. Companies compete by offering a low premium, and also by offering various supplementary benefits.

Cream skimming

The problems mentioned – moral hazard, collective risk and adverse selection – are technical in nature. There are also non-technical problems related to the kind of economic policy pursued in a country. As an example we would like to mention an obligation for insurance companies to charge all customers the same premium in spite of the fact that there are different risk groups. Such an obligation does not have to be explicit. For example, nowadays many demand a law preventing Swedish insurance companies having different premiums in pension plans for men and women.

Objections to differentiated premiums are typically raised on equity grounds. True enough, differentiated premiums would mean higher payment from people exposed to high risks. But there would at least be insurance available. In the case of a uniform premium independent of risk, high-risk persons might have difficulties finding any insurance at all. From the point of view of the insurance companies, high-risk persons are in this case bad risks one should try to avoid. There are various means for companies to do that. For example, advertising could be organised in such a way that women (or other 'bad risks') prefer to buy insurance elsewhere.

The result of such cream skimming may be anything but equitable.

7.3   Sickness insurance

In the Swedish sickness insurance scheme individuals are compensated for loss of income due to temporary illness. Compensation is given irrespective of the cause of illness. Thus, no distinction is made between illness caused by a common cold, a work or traffic accident, sports activities, etc. The compensation is given in two parts: (1) sick pay from the employer during the first two weeks of a sickness episode, the sick pay period, and thereafter (2) a sickness benefit from the social insurance. There is no formal limit for how long a period one can receive sickness benefit in Sweden. However, in case an individual's working capacity is permanently reduced the sickness benefit will be replaced by a disability pension. Presently there is one waiting day, meaning that no compensation is paid for the first day of a sickness episode.

Law carefully regulates both parts of the compensation. Thus, employers are not free to have a higher or lower sick pay than stipulated. Equity as well as efficiency arguments are used in favour of this regulation. Its purpose is to make sure that the rate of co-insurance is kept reasonably high and the same for all workers. There are some concerns that generous rules during the sick pay period will induce a higher cost during the sickness benefit period, i.e. that more absence during the first two weeks would induce more absence also from the fifteenth day onwards.

There are two main advantages of having insurance in the hands of competing private insurance companies:
- *differentiation*: competing insurance companies are likely to take all steps possible to promote prevention on the part of the insured;
- *diversification*: competing insurance companies are likely to offer policies adapted to the preferences of various groups in society (not only the majority).

We now look at these in turn.

Differentiation

An important role for insurers is to promote prevention. When moral hazard is present, co-insurance is an obvious incentive to this end. Alternatively, provided that risk groups can be identified, one could stimulate prevention by having premiums differentiated according to risk. Prevention is promoted by both models, but only to the extent that the risk in question really depends on manageable factors. Should the risk of illness be independent of working conditions, eating habits, etc., there is no scope whatsoever for prevention.

In our view, a general sickness insurance scheme with risk-adjusted premiums is a rather poor instrument to achieve risk consciousness and active prevention on the part of policyholders. Our main reason is that premium differences due to ordinary illness to a large extent would reflect risk factors that people cannot do much about. A higher than normal risk has been observed for women, single parents, the foreign born, the poorly educated, and persons with congenital problems like diabetes and rheumatism. Premiums differentiated according to such factors are debatable from an equity point of view without having positive effects with respect to efficiency.

A better alternative would be to design *partial* insurance schemes for areas where prevention comes naturally and the insurance contract could be used as an incentive. An obvious candidate for an arrangement of this sort would be insurance related to *work injuries*. In fact, most industrial countries have a separate insurance for such damages, often under private administration.

An optimal arrangement in this context would be an insurance which is compulsory for employers, covers all kinds of damages – not only the loss of income, but also costs for health care and rehabilitation, and physical suffering – and which is financed by strictly risk-differentiated premiums.[3] Such an arrangement would give employers a strong incentive to apply preventive measures in order to make working conditions reasonably safe and healthy. Compared to the present Swedish system, where the social insurance only covers a part of the income loss and is financed by a tax in proportion to the wage bill, workplaces with poor

---

[3] Following the Coase theorem (Coase, 1988) one might argue that it does not matter whether this type of insurance is compulsory for employers or employees, but we think that the employer is the more suitable party to carry the risk. One important reason is that the employer has more control over working conditions and more knowledge about risks at the workplace. Hence, transaction costs are lower when the employer is responsible for the insurance than when the responsibility rests with the employees. For an overview of these issues in the context of work injuries and diseases, see Diamond (1977).

working conditions would be charged with a higher premium and have a less favourable market position. This, we believe, would be good for working conditions in general.[4]

There are two types of work injuries: accidents and diseases. For accidents it is often possible to determine when and where the injury has arisen. It is therefore relatively easy to charge the appropriate employer with the costs. Injuries caused by diseases are more difficult to handle. As a rule, diseases are insidious and might even be a result of risks in more than one workplace. It is therefore, in our view, reasonable to keep the two types of injuries separate. While damages due to accident are well suited for insurance offered by competing private insurance companies, damages caused by diseases are rather difficult for them to handle. The main problem is that private insurance companies must be prepared for the possibility that activities today may cause illness many years from now, some not yet known. The only way they can do that is to increase premiums in order to build a sufficiently large fund. This is the situation in, for example, Norway where the work injury insurance was handed over to private administration in the 1990s. Denmark and Finland also run this insurance privately. They all have problems with the 'disease part'; for details, see Söderström et al. (1996). Hence, it might be better to leave this part of the workers' compensation in the public sector, where funds are unnecessary.

Even with a limitation to accidents, private insurance for work injuries would imply large differences in premiums for employers in different branches. An estimate of possible premiums in a private system replacing the ordinary sickness insurance and disability pension shows that the yearly premium per employee would vary from a few hundred SEK up to more than ten thousand SEK per year (Söderström et al., 1996). This would give employers in high-risk industries a strong incentive to improve the working environment and to rehabilitate injured employees as quickly as possible, thereby lowering future premiums.

Traffic insurance is another candidate for separate private administration. In Sweden there is at present, as previously mentioned, a compulsory third party motor insurance provided by private insurance companies. This insurance covers damages to cars, etc. Damages in the form of income loss are covered by the general sickness insurance scheme and health care costs are covered by local/regional government budgets. In our view, one should consider enlarging the third party motor insurance to something similar to the hypothetical work injury insurance mentioned above.

---

[4] For a critical examination of environmental regulations in the United States, see Viscusi (1992). He claims that these regulations, with respect to work environment, have been relatively ineffective.

In this case car owners (as well as owners of other vehicles) would be charged with a premium that covers expected costs for income compensations in the form of sickness benefits, disability pensions and possibly also health care costs.

We do not know what the premiums would look like for this type of traffic injury insurance, but we suspect that they would be relatively high, for example, for heavy motorcycles. As private insurance companies carry these costs the public budget will be burdened correspondingly less.

Diversification

The second argument in favour of private insurance mentioned above is that private insurance companies would be eager to customise insurance plans according to individual preferences. As an example we now look at the design of sickness insurance with respect to two important parameters: the number of waiting days and, when the payment of benefits starts, the compensation ratio. It is possible to combine these parameters in such a way that the total amount of expected benefits (and therefore also the average premium) will be the same. It could be expected that individuals prefer different combinations along such an 'iso-cost curve'.

In an attempt to find out which mixture of waiting days and compensation rate people prefer, and the factors influencing people's preferences for fewer waiting days over high compensation, Daniel Eek and Klas Rikner conducted a questionnaire survey. Participants in the survey were presented alternatives with approximately the same aggregate expenditures according to data from the National Social Insurance Board (NSIB) for the year 1988. In this year there was no sick pay: all compensations were in the form of sickness benefits. For a detailed description of the survey, see Rikner (2002).

The data were used to count the share of total absence for day no. 1 in all sickness episodes, and the same for day no. 2, day no. 3, etc. From these estimates it was found that introducing one qualifying day leaves about 10 per cent less time to compensate. Thus, a system with 90 per cent compensation from day no. 1 would cost about the same as a system with one qualifying day and then a 100 per cent compensation from day no. 2. Similarly, a system with 75 per cent compensation from day no. 1 would cost about the same as a system with three waiting days and 100 per cent compensation from day no. 4. To visualise a number of combinations of waiting days and compensation rates that give approximately the same costs within the system, iso-cost curves are shown in figure 7.1.

Alternatives concerning the number of waiting days were in the survey limited to 0, 1 and 3 days; the corresponding rates are shown in the third

Table 7.2 *Combinations of waiting days and compensation rates used in the survey*

	Qualifying days	Compensation rate (%)	Alternate rate (%)
Combination A	0	65	60
Combination B	1	75	70
Combination C	3	90	85

Iso-cost curves

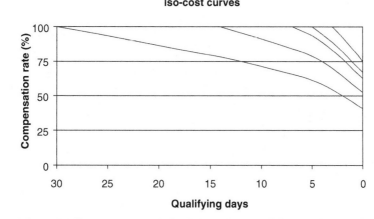

Figure 7.1 Iso-cost curves derived from 1988 statistics on absence due to sickness

column of table 7.2. Combination B was the system prevailing when the survey was conducted, with one qualifying day and 75 per cent compensation thereafter. Three alternative rate choices were also available (shown in the last column of the table) in order to test how strong preferences were. The respondents were asked to rank the combinations A, B and C, including the alternative rate choices, from 1 to 6, with the most preferred alternative equal to 1.

It turned out that most people preferred the actual system. Approximately 56 per cent of the respondents preferred a system with one waiting day as the best alternative, about 20 per cent preferred a system without waiting days, and almost 25 per cent preferred three waiting days as the best alternative (see table 7.3).

Preferences seem to mirror the respondents' absence profile as well as their capability of managing risks. For example, in the statistical analysis the sign of age was positive, which means that older people prefer

Table 7.3 *Results from the study of preferences, referring to the respondents' most preferred alternative (%)*

No waiting day	1 waiting day	3 waiting days	1 waiting day as both best *and* next-best alternative
19.6	55.6	24.8	40.7

more waiting days followed by a higher compensation rate. Since older people have relatively more long-term absences this result was expected. Employment status was another important factor. Both self-employed and temporary employed had strong preferences for more rather than fewer waiting days; a possible explanation might be that these groups are better prepared to handle short-term fluctuations in income.

Given that people, in line with the results from the survey, to some extent form their preferences in accordance with their own expected absence profile, a conclusion is that expenditures for a flexible system would increase relative to a system where all individuals are offered the same scheme. We do not know how much expenditures would be affected and to what extent people actually would be prepared to pay a higher price for customised insurance.

Longer period of sick pay

The present Swedish system is a combination of mandatory private insurance (the sick pay period) and public insurance (the sickness benefit period). A particular advantage with this type of combination, as we have pointed out before, is that private insurers do not have to worry about the long tail of the risk distribution. They can concentrate on normal variations in sickness absence. Another positive effect of a (longer) sick pay period is that it gives the employer an incentive to care about the working conditions for employees. Besides prevention against work injuries it is also important that employers create a stimulating working environment. Employees who are satisfied with their working conditions will probably have less absence than others will. In our view, this feature of the present system, with both a sick pay period and a sickness benefit period, is worth preserving. By doing so the role of differentiation and diversification can be limited to just the sick pay part of the insurance. It is, however, nothing that formally prevents differentiation and diversification also in a public system.

Of course, one has to decide how long the sick pay period should be. With a longer sick pay period claims would be transferred from the social

Table 7.4 *Proportion of absence due to illness within a certain number of days in 1990*

Number of days	Proportion of total absence (%)
14	40
29	49
59	58
89	64
179	74
364	85

Source: Own calculations based on statistics from the National Social Insurance Board.

insurance scheme to the employers' budget. Table 7.4 shows the proportion of absence days due to sickness that would be under the employers' responsibility depending on the length of the sick pay period. For example, increasing the sick pay period from two weeks to one month would increase the sick pay period's share of absence days from about 40 per cent to about 50 per cent. Since high-income workers usually have a shorter absence period than low-income workers, the employers' share of expenditures would probably be higher than their share of days.[5]

The sick pay period in Sweden was two weeks from 1992 until 1996, and then prolonged to four weeks. This increase in the employers' responsibility was heavily criticised, and in 1998 the sick pay period was reduced to two weeks again. It was feared that small firms in particular – and the self-employed – would be hurt by the longer period. They would be exposed to a higher risk and forced to take precautions, for example avoiding hiring individuals in high-risk groups. For example, in Switzerland, where employers do bear much of the cost for sickness absence, many firms do not accept new employees unless they have passed a medical examination (Rikner and Strumpf, 1998). In the Netherlands the employer period has been twelve months since 1996. The result seems to be that sickness absence is somewhat reduced but, at the same time, that it has become harder for people with health problems to find a permanent job (see Hoegelund and Veerman, 2000; Nordisk Försäkringstidskrift, 2000).

[5] These figures refer to 1990 when there was no waiting day for benefits. Since the first day of sickness episodes on average account for about 10 per cent of total absence, the proportion of absence during the sick pay period would be reduced correspondingly.

7.4   Pensions

The Swedish pension system has three parts: a social pension scheme, supplementary negotiated pension schemes, and individual pension plans. The social scheme is public and the two others are private, the difference between them being that the negotiated schemes are collective, similar or identical for all members of the respective group, while individual plans are adapted to each person's preferences. The three parts are closely interrelated. The negotiated schemes and individual plans are to a large extent merely supplements to the social scheme and will therefore, if possible, also change as a consequence of changes in the social scheme.

Social pension schemes are as a rule mandatory. This is particularly important in a welfare state. Since citizens can count on the state (or the respective municipality) to provide for their welfare when needed, there is a temptation to postpone financial arrangements for one's old age or even skip such provisions altogether ('free riding'). It is therefore very much in the interest of taxpayers to mandate a system that requires everyone to pay into a scheme that provides adequate coverage in old age. The adequate level should at least include subsistence needs.

Social pension schemes

There are several models for a mandated social pension scheme. Given that pensions one way or the other are financed out of current earnings the following macroeconomic relationship must in the long run hold for any pension scheme (it does not matter whether they are organised as a pay-as-you-go scheme or a capital reserve scheme):

$$RP = sNW \tag{1}$$

or equivalently

$$s = (R/N)(P/W) \tag{2}$$

where R = number of pensioners, P = average pension, N = number of employed persons, W = average earnings, and s = the proportion of earnings being used for pensions. In a tax-financed system with a proportional pay roll tax, s is the tax rate. As seen in (2) the tax rate is equal to the product of the *dependency ratio* (R/N) and the *replacement ratio* (P/W). If, for example, there are six pensioners for every ten employed, $R/N = 0.6$, and pensions make up 70 per cent of an average salary, $P/W = 0.7$, then 42 per cent of current earnings must be transferred into the hands of pensioners, $s = 0.42$. Of course, the dependency ratio (R/N) is not given exogenously. A more generous pension scheme is likely to stimulate early retirement and a higher dependency ratio. As shown by, for example, Gruber and Wise (1997), there is a strong correspondence between the age at which benefits are available and departure from the labour force. This observation was based on evidence in eleven industrialised countries.

An important distinction can be made between pension schemes that are *defined benefit* (DB) and schemes that are *defined contribution* (DC). To put things simply, we can say that a DB scheme takes the pension level (or the replacement ratio) as given and then fits the premium/tax gradually according to equation (1), while a DC scheme takes the premium/tax as given and gradually adapts the pension level (or replacement ratio) according to the same equation. In the first case, workers cannot be sure how large a part of earnings they will have to hand over to pensioners; and in the second case, pensioners (or at least potential pensioners) cannot be sure what the pension will be. Hence, demographic and macroeconomic risks are placed differently in the two types of schemes.

Most countries have the social pension scheme organised in line with the DB principle, but in recent years there has been a tendency to switch to the DC principle, at least for some part of the social pension scheme, as recommended by the World Bank (1994). Pure DB schemes are likely to become too expensive over time (see below), and are therefore considered unreliable. A compromise between the two principles is that pension benefits are fixed at the time when individuals retire; whatever contribution an individual has made during his working life will then be converted to an annuity lasting for the rest of his life.

Sweden has also changed to the DC principle, but only partly. An important feature of the new Swedish social pension system is that everyone should have subsistence needs covered by a 'guaranteed pension'.[6] This guarantee follows the DB principle and is financed from the general state budget. With a growth rate around 2 per cent per year, about 20 per cent of Swedish pensioners are expected to receive some benefit from the guarantee. With a growth rate above 3 per cent this proportion will be down to about 12 per cent (National Social Insurance Board, 1999). Very few are expected to get the entire pension from the guarantee. Low-income earners will benefit from both the ordinary social pension scheme and the guarantee. To the extent that a person gets an earned pension in the social pension scheme there will be a reduction in the amount he can get from the guarantee: the reduction ('marginal tax') is 100 per cent

---

[6] It is required that one has been a Swedish resident for at least forty years. Social assistance will support people who have stayed in Sweden a shorter period.

of the earned pension up to a certain limit, and 48 per cent above the limit.

There are two types of pension schemes based on the DC principle. In Góra and Palmer (2001) these types are called *Financial Defined Contribution* (FDC) and *Notional Defined Contribution* (NDC), respectively. A NDC scheme is described in the following way (Góra and Palmer, 2001: 7):

- Contributions based on individual earnings create account values.
- Account balances from the close of the preceding period earn a rate of return based on the growth of the sum of paid contributions. In other words, accounts are credited with an 'interest' equal to the rate of growth in earnings.
- Accumulated account values are annuitised at the time of retirement.
- Annuities are calculated on the basis of accumulated capital and life expectancy at the age of retirement.
- Annuities may be indexed as long as the index used does not surpass the growth of the contribution base (i.e. the wage sum).
- Demographic reserves are created when relatively large cohorts are working. These reserves, which are used up as the same cohorts retire, are the only reserves in a NDC scheme.

In a FDC scheme, on the other hand, there are also the traditional capital reserves set aside to cover future claims by those who contribute to the scheme. These reserves can include equities in private companies as well as government bonds, etc. The rate of return on such reserves may be larger or smaller than the rate of return in a NDC scheme, that is, the development of the wage bill. If reserves in a FDC scheme consist of government bonds yielding a return equal to the growth of the NDC contribution base (that is, the wage bill), both types of scheme would have the same rate of return.

Most of the Swedish social pension system was recently converted from a DB scheme to a NDC scheme. Both schemes may be characterised as pay-as-you-go (PAYG), but they are fundamentally different. Individual claims were in the old system determined on an *ad hoc* basis and in the new system are determined by each individual's own contribution. The old system had redistribution as an essential goal. In the new system the redistribution aspect has been deferred to the guaranteed pension that, as pointed out before, is financed outside the NDC scheme.[7]

---

[7] The NDC scheme attracts much attention these days. See, for example, the *World Bank Pension Reform Primer* (2000) with contributions by Richard Disney, Marek Gora, Edward Palmer and others. As far as we know, Söderström (1990) was first to suggest that a NDC scheme should replace a traditional DB scheme.

Alongside the new NDC scheme Sweden has also introduced a minor FDC scheme, using 10–15 per cent of total contributions. In this supplementary scheme individuals are free to compose a capital reserve of their own taste. There are several hundred funds of different types to choose from.

Privatisation

There are many things one can do under the heading privatisation. Góra and Palmer list the following four issues of privatisation: (1) private versus public administration; (2) well-defined contracts versus political promise; (3) direct versus indirect claims; and (4) public debt versus private equities.

The transition of the Swedish social pension from a DB scheme to a NDC scheme is in our view a major privatisation step, irrespective of the fact that the system is still under public administration. As a consequence, benefits are now defined by precise contracts instead of vague political promises. This does not mean that law cannot change the rules of the game, but it is generally believed that a DC scheme can resist political pressures better than a DB scheme. This is especially true for a NDC scheme, since there will be no real reserves to tap. The introduction of explicit capital reserves with possibilities for individuals to choose a portfolio of one's liking is a further step of privatisation. With these steps Sweden has come a long way in privatising the social pension system. The question now is, how much further can one go?

An obvious next step would be to allow private management of the capital reserve part of the social pension scheme. The reserves are already kept in the form of equity funds, etc., under private administration, so what is needed is that private agents are given responsibility for the collection of contributions and to keep a record of each individual's contributions and capital reserve. Traditionally this has been a task for public agents.

A final step of privatisation would be to enlarge this model to the entire social pension scheme (except the guarantee part), that is, to transform the entire social pension scheme from a NDC scheme to a FDC scheme and let all the corresponding capital reserves be managed by private agents. As suggested by James Buchanan, and tried, for example, in Chile, the transformation could take place gradually as new cohorts retire. In this case there is a NDC scheme for the working population and a FDC scheme for pensioners. At the time of retirement, government bonds are used to convert the accumulated account value on individual accounts to a real capital reserve. A consequence is that an implicit public debt becomes explicit (Buchanan, 1968).

Real capital reserves in the form of government bonds represent claims on future taxes. An alternative might be to convert accumulated account values into shares traded on the stock market. Provided that such shares support all pension benefits, it might be hard to find a reasonable return on the capital. In order to cover all claims in the present Swedish social pension scheme capital reserves would have to be of the order three times GDP. Hence, the social pension system would take up a very large part of the Swedish capital market and become a major owner of companies in the country. (As long as few countries follow this route it might seem that there are unlimited investment opportunities abroad, but this is not true. The amount of investments a country can make abroad is limited by its trade surplus.)

Political aspects

We like to point out that these privatisation steps include a considerable political risk. This risk is clearly illustrated by the pension reforms implemented as a part of Roosevelt's New Deal (Sjoblom, 1985). At first the pension system was meant to have FDC properties, but gradually its character was changed into a simple DB scheme without any reserves at all ('social security'). Sweden had a similar experience with the public pension system of 1913. The political risk can be explained in the following way (Söderström, 1990).

For the sake of the argument we assume that the social pension has been organised according to the FDC scheme, and that it is left to the median voter to decide changes in the scheme. We also assume that the market rate of interest is high relative to the rate of growth in earnings. The issue is what the social pension will look like. What does the median voter want? Will the FDC scheme be maintained, or will there be a shift to some other type of scheme?

Windfall gain   It is certainly not sufficient that funds in the FDC scheme have a high rate of return. A shift to a type of scheme that does not need any funds would give rise to a windfall gain for the present generation. For those who have had time to obtain capital reserves in the old system, the profit is visible in that they can receive two pensions. Roughly calculated, the windfall gain is as large as all existing capital reserves in the FDC scheme. In extreme cases these reserves cover something like a quarter of an individual's life income, which is to say about ten years of earnings. The temptation to obtain additional income that size is naturally hard to resist.

Should the transition be immediate and without special exceptions, today's pensioners would be strongly tempted to vote for a reform. They would receive a double pension. It is just as clear that the young would vote against. Because they have not had the time to save in the FDC scheme, they have no part in the windfall gain. Since the market rate of interest is relatively high, according to our assumption, the young are better off in the FDC scheme. With pensioners for and young against, the decision rests with those who are middle-aged. As the windfall gain rises with age, the oldest are most positive to a reform. The median voter would be a person around fifty years of age.

Tax rate and pension level   It must also be decided which level the pension should have. In a DB scheme this is a purely political issue. Which tax rate and thus pension level does the median voter prefer? There is obviously a trade-off between present and future consumption. Most in favour of raising the tax are pensioners who receive a correspondingly higher pension without having to pay anything at all. Middle-aged persons are the next most favourable to a higher tax rate. In exchange for paying a higher tax in a few years they receive a higher pension for the rest of their lives. Young people prefer a relatively low tax rate, well below the level preferred by the median voter, which is the level of taxation decided by the political system. Thus, the young generation will be forced to have an inefficient consumption profile, consuming too little when young and too much when old. If the median voter looks beyond self-interest and considers their children's interest, then she or he would act more as a twenty-year old individual. If everyone considers everyone, in other words perfect altruism, then the result would be the same as if everyone were twenty-years old and only considered themselves.

Promise of future pensions   The transition to the DB model and the following tax increase does not have to be made so that pensioners are the most favoured group. It is possible to get the majority to vote for a reform implying that a major part of the windfall gain goes to those who are middle-aged. This is achieved by allowing the transition to be made through promises of *future* pension benefits. An example is the Swedish supplementary pension system (ATP) introduced in 1960 and now abolished, where a qualification time of thirty years of employment was required to receive a full pension (in relation to one's salary). Such requirements prevent pensioners from receiving anything of the windfall gain at the same time as the gain for middle-aged persons is cut back.

An arrangement of this type is significant for the pension level. Since the main focus among decision-makers descends into younger age groups, preferences for tax increases lessen. The pension system will be more in line with the desires of the youngest generation. This means lower pensions and a correspondingly reduced burden on the national economy. Notice, though, that we are still discussing an oversized system with too much saving from the point of view of the youngest generation. Only when the decision is left to the very young will the result be optimal with respect to each individual's entire life cycle.

The guarantee pension

As mentioned before, a problem with DC schemes is that some individuals do not manage to make enough contributions to receive a decent pension. One reason could be that they have immigrated late in life. For these individuals there must be a supplementary scheme in the form of social assistance. In the Swedish case, the supplementary scheme has been incorporated in the pension scheme as a particular guarantee pension.

We do not think that the guarantee pension scheme should be privatised in the way described earlier. This scheme is very different from ordinary private insurance arrangements. There is no alternative to have the guarantee pension in line with the DB principle without any connection at all between contributions and benefits. Otherwise this pension would not fulfil its purpose to supplement pensions organised according to the DC principle.

7.5   How much?

It is not easy to estimate the potential savings in the public social protection budget from a privatisation of just *a part* of certain insurance and not the entire insurance. A rough estimate says that a sick pay period of two weeks would reduce the public costs for the sickness insurance by about 25–30 per cent compared to a public insurance that compensates from the second day of absence. A sick pay period of four weeks would reduce the public costs by about 35–40 per cent. More than four weeks seems to be excessive since a long sick pay period would make it more difficult for high-risk groups to get employment.

Cash benefits in connection with work accidents amount to about 3 per cent of the social insurance budget for cash benefits, or slightly below 0.5 per cent of GDP. Including traffic insurance yields an overall potential between 0.5 and 1 per cent of GDP.

In the pension system it is even more difficult to estimate potential savings in the public budget. A possibility is to convert the guarantee pension to a basic pension precisely above the subsistence level, and to put the rest of the social pension scheme under private administration. A rough estimate is that such a reform would reduce public expenditures for pensions by about 50 per cent. This is a very uncertain figure. Among other things, we do not know how people would react to the reform.

Another, in our view 'deeper', form of privatisation is to privatise social insurance schemes themselves, either by introducing consumer choice with respect to the construction of benefits or by introducing individual responsibility for the financing of benefits. We have given examples of this type of privatisation within the sickness insurance scheme and the old age pension scheme. In our view, this type of privatisation should be used much more than at present.

References

Borch, Karl, 1990, *Economics of Insurance*, Amsterdam: North-Holland.
Buchanan, James M., 1968, 'Social insurance in a growing economy: a proposal for radical reform', *National Tax Journal*, 21, 386–95.
Coase, Ronald H., 1988, *The Firm, the Market and the Law*, Chicago: University of Chicago Press.
Diamond, Peter A., 1977, 'Insurance theoretic aspects of workers compensation', in Alan S. Blinder and P. Friedman (eds.), *Natural Resources, Uncertainty, and General Equilibrium Systems*, New York: Academic Press, 67–90.
Góra, Marek and Palmer, Edward, 2001, 'Shifting perspectives in pensions', working paper received from *Mgora@sgh.waw.pl*.
Gruber, Jonathan and Wise, David, 1997, 'Social security programs and retirement around the world', NBER working paper 6134.
Haslinger, Franz and Horgby, Per-Johan, 1997, 'High cost-protection in health insurance: a proposal for a reorganisation of health insurance in the presence of asymmetric information', *FinanzArchiv*, 54, 1–25.
Hoegelund, Jan and Veerman, Theo J., 2000, 'Reintegration: public or private responsibility: the Dutch and Danish reintegration policy towards work incapacitated persons'. Paper presented at the ISSA conference on Social Security in the Global Village, Helsinki, 25–27 September 2000.
Horgby, Per-Johan and Söderström, Lars, 1998, 'Social risk in health insurance: a reflection on the economics of scale and scope in health insurance', *Australian Economic Papers*, 37, 185–94.
Ministry of Social Affairs, 2001, *Välfärdsfakta Social*, 24 April.
National Social Insurance Board (1999), *Den nya allmänna pensionen*, RFV Redovisar, 12.
Nordisk Försäkringstidskrift (2000), 'Holländsk sjukförsäkring – offentligt system i privat regi', 4/2000, 359–67.
Rikner, Klas, 2002, 'Sickness insurance: design and behaviour', PhD thesis, Lund Economic Studies no. 103, Department of Economics, Lund University.
Rikner, Klas and Strumpf, Michael, 1998, 'Compensation for health-related loss of income', in Peter Zweifel, Carl Hampus Lyttkens and Lars Söderström

(eds.), *Regulation of Health: Case Studies of Sweden and Switzerland*, Boston: Kluwer.

Sjoblom, Kriss, 1985, 'Voting for social security', *Public Choice*, 45, 3, 226–40.

Söderström, Lars, 1989, 'Almost genuine insurance schemes as an alternative to tax-financed pensions and other social security benefits', in Ando Chiancone and Kenneth Messere (eds.), *Changes in Revenue Structures*, Wayne State University Press / International Institute of Public Finance.

—1990, 'Avgiftsbestämd tilläggspension – ett alternativ till ATP', in Lars Jonung (ed.), *Nya Fält för Marknadsekonomin, En Bok Tillägnad Ingemar Ståhl*, SNS Förlag, 25–43.

—1997, 'Moral hazard in the welfare state', in Herbert Giersch (ed.), *Reforming the Welfare State*, Springer Verlag / Egon-Sohmen-Foundation.

Söderström, Lars, Rikner, Klas and Turtell, Klas, 1996, 'Om förutsättningarna för en privat arbetsskadeförsäkring', *Working Papers in Public Economics, Labour Economics, and Human Capital Research*, 2, Department of Economics, Göteborg University.

Viscusi, W. Kip, 1992, *Fatal Tradeoffs, Public and Private Responsibilities for Risk*, Oxford: Oxford University Press.

World Bank, 1994, *Averting the Old Age Crisis, Policies to Protect the Old and Promote Growth*, Washington DC: World Bank.

—2000, *World Bank Pension Reform Primer*, Washington DC: World Bank.

8   Occupational welfare

Ann-Charlotte Ståhlberg[1]

8.1   Alternative and supplement

Several studies indicate that occupational and private welfare can be a substitute for or supplement to social welfare. In Forssell et al. (1999), social insurance transfers to older people are compared with non-state employment-related (occupational) transfers in eight European countries (Denmark, Finland, France, Germany, the Netherlands, Norway, Sweden and the UK). Denmark and the Netherlands have social insurance pension schemes that bear no relation to earnings at all, and in the UK social insurance pensions are only weakly related to earnings. These are the countries in the study with the most comprehensive occupational pensions. Germany and France, with state pension schemes based on the corporate model, provide good standard protection with high rates of replacement even for those who have had high salaries. Non-state employment-related pensions are less important in France and Germany than in the other countries in the study. A comparison of the Nordic countries shows a varied choice of solutions to the problem of providing for old age in spite of the fact that they are similar in many respects. All have a basic provision given to everyone irrespective of income. Finland, Norway and Sweden, but not Denmark, have national supplementary pensions based on the principle of compensation for loss of income. However, as the replacement rate is higher in Finland than in the other Nordic countries, there is little scope there for occupational pensions, which are most comprehensive in Denmark. The study shows that average disposable income for the group of elderly people as a whole does not vary very much from country to country. This is in spite of the large differences in public spending on pensions and benefits, and in spite of the fact that the public pension systems follow completely different principles in linking the level of compensation to previous income. However, the proportion of elderly people with low incomes is lower in

[1] I am grateful for comments on earlier versions from the participants at two SNS meetings at the Krusenberg Manor.

the countries that have guaranteed basic pensions. Similar results are found in OECD (1998).

In Rein and Wadensjö (1997), a comparison between social insurance and occupational pension schemes in nine industrialised countries (Austria, France, Germany, Italy, Japan, the Netherlands, Sweden, the UK and the USA) shows that among the countries with social insurance pension schemes providing high replacement rates, there is wide variation in the extent of occupational pension schemes. However, the three countries with the lowest replacement rates from their social security systems – Japan, the UK and the USA – all have extensive occupational pension schemes.

The organisation of public pensions varies widely, yet the overall income situation of older people could be similar. Less social insurance compensation might result in individuals and organisations trying to find other, non-state solutions to the security problem. These can be arrangements related to employment, such as collective and individual insurance schemes provided by the employer (occupational welfare). Alternatively they can be private personal insurance schemes, bank accounts, etc. (private welfare).

Non-state employment-related insurance schemes might reflect the interests of the state, unions, employers, employees and insurance companies. Collective insurance schemes attached to wage contracts can provide unions with new ways of attracting and keeping members. It may be in the interests of the state to relieve itself of some of the economic responsibility for insurance protection, for example by providing tax incentives for occupational insurance schemes to encourage their development. Wage compensation in the form of insurance rights instead of money is attractive to the employer if the payroll tax is lower for insurance contributions than for money wages. It is attractive to the employee if a lower tax rate is payable on insurance contributions than on equivalent money wages. Owing to the progressive nature of income tax, tax relief for non-state insurance has a distributive impact. Agulnik and Le Grand (1998) show a strongly regressive pattern for the UK. Half the benefit of tax relief on pension contributions goes to the top 10 per cent of taxpayers, and a quarter to the top 2.5 per cent (see also Sinfield, 2000). Occupational insurance is adaptable to the special desires of different groups. It may be a means for employers to attract and retain certain employees. Often, non-state employment-related insurance schemes give higher insurance rights as a percentage of money wages to higher-paid workers than to lower-paid. In such cases, the dispersion in employees' *total* remuneration for work is higher than the dispersion in money wages alone. When this wage benefit is not included in traditional wage statistics, occupational insurance schemes may be used as a tool to hide wage drift and to circumvent anti-discrimination laws and agreements.

Although social insurance and occupational insurance are similar in some ways, they differ in a number of respects. The link between the benefits that an individual can expect and what he or she pays for this protection may be more or less strong, and there are differences in replacement rates, coverage, qualification rules, administrative costs, transparency, etc. Occupational insurance schemes are supposed to affect efficiency, income distribution and gender equality differently than the social insurance system. This is proved in the following by means of the Swedish old age pension, survivors' pension and sickness benefit insurance systems. The Swedish non-state employment-related insurance schemes cover the same areas as the social insurance system. They raise the level of compensation especially upon illness and retirement. They also compensate for loss of income above the level of earnings covered by social insurance.

Unfortunately, there are few studies of occupational insurance, in Sweden and the rest of Europe (see for example Edebalk, Ståhlberg and Wadensjö, 1996, 1998; Shalev, 1996; Rein and Wadensjö, 1997). One reason could be the lack of individual data; another the fragmentary nature of occupational schemes, which complicates the analysis.

8.2   Coverage and inclusion

While available data are far from complete, it is evident that national differences in the scope of occupational welfare are greater than the differences in social welfare. Shalev (1996) presents data, for instance, from studies by Rein and Reinwater (1986), Turner and Dailey (1990), Dailey and Turner (1992) and Pestieau (1992). The Rein and Reinwater study indicates that whereas in France, Germany and England 20–25 per cent of overall social expenditure took the form of occupational benefits, the corresponding proportions for Sweden were 6 per cent and for the USA 33 per cent. In the late 1980s the participation rate of the private sector labour force in occupational pension plans ranged from 20–30 per cent in the UK, Australia and Canada, to 90 per cent in Switzerland and 46 per cent in the USA, according to Dailey and Turner. Pestieau focuses on middle-income households with heads aged 65–74. For this population, occupational pensions contributed about 20 per cent of household income in Canada, Australia, Germany and Switzerland. The corresponding ratio was 17 per cent in the USA, 27 per cent in the UK and 35 per cent in the Netherlands.

Rein and Wadensjö (1997) find that the general trend is towards an expanded role for occupational and personal pensions as against national pension schemes. In 1989, between 0.2 and 5 per cent of GDP was spent on occupational pensions. In some countries a value of five percentage points means that almost half of total pension spending comes from occupational pensions. The high-spending countries (4–5 per cent of GDP) include the Netherlands, the UK and the USA; the low-spending countries (less than 1 per cent of GDP) are Austria and Italy; medium-spending countries (about 2 per cent of GDP) are Germany, France and Sweden.

Comparative studies indicate that occupational insurance schemes are found mainly in large companies. Mooslechner and Url (1995) estimated the correlation between company size and occupational pensions in Austria. They found that the larger the company, the greater the probability that it offers occupational pensions. As many as 85 per cent of companies with more than 100 employees do so, as against only 3–5 per cent of the small companies. According to Schmähl (1997), many German private-sector companies routinely offer occupational old age pensions as a supplement to the mandatory pension scheme. But the extent to which pension schemes are offered is highly dependent on company size and branch of industry. Among companies with more than 1,000 employees, about 95 per cent have occupational old age pension schemes, compared to only 50 per cent of small enterprises with 10–99 employees.

When we look at how many individuals meet the qualification requirements and actually receive an occupational pension in practice, the figures for small enterprises are even lower compared with large companies. Rosner et al. (1997) study the pension system in Austria. They find that in relatively small enterprises, only about 25 per cent of the employees meet the qualification requirements, whereas about 80 per cent of the employees in large companies qualify for an occupational pension. In general, minimum income and minimum working hours requirements discriminate against part-time employees. Disqualification because of stopping work and vesting rules that require several years of employment by one and the same employer put women at a disadvantage, as they are often forced to change jobs during the period when they have young children because of intolerance to employment interruptions.

8.3   Coverage in Sweden

Sweden has quasi-mandatory occupational insurance schemes where the mandate is not a legal requirement imposed by the state, but the result of contractual agreements between labour unions and employers.[2] What

---

[2] The Netherlands is another example of this approach.

is unusual about the situation in Sweden is that practically all employees are covered by occupational insurance that is drawn up in a very small number of occupational schemes. There are four main schemes: one for private-sector white-collar workers, one for private sector blue-collar workers, one for state employees, and one for local authority and county council employees. Those who are not covered are employees of companies lacking collective agreements. In occupational insurance, as opposed to social insurance, type of employment and working hours may be questions of vital importance. People working less than 40 per cent of full-time hours or on a temporary or casual basis do not qualify for benefits in certain occupational insurance schemes. These restrictions primarily affect women and young people. Temporary or casual work is more frequent among women than among men and the risk of becoming a permanently temporary/casual worker (moving solely between such jobs) is also higher among women than among men (Håkansson, 2001; Nelander and Bendetcedotter, 2001). The proportion of temporary or casual workers increased by 32.5 per cent during the period 1987–99, from 12 per cent of all employed in 1987 to 15.9 per cent in 1999 (Håkansson, 2001).[3] According to Nelander and Bendetcedotter (2001) the rate of increase was higher among men than among women during the 1990s.

Table 8.1 shows temporary/casual workers of different age and gender in 1999. Eighteen per cent of all employed women and 13 per cent of all employed men had a temporary job. Young people were temporarily/casually employed to a greater extent than older people. In 1999, 58 per cent of all employed women and 43 per cent of all employed men between the ages of sixteen and twenty-four were temporary or casual workers. Those employed by the hour are especially vulnerable. In the course of a ten-year period, this category has more than trebled its share of the temporary/casual group, from 5.7 per cent in 1987 to 19.2 per cent in 1999 (Håkansson, 2001). Two-thirds of those employed by the hour are women.

Thus, some young, short-hour and temporary workers receive less *total* remuneration from work per hour than older and full-time workers in spite of equal work, hourly money wages and risk. Private-sector white-collar workers who are employed by the hour are not eligible for an occupational old age pension or occupational survivors' pensions. Private-sector blue-collar workers who have reached the age of twenty-one meet the qualification requirements for an occupational pension. For local government and state employees similar stipulations are to come into force in the near future. This means that occupational pension agreements in

---

[3] The data do not separate temporary workers from non-temporary workers before 1987.

Table 8.1 *Temporary or casual workers 1999 by age and gender. % of all employed.*

	Women	Men
16–24	58	43
25–34	24	15
35–44	14	9
45–54	9	7
55–64	7	6
16–64	18	13

Source: Håkansson (2001).

industries where employment by the hour is most frequent – hotels and restaurants, care of the elderly and wholesale and retail trade – do not discriminate against part-time and temporary workers.

When ill, those employed by the hour have less economic protection. Sick pay is mandatory for the first fourteen days of sick leave (with one no-benefit day), but in practice it is not particularly difficult for the employer to avoid sick pay to temporary workers.

As we have seen, occupational insurance in general may promote inequalities and favour employees in large companies. Having said that, the Swedish quasi-mandatory occupational insurance covers almost all employees. However, in practice, qualification requirements exclude certain temporary and part-time workers.

8.4   The Swedish old age pension

The old age pension, the purpose of which is largely to even out consumption potential between the different phases of a person's life, incorporates a smaller element of risk-spreading or insurance and a larger element of saving than the other security insurance schemes. The redistribution of incomes between individuals is the main purpose of the national basic or guaranteed minimum pension. In 1999, a new national income-related old age pension was introduced. The defined benefit system was changed into a notional defined contribution (not funded) and a defined contribution (funded) system.[4] The pension is in the main actuarially fair as long as annual incomes are below the social insurance ceiling[5] (with some exceptions, such as free pension rights for parents with young children,

---

[4] The pension contribution is 16 per cent of a worker's wage to the NDC scheme and 2.5 per cent to the DC system.
[5] The social insurance ceiling is about SEK 24,000 per month in 2002.

students and those performing compulsory military service, payment by the state of pension contributions on unemployment benefits, sickness benefits, etc.). There is no ceiling on contributions. Since contributions on income above the ceiling do not result in any pension benefits they are regarded as a pure tax on high incomes.

The great majority of the occupational pension schemes have undergone a radical change since the late 1990s, from defined benefit to defined contribution systems. For private-sector blue-collar workers, the entire income is pensionable and temporary and part-time workers have the same right to pensions as other workers. For state and local government employees, the occupational pension is defined contribution and in all essentials actuarially fair on portions of wages below the social insurance ceiling. It is defined benefit and non-actuarial on portions of wages above the ceiling, that is, a wage benefit only for those with high incomes. For private-sector white-collar workers, the occupational pension is still defined benefit and on the whole has an actuarial design. The premium as a percentage of the money wage is higher for those in careers with strong wage growth and those earning wages above the social insurance ceiling than for those with wages below the ceiling and weak wage growth.[6]

Pension rights are transferable between jobs. In practice, the fact that the occupational pension schemes of private-sector white-collar workers and public-sector high-income earners are defined benefit presents an obstacle to mobility. In occupational sectors with defined benefit pensions it may be expensive to employ older workers coming from sectors with defined contribution schemes.

Occupational pensions for governmental and municipal employees alongside the social insurance pension were long organised as pay-as-you-go systems, but a reorientation towards funded systems is in progress. The choice of funds is up to the individual. Persons with a high degree of risk aversion are free to choose conservative funds, while persons who want to take greater risks can do so.

On the whole, the link between benefits and costs at the individual level has become stronger in occupational pensions. (The approach is similar within the social insurance income-related pension system.) By comparison with private personal insurance, the administrative costs (marketing costs, etc.) are lower for collective insurance.

Besides the occupational pensions based on collective agreements in the labour market there are occupational pensions based on individual

---

[6] The wage benefit that the insurance represents is higher for those in careers with strong wage growth and wages above the social insurance ceiling than for those with wages below the ceiling and weak wage growth. This should be taken into account when comparing remuneration from work in different groups (see Selén and Ståhlberg, 1996, 1998).

contracts. A portion of the wage is exchanged for a personal private pension premium. These pension contracts have become popular among high-income earners after special tax relief for occupational pensions changed in the late 1990s (see Granqvist and Ståhlberg, 2002).

8.5   The survivors' pension in Sweden

The social insurance widow's pension was abolished in 1990, with certain transitional rules, and replaced by an adaptation pension for both men and women payable for a short period. In the old scheme, only widows received a pension from the social insurance system, whereas widowers' pensions came from the occupational schemes. Only the occupational scheme for private-sector blue-collar workers did not include a survivors' pension.

The social insurance survivors' pension from 1990 on consists of an adaptation pension for six months payable to the deceased person's wife/husband or cohabitee if they have children in common. There is also a child's pension until the age of (at most) twenty. The pension amount is based on the deceased's old age pension rights in the social insurance system and therefore on income below the ceiling. In addition, people are free to give away their DC (defined contribution) pension rights to their husband or wife. So far, this option has been very little used. A voluntary survivors' pension in the DC pension programme is in operation. Those who want such coverage pay into this system themselves. The premium is deducted from their pension contribution. Unlike a private survivors' pension no health test is required, which means that adverse selection problems will turn up. Those who have weak health and consequently a higher mortality rate than the average would have to pay more in the private market than healthy persons and so prefer the voluntary non-market survivors' pension. Those who are locked out of the private market would tend to choose it. People at low risk are able to find cheaper alternatives in the market.

The survivors' pension from the occupational schemes has several components. Besides occupational life insurance, which is the same for all sectors and categories, occupational pensions are paid to widows, widowers (sometimes cohabitees) and children in all occupational schemes, but the design differs significantly between the different schemes. The defined contribution scheme includes a voluntary survivors' pension. In addition, survivors of well-paid white-collar workers receive a mandatory pension for the rest of their lives, on condition that they do not remarry.

We cannot directly observe the individual value of a mandated collective insurance scheme. However, Selén and Ståhlberg (2001a) have estimated the individual actuarial value of the survivors' pension from the 1995 occupational schemes and the social insurance scheme.[7] The calculation was made on the basis of a representative sample of the Swedish adult population (about 6,500 individuals), taking into account differences in occupational sector, income, age, sex, life expectancy, age of the spouse/cohabitee, his or her life expectancy, number of children and the children's ages.[8] Since the insurance schemes are mandatory and not marketable, there is a problem of valuation. This should be kept in mind when the actuarial values of individual insurance rights are compared with money wages.

Firstly, the estimation shows that the actuarial value of the survivors' pension from the occupational and social insurance systems makes up only a small part of the money wage. The actuarial value of the survivors' pension from occupational insurance is estimated at 1–1.5 per cent of the money wage on average, and from the social insurance system at 0.5 per cent of the money wage.

Secondly, it is shown that there are differences between occupational groups, between men and women, and between married employees with children and unmarried, childless persons. The actuarial value as a percentage of the worker's money wage is higher for white-collar workers than for blue-collar workers, and higher for state employees than for employees in the private sector and for local government employees. It is higher for

---

[7] In 1995 the rules of the occupational schemes were somewhat different from the 2002 rules. The survivors of private-sector white-collar workers or state employees received a mandatory pension on portions of the deceased's wage above the social insurance ceiling. The spouse received a lifetime pension. In addition, survivors of state employees received a mandatory pension on portions of the deceased's wage below the ceiling. This was paid for a maximum period of five years. For survivors of local authority and county council employees a mandatory survivors' pension was paid for five years.

[8] The authors have calculated the actuarial value of the occupational survivors' pension $\Pi^{Occ}_{i,j}$ for each individual i who belongs to the occupational insurance scheme j, and the actuarial value of the survivors' pension from the earnings-related social insurance system Π^{Soc}_i for each individual i.

$$\Pi^{Occ}_{i,j} = p_i \times B^{Occ}_{i,j} + A^{Occ}_j$$
$$\Pi^{Soc}_i = p_i \times B^{Soc}_i + A^{Soc}$$

p_i is the probability of the insurance situation occurring, that is, the mortality risk. This is calculated by age and sex. $B^{Occ}_{i,j}$ and B^{Soc}_i are the discounted values of the expected benefit amounts from occupational insurance and social insurance respectively, and are determined by the rules of construction. $B^{Occ}_{i,j}$ depends on the individual's age, whether married/cohabitee, annual wages, the marginal tax rate (some benefits are exempt from taxes, others not), the age of spouse/cohabitee, the mean life expectancy, the number of children, the children's ages and the rate of discount. B^{Soc}_i depends on whether married/cohabitee, pension points in the national supplementary old age pension scheme (ATP), number of years with pension points, the marginal tax rate, the number of children, children's ages and the rate of discount. A^{Occ}_j and A^{Soc} are administrative costs. It is assumed that $A^{Occ}_j = A^{Soc} = 0$.

Table 8.2 *The actuarial value of occupational and social survivors' pensions. Share of the money wage. Average ratios in per cent.* *

Category	Men	Women	Age 18–27	Age 28–40	Age 41–50	Age 51–64	No child	One child	Two or more children
Blue-collar workers									
State	1.8	(0.8)	(0.2)	1.5	(2.4)	(1.7)	0.9	(1.2)	(3.1)
Local	1.9	1.1	0.3	1.3	1.3	1.6	0.8	1.1	1.9
Private	1.3	0.7	0.3	1.1	1.5	1.6	0.6	1.3	2.4
White-collar workers									
State	2.7	1.2	0.2	1.5	2.4	2.4	1.1	1.9	3.9
Local	2.1	1.1	0.2	1.2	1.6	1.5	0.9	1.2	2.4
Private	2.0	0.9	0.2	1.3	2.0	2.0	0.9	1.7	2.8

Note: Parentheses indicate that the number of observations is less than 20.
* The calculations are based on 1995 rules.
Source: Selén and Ståhlberg (2001a).

Table 8.3 *The actuarial value of occupational and social survivors' pensions. Share of the money wage. Average ratios in per cent.* *

Category	Annual money wage > social insurance ceiling	Annual money wage ≤ social insurance ceiling	Married with children and money wage > social insurance ceiling	Unmarried without children and money wage ≤ social insurance ceiling
Blue-collar workers				
State	(3.7)	1.3	(3.8)	(0.4)
Local	(1.3)	1.2	(1.4)	0.4
Private	1.9	1.1	3.1	0.4
White-collar workers				
State	3.3	1.6	4.7	0.4
Local	2.2	1.3	3.7	0.5
Private	2.3	1.2	3.4	0.4

Note: Parentheses indicate that the number of observations is less than 20.
* The calculations are based on 1995 rules.
Source: Selén and Ståhlberg (2001a).

men than for women and increases with age and with number of children. It is highest for those who are married (cohabitees), have many children and an annual wage above the social insurance ceiling. The lowest value is found for those under twenty-eight who do not qualify for a family

Table 8.4 *A regression description of the ratios of extended wages (money wage (MW) including the wage benefit of the occupational (OW) or the social (SW) survivors' pension) to the money wage in per cent. Regression coefficients and R-squared. Insignificant factors in italics (p > .01).* *

		Share of money wage for		
		MW + OW	MW + SW	MW + OW + SW
Intercept		102.08	101.01	103.10
Class	Blue-collar	−0.11	−0.04	−0.15
	White-collar	0	0	0
Sector	State	0.40	*0.00*	0.41
	Local	0.14	*−0.00*	0.13
	Private	0	*0*	0
No. of children	0	−1.65	−0.47	−2.12
	1	−0.91	−0.31	−1.23
	2 or more	0	0	0
Sex	Men	0.59	0.29	0.89
	Women	0	0	0
Age	18–27	−0.73	−0.64	−1.37
	28–40	−0.86	−0.61	−1.47
	41–50	−0.42	−0.40	−0.82
	51–65	0	0	0
Married/cohab	Yes	0.26	*0.00*	0.26
	No	0	*0*	0
R-squared		0.484	0.465	0.517

* The calculations are based on 1995 rules.
Source: Selén and Ståhlberg (2001a).

pension or child pension in the 1995 occupational schemes (see tables 8.2 and 8.3).

Table 8.4 describes the results of multivariate descriptions of the actuarial value of the insurance protection relative to the money wage. For the factors used – class, employment sector, number of children, sex, age and marital status – the coefficients show the average differences between the categories within each factor, holding other factors constant. The reference category is the last within each factor and the coefficients show the differences relative to that category. The estimates are calculated by least squares and observations are weighted according to the different sampling probabilities. All factors are significant except employment sector and marital status for the social insurance component; in the social insurance system these factors are not accounted for. In the table, we can see that occupational insurance is to the advantage of men, those employed by the state and white-collar workers, and that married individuals are favoured as well as those with children and those in the older age classes.[9] All this is in agreement with the principles underlying the construction of the survivors' pension systems.

The occupational survivors' pension is financed by a uniform contribution rate (within one and the same occupational scheme). Therefore, there is a redistribution of income from unmarried and childless employees to married persons/cohabitees and employees with children, and also, when the actuarial value as a percentage of money wages is higher for those with income above the social insurance ceiling, a redistribution to high-income earners from low-income earners. Those who are most favoured are well-paid older men who are married to much younger women and have several young children. The premium would have been significantly higher in market insurance differentiated by age and family situation.

8.6   The sickness benefit system in Sweden

The employer pays sick pay for the first fourteen days of sick leave (with one no-benefit day) at a replacement rate of 80 per cent (both below and above the ceiling). From day fifteen, social insurance pays 80 per cent of income up to the social insurance ceiling, while occupational sickness insurance adds a supplement. These rules are similar for both private- and public-sector white-collar workers. Their occupational sickness benefit insurance systems have a lower rate for earnings below the social insurance ceiling (10 per cent) and a higher rate for earnings above the ceiling (90 per cent, falling to 80 per cent after three months in most cases).

The social insurance contribution is not risk diversified; thus, it aims to redistribute incomes from people who are at low risk of sickness to those who are at high risk. The risk of sickness differs between individuals due to age, sex and socio-economic group, as is shown in, e.g., Edgerton, Kruse and Wells (2000). Average sick leave incidence rates, which can be interpreted as the probability of being absent in a specific week, are described for the periods 1987–91, 1992–3, 1994–7 and 1998–9, the periods being chosen so as to reflect the main changes in the sickness

[9] The authors do not take into account differences in death risks between classes. These are to the disadvantage of blue-collar workers, according to studies made (see Vågerö and Lundberg, 1995), and would increase their values if included.

Table 8.5 *Sick leave incidence rates by sex and age 1987–1999 (%)*

Period	Sex	Age 20–24	Age 40–44	Age 50–54	Age 60–64	All
1987–91	Men	6.1	7.1	10.2	13.5	7.9
	Women	8.6	10.0	12.3	14.0	9.7
	All	7.3	8.6	11.3	13.7	8.8
1992–93	Men	4.2	5.2	7.5	12.1	5.8
	Women	4.8	8.2	10.2	16.9	8.0
	All	4.5	6.8	8.9	14.6	6.9
1994–97	Men	2.3	3.7	5.2	7.7	4.2
	Women	3.9	6.2	8.2	7.9	6.2
	All	3.1	5.0	6.8	7.8	5.2
1998–99	Men	2.7	2.9	3.8	9.9	3.6
	Women	3.9	6.2	7.5	9.2	5.9
	All	3.2	4.6	5.7	9.5	4.8

Source: Edgerton, Kruse and Wells (2000).

benefit insurance system.[10,11] Table 8.5 shows that the sickness rate is much higher for women than for men and increases with age. Table 8.6 shows the differences in sick leave between socio-economic groups, the rate being higher for blue-collar workers than for white-collar workers and higher for lower-level white-collar workers than for upper-level white-collar workers.

Occupational insurance schemes all share a similar design. The contribution rate is uniform (within one and the same scheme), but the risk of sickness differs between companies and individuals. Private-sector white-collar workers, state employees and certain local government employees receive sick pay from the employer instead of occupational insurance.

The individual value of the security provided in times of sickness is estimated in Selén and Ståhlberg (2001b). They have calculated the actuarial value of sickness benefit rights when the risk of sickness is diversified according to sex, age, socio-economic group and occupational sector.[12]

---

[10] The presentation is based on Labour Force Survey (AKU) data on roughly 14,000 individuals. The individual is asked about her/his activities in a certain week. If employed, the person is asked about contracted time and actual worked time. The reason for absence is asked where applicable.

[11] From 1987 to March 1991 sickness benefits were very generous with full compensation from the very first day. In 1991 the replacement rate from social insurance was reduced and in the following years changed a number of times for different days in the sickness period. Sick pay was introduced in 1992, that is, the employer took over compensation for the first fourteen days of a sick leave period from the social insurance system. The first day became a no-benefit day in 1993.

[12] It is assumed that there are no administrative costs.

Table 8.6 *Sick leave incidence rates by socio-economic group during the 1990s*

Category	1990–91	1992–93	1994–97	1998–99
Blue-collar workers	10.9	8.3	6.6	6.1
Lower white-collar workers	7.2	6.3	4.4	4.4
Upper white-collar workers	5.0	3.3	2.8	2.2
All	8.9	7.0	5.2	4.8

Source: Edgerton, Kruse and Wells (2000).

The data used emanate from the database for labour market analysis at the Swedish Trade Union Research Institute (FIEF). This database, compiled in cooperation with Statistics Sweden, contains information on all individuals participating in the labour force surveys in 1990–5, in total just over 200,000 individuals, with register information from the tax authorities, the Labour Market Administration and the National Social Insurance Board for the years 1990–7.

Selén and Ståhlberg estimated the average actuarial value of the benefit rights in all sickness benefit schemes at 5.8 per cent of the money wage. This percentage differs between occupational groups. The average sickness benefit rights for private-sector blue-collar workers is 7.4 per cent of the money wage, for private-sector white-collar workers 3.4 per cent, for state employees 4.2 per cent, and for local government employees 6.6 per cent. Sickness benefit rights are highest for blue-collar women in the private sector, at around 10 per cent of the money wage, and lowest for state-employed white-collar workers aged 18–27, at around 2 per cent (see table 8.7). Table 8.8 shows the actuarial value of occupational insurance, social insurance and sick pay respectively. The actuarial value of social insurance differs significantly between different occupational groups whereas the differences are relatively small where occupational insurance and sick pay are concerned.

If occupational insurance covered all sickness benefits, the contribution rate would differ between the occupational insurance schemes, given the current total replacement rates. The contribution rate would then be much higher for private-sector blue-collar workers and local government employees than for private-sector white-collar workers and state employees. This would result in higher costs for the employer for private-sector blue-collar workers and local government employees on the one hand, than for private-sector white-collar workers and state employees on the other hand, compared to the current situation with social insurance. Within each occupational scheme the risks are very unequally distributed

Table 8.7 *The actuarial value of occupational insurance, social insurance and sick pay. Share of the money wage. Average ratios in per cent.*

Class	Sector	Men	Women	18–27	28–40	41–50	51–64	All
		\multicolumn{2}{c}{Sex}		\multicolumn{5}{c}{Age}				

Class	Sector	Sex Men	Sex Women	Age 18–27	Age 28–40	Age 41–50	Age 51–64	Age All
Blue-collar	State	4.8	6.8	4.5	5.3	5.5	6.9	5.5
	Local	6.7	8.6	8.5	8.5	7.4	9.1	8.3
	Private	6.1	10.4	6.1	7.3	7.6	9.4	7.4
	All	6.0	9.3	6.6	7.5	7.3	9.1	7.5
White-collar	State	2.3	4.8	2.2	3.3	3.2	4.7	3.5
	Local	3.3	5.5	5.5	5.3	3.7	5.6	4.9
	Private	2.5	4.6	3.4	3.3	2.7	4.7	3.4
	All	2.6	5.0	3.7	4.0	3.1	5.0	3.9
Sector								
State		3.2	5.3	3.3	4.0	3.8	5.3	4.2
Local		4.6	7.2	7.6	6.8	5.3	7.3	6.6
Private		4.7	7.3	5.3	5.4	5.0	7.2	5.6
All		4.5	7.1	5.7	5.7	4.9	7.0	5.8

Source: Selén and Ståhlberg (2001b).

Table 8.8 *The actuarial value of occupational insurance, social insurance and sick pay. Share of the money wage. Average ratios in per cent.*

Sector	Sick pay	Social insurance	Occupational insurance	All
Private blue-collar	1.7	5.3	0.4	7.4
Private white-collar	1.1	2.1	0.2	3.4
Local	1.6	4.7	0.4	6.6
State	1.3	2.6	0.3	4.2
All	1.4	4.0	0.3	5.8

Source: Selén and Ståhlberg (2001b).

between different enterprises, but the premium is uniform, and for this reason the employers' economic incentives to reduce absence due to sickness are weak. Therefore, it is probable that this difference in costs would have a direct impact on wage formation, i.e., the cost differentials for sick leave would be reflected in wage differentials between blue-collar workers and white-collar workers. Since women dominate among local government employees (80 per cent are women) wage differences between women and men would, *ceteris paribus*, also increase.

A private sickness insurance system that replaced the current system and differentiated with respect not only to sector and class but also to sex and age, would entail very large premium differences between women and men and between persons of different ages – according to the estimations in table 8.7, at most, premiums could be five times higher.

A private or occupational sickness insurance system would give rise to differences that are probably too large to be accepted from a redistribution point of view.

8.7   Can occupational welfare be a substitute for social welfare?

We have asked the question whether occupational welfare could take over some social security commitments and relieve the state of some of the economic responsibility for insurance protection. The usual objections against occupational welfare are that it is inadequate, that it does not cover all employees and that its redistribution pattern is different from that of social welfare.

We have found that the mix of social, occupational and personal systems of protection might vary, rather than total protection as a whole, if social insurance were to change. A lower social insurance ceiling, for example, would increase the scope for occupational insurance.[13] What is unusual about the situation in Sweden is that practically all employees are covered by occupational insurance. Occupational pensions in Sweden are neutral from a redistribution point of view, as are the income-related pensions in the social insurance system. An employee's pension benefits would not be affected if the social insurance component of the defined contribution pension scheme (2.5 per cent of a worker's wage) were taken over by the occupational scheme. The redistribution pattern of occupational sickness insurance, however, is different from that of social insurance and the redistribution pattern of occupational survivors' pension is a bit odd. The current mandatory occupational survivors' pension favours married employees with high incomes and young children at the expense of unmarried and childless employees. It is debatable whether a survivors' pension has to be mandatory, covering married as well as unmarried people, or whether it should be a private responsibility of the family. The average occupational survivors' pension premium has been estimated at 1–1.5 per cent of a worker's wage. If this money went into

[13] According to the pension enquiry in the 1990s pension payments from the social insurance system would decrease by 0.4 per cent of GDP if the social insurance ceiling had to follow the price index instead of the wage index. See SOU 1990, 128–9.

the occupational old age pension instead, this would relieve the state of some of the economic responsibility for old age pensions.

An occupational sickness insurance system that replaced the current social and occupational systems would give rise to differences in premiums that are probably too large to be accepted from a redistribution point of view. The estimated premium is 5.7 per cent of the money wage for private blue-collar workers and 2.3 for private white-collar workers. It is 5.1 per cent for municipal employees and 2.9 for state employees. With a lower social insurance ceiling, however, occupational schemes might be a substitute for some of the social insurance sickness benefits.

References

Agulnik, P. and Le Grand, J., 1998, 'Tax relief and partnership pensions', *Fiscal Studies*, 19, 4, November, 403–28.
Dailey, L. M. and Turner, J. A., 1992, 'US private pensions in world perspective: 1970–1989', in J. A. Turner and D. J. Beller (eds.), *Trends in Pensions 1992*, Washington DC: GPO.
Edebalk, P. G., Ståhlberg, A. and Wadensjö, E., 1996, 'Avtalsreglerade trygghetssystem vid sjukdom, arbetsskada och förtidspension', *SOU*, 113, 2, 127–96.
—1998, *Socialförsäkringarna*. Stockholm: SNS Förlag.
Edgerton, D., Kruse, A. and Wells, C., 2000, 'Designing an optimal sickness insurance. Some evidence from the Swedish experience'. ESPE meeting.
Forssell, Å, Medelberg, M. and Ståhlberg, A., 1999, 'Unequal public transfers to the elderly in different countries – equal disposable incomes', *European Journal of Social Security*, 1, 63–89.
Granqvist, L. and Ståhlberg, A., 2002, *De nya avtals-och tjänstepensionerna: Ökad jämställdhet – men fortfarande sämre pension för kvinnor*, Stockholm: Pensionsforum.
Håkansson, K., 2001, 'Språngbräda eller segmentering? En longitudinell studie av tidsbegränsat anställda', working paper 1, IFAU – Institutet för arbetsmarknadspolitisk utvärdering, Uppsala.
Mooslechner, P. and Url, T., 1995, 'Betriebliche altersvorsorge in Österreich', Vienna: WIFO-Gutachten.
Nelander S. and Bendetcedotter, M., 2001, 'Anställningsformer och arbetstider', LO/Löne-och välfärdsenheten, August.
OECD, 1998, 'Maintaining prosperity in an ageing society: the OECD study on the policy implications of ageing', working paper AWP 4.3.
Pestieau, P., 1992, 'How fair is the distribution of private pension benefits?' Luxembourg Income Study (LIS) working paper, no. 72, April.
Rein, M. and Reinwater, L., 1986, 'The institutions of social protection', in M. Rein and L. Reinwater (eds.), *Public/Private Interplay in Social Protection: A Comparative Study*, Armonk NY: M. E. Sharpe.
Rein, M. and Wadensjö, E. (eds.), 1997, *Enterprise and the Welfare State*, Cheltenham: Edward Elgar Publishing, Inc.

Rosner, P., Url, T. and Wörgötter, A., 1997, 'The Austrian pension system', in M. Rein and E. Wadensjö (eds.), *Enterprise and the Welfare State*, Cheltenham: Edward Elgar Publishing, Inc.

Schmähl, W., 1997, 'The public-private mix in pension provision in Germany', in M. Rein and E. Wadensjö (eds.), *Enterprise and the Welfare State*, Cheltenham: Edward Elgar Publishing, Inc.

Selén, J. and Ståhlberg, A., 1996, 'Non-wage benefits in Sweden', working paper 2/1996, Swedish Institute for Social Research, Stockholm University.

—1998, 'Pension rights and wages', *Labour*, 12, 191–209.

—2001a, 'Survivors' pension rights in occupational and social insurance: the Swedish experience', *European Journal of Social Security*, 3, 2, 117–36.

—2001b, 'The importance of sickness benefit rights for a comparison of wages', ESPE meeting 2001, working paper 1/2002, Swedish Institute for Social Research, Stockholm University, www.sofi.su.se.

Shalev, M. (ed.), 1996, *The Privatization of Social Policy?*, Basingstoke: Macmillan Press Ltd and New York: St. Martin's Press, Inc.

Sinfield, A. (2000), 'Tax benefits in non-state pensions', *European Journal of Social Security*, 2, 137–67.

SOU, 1990, *Allmän pension*, Stockholm.

Turner, J. A. and Dailey, L. M., 1990, *Pension Policy: An International Perspective*, Washington DC: GPO.

Vågerö, D. and Lundberg, O., 1995, 'Socio-economic mortality differentials among adults in Sweden', in A. Lopez, G. Caselli and T. Valkonen (eds.), *Adult Mortality in Developed Countries: From Description to Explanation*, Oxford: Clarendon Press, 222–42.

9 Pathways to retirement and retirement incentives in Sweden*

Mården Palme and Ingemar Svensson

9.1 Introduction

The trend towards earlier exit from the labour force, in particular among men, has been one of the most important changes in the composition of the labour force in industrialised countries over the past forty years. Because this trend has been going on at the same time as a trend towards increased longevity, the financial stability of most social security systems around the world has been threatened.

Since the decline in labour force participation has coincided with the build-up of income security systems in most countries, the economic incentives to exit the labour force inherent in these schemes has been suggested as an explanation for the trend towards earlier retirement. One way to examine this hypothesis is to model the retirement decision econometrically, and a growing literature of studies that try to do this exists (see Lumsdaine and Mitchell, 2000, for an overview). Palme and Svensson (2003) and Karlström, Palme and Svensson (2002) follow this approach using Swedish data.

This study follows a somewhat different approach: instead of modelling the retirement decision we describe in detail the retirement behaviour in different groups of the labour force. We then describe the economic incentives to exit from the labour market in these groups. The idea behind this approach is that, rather than doing a causal analysis of retirement, we study to what extent the observed retirement behaviour matches up with the observed retirement incentives. This approach also enables us to investigate which policies – the social security system, labour market insurance, occupational pensions, income taxes or housing allowances to the elderly – affect the economic incentives for additional work of older workers.

* We are grateful to Annika Sundén and the two editors of this volume for constructive comments. Mården Palme acknowledges financial support from the Swedish Council for Social Research.

In a previous study (Palme and Svensson, 1999), we also used a descriptive approach of economic incentives and retirement behaviour: the economic incentives facing a number of representative individuals were described at different ages. The present study extends several dimensions of this study. First, we use real, rather than synthetic, earnings histories for a large sample of individuals collected from a large panel data set (LINDA). Earnings histories can be observed from 1960–97. This long series enables us to study heterogeneity in incentives, and also within groups of workers. Second, we study incentives for all major occupational pension programmes, rather than just for blue-collar workers in the private sector as in the previous study, and all major labour market insurance programmes, rather than just the disability insurance programme. Finally, we use a forward-looking measure for the economic gain of remaining in the labour force, the peak value measure, in addition to social security wealth and one-year benefit accruals.

The chapter is organised as follows. Section 9.2 briefly describes Sweden's income security system, income taxes and housing allowances to elderly. Section 9.3 describes the data. Section 9.4 first shows trends in labour force participation rates among older workers and then exit paths and timing of retirement for different groups in the labour force. Section 9.5 describes the economic incentive measures for additional work of older workers. Section 9.6 concludes.

9.2   Sweden's income security system

The income security system in Sweden consists of two main parts: the public old age pension system and the compulsory labour market insurance programmes. Both these parts are, to about the same extent, used for financing exits from the labour market. In this sub-section we briefly describe the design of these programmes.[1] The description is based on the rules pertaining to the persons covered in the study. We start with the public old age pension programmes and the occupational pension schemes. We then describe the disability, sickness and unemployment insurance programmes.

Old age pension programmes

Sweden's old age pension programme consists of two main parts: the public old age pensions and occupational pensions. The occupational pension programmes are compulsory for the approximately 95 per cent

---

[1] For a more complete description, see Palme and Svensson (1999, 2003).

of the labour market covered by central agreements. Table 9.1 summarises how the benefits are determined in each programme and the actuarial adjustments, i.e., the key facts on how these programmes will affect economic incentives for older workers to remain in the labour force.

As can be seen in table 9.1, all pension benefits are defined in basic amounts (BAs). The basic amount follows the CPI closely. In the year 2001 the level of one BA was 36,900 SEK.[2]

Disability, sickness and unemployment insurance

Eligibility for disability insurance (DI) requires that an individual's capacity to work is permanently reduced by at least 25 per cent. Full compensation requires that work capacity is completely lost. Work capacity is in general determined by a physician, and eligibility for disability insurance is determined by the local social insurance administration. Between 1970 and 1991 disability insurance could be granted for labour market reasons. Disability benefits consist of a basic pension and a supplementary pension (ATP). The level of the basic pension is the same as for the old age scheme and the supplementary pension is determined in the same way as for the old age scheme with no actuarial reduction for early retirement. 'Assumed' pension points are calculated for each year between the date of retirement and age sixty-four.

Sickness insurance (SI) replaces a share of lost earnings due to temporary illnesses up to the social security ceiling. The replacement level in the insurance has been changed on several occasions during the time period covered by this study. A reform in 1987 set the replacement level to 90 per cent of the worker's insured income. Since then, the replacement has been changed several times. In 1991 it was decreased for short sickness spells. In 1996 it was set to 75 per cent of the insured income for long sickness spells, and in 1998 it was raised to 80 per cent.

The unemployment insurance (UI) benefit consists of two parts: one basic part, which is unrelated to the worker's insured income, and one part which requires membership in an unemployment benefit fund and is related to the worker's insured income. Unemployed workers who actively search for a new job are eligible for compensation. The main difference between the benefit level in the unemployment and sickness insurance is the ceiling. The ceiling of the latter is the same as for other parts of the social insurance system, while that of the former is subject to discretionary changes, and is lower than the ceiling for the sickness benefit. The replacement rate for unemployment insurance has also been changed on

---

[2] In 2001 the exchange rate was 1$ = 10 SEK.

Table 9.1 *Old age pension programmes in Sweden*

Benefit	Determination of normal benefit	Actuarial adjustment	Eligibility
State old age pension			
Basic	unrelated to previous earnings; 96% of BA for unmarried; 78.5% of a BA if married	0.5% reduction for each month if claimed before the 65th birthday; 0.7% increases for each month delayed.	age 60
ATP	60% of average earnings of the 15 best years below the social security ceiling; proportionately reduced if less than 30 years of contributions	same as for basic pension	age 60; three years of earnings
Special supplement	supplement for pensioners with no or low ATP		
Occupational pensions			
Blue-collar workers (STP) [1]	10% of average earnings of the 3 best years between age 55 and 59.	cannot be claimed before age 65	three years of earnings between age 55 and 59
White-collar workers (ITP) [2]	earning the year before retirement; 10% below 7.5 BA; 65% 7.5 − 20BA; 32.5% 20 − 30 BA	normal retirement age 65; can be claimed with an actuarial adjustment of about 6% per year	age 60; individual actuarial

| Employees in central government [3] | average earnings during the five years preceding retirement; 10% below 7.5 BA; 65% between 7.5 and 20 BA; 32.5% between 20 and 30 BA | for most occupations normal retirement age 65; actuarial adjustment of about 6% per year | in general age 60; if the worker retires before age 60, a life annuity is paid out starting at age 65 |
| Employees in local governments [4] | average earnings of the best 5 of 7 years before retirement; 96% below 1 BA, 78.5% 1 – 2.5 BAs, 60% 2.5 – 3.5 BAs, 65% 7.5 – 20 BAs, 32.5% 20 – 30 BAs | normal retirement age 65; can be claimed with an actuarial adjustment of about 6% per year | adjustment if claimed before in general age 60; if the worker retires before age 60, a life annuity is paid out starting at age 65 |

[1] Currently being replaced by a fully funded scheme. Workers born 1938–40 in a 'transition scheme'.

[2] Also contains a funded scheme ITPK.

[3] Also contains a funded scheme 'Kåpan'.

[4] Calculated as a 'gross' pension. Pension from the public schemes included in the benefit amounts.

several occasions during the time period analysed in this empirical analysis. These changes have roughly followed the changes in the sickness insurance.

There are also negotiated occupational insurance programmes for unemployment, disability and long-term sickness. These programmes cover the same groups as the occupational pensions. The replacement levels are similar to those of the occupational pensions which are shown in table 9.1, i.e., they are complements to the public insurance programmes and the replacement levels are higher above the social security ceiling.

Income taxes and housing allowances

Sweden went through a major income tax reform in 1991. Before the reform, all income was included in the same tax base and taxed with a proportional local government tax (around 30 per cent depending on municipality) and a progressive national tax. The maximum marginal tax rate was set to 75 per cent. A main feature of the tax reform was that the tax base was divided into capital income and earned income. Income from capital is subject to a 30 per cent national tax while earned income is subject to a local government tax and above a certain break-point a 20 per cent national tax.

Old age, disability and survivors' pensioners with low income are entitled to a housing allowance. In 1995, this allowance was at most 85 per cent of the housing cost up to a ceiling. About 30 per cent of all old age pensioners received housing allowances in 1995.

9.3   Data

We use the Longitudinal Individual Data (LINDA) panel. LINDA is a sample drawn from administrative records. It contains data from Statistic Sweden's Income and Wealth register, which is a register containing data from income tax returns for the entire Swedish population; the Population Census, which is data primarily on occupation and housing conditions from mailed questionnaires distributed every five years to the entire population; and the National Social Insurance Board registers, which contain data on contributions to the public pension schemes.

The total sample size of LINDA is about 300,000 individuals. Detailed income components are available from 1983. Data on earnings below the social security ceiling are available from 1960.

Our sample consists of men born between 1927 and 1940. We have excluded individuals younger than age fifty. For example, the youngest

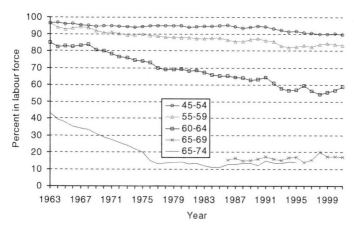

Figure 9.1 Historical trends in labour force participation in different age groups of older men in Sweden
Source: Swedish Labour Force Survey, Statistics Sweden.

cohort, born in 1940, are just forty-three years old in 1983 and we therefore exclude the first seven observations for each individual from this cohort. We have also excluded the self-employed because the quality of the income data for this group can be questioned.[3] Furthermore, LINDA does not include information on their pension rights.

Using these criteria 15,619 individuals remained from the original 22,375 for the cohorts included in the study. The total number of observations is 127,390.

9.4 Trends in labour force participation rates and pathways to retirement

Historical trends in labour force participation rates among older workers

Figure 9.1 shows trends in labour force participation for men in different age groups. These figures reveal several distinct patterns. The male labour force participation rate has decreased in all these age groups over the past decades. However, the development is most dramatic in the age group between sixty and sixty-four. In 1963, the labour force participation rate in this age group was almost as high as in the younger age groups at about 85 per cent. Almost forty years later, in 2001 the corresponding figure is

---

[3] The self-employed are always able to accumulate wealth within their own business.

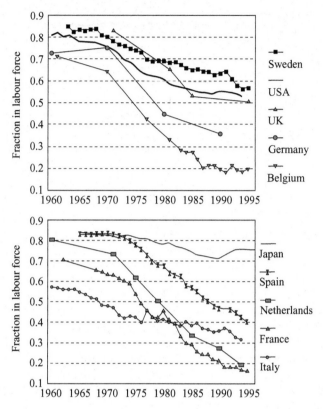

Figure 9.2 Historical trends in labour force participation rates in the 60–64-year-old age group in different OECD countries
Source: Gruber and Wise (1999).

below 60 per cent. The development of labour force participation rates for the age group sixty to sixty-four is dramatic in the sense that almost one-third of the labour force in this group has disappeared. However, as is shown in figure 9.2, the same pattern has emerged in most comparable countries and has been even more dramatic.

Figure 9.3 shows the trends in labour force participation rates by age groups for women. Compared to the corresponding graphs for men, the trends for women are more complex. Among women, labour force participation rates increase at a decreasing rate in most age groups. The most likely explanation for this pattern is that there is an underlying 'cohort effect' of increasing female labour force participation, combined with a 'period effect' towards earlier exits from the labour market. The graphs

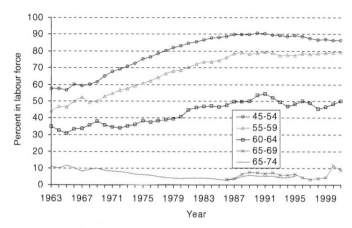

Figure 9.3 Historical trends in labour force participation in different age groups of older women in Sweden
Source: Swedish Labour Force Survey, Statistics Sweden.

show that the labour force participation rates seem to be fairly stable among women since the early 1990s.

Timing of the exit from the labour force in different groups of the labour force

Although no direct information on date of exit from the labour market is available in our data set it is possible to measure this date indirectly from the individual information on income components in the data. We measure exit from the labour market as the year when the worker permanently starts to earn less than one *basic amount* (BA) from labour. An alternative measure is the year when the worker starts to claim income security benefits. However, in most old age pension systems in Sweden, the worker is able to continue to work while claiming benefits without any reductions in benefits. This means that using claim of benefits will be a misleading measure of labour market status for individuals who continue working. A worker can leave the labour force in two ways: the worker can either retire or die. We will not distinguish between these modes when we present the results. Because the mortality among the individuals who remain in the labour force is quite low (only about 5 per cent can be estimated to leave the labour force due to death), the main differences between the groups shown in this section are due to differences in retirement behaviour.

Table 9.2 *Labour force participation rates for different groups of workers*

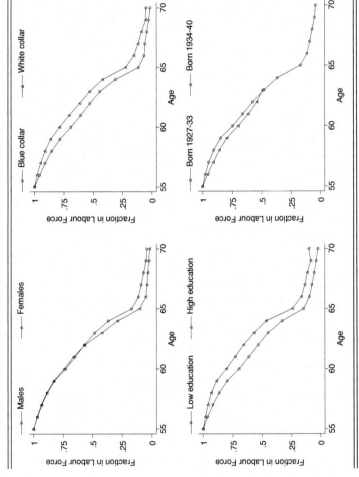

Source: Authors' calculations form the LINDA panel survey.

Table 9.2 shows survival functions, i.e., the share remaining in the labour force in the one-year age groups between age fifty-five and seventy conditional on being in the labour force at age fifty-five, for different groups in the Swedish labour market. The north-west panel compares male–female timing of retirement. Until age sixty-two the survival functions for labour force participation are almost identical for men and women respectively. However, starting at age sixty-three, labour force participation rate among men is about five percentage points higher than among women. Very few women work beyond age sixty-five.

The north-east panel compares labour force participation for male white-collar workers with blue-collar workers in the private sector. The graph shows a clear difference between the two groups: white-collar workers retire on average later and the difference is mainly due to a higher retirement rate for workers aged fifty-six to fifty-nine. This difference can be attributed to a large number of differences between these two groups, such as in health, preferences, job characteristics or economic incentives as well as differences in income levels and occupational pensions schemes. The south-west panel shows that the difference between the survival function for labour market participation is even larger between groups with low and high education levels respectively. For example, at age sixty-two the difference in the labour force participation rates between these two groups is thirteen percentage points. Finally, the south-east panel shows that the trend towards earlier retirement seems to be present also in our data set since the survival function for the cohorts born later is below the corresponding graph for the cohorts born earlier.

Pathways to retirement

The sources of income after the exit from the labour market provided by the Swedish income security system can be divided into two groups: old age pensions and benefits from labour market insurance (unemployment, sickness and disability insurance).

Table 9.3 shows the share of workers who receive their main income (more than 50 per cent of their total non-labour income) from one of ten different sources of income after retirement. The table is constructed for the individuals who are born between 1927 and 1932. Since these birth cohorts have reached the 'normal' retirement age of sixty-five at the end of the period under study (1997) their pathway to retirement is known. The programmes that are designed to serve as old age pensions programmes are: the state old age pension (1), occupational pensions (2), pensions provided by the employer or severance payments (6), private pensions (7) and partial retirement benefits (10). The insurance programmes that cover income loss from poor health or unemployment, that can be used

Table 9.3 *Percentage share of the pathways to permanent exit from the labour market showing main source of income (more than 50 per cent from the indicated source); cohorts born 1927–32*

Source	Men	Women
1. State old age pension	33.70	26.94
2. Occupational pension	13.68	14.21
3. Disability pension (DI)	6.55	6.59
4. Survivors' pension	–	3.99
5. Wife's supplement	0.02	2.0
6. Severance payments from employer	0.60	0.69
7. Private pension	0.86	0.76
8. Sickness insurance	20.53	26.88
9. Unemployment insurance	8.35	6.42
10. Partial retirement benefit	10.04	6.83
11. No income source more than 50%	5.67	4.64

Note: The 10.02 per cent of the male sample and the 6.11 per cent of the female sample who not yet retired by the end of the panel are included in source 1. Source 5 also includes some other minor benefits in addition to wife's supplement.

to finance retirement, are disability insurance (3), sickness insurance (8) and unemployment insurance (9).

Table 9.3 shows that the labour market insurances (3, 8 or 9) as initial source of income after retirement account for about 35 per cent of the male and about 40 per cent of the female sub-sample for these birth cohorts. Sickness insurance is the most common insurance as the initial source of income, accounting for 20 per cent of all labour market exits for men and 27 per cent for women. Among the old age pension programmes, the national old age pension dominates with 34 per cent for men and 27 per cent for women. Occupational pensions are also important as an initial source of income after retirement – about 14 per cent of both men and women use this pathway.

The pathways to retirement differ significantly between workers belonging to different occupational pension schemes and education levels. Table 9.4 shows the initial source of income after retirement among workers with different occupational pension schemes, and table 9.5 shows the corresponding figures for different educational groups.

According to table 9.4, among blue-collar workers in the private sector the most common initial source of income after retirement is sickness benefits. Sickness insurance accounts for 31 per cent of all labour force exits in the male sub-sample, and 35 per cent in the female sub-sample.

Table 9.4 *Main source of income after exit from the labour force by group of occupational pension scheme*

Source	Men					Women				
	1	2	3	4	5	1	2	3	4	5
1. State old age pension	25.7	36.2	28.3	41.1	48.9	24.3	31.0	25.9	25.4	41.6
2. Occupational pension	5.1	19.5	32.0	16.9	4.4	4.2	12.6	16.4	20.5	5.8
3. Disability pension	7.1	4.4	8.9	5.7	9.0	6.0	5.3	10.8	6.4	5.2
4. Survivors' pension			0.3			2.7	3.3	3.7	4.8	5.5
5. Wife's supplement	0.1					2.8	0.2	1.9	1.9	4.8
6. Severance payments from employer	0.1	1.7		0.8	0.1	0.3	3.1	0.3	0.2	1.0
7. Private pension	0.4	1.0		0.4	3.1	0.3	0.8		0.6	4.8
8. Sickness insurance	31.1	12.6	14.0	17.0	17.8	34.8	18.8	22.4	28.3	16.8
9. Unemployment insurance	13.1	7.7	4.8	2.5	5.7	14.1	8.6	5.4	1.8	6.9
10. Partial retirement benefit	12.9	8.8	7.3	9.3	7.7	6.2	10.3	9.0	5.7	3.1
11. No income source more than 50%	4.6	8.3	4.5	6.3	3.3	4.5	6.1	4.2	4.3	4.5

Note: 1 = blue-collar workers in private sector; 2 = white-collar workers in private sector; 3 = employees in central government; 4 = employees in local government; 5 = self-employed.

Table 9.5 *Main source of income after exit from the labour force by education level*

Source	Men				Women			
	1	2	3	4	1	2	3	4
1. State old age pension	30.2	32.1	37.3	47.8	23.2	27.7	31.7	37.9
2. Occupational pension	8.1	14.2	22.4	22.9	9.4	16.9	20.6	18.3
3. Disability pension	6.5	8.1	5.5	4.9	6.2	6.6	5.7	10.2
4. Survivors' pension					3.7	5.0	3.2	1.8
5. Wife's supplement		0.1			3.4	1.4	0.3	
6. Severance payments from employer	0.2	0.6	1.1	1.4	0.5	0.7	1.7	0.5
7. Private pension	0.8	1.0	0.9	0.7	0.8	0.5	1.2	1.5
8. Sickness insurance	27.0	21.2	10.4	7.0	33.0	25.5	19.4	10.2
9. Unemployment insurance	10.5	8.2	6.9	1.2	9.7	4.7	3.2	1.5
10. Partial retirement benefit	11.8	9.1	9.2	5.6	6.5	6.9	7.0	7.9
11. No income source more than 50%	4.9	5.4	6.5	8.6	3.7	4.3	6.0	10.2

Note: 1 = compulsory education only; 2 = vocational schooling; 3 = highschool; 4 = college or university education.

Unemployment insurance and, for men, partial retirement benefits, are also important. Other groups that are likely to use insurance programmes other than old age pensions to exit the labour market include women in the public sector – both central and local government. For female local government employees, sickness insurance is the dominant initial source of income.

The differences between educational groups are also large as shown by table 9.5. The frequency of the national old age pension as the initial source of income increases with education, from 30 per cent of all exits among men with only compulsory education to 48 per cent among men with college or university education. The corresponding figures for women are 23 and 38 per cent. The opposite pattern is true for sickness and unemployment insurance. The data also indicate clear gender differences with respect to the importance of sickness insurance and the state old age pension. Women are more likely to retire using sickness benefit and less likely to retire using the national old age pension than men.

So far we have only described the initial main income source after retirement. Within the Swedish income security system many possibilities to combine and switch between the different labour market insurance and retirement programmes exist, for example, from UI to SI to DI and then finally to old age pensions. Those who start to receive state old age pension benefits at retirement are most likely to continue to do so, and those who leave the labour force with disability insurance as their main source of income will be transferred to old age pensions at age 65. Those who start with occupational pensions are also likely to switch to state old age pensions as the main source at age sixty-five.

In Palme and Svensson (2003) we show a detailed analysis of the frequency of transitions to other income sources for those who start with sickness or unemployment insurance as their main income source after retirement. It was found that in most cases a transition to disability pensions takes place after one to two years. This finding was used in Palme and Svensson (2003) to construct two stylised pathways to retirement for the purposes of incentive calculations: the old age pensions pathway and the labour market insurance pathway.

Table 9.6 shows the distribution of the number of years between retirement and the transition to disability pensions for different age groups. A majority of those who initially left the labour force with sickness or unemployment benefit make the transition within two years after they retired. Those who retire at relatively older ages make a faster transition to disability insurance.

The east panel of table 9.7 shows the labour force participation survival functions for males conditional on financing the labour force exit by

Table 9.6 *Percentage distribution of the number of years after permanent exit from the labour force before DI becomes the main income source. Retirees with initial income from sickness/unemployment insurance only*

| | Number of years before DI as main income source | | | | | |
	1	2	3	4	5+	Mean
Age 50–55						
Sickness insurance	9.09	37.60	33.47	9.09	10.74	2.75
Unemployment insurance	–	7.69	30.77	15.38	46.15	4.00
All	8.91	35.66	33.33	9.30	12.79	2.81
Age 55–60						
Sickness insurance	20.10	42.44	27.17	6.67	3.62	2.31
Unemployment insurance	3.92	40.20	38.24	13.73	3.92	2.74
No income source more than 50% alone	51.02	18.37	24.49	6.12	–	1.86
All	18.91	41.21	28.70	7.66	3.53	2.36
Age 60–65						
Sickness insurance	49.31	40.79	9.95	–	–	1.60
Unemployment insurance	10.42	64.58	25.00	–	–	2.15
No income source more than 50% alone	75.56	18.89	5.56	–	–	1.30
All	49.74	39.48	10.78	–	–	1.61

old age pension and labour market insurance, respectively. For obvious reasons, those who use labour market insurances retire on average much earlier than the old age pension group. The graph of the survival function for those who retire by old age pensions changes slope at age sixty. This is probably due to the fact that sixty is the eligibility age for benefits in most old age pension schemes.

The west panel of table 9.7 shows that for old age pensioners the behaviour is remarkably similar between the two groups, although a somewhat larger share of the white-collar workers stay after age sixty-five. This means that the difference in timing of retirement between white- and blue-collar workers can be explained by workers who finance their labour market exit by labour market insurance.

9.5 Measuring income security incentives for retirement

A compulsory old-age pension scheme affects labour market behavior of older workers in at least two ways.[4] First, it creates individual wealth, the

---

[4] We have, in order to save space, restricted the presentation of results in this section to men. However, the main conclusions apply also to women.

Table 9.7 *Labour force participation rates for male workers conditional on being in the labour force at age 55. West panel: old age and labour market insurance paths to retirement. East panel: blue- and white-collar workers in the private sector conditional on taking the old age pension path to retirement*

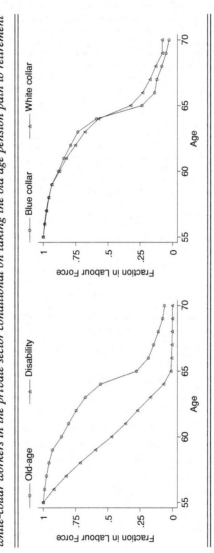

Source: Authors' own calculations from the LINDA panel survey.

expected present value of future benefit payments, which, provided that leisure as retired is a normal good, creates an incentive for the worker to exit from the labour force. For at least some workers, this wealth is likely to be greater than the wealth that they would have had saved for their retirement in absence of an old age pension scheme. Second, the actuarial reductions for early withdrawal of benefit and general rules on contributions to the pension scheme for determining the level of the benefits may, on the other hand, create incentive for the worker to stay in the labour force. Thus, to study individual incentives to exit from the labour force generated by the income security system we need two different measures: one for the size of the wealth at different ages and one for the change in wealth from staying an additional year in the labour force.

Income security wealth is defined as the expected present value of a worker's future pension benefits at year t if he retires at age r, i.e.,

$$ISW(t, r) = \sum_{s=r}^{\max age} \delta^{s-t} E_t B(s, r), \tag{1}$$

where δ is the discount factor which we set to 0.97 in the empirical analysis, i.e., 3 per cent interest rate, and $E_t B(s, r)$ is the expected benefit at age s if the worker retires at age r, i.e.,

$$
\begin{aligned}
E_t B(s, r) = & \; p(s \mid t) q(s \mid t) BM(s, r) \\
& + p(s \mid t)(1 - q(s \mid t)) BS(s, r) \\
& + (1 - p(s \mid t)) q(s \mid t) S(s, r, t),
\end{aligned}
\tag{2}
$$

where $BM(s, r)$ is the worker's pension benefit at age s if he is married and retires at age r; $BS(s, r)$ is the worker's pension benefit at age s if he is not married and retires at age r; $S(s, r)$ is the survivor's benefit when the worker would have been aged s and retired at age r; $p(s \mid t)$ is the probability of survival at time s conditional on survival at time t; $q(s \mid t)$ is the probability of the spouse surviving at age s conditional on survival at age t. $S(s, r, t)$ depends on the spouse at time t as well as the retirement age r, while $BM(s, r)$ and $BS(s, r)$ are not dependent on t since we assume perfect foresight about wages. We also disregard the possibility of divorce.

Table 9.8 shows income security wealth for the old age pension path of retirement for ages between fifty-five and seventy for the average in the first, fifth and tenth decile of predicted permanent income, respectively. Permanent income is calculated as the sum of predicted income[5] for the

---

[5] Predicted income equals actual income when observed. If it is not observed, e.g. because the worker has retired, it is calculated as the average of the earnings the three years preceding the missing observation. We have predicted earnings for each missing individual observation over the fifteen years between 1983 and 1997 covered by the data.

Table 9.8 *Average income security wealth by age for different income concepts. 1st (a), 5th (b) and 10th (c) decile in the distribution of permanent income*

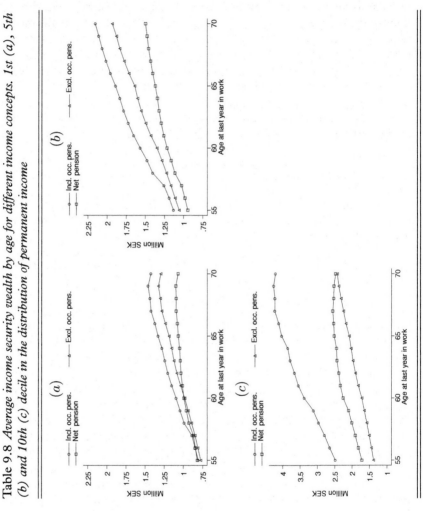

fifteen years that we are able to observe labour income in the data set. Each figure contains three graphs: one showing the wealth from the public pension system, one which, in addition to the public system, also includes occupational pension, and, finally, the net income security wealth, i.e., the wealth corresponding to benefit income net of income taxes and housing allowances. The differences between the first two graphs shows the importance of occupational pensions, and the difference between the second and third graph shows the effect of income taxes and housing allowances.

The results in table 9.8 show that there are considerable differences in the size of the income security wealth between the income groups. If a worker retires at age sixty-five, mean income security wealth is 1.3 million SEK in the first decile, compared to about 2 million in the fifth and more than 4 million in the tenth decile. This shows that the Swedish public and compulsory occupational schemes insure the incomes for all deciles in the income distribution. It is clear from the graphs that the occupational pensions are much more important for the high-income earners: it corresponds to more than half of the income security wealth in the tenth decile, but only about 10 per cent in the fifth decile. The reason for these results is that most high-income earners have earnings above the social security ceiling, which are not covered by the public income security system but are covered by occupational pensions.

Table 9.9 shows mean income security wealth by age for different occupational pension groups: white- and blue-collar workers in the private sector and employees in central and local governments, respectively. Each figure shows two different graphs: one for the public old age pension system and one where the occupational pension is also included. The results show that the occupational pension is most important for white-collar workers in the private sector. The explanation for this result is the fact that this group has the most generous pension scheme and that the share of workers above the social security ceiling is the largest in this group.

The income security system affects retirement behaviour not only through the old age pension scheme but also through unemployment, sickness and disability insurance. Typically, the worker has access to an old age pension scheme once a minimum age requirement is met. The labour market insurance schemes have additional eligibility requirements. Access to the unemployment insurance schemes requires active search for a new job. Access to compensation from the disability insurance requires that the worker permanently has lost his ability to do his regular work due to health reasons. Therefore, these insurance schemes affect the retirement behaviour both through the strictness in giving access to these schemes and the general economic incentives inherent in the schemes.

Table 9.9 *Average income security wealth by age for the old age pension path to retirement. Including occupational pension versus excluding this income source. (a) blue–collar workers in the private sector; (b) white–collar workers in the private sector; (c) employees in central government; (d) employees in local governments*

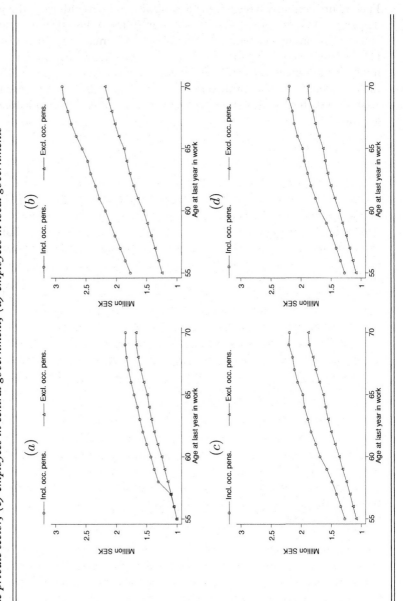

Table 9.10 compares income security wealth between the old age pension and labour market insurance paths to retirement for the first, fifth and tenth permanent income deciles, respectively. We use the stylised pathway to retirement through the labour market insurance programmes as we described in section 9.4.[6] The same mortality risks are used in both cases in order to show the difference in incentives for the same individual.

It is clear from these graphs that there is a huge gain in wealth, in all income groups, from being admitted to a labour market insurance programme, rather than retiring through the old age pension system, if a worker would like to retire at a relatively young age. If a worker retires at age fifty-five, this difference in wealth ranges from 0.75 SEK in the first decile to 1.5 million in the tenth decile. These results imply that not only the old age pension schemes, but also the labour market insurances cover the incomes in all deciles of the income distribution.

We use two different measures for the gain of staying in the labour force compared to retiring in the current period. The first one, the *benefit accrual* measure, is simply the change in the income security wealth of staying one additional year in the labour force compared to retiring in that period. At age t this measure is defined as

$$ACCR(t) = \sum_{s=t+2}^{\max age} \delta^{s-t} E_t B(s, t+2) - \sum_{s=t+1}^{\max age} \delta^{s-t} E_t B(s, t+1). \qquad (3)$$

The benefit accrual measure has been criticised for being myopic in the sense that, although it considers all expected future benefit payments to the individual, it disregards the possibility that the individual may have a greater gain from staying in the labour force some years ahead of the decision period. Since the retirement decision in most cases is irreversible and future gains of staying in the labour force may be an important aspect of the economic incentive, this omission may be misleading for measuring the economic incentives to stay in the labour force.

An example where this aspect may be important is the STP pension scheme for blue-collar workers in the private sector. The benefit from this scheme is, as described in section 9.2, equal to 10 per cent of the average of the three best years of earnings below the social security ceiling between ages fifty-five and fifty-nine. If the worker contributes less than three years to the scheme he or she will not be eligible for any pension at all. This means that the benefit accrual for the first two years are zero while it will be quite large for the third year, i.e., for working between ages fifty-seven and fifty-eight. The large accrual in the third year is, however,

---

[6] See Palme and Svensson (2003) for a detailed description of how this pathway is constructed.

Table 9.10 *Income security wealth by age. Old age pension and labour market insurance paths to retirement. Averages for 1st (a), 5th (b) and 10th (c) decile groups in the distribution of permanent income*

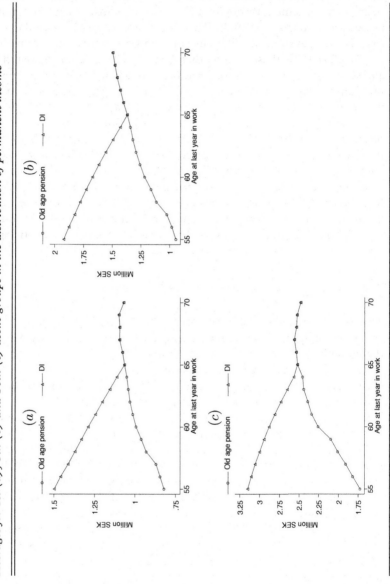

likely to affect the retirement decision the first two years as well, although it is not taken into account in the benefit accrual measure.

There are different ways to construct 'forward looking' incentive measures. One of the most commonly used is the Stock and Wise (1990) *option value* measure, i.e., a measure of the value of the option of retiring at some later time than in the current period. The option value measure requires estimation of a number of parameters. Since this is beyond the scope of this chapter, we will use a simplified version of the option value measure, the so-called *peak value* measure (see Coile and Gruber, 2000). The peak value is defined as social security wealth (SSW) at its maximum value minus SSW at time t, i.e.,

$$PEAK(t) = \max_{r=t+2,...,71} \sum_{s=r}^{\max age} \delta^{s-t} E_t B(s, r) - \sum_{s=t+1}^{\max age} \delta^{s-t} E_t B(s, t+1).$$

This measure is forward-looking in the sense that rather than measuring the immediate accrual in SSW of working one additional year, it measures the maximum gain of staying in the labour force in the future.

Table 9.11 shows the benefit accrual and peak value measures for benefit income by age for the first, fifth and tenth deciles in the permanent income distribution. The results from the first and fifth deciles show a very similar pattern: a spike in the benefit accrual measure of working one additional year at age fifty-seven and a steeply declining peak value measure until age sixty, where the negative slope becomes flatter. The explanation for the spikes at age fifty-seven is the eligibility rules in the STP scheme for blue-collar workers in the private sector, as discussed above. The fact that blue-collar workers dominate both the first and fifth decile in the permanent income distribution explains why this spike is apparent in both graphs.

The change in the slope of the peak value measure at age sixty, for the tenth decile in the distribution of permanent income shown in panel (c) in table 9.11, is due to the fact that old age pensions from pension schemes for public employees cannot be claimed if the worker retires before age sixty. The graphs for benefit accrual and peak value start to coincide at age sixty for the first and fifth decile, but not until age sixty-four for the tenth decile. The reason for this pattern is that the maximum accrual in the future coincides with the one-year change for the first and fifth per centile. The difference in this respect in the tenth decile is likely to be due to more heterogeneity in the benefit accrual pattern in this group.

A negative benefit accrual, that is, when the value of the forgone benefit payments is greater than the expected increase in benefits later on by staying one additional year in the labour force, can be interpreted as a

Table 9.11 *Peak value and benefit accrual rates by age at last year of work. Averages for the 1st (a), 5th (b) and 10th (c) decile in the distribution of permanent income*

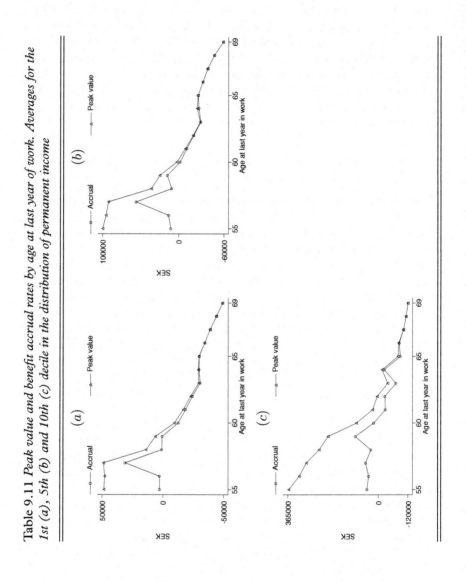

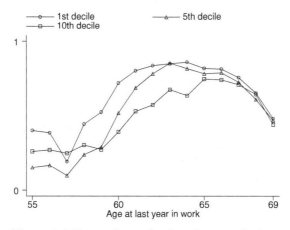

Figure 9.4 Share of negative benefit accrual observations by age at last year of work for different decile groups in the permanent income distribution

tax on additional work from the social security system. As can be seen in table 9.11, the benefit accrual becomes negative after age fifty-nine in the first decile and after age sixty in the fifth and tenth deciles. This difference and the, in general, lower accrual rate in the first decile, can probably be explained by the greater progressivity of the income taxes for low-income retirees and the means-tested housing allowance system for the elderly. Comparing the fifth and tenth deciles, it can be seen that although the benefit accrual measure is on average zero at age sixty, the peak value measure is still on average positive at that age in the tenth decile. This result implies that workers in the tenth decile have, compared to those in the fifth decile, on average more incentives to additional work at this age.

Figure 9.4 shows the share of negative benefit accrual observations by age for each of the three decile groups. These graphs confirm the general picture of the incentives presented in table 9.8: the share of negative observations increases rapidly at age sixty and the share of negative observations are in general highest among the low-income earners in the first decile.

To sum up, let us compare the results from benefit accrual with those of the peak value measures. The peak value measure, being forward-looking, gives less 'noisy', more realistic results: the incentives to stay in the labour force decrease rapidly at age sixty in all three groups. To the extent that workers are forward-looking when making decision about retirement, the peak value measure can be expected to work better in modelling retirement behaviour econometrically. The results in

Table 9.12 *Benefit accrual rates by age for different retirement income concepts. Old age pension path to retirement. Averages for 1st (a), 5th (b) and 10th (c) decile in the distribution of permanent income*

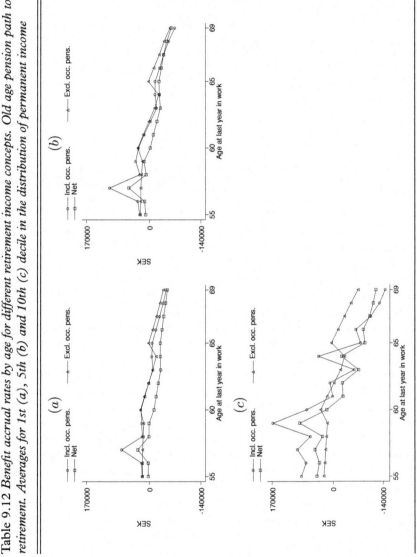

Palme and Svensson (2003) show that the forward-looking measures of economic incentives work slightly better in the sense that the models where they are included gave a higher log-likelihood compared to the models that included benefit accrual. For descriptive purposes the measures convey similar information. However, the benefit accrual measure reveals more clearly the discontinuities, the 'spikes', created by different rules in the social security system. Therefore, in order to save space, we confine ourselves henceforth to just show the results from the benefit accrual measure. We should, however, keep in mind how these results should be interpreted in the peak value framework.

To study how the public old age pension system, occupational pensions, housing allowances and income taxes affect the benefit accruals, we do the same decomposition analysis as we did above for social security wealth. Table 9.12 shows separate graphs for benefit incomes from the public system only, incomes from the public system and occupational pensions and, finally, net from housing allowances and income taxes for the averages in the first, fifth and tenth decile in the permanent income distribution.

Table 9.12 shows several interesting results. First, it can be seen that the graphs for the public old age pension systems in all three groups show a very similar pattern. The accrual is on average positive up to age sixty, but beyond that age the actuarial adjustment for early withdrawal is on average too small to make the system actuarially fair in the sense that benefit accrual is zero.[7] There is a small spike of working the last year at age sixty-five. This is due to the asymmetry in the actuarial increase from delaying withdrawal of pension benefits: a 0.7 per cent increase for each month before the sixty-fifth birthday compared to a 0.5 per cent reduction for each month of early withdrawal. A second interesting result is the relatively large effect of income taxes and housing allowances in all three groups. A general result is that the income tax and housing allowances 'smooth out' spikes in the accrual rate. This will have a more permanent and apparent effect on the peak value measure. Comparing the first and fifth decile groups, it can be seen that the lower accrual rates shown in table 12 (a) and (b) are due to the effect of income taxes and the means-tested housing allowances to the elderly.

To isolate the effect of occupational pensions, table 9.13 shows the average benefit accrual rates by age within each of the four occupational pension groups. Each figure contains two graphs: one where only the public pension system is considered and one where occupational pensions are also included. We have already discussed the spike for working the last

---

[7] Remember that this is conditional on the chosen discount rate.

Table 9.13 *Benefit accrual rates by age. Old age pension path to retirement. Averages for blue-collar workers in the private sector (a); white-collar workers in the private sector (b); employees in central government (c); local governments (d)*

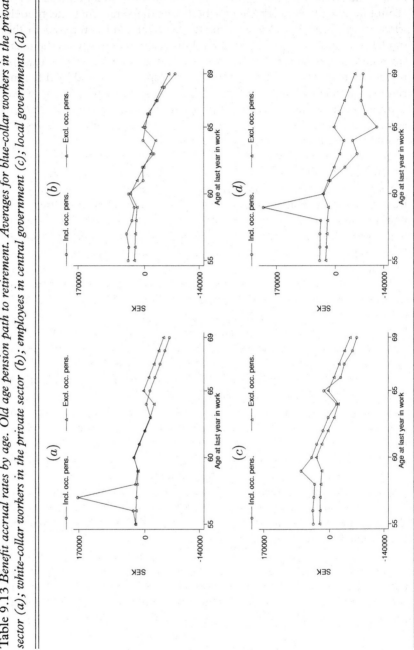

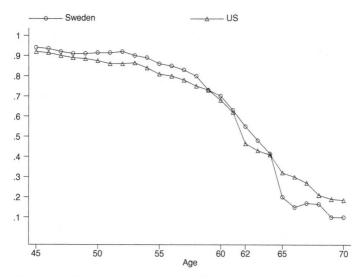

Figure 9.5 Male labour force participation rates by age in Sweden compared to the USA.

year at age fifty-seven for blue-collar workers. Graphs (c) and (d) show similar spikes for workers in the public sector of working the last year at age fifty-nine. The reason for these spikes, which are more pronounced for local government employees, is that, as we described in section 9.2, public-sector employees can only claim their old age pension at retirement before age sixty as a life annuity which is paid out starting at age sixty-five with an actuarial reduction.

In sum, the analysis of the accrual measures shows that there are large actuarial penalties for workers who retire one, two or three years before age sixty. To what extent does this observation on the incentives to stay in the labour force match up with the observed retirement behaviour? One piece of evidence that these discontinuities actually do matter for the retirement behaviour is the labour force participation rates by age shown in table 9.7 in section 9.4. The slope of the graph for those who retire through the old age pension path changes markedly at age sixty. Another way to assess the importance of these incentives is to compare the retirement behaviour with another country with different incentives.

Figure 9.5 compares labour force participation rates in Sweden and the United States for men by age. In the United States there is a stronger element of private pension which supposedly is more closely tied to the contribution made to the insurance than the defined benefit schemes in Sweden. The graphs in figure 9.5 show that Sweden has a higher labour force participation rate up to age fifty-nine. Between age sixty and sixty-four the graphs intersect at several ages, with the US labour force participation rate dropping at a faster rate at the early eligibility age of social security at age sixty-two. After age sixty-four there is a higher labour force participation rate in the USA. One interpretation of this pattern is, again, the large actuarial penalties in Sweden for retiring before age sixty.

9.6   Conclusions

Although labour force participation among older workers in Sweden has decreased substantially in recent decades, this decrease has been quite modest, viewed in an international perspective. In this study we have shown that the different old-age pension systems in Sweden create several discontinuities, 'spikes', in the incentives to stay in the labour force. These are concentrated in the ages before sixty and the observed participation rates suggest that these discontinuities are important for participation behaviour.

A second finding in the study is the importance of income taxes and housing allowances for the retirement incentives. By decomposing the incentive measures it was seen that, in particular for low-income earners, progressive income taxes and means-tested housing allowances, policies designed to make the income distribution among pensioners more equal, counteracted the actuarial adjustments in the pension schemes.

A third finding is the importance of labour market insurance programmes. Most workers who retire before age sixty-five use labour market insurance programmes. Our calculations show that eligibility to these insurance programmes increases the value of the income security wealth by about 1.5 million SEK at age fifty-five for a median income earner and by much more for high-income earners. These generous insurance programmes create strong incentives for workers to exit from the labour force and highlight the importance of the rules for access and their application.

Sweden is currently going through a reform of the old age pension system: the old defined benefit scheme is being replaced by a notional defined contribution system (see Palmer, 2001 for a detailed description). Also several of the occupational pension programmes are changing to a defined contribution scheme. In light of the results from this study, alleviating the discontinuity in the benefit accrual, which is an effect of the latter reform, may actually weaken the incentives for workers to stay in the labour force until age sixty. Our results also show that considering the incentives generated by the old age pension scheme alone may be misleading: income taxes, housing allowances and labour market insurance programmes are also very important in determining the overall incentives for older workers to stay in the labour force.

References

Coile, Courtney and Gruber, Jonathan, 2001, 'Social security incentives for retirement', in David A. Wise (ed.), *Themes in the Economics of Aging*, Chicago: University of Chicago Press.

Gruber, Jonathan and Wise, David, 1999, *Social Security and Retirement around the World*, Chicago: University of Chicago Press.

Karlström, A., Palme, M. and Svensson, I., 2002, 'The timing of retirement and social security reform: measuring individual welfare changes', mimeo, Stockholm School of Economics.

Lumsdaine, Robin L. and Mitchell, Olivia S., 1999, 'New developments in the economic analysis of retirement', in Orley Ashenfelter and David Card (eds.), *Handbook of Labor Economics*, Amsterdam: North-Holland.

Palme, Mårten and Svensson, Ingemar, 1999, 'Social security and occupational pensions in Sweden', in Jonathan Gruber and David Wise (eds.) *Social Security and Retirement around the World*, Chicago: University of Chicago Press.

—2003, 'Income security programs and retirement in Sweden', in Jonathan Gruber and David Wise (eds.), *Social Security and Retirement Around the World: Micro-Estimation*, Chicago: University of Chicago Press.

Palmer, Edward, 2001, 'Swedish pension reform: how did it evolve and what does it mean for the future?', in Martin Feldstein and Horst Siebert (eds.), *Coping with the Pension Crisis: Where Does Europe Stand?*, Chicago: University of Chicago Press.

Stock, J. and Wise, D., 1990, 'Pensions, the option value of work, and retirement', *Econometrica*, 58, 1151–80.

10   Social insurance and redistribution[1]

Pierre Pestieau

10.1   Introduction

Social protection and, more generally, the welfare state have wide-ranging objectives. It is not surprising that each should appear to be a patchwork of diverse sources of financing and manners of delivery. Yet, it is possible to focus on two specific kinds of objectives: efficiency and equity, keeping in mind that in a market economy the market is the norm, and that a case can be made for government intervention. When the markets don't function efficiently, public intervention is justified if it can be corrective.

Indeed, there are a number of market failures in the areas traditionally covered by the welfare state: education, health, retirement, disability. But increasingly, there is a sense that these failures of the market are less pervasive than they were several decades ago, when the framework of the welfare state was first developed. This is because they tend to be less severe than alternative government failures, or because they can be corrected through the legal process. Regardless of the reasons, the efficiency function of the welfare state is not as convincing today as it was in the past.

The equity failure, on the other hand, is a totally different matter. Even the most efficient market economy cannot achieve desirable distribution of resources – unless it be by chance – because that is not its objective. Here the case for government intervention is incontrovertible. The only question is the form that this intervention should take.

There is an idea, still ingrained in the mind of today's policy-makers and economists, that redistribution can be achieved through the tax system, particularly income taxation. Accordingly, if the government is to intervene in spending programmes such as health, retirement, disability or education, it should do so according to the market rules, or at least according to the so-called benefit principle. This tradition has been

[1] An earlier version of this paper was presented in the workshop on the public sector project, 4–6 May, Krusenberg Manor. I am grateful to T. Andersen and P. Molander for their helpful comments.

238

most eloquently advocated by Musgrave (1959) in his classic separation between the allocative and the distributive functions of government.

An observation of the real world gives a different picture. In most countries, whether developed or developing, the evidence is that there is more redistribution being achieved by the various components of the welfare state – public education, guaranteed old age pensions, health care insurance and others – than by the tax system. Why is this? Two reasons can be advanced. They pertain to the theory of 'second best' and to the political economy approach. The Musgrave separation of functions implicitly assumes that we are in a 'first best' setting wherein tax redistribution involves no allocative distortion. When taxation is distortionary, that is, when it has clear disincentive effects on education, effort, saving and risk taking, then the use of specific public spending, or social protection, can be shown to be desirable.

If we leave the normative perspective of social welfare maximisation, we find yet another argument for using social protection and social production for purposes of redistribution. Voters seem to be readier to support redistributive programmes than redistributive taxation. The reason may be found in some kind of paternalistic altruism. In addition, we can show that voting for tax rates as well as social programmes can result in a more progressive outcome than just voting on taxes.

The purpose of this chapter is to explore these explanations in favour of redistributive social spending. In section 10.2 we define the concepts of social protection, social insurance and welfare state. We also briefly discuss the allocative rationale for having social protection programmes. In section 10.3 we develop the second best argument for providing social insurance with moral hazard from an exclusively normative viewpoint. In the concluding section we deal with certain aspects of political economy.

10.2   Social protection, private insurance and redistribution

Definition and data

Social insurance is the focus of this chapter. How does it relate to the more comprehensive concepts of social protection and the welfare state? The welfare state consists of a number of programmes through which the government pursues the goal of social protection on behalf of citizens against certain categories of risk. It provides social assistance to the needy and encourages the consumption of certain services such as education, housing and child care.

These programmes were introduced to meet certain objectives, the two most important being relief of poverty and a sense of security for everyone.[2] When assessing the performance of the welfare state it is important to do so with respect to these goals. But assistance and insurance are not the only objectives of the welfare state. Some of its programmes also affect macroeconomic stabilisation and growth. Conversely, some assistance and some insurance can be achieved by institutions other than the government. Insurance can be provided by the market, and both insurance and assistance can be provided by the family, and more broadly by the non-profit sector. While it is true that neither the market nor the family has the negative impact on the workings of the economy that is attributed to the welfare state, the scope of the family and of the non-profit sector is much narrower than that of the welfare state. It is significant that the market affects little redistribution, if any.

It is difficult to generalise about a 'European model' of the welfare state, in view of the diversity of welfare states in the European Union developed largely after 1945. This diversity is reflected in the scale of expenditures on social protection systems, in the division of expenditures between programmes, in the structure and design of benefits, and in the organisation and the sources of financing. What all these welfare states have in common is that they are subject to an increasing scepticism regarding their performance. So much so that they are currently being threatened with downsizing, or even dismantling, in a number of countries.

Private versus social insurance

It is not possible to study social protection, specifically social insurance, without reference to private insurance. This is particularly true today. We believe that these two types of insurance are not comparable, as they were fifty years ago at the start of the welfare state. Social insurance is now experiencing a number of difficulties. Some of these are linked to recent developments such as fiscal competition, the declining credibility of the state, evolving labour markets, public opinion resisting redistributive policy and an increasing demand for protection. Other difficulties pertain to the fact that some market failures have been overstated, or that they are no worse than corresponding government failures. This is surely the case with moral hazard, or even adverse selection.[3]

Let us begin by clarifying some conceptual issues and give some figures regarding the evolution and the relative strength of social versus private insurance. What is specific to social insurance relative to private insurance? As observed by Atkinson (1991), there is no easy answer to this question.

[2] See on this Barr (1992, 1993) and Sandmo (1991, 1995).
[3] This is developed by Pestieau (1994).

Is it the public quality of provision? Not really, since one can have social insurance benefits distributed to individuals by private organisations. Such is the case in Belgium for health care. On the other hand, in many countries like France there are a number of state-owned insurance companies involved in private insurance.

Is it the mode of financing? Even though social insurance is often associated with the functioning of the labour market and financed by payroll taxes, there are countries such as Denmark where it is almost exclusively financed by general revenue. In this regard, we should add that the decline in regular salaried employment contributes to loosening the connection between social insurance and the labour market.

Undoubtedly the most specific feature of social insurance is that it is mandatory and universal. But as stated by Stiglitz (1983b), one often confuses 'the question of whether individuals are to be insured with the question of who is to provide the insurance. The view that society must take measures to insure that everyone is insured against certain major risks does not, in itself, imply that the government should directly provide that insurance.' Obligation is not enough to characterise social insurance. In a number of countries car insurance and fire insurance are compulsory, and yet one would not refer to them as social insurance. This leads us to an additional specificity: social insurance is not based exclusively on an actuarially sound basis. Rather, it involves some redistribution. In other words, social insurance can be explained not only by a 'merit good' kind of argument, but also by equity considerations. This latter feature is a prerequisite for universal access.

In figure 10.1 we contrast spending on social insurance and on private insurance across countries. This calls for three remarks. First, social insurance proxied by social protection spending dominates private insurance; it is almost five times as important. Second, in terms of trends, whereas social insurance seems to have reached a ceiling, and even to have decreased in some countries, the role of private insurance is increasing everywhere steadily, albeit slowly.

Finally, one notes two main features. There is an income effect that implies that the richer the country the higher its expenditure on both types of insurance. There is also a taste-specific effect according to which some countries like Ireland, the United Kingdom and Luxembourg have a more active private insurance market than others. On the other side of the regression line one finds the Scandinavian countries, which have a clear preference for social insurance.

Figure 10.1 indicates a small negative correlation between the two types of insurance across countries. It is interesting to note that such a relation pointing to a certain substitutability between the two schemes has

Table 10.1 *Comparative advantage of social over private insurance*

Argument	Advantage
Large risk	Nil when reinsurance is possible
Intergenerational smoothing	High
Moral hazard	Negative
Adverse selection	Nil if insurance is made mandatory
Administrative cost	Noticeable particularly in the field of health care
Redistribution	High
Financing	Negative because of tax competition
Commitment	Negative
Single provision	High in the field of health care

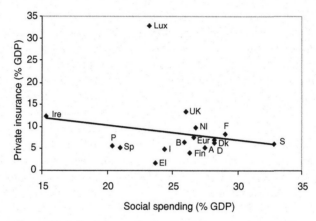

Figure 10.1 Social spending and private insurance, 1998
Source: Eurostat and OECD.

been evolving over time. On the basis of panel data covering the period 1970–88, we find that there was first a positive correlation between the two types which progressively turned negative, indicating a trend from complementarity to substitutability.[4]

In an earlier paper (Pestieau, 1994) we have shown that a number of arguments traditionally put forward in favour of social insurance might have been overstated. Table 10.1 summarizes the pro and con arguments.

---

[4] Admittedly our comparison is questionable. In the concept of social spending there are a number of expenditures which are not related to insurance (e.g. family allowances). Also the regression coefficient is sensitive to outliers such as Luxembourg and Ireland. It remains negative, however, if either one is dropped. Finally, the figures are not adjusted for differences in administrative handling and tax treatment. See on this Adema et al. (1996).

In short, the public sector is subject to many of the same incentive problems that lead to the market failures of private insurance. On the revenue side, fiscal competition and economic integration make it increasingly more difficult to maintain 'generous' social protection programmes regardless of their objective: insurance or assistance. The issue of commitment is a difficult one. The private sector does not want to commit itself for the long term; it offers contracts that are both contingent and renegotiable. The government can commit itself but this implies a lot of rigidity to the extent that this precludes adjusting programmes to the emergence of new needs or of new technology.[5] The ideal would be contingent commitment and not rigid entitlements that characterise the welfare state in societies with powerful vested interests. Also, the recent evolution of employment conditions leads to a widening gap between social protection programmes and labour markets. Finally, recent economic and demographic developments call for increased public interventions in the area of redistributive income maintenance.

The lesson drawn from these facts is clear. It is uncertain whether social insurance, or rather social protection, can pursue its two traditional objectives: insurance and assistance. For some time now, and in some countries, such a duality of objectives has not raised any difficulty. However, in a number of countries it is unaffordable today to provide insurance and, at the same time, to take care of the needy. Furthermore, these objectives may interact inefficiently, since redistribution is often used as a veil behind which allocative and even distributional dysfunctionings occur. On the other hand, sticking too closely to the insurance principle, or to put it differently to the Bismarckian idea of social insurance, makes real redistribution difficult.

Consequently, we believe that the two main arguments in favour of social insurance are its redistributive capacity and, to a lesser extent, its lower administrative costs in the fields of health care and old age pensions.

Let us now turn to the central issue of this chapter: the use of social insurance for redistributive purpose along with income taxation.

10.3   Social insurance and income taxation

The problem

As discussed, there are three reasons for public intervention in the field of insurance: transactions costs, market failures and redistribution. In the health care sector and in retirement pension schemes, private insurance

---

[5] There is naturally the question of the credibility of such a commitment.

exhibits higher transaction costs than social insurance. This is partly because of high administrative costs.[6] Market failures, the second reason, come primarily from asymmetric information such as that between insurers and the insured (adverse selection and moral hazard), and between health care providers and health care consumers. It is not certain that the government is necessarily better equipped than the market to face and solve those problems.[7] What interests us is the third reason, the role of social insurance as a redistributive device.

In a full-information world of first best there is little reason for redistribution using social insurance. The distributive and allocative functions of the government can be separated. Thus one could expect income taxation to achieve all the desired redistribution, and social insurance to operate according to the market rule of actuarial fairness. However, we will show that in a second best world of distortionary taxation social insurance can be a powerful device for redistribution, complementing the tax-transfer system.

The literature shows that if risks are negatively related to income in such a way that the poor on average face higher risks, we have an obvious redistributive argument for social insurance. As argued by Rochet (1991) and by Cremer and Pestieau (1996), social insurance combined with a standard distortionary income tax can redistribute more effectively than only income taxation. This is because redistribution through social insurance does not involve the same distortion as income taxation. This is even truer when social insurance is less administratively costly than private insurance.[8]

Rochet's result was developed in a setting where the risk probability is given, and any loss can be compensated for without restriction. In other words, both *ex ante* and *ex post* moral hazard have been assumed away. By contrast, when either one is taken into account, Boadway et al. (2001a) show that the case for social insurance is not as strong, and that full coverage is no longer necessarily socially desirable. Those two types of moral hazard are studied in an economy in which a linear income tax and social insurance can be used jointly, along with private insurance[9] that

---

[6] On this, see Diamond (1992) and Mitchell (1998). The point goes back to Arrow (1963).

[7] The conventional wisdom is that social insurance is better equipped to circumvent the problem of adverse selection but not that of moral hazard.

[8] See also Petretto (1999).

[9] Blomqvist and Horn (1980) also examine the case for public insurance when actuarially fair private insurance is available, and individuals differ in both labour productivity and illness probability. In their paper no labour is supplied when ill, and public insurance consists of a uniform lump-sum benefit to the ill. In Boadway et al. (2001a), illness does not preclude working.

is actuarially fair but possibly costlier than social insurance. (We sketch these arguments below.)

The basic model

Three types of decision-makers make up the economy: households, private insurance firms and the government.[10] Households face an idiosyncratic risk of accident, but they can take hidden actions that affect the size of the loss in the event of an accident (we speak of *ex post* moral hazard), or that affect the probability of the accident occurring (this is then what we call *ex ante* moral hazard). Households differ both in productivity and in accident risk. Insurance companies can observe household risk and provide insurance that is competitive and actuarially fair,[11] except where administrative costs are introduced. The government's objective is to redistribute income among households. But because it cannot observe productivities it is restricted to using distortionary policy instruments. Decision-making can be thought of as occurring sequentially. The government chooses its policies first, followed by the insurance firms and then households. In each case the outcomes of subsequent stages are fully anticipated so that *equilibria* of interest are *sub-game perfect*.

To be more specific we use the case of health insurance as an example, although the analysis is more generally applicable to other types of personal risks faced by households. We consider two states of the world denoted by '0' for good health and '1' for ill health. There are n types of individuals indexed by $i = 1, \ldots, n$, each characterised by a wage rate and a risk characteristic. Wage rate for a type-i person is exogenously given by w_i. In the absence of *ex ante* moral hazard his exogenous probability of illness is π_i. Thus all households of a given wage have the same probability of illness, which simplifies the analysis considerably. With *ex ante* moral hazard type i households can affect the probability of illness according to the function $\pi_i(x_i)$, where x_i is preventive spending that takes place before the state of health is revealed to the household.

In the good state the health status is exogenously given as h^0. In the bad state the health status is $h^1 = \overline{h} + m(z)$, where z is curative expenditures on health improvement and $m(z)$ is strictly concave. Expenditures z chosen by the household in case of *ex post* moral hazard are undertaken after the state of health is revealed to the household. In this case, we assume that

---

[10] We present the model and the results of Boadway et al. (2001a). For further development and proofs the reader can refer to that paper.

[11] That is, there is no adverse selection. Our assumptions are generally designed to ensure that private insurance firms can provide insurance efficiently, thereby eliminating insurance market failure as a reason for government intervention.

$h^1 = \bar{h} + m(z) < h^0$ for all values of z. In other words, treatment cannot bring the health status if ill to a level as high as the health status if not ill. Notice that the parameters h^0 and $\bar{h}$ as well as the function $m(z)$ are the same for all types of households. Only the probabilities of good health differ.

Households have identical state-independent utility functions: $u_i = u(c^i_j, h^i_j, \ell^i_j)$ where c^i_j is consumption, h^i_j is health status and ℓ^i_j is labour supply of a type-i household in state j. Naturally, households maximise expected utility weighted by the probabilities π_i for state 1 (ill health) and $1 - \pi_i$ for state 0 (good health). Households take government policies and private insurance premiums as given. They choose x before the state of health is determined and c, ℓ, z after the state is determined.

Insurance firms are perfectly competitive. They offer insurance policies $\{p_i, P_i\}$ to households of type i where p_i is the proportion of health expenditures z_i covered (reimbursed), and P_i is the total premium. Insurance companies anticipate the effect of their insurance policies on curative expenditures z_i in the case of *ex post* moral hazard, and on preventive expenditures x_i in the case of *ex ante* moral hazard. Initially we ignore administrative costs, in which case competition entails premiums as given by $P_i = \pi_i(x_i) p_i z_i$.

Later we introduce a loading factor k in which case premiums for type-i households are $P_i = (1 + k)\pi_i(x_i) p_i z_i$ (with $k \geq 0$).

The government has two sorts of policy instruments – tax-transfer policies and social insurance. Tax-transfer policy consists of a linear progressive income tax with marginal tax rate of t and a lump-sum poll subsidy of a per household. Social insurance covers a proportion s of curative expenditures z_i financed out of general tax revenues. Notice that the same rate of social insurance applies to all households. Denote total insurance coverage by $\sigma_i = p_i + s$.

As mentioned, there are three main decision-making stages in this economy that represent the sequence in which decisions occur:

Stage 1: The government chooses its policies (t, a, s). It cannot observe individual types or individual demands for goods, leisure or insurance, but it can observe incomes. It knows preferences and the distribution of individuals by type-i. The government anticipates the effect of its policies both on the insurance market and subsequently on households.

Stage 2: The competitive insurance industry sells private insurance to households. Market equilibrium (competition for customers with zero profits) determines p_i and P_i. The insurance industry is assumed to be able to observe household risk types so that there is no adverse selection problem. Thus insurance firms are better informed than the government since they can observe π_i. At this stage (t, a, s) are taken as given, and household behaviour is correctly anticipated.

Stage 3: Households select x_i, c_i^1, ℓ_i^1, z_i, c_i^0, ℓ_i^0. Preventive expenditures x_i are chosen before the state of health is revealed. All other variables are state-specific since they are chosen after the state is revealed (z_i is chosen only in the bad state). Households take $\{t, a, s, p_i, P_i\}$ as given from the previous two stages. The equilibrium is assumed to be sub-game perfect; so we proceed by backward induction.

In the hypothetical case of perfect information and lump-sum transfers, we can easily show that the government does not have to intervene. The Musgravian separation applies: despite moral hazard, actuarially fair insurance can be provided by the private sector, and all redistributive objectives can be accomplished by the tax-transfer system.

This approach is quite intuitive. Thanks to the individualised lump-sum taxes, the marginal utility of income is equalised across types of individuals and with full coverage by private insurance. Thus the marginal utility of income is equalised across states of the world.

Clearly, we are interested in the more realistic case where the government is imperfectly informed, and restricted to pursuing its redistributive objectives using a linear progressive tax. As a benchmark, we present the case first studied by Rochet (1991) where there is no moral hazard.

Labour distortion but no moral hazard

Rochet considers the case where neither private nor social insurance implies moral hazard, but where labour income taxation is distortionary. By assumption, social insurance redistributes from *good* to *bad* risks. Every insuree pays the same contribution, but gets benefits that increase with the risk probability. If such redistribution happens also to go from high- to low-wage individuals (because of a negative correlation between loss probability and labour productivity), then social insurance becomes highly desirable as it effects non-distortionary redistribution.

Assume for simplicity's sake that there is only one value of curative expenditures, and that it fully restores the health status in the ill health state. That is, $\hat{z}$ is such that $h^1 = \overline{h} + m(\hat{z}) = h^0$. Assume also that π_i is exogenously fixed for all i. There is a private insurance market that offers households coverage p_i and that charges a premium P_i adjusted to their illness probability so that $P_i = \pi_i p_i \hat{z}$.

It can be clearly shown that without social insurance each individual will seek full insurance coverage from private insurance ($p = 1$). This comes from three features of the model: risk aversion, actuarial fairness and no moral hazard. With loading cost or with moral hazard there would be no full coverage.

Let us now look at the optimal behaviour of the government. It will implement a linear progressive tax redistributing resources from highly productive workers to poorly productive ones. Such a tax entails allocative distortions that are related to the tax elasticity of labour supply. The question is whether the government wants to interfere with insurance markets.

It is easy to show that the answer to that question depends on the correlation between the two characteristics of workers, labour productivity and loss probability. If the correlation is negative, it is desirable to push s up to its ceiling value, namely unity. Then there is no need for private insurance. This result, which is the polar opposite of the full information case, is the one obtained by Rochet (1991) and Cremer and Pestieau (1996).

This result is again intuitive. With negative correlation social insurance redistributes from 'good risk' individuals, who also happen to be the more productive ones, to 'bad risk' individuals, who are also the less productive ones. This redistribution is non-distortionary as long as there is no moral hazard. Not surprisingly, it dominates income taxation.

The weakness of this analysis is that it implicitly assumes that both social and private insurance have no influence on the size of the loss to be compensated, nor on the probability of the loss π. Examining these two possibilities, we see that the amount of loss that can be recouped depends on each agent's behaviour, and the probability of the loss is also the responsibility of each agent. With these two additions we see that full insurance by the government is no longer desirable. It is useful to treat these two sorts of moral hazard separately.

Labour distortion and moral hazard

First we assume that the π_i's are given (and either negatively or positively correlated with wages w_i), but that individuals can influence their health status following an illness. By investing in curative expenditures z, they can reach a health status $h^1 = \bar{h} + m(z) < h^0$. In other words, they can never fully recoup their original health status h^0. A proportion of expenditures on health improvement is covered by social insurance s and by private insurance P_i. We solve for the sub-game perfect equilibrium by the backward induction described above. The full developments can be found in Boadway et al. (2001a). Skipping them, we provide just the main results.

Full coverage will never happen since it makes no sense. It can only lead to an infinite amount of curative spending without the possibility of ever recouping the original health status.

Similarly, instead of opting for a social insurance coverage, individuals will invariably buy some sort of private insurance that is better adjusted to their specific risk class.

In general, it is difficult to guarantee that there will be social insurance. This depends on two effects: a redistributive effect that is related to the correlation between productivity and probability, and an efficiency effect that is related to the elasticity of curative spending with respect to social insurance coverage. A negative correlation and a low elasticity are factors leading to the desirability of social insurance.

Ex ante moral hazard involves preventive expenditures that can affect the probability of illness. For simplicity's sake, we assume that curative expenditures are fixed at the level $\hat{z}$, and thus the good health status h^0 can be attained in the ill health state. We can therefore exclude the health status variable from the utility function. We proceed as usual by backward induction, looking first at the household's choices, then at private insurance market equilibrium, and finally at the government's optimisation.

Again, for the full development we refer to Boadway et al. (2001a). The formula for the social insurance coverage is the same as with *ex post* moral hazard, and can be interpreted the same way. Social insurance basically depends on two terms: an efficiency term involving the effect of social insurance on preventive spending, and an equity term depending on the co-variance between labour productivity and loss probability that is now endogenous. Under plausible assumptions we expect a positive level of coverage by social insurance. The endogeneity of loss probability makes the case for a negative correlation more likely than with *ex post* moral hazard. High income individuals tend to spend more on preventive care than low income individuals and thus have a lower loss probability.

Administrative cost

As mentioned, it has been documented that there are administrative costs of operating a competitive insurance industry that may be avoided by a single-payer government system. Administrative costs effectively increase the cost of private insurance relative to a public scheme. There are two consequences of this. The first and most obvious one is that this makes social insurance more attractive than private insurance, despite the bad press that usually surrounds the public sector. The second one is that since the cost of private insurance is not actuarially fair, not all households will necessarily purchase private insurance. To illustrate this phenomenon we employ the case of *ex post* moral hazard. The model is the same as above, except for the administrative costs associated with private insurance. In particular, we assume that there is a loading factor equal to a proportion $k > 0$ of insurance premiums.[12] The no-profit condition then becomes

$$P_i = (1 + k)\pi_i p_i z_i.$$

The same three stages of decision-making apply. Household behaviour in Stage 3 is essentially the same as before. In Stage 2 the insurance market equilibrium incorporates the loading factor. We can no longer be sure that there will be an interior solution for p_i, even if $s = 0$. That is, a non-negative constraint on coverage, $p_i \geq 0$, may be binding. Given that, Stage 3 yields a formula for s with two additional terms. These two terms are related to the inefficiency of private insurance: they vanish if $k = 0$. One term reflects the efficiency cost of having individuals purchase expensive private insurance. The other one, involving those households that are quantity constrained, reflects the benefits of providing social insurance to those households for whom private insurance coverage is too expensive. Overall, the existence of administrative costs of private insurance tends to increase the desirability of public insurance coverage, which is not at all surprising.

Main findings

This section started with Rochet's (1991) finding that, with distortionary income taxation, social insurance is desirable as a redistributive device. The core of his argument is the distortionary feature of income taxation. With a non-distortionary redistributive tax there is no need for social insurance in so far as it is not cheaper than market-provided insurance.

We then explored the robustness of this finding when introducing moral hazard. We distinguished between *ex ante* and *ex post* moral hazard, and showed that the case for public intervention in insurance markets remains a reality. However, while in Rochet's analysis optimal social insurance is complete and crowds out private insurance, in the presence of moral hazard that is no longer the case. Public and private insurance will generally exist side by side. We also introduced the idea that social insurance could be less costly than private insurance, which clearly strengthens the case for social insurance.

Even though with moral hazard a negative correlation between labour productivity and loss is probably neither a sufficient nor a necessary condition for positive social insurance, it is clear that this correlation plays

---

[12] We assume that $k > 0$. Positive loading factors in private health insurance are well documented in the literature. For instance see Phelps (1992), ch. 10. In some sectors private insurance might be less costly than social insurance. The results should then be modified accordingly.

Table 10.2 *The case for social and private insurance*

	s	p_i	σ_i
Full information and moral hazard	0	$0 < p_i < 1$	$= p_i$
Asymmetric information without moral hazard	1	0	1
Ex post moral hazard	$0 < s < 1$	$0 < p_i < 1$	< 1
Ex ante moral hazard	$0 < s < 1$	$0 < p_i < 1$	< 1
Administrative cost in private insurance	$0 < s < 1$	$0 \leq p_i < 1$	< 1

an important role. Thus it is interesting to explore what we know about the relation between income and loss probability. Unfortunately, there is little evidence on these issues when distinguishing types of risk: unemployment, health, disability, mortality. The conventional wisdom is that unemployment, health status and disability are negatively correlated with earnings. By contrast, longevity and use of preventive medicine are positively correlated with earnings.[13] In other words, since we are not dealing here with retirement, it is not unreasonable to assume that there is some negative correlation between π and w.

Another point worth emphasising is that income taxation does not redistribute across states of nature, unlike insurance whether private or public. In other words, even with a non-distortionary labour income tax there is still a case for social insurance.

In Table 10.2 we summarise the main findings presented in this chapter. These findings hold under rather plausible assumptions.

10.4 Conclusion

The purpose of this chapter was to provide some normative arguments as to why social and private insurance coexist in so many countries. We first gave a quick overview of the relative importance of these two types of insurance in European countries. Then, we turned to the rationale for their development. We argued that the most convincing rationale for social insurance is to improve redistribution, rather than to correct for traditional market failures. We presented a normative model showing that, even with moral hazard, the case for social insurance remains strong even where it competes with an actuarially fair private insurance.

---

[13] In the macroeconomic work on business cycles people use data from panel studies to grasp some of these correlations among risks. See Storesletten et al. (2000). The evidence so obtained is questionable for the microeconomic problem at hand. To make significant simulation and obtain relevant results one would need evidence on generic characteristics – innate ability, *ex ante* probability – which is not available.

Our survey chapter is not exhaustive. A number of aspects have not been touched, partly because of space constraints, but also because the current research is lacking. These untouched aspects include the effect of globalisation on social protection[14] and the effect of adverse selection in the private market on the level of social insurance. It is expected that the introduction of adverse selection in the private insurance market will strengthen the case for social insurance.[15]

We have focused exclusively on a normative viewpoint that gives us a kind of reference solution. We can distinguish two rationales for social protection: the pursuit of social justice as an ethical imperative, and the exercise of self-interest through the coercive power of the state.[16] The first rationale, the normative one, is the basis of this chapter, and it has been dealt with by using a social welfare function. The second rationale is a positive one. It starts from the observation that unless it is Pareto improving (and even then), social protection is an inherently political matter that may involve direct democracy. Direct democracy can be contrasted with other forms of democracy in that no politician, bureaucrat or lobbyist can interfere in any substantive way with the preferences of the citizens and the choice of policy. Collective decision-making is simply a matter of moving from individual preferences to the selection of a collective solution. Many rules obtain.

The majority rule is the one generally adopted in the literature. Some work exists, although not much, that deals with the political economy of the public provision of insurance, in particular health insurance (Gouveia, 1997; Petretto, 1999; Epple and Romano, 1996) and social security (Browning, 1975; Casamatta et al., 2000a, b; Boadway et al., 2001b; Persson and Tabellini, 2000).

In general, uncertainty is assumed away. What is dealt with is the issue of political support for the public and the free provision of services that have many of the characteristics of private goods. Whether the public sector is the sole provider or not is crucial. In many contexts – old age, health, education, etc. – households have the choice of purchasing some insurance or service for themselves as a top-up to the 'rationed' amount offered by the public sector. In some countries they can even opt out, but are still partially responsible for paying the taxes that finance the benefits of those who remain in the system. The general conclusion of this literature is that there is a good case to be made for some coexistence between private and public insurance. At the same time, it is clear that there is much work to be done on this important question.

---

[14] Cremer et al. (1998).   [15] Dahlby (1981).   [16] Boadway and Keen (2000).

As a final remark let us recall the underlying assumption made in this chapter, namely, that of a utilitarian government that seeks maximum social welfare. We show that, in most cases, asymmetric information regarding ability and risk implies that there is some positive social insurance acting as a substitute for income taxation. However, in the absence of such an assumption, and if one is not ready to entrust the government with such a responsibility, neither social insurance nor progressive income tax are desirable.

References

Adema, W., Einerhand, M., Eklind, B., Latz, J. and Pearson, M., 1996, 'Net public social expenditures, labor market and social policy', OECD Social Policy Papers, no. 13.

Arrow, K. J., 1963, 'Uncertainty and the welfare economics of medical care', *American Economic Review*, 53, 942–73.

Atkinson, A. B., 1991, 'Social insurance', *The Geneva Papers on Risk and Insurance Theory*, 16, 113–32.

Atkinson, A. B. and Stiglitz, J. E., 1980, *Lectures on Public Economics*, New York: McGraw-Hill.

Barr, N., 1992, 'Economic theory and the welfare state: a survey and interpretation', *Journal of Economic Literature*, 30, 741–803.

—1993, *The Economics of the Welfare State* (2nd edition), London: Weidenfeld and Nicolson.

Blomqvist, A. and Horn, H., 1980, 'Public health insurance and optimal income taxation', *Journal of Public Economics*, 24, 352–71.

Boadway, R. and Keen, M., 2000, 'Redistribution', in A. Atkinson and F. Bourguignon (eds.), *Handbook of Income Distribution*, Amsterdam: North Holland.

Boadway, R., Leite Monteiro, M., Marchand, M. and P. Pestieau, P., 2001a, 'Social insurance and redistribution', in S. Cnossen and H. W. Sinn (eds.), *Public Finance and Public Policy in the New Millennium*, Cambridge, MA: MIT Press.

—2001b, 'The political economy of social insurance with moral hazard', unpublished.

Browning, E. K., 1975, 'Why the social insurance budget is too large in a democratic society', *Economic Enquiry*, 13, 373–88.

Casamatta, G., Cremer, H. and Pestieau, P., 2000a, 'Political sustainability and the design of social insurance', *Journal of Public Economics*, 75, 315–40.

—2000b, 'The political economy of social security', *Scandinavian Journal of Economics*, 102, 503–22.

Cremer, H. and Pestieau, P., 1996, 'Redistributive taxation and social insurance', *International Taxation and Public Finance*, 3, 259–80.

—1998, 'Social insurance and labour mobility: a political economic approach', *Journal of Public Economics*, 68, 397–420.

Cremer, H., Fourgeaud, V., Leite Monteiro, M., Marchand, M. and Pestieau, P., 1998, 'Mobility and redistribution: a survey of the literature', *Public Finance*, 51, 325–52.

Dahlby, B. G., 1981, 'Adverse selection and Pareto improvements through compulsory insurance', *Public Choice*, 37, 547–58.

Diamond, P., 1992, 'Organizing the health insurance market', *Econometrica*, 60, 1233–54.

Epple, D. and Romano, R., 1996, 'Public provision of private goods', *Journal of Political Economy*, 104, 57–84.

Gaynor, M., Haas-Wilson, D. and Vogt, W. B., 2000, 'Are invisible hands good hands? Moral hazard, competition and the second-best in health care markets', *Journal of Political Economy*, 108, 992–1005.

Gouveia, M., 1997, 'Majority rule and the public provision of a private good', *Public Choice*, 93, 221–44.

Hindriks, J. and De Donder, P., 2000, 'The politics of redistributive social insurance', unpublished.

Mirrlees, J. A., 1971, 'An exploration in the theory of optimum income taxation', *Review of Economic Studies*, 38, 175–208.

Mitchell, O., 1998, 'Administrative costs in public and private retirement systems', in M. Feldstein (ed.), *Privatising Social Security*, Chicago: University of Chicago Press.

Musgrave, R. A., 1959, *The Theory of Public Finance*, New York: McGraw-Hill.

Persson, T. and Tabellini, G., 2000, *Political Economics: Explaining Economic Policy*, Cambridge, Mass: MIT Press.

Pestieau, P., 1994, 'Social protection and private insurance: reassessing the role of public versus private sector in insurance', *The Geneva Papers on Risk and Insurance Theory*, 19, 81–92.

Petretto, A., 1999, 'Optimal social health insurance with supplementary private insurance', *Journal of Health Economics*, 18, 727–45.

Phelps, C. E., 1992, *Health Economics*, New York: HarperCollins.

Rochet, J.-Ch., 1991, 'Incentives, redistribution and social insurance', *The Geneva Papers on Risk and Insurance Theory*, 16, 143–66.

Sandmo, A., 1991, 'Economists and the welfare state', *European Economic Review*, 35, 213–39.

Sandmo, A., 1995, 'Introduction: the welfare economics of the welfare state', *Scandinavian Journal of Economics*, 97, 469–76.

Stiglitz, J., 1983a, 'Risk, incentive and insurance', *The Geneva Papers on Risk and Insurance Theory*, 8, 4–33.

Stiglitz, J. 1983b, 'On the social insurance: comments on "The state and the demand for security in contemporary societies" ', *The Geneva Papers on Risk and Insurance Theory*, 8, 105–10.

Storesletten, K., Telmer, Ch. and Yorn, A., 2000, 'The welfare cost of business cycles revisited: finite lives and cyclical variations in idiosyncratic risk', NBER working paper No. 8040.

11 Assessing the effect of introducing welfare accounts in Sweden

Stefan Fölster, Robert Gidehag, Mike Orszag and Dennis J. Snower[1]

11.1 Introduction

Sweden recently implemented a pension reform that includes a system of individual accounts giving individuals substantial flexibility in their choice of investments. At the same time, other Swedish social insurance systems such as unemployment insurance, sickness benefits and parental leave have remained unchanged. Like numerous other OECD countries, Sweden faces a serious challenge in welfare policy-making. Existing welfare benefits are associated with substantial market distortions and create disincentives to work.

This chapter examines the possible effects of introducing a large-scale welfare reform in Sweden, namely, the introduction of comprehensive welfare accounts. Under this policy, individuals make mandatory contributions to accounts, which they can top up with voluntary contributions. In return, individuals' welfare benefits are paid from their accounts. Moving from the traditional tax-financed welfare systems to a welfare account-based system involves replacing general taxes by mandatory saving to finance the requisite welfare benefits. The welfare accounts are hence like ordinary savings accounts with two key exceptions. First, to avoid problems of moral hazard, there are restrictions on withdrawals from the welfare accounts. And second, the welfare accounts also serve a redistributive function, so that individuals receive specific minimum welfare benefits regardless of how low their account balances may be.[2] Such accounts are in place on a comprehensive basis in Singapore, and for specific benefits such as unemployment, health and education in the US, Chile and Brazil.

---

[1] Any opinions in this chapter are of the authors alone and do not necessarily represent those of their employers.

[2] The welfare accounts would hence operate somewhat like the new Swedish premium pension accounts but would apply to benefits more generally.

In order to motivate the introduction of welfare accounts,[3] we note that social insurance programmes involve a combination of savings, insurance and redistribution. In traditional social insurance programmes, this combination is often far from transparent to the average consumer (or anyone else, for that matter!). The Swedish welfare system is a case in point. Individuals receive a panoply of benefits but neither the cost of each nor the degree of cross-subsidy is transparent. Even the new Premium Pension system is not entirely transparent on how movements in mortality are smoothed into changes in retirement benefits.

In addition to lack of transparency, another problem with traditional welfare systems is lack of flexibility. Whereas private compensation and benefit arrangements have moved increasingly towards benefits that are responsive to individuals' personal circumstances, public welfare benefits remain relatively rigid in this regard.

The lack of transparency and flexibility in the traditional welfare systems has adverse incentive effects, since individuals do not have to bear the consequences of their own actions. If an individual claims insurance, it does not affect his or her subsequent contribution rates. The costs of claiming social insurance are thus not internalised and as a result have excessive incentives to claim social benefits.

Yet another major problem is that the benefits provided by traditional welfare systems are devoted, in large part, to redistribution across individuals' life cycles, rather than to promoting income equality or providing insurance against adverse economic circumstances in a lifetime perspective. We will argue that life-cycle redistribution – enabling income smoothing over an individual's lifetime – can be performed more efficiently through comprehensive welfare accounts than through traditional welfare benefits. A major insight in recent economic research is that lifetime income tends to be much more equally distributed than income in any particular year. An OECD study on income mobility, for example, indicates that the majority of individuals in the lowest income quintile in 1986 had moved up five years later (Sawyer, 1997). In fact, one in five had moved up at least two quintiles. A Swedish study (Hussénius and Selén, 1994) that estimated income distributions over the entire life cycle concluded that the lowest quintile only had 31 per cent lower lifetime income than the highest quintile, while annual incomes were four times higher in the highest quintile than in the lowest.

Studies from several welfare states indicate that as little as 20–25 per cent of social transfers may actually redistribute between individuals,

---

[3] Theoretical analyses of welfare accounts are presented in Fölster and Trofimov (1999); Orszag and Snower (1997), and Orszag et al. (1999).

while the remaining 75–80 per cent merely smooths income over the individual's life cycle (Hussénius and Selén, 1994; Fölster, 1998). The taxes that need to be levied to finance these transfers inevitably distort economic incentives, reducing the incentive to work, save and invest. In addition, the tax and transfer systems are run by costly bureaucracies. Thus, there could be substantial efficiency gains from a reform that focuses public welfare provision on the 20–25 per cent of current expenditure devoted to the achievement of interpersonal redistribution and social insurance against adverse economic circumstances with significant lifetime income implications.

In order to enable individuals to use their welfare accounts to perform life-cycle redistribution, the government must permit them to have negative balances on their welfare accounts during their working lifetimes, thereby enabling them to shift purchasing power through time. In accordance with the government redistributive objectives, people with negative account balances at the end of their working lives are eligible for public support. For those people, the incentives to work and save will inevitably be impaired, but – as we will see below – they may be expected to be small in number in comparison with those who have negative account balances in any particular year. Since lifetime incomes are distributed more equally than annual incomes, as noted, welfare accounts tend to impair incentives of far fewer people than do the traditional tax-based systems.

When the welfare state was first introduced, family structures were more uniform, benefits were more basic and technology was simpler. In such a setting it was both unnecessary to have differentiated benefits and technologically not possible. Flexible benefits and transparency requires good and transparent information technology. While it would have been inconceivable to implement a transparent, flexible benefits policy in the inter-war period or even in the 1950s and 1960s, it is technologically possible today.

In short, welfare accounts promise a number of significant advantages over the traditional welfare systems. In particular, by permitting the government to focus on interpersonal redistribution and social insurance against economic circumstances with significant lifetime income implications, the reform may allow substantial reductions in taxes and thereby improve people's incentives to work, save and invest. Furthermore, by helping people internalise the social cost of their welfare expenditures, welfare accounts discourage people from making excessive welfare claims. In so doing, welfare accounts also improve people's incentive to work.

This chapter uses a large panel of individual income data to examine how the adoption of universal welfare accounts may affect economic

Table 11.1 *Welfare accounts versus tax-financed benefits in the absence of redistribution (under flat-rate guaranteed minimum income)*

People	1	2
A	y	0
B	0	y
Tax rates	t_{TB}	t_{AB}
	β	0

activity. We find that this policy could be designed so as to reduce social insurance expenditure considerably, improve the incentives to work and save, all with relatively small redistributive impact. Our simulations indicate that when the redistribution among welfare account balances is sufficient to ensure that people receive at least as much as under the current system, the move to universal welfare accounts is associated with substantial reduction in taxes, rises in after-tax incomes, and improvements in work incentives.

11.2   Simple examples

It is useful to illustrate the effects of moving from tax-financed welfare benefits to individual welfare accounts with a sequence of simple examples. The data for the first are given in table 11.1. In each period of analysis, there are equal numbers of individuals of two types who live for just two periods. Individual type A has income y in the first period and zero income in the second, whereas individual type B has zero income in the first period and income y in the second. Within each period their incomes are therefore characterised by a high degree of inequality. Observe, however, that lifetime income is equally distributed, if we ignore time discounting.

Suppose that the government specifies that when income drops to zero, the person is entitled to a benefit of βy. We assume, plausibly, that $\beta < \frac{1}{2}$, i.e., the replacement ratio is less that half of the income of the richest individual. A conventional tax-financed welfare system requires that the per-period benefit βy be financed through taxes on the income earners. Thus the government's budget constraint is $\beta y = t_{TB} y$, where t_{TB} is the tax rate under the 'tax-based' (TB) welfare system. Thus the tax rate is $t_{TB} = \beta$.

In an account-based social insurance system, individuals use their welfare accounts to shift income between periods. Individual A saves in the

Table 11.2 *Welfare accounts versus tax-financed benefits with redistribution (under flat-rate guaranteed minimum income)*

People	1	2
A	y	0
B	0	θy
Tax rates	t_{TB}	t_{AB}
	$2\beta/(1+\theta)$	$2\beta - \theta$

first period and withdraws money in the second; whereas individual B borrows in the first period and repays in the second.[4] Since lifetime incomes are equal across the two individuals, the tax rate t_{AB} under the account-based system (where subscript AB stands for 'account-based') is zero. The core reason that accounts could improve economic outcomes is that this lower tax rate provides better incentives for all to work.

Next consider a second example, in which the individual's lifetime incomes are not equal. Here the redistributive function of welfare accounts comes into play. In particular, individual A once again has income y in the first period and zero income in the second, but individual B now has zero income in the first period and income θy in the second. Thus, whereas the lifetime income of A is y, that of B is θy.

Under the tax-based welfare system, the tax rate t_{TB} is imposed on the incomes y and θy to pay for the welfare benefit β per person per period. Thus the government budget constraint is $t_{TB}(y + \theta y) = 2\beta y$. Thus the tax rate is $t_{TB} = 2\beta/(1 + \theta)$.[5]

Under the account-based welfare system, by contrast, the redistribution is over lifetime incomes rather than per-period incomes. The lifetime income of individual A is y, and that of individual B is θy. We have supposed that guaranteed minimum income is βy; and thus the guaranteed minimum lifetime income is $2\beta y$. If $2\beta y < \theta y$ (i.e. the guaranteed minimum lifetime income is less than the lifetime income of the poorer individual), then the tax rate t_{AB} under the account-based system is zero. On the other hand, if $2\beta y > \theta y$ (i.e. the guaranteed minimum lifetime income is greater than the lifetime income of the poorer individual), then

---

[4] In this particular example shifting income over time could of course be achieved in a private capital market. As soon as there is some redistribution, however, there has to be some government involvement in administration of welfare accounts.

[5] We assume here that the government can borrow or invest in international capital markets between periods. Alternatively one can think of the example as representing an overlapping generations structure. In period 1, there are two As, one in the first and one in the second period of his life. Similarly, there are two Bs. This will then balance the government budget in each period.

Table 11.3 *Welfare accounts versus tax-financed benefits under stochastic incomes and flat-rate guaranteed minimum income*

People	Expected income	
A	$(1 - u)y$	
B	$(1 - u)\theta y$	
Tax rates	t_{TB}	t_{AB}
	$2(u/(1 - u)\,(\beta/(1 + \theta)$	$(\beta/(1 - u)) - \theta$

the tax rate on the richer individual must be such as to cover the difference between the guaranteed minimum lifetime income and the actual lifetime income of the poorer individual. Thus, the tax rate t_{AB} fulfils the following government budget constraint: $t_{AB}y = 2\beta y - \theta y$. Thus the account-based tax rate is $t_{AB} = 2\beta - \theta$.

Observe that $t_{AB} < t_{TB}$, since $2\beta - \theta < 2\beta/(1 + \theta)$ is implied by $\beta < (1 + \theta)/2$, which holds since $\beta < \frac{1}{2}$.

Whereas the two examples above have been deterministic, our last example concerns risky income streams. Suppose that the individuals A and B both face the probability u of being unemployed and receiving zero income – in the absence of government intervention – and the probability $1 - u$ of being employed. If employed, individual A receives income y and individual B receives income θy. Suppose that both individuals live sufficiently long so that their average per-period incomes can be closely approximated by their mean incomes. Then the expected per-period income of individual A is $(1 - u)y$, and that of individual B is $(1 - u)\theta y$.

Under the traditional tax-based welfare system, the average tax receipts per period are $t_{TB}(y + \theta y)\,(1 - u)$ and the average transfers per period are $\beta y u$ (where βy is the minimum guaranteed income per period). Thus the government budget constraint is $t_{TB}(y + \theta y)\,(1 - u) = 2\beta y u$. The associated tax rate is $t_{TB} = 2(u/(1 - u)\,(\beta/(1 + \theta))$.

Under the account-based system, the tax receipts from the richer individual, $t_{AB}(1 - u)y$, are used to finance the difference between the minimum guaranteed income (βy) and the expected income of the poorer individual $((1 - u)\theta y)$, provided that the former is greater than the latter (i.e. $\beta > ((1 - u)\theta)$. Moreover, we assume – plausibly – that $\beta < \theta$, i.e. the minimum guaranteed income is less than the income earned by the poorer individual when employed. Thus the associated government budget constraint is $t_{AB}(1 - u)y = \beta y - (1 - u)\theta y$, and the tax rate therefore is $t_{AB} = (\beta/(1 - u)) - \theta$.

Once again, the tax rate under the account-based system is less than that under the tax-based system. To see this, note that $t_{AB} < t_{TB}$ implies that $= (\beta/(1 - u)) - \theta < 2(u/(1 - u)) (\beta/(1 + \theta))$, which in turn implies that $\Omega = (\beta/(1 - u)) (1 - 2u/(1 + \theta)) < \theta$. Observe that $d\Omega/du < 0$, so that Ω attains its maximum when $u = 0$. This maximum value of Ω is β, which is less than θ.

It is important to note that, although the move from a tax-based to an account-based welfare system may improve the trade-off between equality and incentives, it certainly does not eliminate it. The more an account-based system attempts to equalise lifetime incomes across individuals, the weaker will be the relation between a person's productivity and income and thus the lower the incentive to be productive. In the previous example, for instance, the tax rates $t_{TB} = 2(u/(1 - u)) (\beta/(1 + \theta))$ and $t_{AB} = (\beta/(1 - u)) - \theta$ both rise with β. Moreover, for plausible unemployment rates (e.g. $u < \frac{1}{2}$), the tax rate under the account-based system rises faster than that under the tax-based system, so that the relative tax advantage of welfare accounts is eroded.

Furthermore, it needs to be emphasised that welfare accounts are not meant to be a substitute for insurance against risks. The point is rather that some risks are more effectively insured in a lifetime perspective than on a day by day basis.[6]

Yet welfare accounts have a number of important problems. Their increased transparency may lead to calls for less redistribution, thereby harming those less well off. Where individuals have more choice and flexibility, there could be additional selection effects from accounts, raising the cost of provision. Finally, despite advances in modern technology, accounts may be more expensive to administer than traditional social welfare systems. In practice, the size of these costs depends heavily on the detailed provisions determining the way in which the welfare account reform is to be implemented.

11.3   Application to Sweden

Our analysis focuses on a comprehensive reform of the entire Swedish social insurance system. The components of the welfare system we replace with welfare accounts are listed in table 11.4 below. In all, the reform we examine involves roughly 21 per cent of Swedish GDP of which slightly less than half is non-pension benefits.

For our analysis, we used LINDA, a longitudinal Swedish data set containing information on 300,000 individuals and members of their households. The sample of individuals is representative for the population during the period 1960 to 1996. The core of the data are the income

[6] Also, a welfare account still allows the government to target expenditure on health insurance by regulating which types of expenditure the account can be used for.

Table 11.4 *Benefits and public services encompassed by our analysis* [1]

Benefit	% of GDP
Unemployment benefit [2]	3.7
Parental leave	1.5
Sick benefit	1.3
Child benefit	1.2
Welfare	0.93
Housing	0.62
Pensions	12.2

[1] Not counting public costs of insuring the account.
[2] Includes benefits for training during unemployment (AMU).

registers (Inkomst-och Förmögenhetsstatistiken) available annually from 1968 to 1996, and population census data available every fifth year from 1960 to 1990. For each year information on all family members of the sampled individuals are added to the data set, but they are included only for as long as they stay in the family.

While LINDA primarily consists of a panel, the sample outflow has been matched by a representative inflow, so that the included individuals are both longitudinally and cross-sectionally representative of the population. Of the 300,000 individuals available each year, about 100,000 are in the sample over the entire period from 1968 to 1996.

Since we have such rich historical data on welfare benefits, most of our analysis is retrospective, assuming that welfare reform was actually implemented in 1978 and imputing how accounts would have worked. We also implemented a model which projects costs forward.

We assume that accounts are implemented for individuals up to the age of forty-five in 1978. In the initial year individuals start with an account balance that roughly matches what they would have had if the account had been in existence all along. The initial deposit is calculated as a function of the average amount accumulated per person and year multiplied by the number of years that the individual exceeds eighteen years of age. The average account accumulation is calculated by simple linear regression. [7]

[7] Using a panel with every individual's account balance during each of the nineteen years in the panel a simple OLS regression was run:

$$\text{Balance} = \beta^* \text{ (number of years in working life)} + \varepsilon$$

In this regression, β is 52,000 kronor and significant. This means that the average account balance is accumulated at a rate of 52,000 kronor per year the individual is working. Based on this information we have calculated an imputed value on the account 1978 for each individual in our database.

This procedure resembles the type of transition rules often used when savings-based social insurance replaces a conventional system.

There were a number of practical problems in doing the analysis. In particular, the sample cannot be used in the same form over the entire period, as the data become richer over time. From 1968 there is annual information on income, but some components of income, such as social assistance, are shown separately first after 1977. For most of the analysis described below we therefore focus on the period 1978–96, and on the group of people who were eighteen to thirty-four years old in 1978. They were thirty-six to fifty-two years old in 1996.

The following variables are central to the analysis:
- wage income before taxes (Y)
- taxable government transfers before taxes (B)
- income taxes (T) paid on wage income and on taxable government transfers, and
- non-taxable government transfers, such as social assistance (A).

All economic variables are stated relative to GDP. We further use the long-run equilibrium assumption that the return on accounts is equal to the growth of GDP. The reason for this is that with perfect capital markets, this should be the rate of return both on funded accounts and pay as you go accounts.

Disposable income for individual i during year t is

$$I_{i,t} = Y_{i,t} + B_{i,t} - T_{i,t} + A_{i,t} \tag{11.1}$$

The basic system we examine as an alternative to the current tax system requires each individual to save a fraction of his or her wage income in a welfare account. For simplicity, it is assumed that payments into the account replace current social insurance fees (equal to employers' taxes).[8] These have fluctuated between 27 and 39 per cent. We use the actual rate that applies each year, denoted σ_t. To be precise, the payments into the welfare account $T_{i,t}^a = \sigma_t Y_{i,t}$, and withdrawals from the account equal $W_{i,t} = B_{i,t} + A_{i,t}$. As noted above, the withdrawal $B_{i,t}$ is taxed as in the current system, and these taxes are included in $T_{i,t}$. The balance on the account $(b_{i,t}^a)$ in units of current real per capita GDP then develops as

$$b_{i,t}^a = b_{i,t-1}^a + T_{i,t}^a - W_{i,t} \tag{11.2}$$

In this most simple version of the welfare account, the disposable income under the account system equals disposable income under the current income up until retirement. The difference between contributions and

[8] Sweden did not have employees' contributions during the sample period. Otherwise, they would have been included here as well.

withdrawals lies in the accumulation of assets on the account. Since the accumulation on the account provides retirement income it is then necessary to compare the balance on the account with the individuals' implicit wealth provided in the current pension system, $P_{i,t}$. This is calculated as the expected present value of retirement benefits.

If the funds in the account are not sufficient to pay the benefit, the government lends the necessary amount to the individual account. The account system in aggregate is calibrated, however, to ensure that the government's budget is balanced. To calibrate this we have simply calculated the public sector costs, during the entire period we examine (1978–96), of the welfare systems within the account system. This cost is then compared with the tax cut (whole period) the account reform implies. The money the public sector gains in the years 1978–96 from not handling the welfare systems in the account system very well balance the income loss from the tax cut of social insurance fees in the similar period. At retirement age the funds in the account would be converted into an annuity that supplements pension income.

In initial calculations we show how the individual is affected by introducing an account that has no insurance elements at all. We do not believe this to be politically feasible or desirable, but it helps to illustrate how the account system works. It also allows a calculation of how much redistribution the tax-financed system actually has achieved. In later steps a number of insurance elements are introduced. First, the government guarantees a minimum pension to those that retire with insufficient balances. Second, more generous redistribution is considered.

We assume that total payments into the account and withdrawals from the account match, so that no fiscal deficit arises. All current employer and individual social insurance taxes are hence deposited in the individual accounts and the accounts are used to finance all household transfers including pensions. Because the contributions replace taxes, we follow the convention that there is no tax arising from the contributions. This mirrors the fact that in most pension account systems contributions are not taxed, but withdrawals are.

The budget constraint requires that $\Sigma_{i,t}G_{i,t} = \Sigma_{i,t}(B_{i,t} + A_{i,t})$ where again $G_{i,t}$ is government expenditure on transfers which is composed of non-taxable transfers, and A and B are the taxed withdrawals from the account. Over the period 1978–96 transfers to households averaged 14.3 per cent (net of income taxes, 20.4 per cent before income taxes) of GDP, while employer tax revenue averaged 14.1 per cent of GDP.

The feasibility of welfare accounts depends on the extent to which insured events are concentrated in a sub-group of the population. In the extreme, if one group of individuals never earned any wage income and lived entirely off social insurance, while all others never required transfers, then the use of a welfare account would be irrelevant. Those who collect benefits would live entirely on the government guarantee. This is a potentially serious problem that could make accounts unworkable. Therefore it is important to assess the extent to which current benefits are paid to people who would end up with a negative account balance. It is important to note in this context that, under the proposed system of universal welfare accounts, people would be allowed to run negative welfare account balances during their working lives. This possibility would not pose a budgetary problem for the government, provided that in aggregate the welfare accounts do not run into deficit on this account.

To examine how many people might end up with negative account balances, we consider the following experiment. We credit accounts with what were previous employer contributions and debit accounts with individual-specific social insurance expenditure.[9] We show the results in table 11.5 which shows the average account balance ($b_{i,t=1996}$ as defined earlier) for all individuals in each decile, where the deciles are based on the account balance at the end of our period divided into deciles.

Table 11.6 shows the same same exercise for guaranteed accounts. The previous experiment has the drawback that it does not include guarantees on account balances so that individuals could conceivably end up with negative account balances and hence might not be able to finance crucial social insurance expenditure. Here, we consider an account system with a guarantee fund financed out of payroll taxes. The tax provides the same guarantee as the current system, that is, those people who under the current system are subsidised are guaranteed the same pension that they would have received under the current system. This subsidy is given to about 30 per cent of all people.

The tax rate out of compulsory contributions necessary to finance the guarantee in our sample of individuals turns out to be 13.08 per cent of payroll. This should be compared to the current rate of 33 per cent (of which 27.4 per cent should be considered non-actuarial, see section 11.4).

Tables 11.5 and 11.6 also show the total income accumulated over the nineteen years in the account system and in the current system. In the account system the total income is the sum of individuals' disposable income and the accrued account balance. In the current system the comparable measure is the sum of disposable income and accrued pension rights.[10]

---

[9] As previously noted, we credit balances in 1978 based on imputed rights. Therefore, this analysis is that of a steady state with fully implemented accounts rather than the effects of accounts starting from scratch.

[10] The accrued pension right is calculated according to the rules in the old pension system (ATP-system) since these are the rules that are relevant for the age group in our sample. In addition, drawing rights upon early retirement and sickness benefits have been considered, based on expected values of these benefits for each age and income level.

Table 11.5 *Account balance in 1996 assuming no insurance provided,*
average balance per decile, Swedish kronor

Decile	Disposable income during working life	Account balance 1996	Sum of disposable income and account balance in the account system	Sum of disposable income and accrued pension rights in the current system
1	2,702,452	−1,067,704	1,099,964	4,359,943
2	2,365,740	225,505	2,704,194	3,974,105
3	2,323,020	832,684	3,572,773	4,068,686
4	2,440,630	1,228,168	4,283,955	4,389,799
5	2,595,759	1,553,069	4,926,719	4,734,779
6	2,858,347	1,840,225	5,620,292	5,820,186
7	3,132,159	2,130,045	6,329,087	5,850,476
8	3,380,445	2,464,883	7,079,922	6,444,781
9	3,813,998	2,924,685	8,203,579	7,015,070
10	4,939,076	4,069,698	11,047,177	8,206,156

Note: The decile partition is computed based on account balances. As can be seen
disposable income during working life is not perfectly correlated with final account
balances.

Table 11.6 *Account balance in 1996 assuming guaranteed accounts, average*
balance per decile, Swedish kronor. Under guaranteed accounts the same
pension as in the current system is guaranteed to the 30 per cent of people
whose pensions are subsidised in the current system

Decile	Disposable income during 1978–96	Account balance 1996	Sum of disposable income and account balance in the account system	Sum of disposable income and accrued pension rights in the current system
1	2,702,452	1,657,491	4,359,943	4,359,943
2	2,365,740	1,657,491	4,023,231	3,974,105
3	2,323,020	1,657,491	3,980,511	4,068,686
4	2,440,630	1,757,491	4,198,121	4,389,799
5	2,595,759	1,979,451	4,575,210	4,734,779
6	2,858,347	2,778,565	5,636,912	5,820,186
7	3,132,159	2,714,831	5,846,990	5,850,476
8	3,380,445	3,141,596	6,522,041	6,444,781
9	3,813,998	3,727,632	7,541,630	7,015,070
10	4,939,076	4,040,102	8,979,178	8,206,156

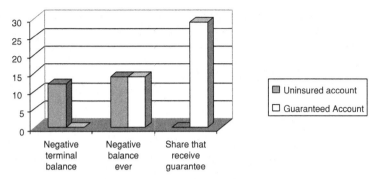

Figure 11.1 Share of individuals with negative terminal balances, negative balances ever, and share of individuals that receive compensation in the guaranteed system

Figure 11.1 shows some summary statistics for the sample. The number of people ending up with negative balances is about 12 per cent. This can be contrasted with Feldstein and Altman's (1998) analysis of an unemployment savings account using the Panel Study of Income Dynamics in the USA. They find that 5 per cent would retire or die with negative balances. One important difference is that in their study all people initially included in the sample work. In our sample, in contrast, all people who due to various disabilities never work are included. Another important difference is, of course, that the account here has a wider scope.

Due to the initial deposit on the account most people that have drawn down their account so much that they have negative balances in any year of the period are people with long-term income losses and tend also to have negative balances at the end of the period. If the initial deposit is excluded, however, a large group of people (34 per cent) have negative balances at some point over the period, but many (13.5 per cent) recover and end up with positive balances.

Turning now to the distributional consequences of the account system, table 11.7 shows how total income including accrued pension rights are affected by a switch to the account system. As expected, the distributional consequences are considerable as long as no insurance element is added. Interestingly, however, the sum of individual losses is only a small fraction (18 per cent) of the total employer's tax collected over the period. This supports the argument made above, that only a small share of taxes is actually needed to redistribute between individuals in a lifetime perspective. The figure indicates the level of balances with guarantees as a function of income deciles. The LINDA data set as a historical data set encompasses an ageing population and therefore the positive gains need to be offset by

Table 11.7 *Share of individuals that move up or down lifetime disposable income deciles when an account system is introduced (%)*

Income decile in current system	Move down 3 deciles	Move down 2 deciles	Move down 1 decile	Unchanged	Move up 1 decile	Move up 2 deciles	Move up 3 deciles
1–5 decile	0	2	4	81	9	3	1
6–10 decile	1	2	7	84	4	2	0
All deciles	1	2	6	82	6	3	0

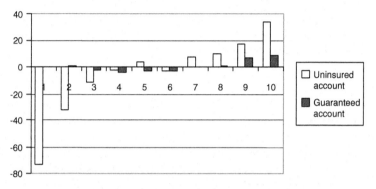

Figure 11.2 The change in lifetime disposable income when moving to either an uninsured or a guaranteed account system, percentage change

the costs of future liabilities of social expenditure for an ageing population. We did the offset for pensions but not for other social insurance benefits because of the complexity of forecasting age-dependent social insurance benefits into the future. The bottom line is that redistribution based on wealth levels can be much cheaper to finance than the current system of redistribution based on period by period income.

The distributional effects of the uninsured and guaranteed account systems are also illustrated in figure 11.2.

Thus far we have focused on calculations for income deciles. This gives a good picture of how the overall distribution of incomes changes. But probably even more important is how individuals are affected. Does the switch of social insurance system cause great upheaval in the sense that many people move to other income deciles? Do such moves reflect poor insurance or other factors? These questions turn out to be quite difficult conceptually. Table 11.7 shows how individuals' lifetime disposable income is affected by a switch from the current system to an account system. The table shows how many individuals move up or down.

This table, however, does not settle the issue of whether individual changes are motivated. In the current system insurance has a considerable arbitrary element. A person on parental leave while receiving a high wage will also receive high parental leave compensation. A similar person who has a child while studying receives no compensation – even though this may delay his career and thus cause an income loss as large as the first person's. Similarly, a person who is disabled while working may be fully compensated, while a person who is disabled just a few months before she starts working, receives nothing or only welfare benefits.[11]

In the account system, insurance is less arbitrary. On the other hand, high-income earners tend to be less well insured in the sense that a person who has accumulated a large balance on the account and then is disabled or unemployed for long periods, will lose much of the accumulated balance.

As mentioned above, the panel data cannot be used directly to calculate marginal tax effects of introducing welfare accounts. In a companion paper, however, these have been calculated in a simulated panel of individual life cycles.[12] On average, it was shown that marginal effects of taxes and transfers fall from 74 per cent to 61 per cent. In the next section we turn to some macroeconomic effects of introducing welfare accounts.

11.4 Simulations of macroeconomic effects

This section addresses two macroeconomic effects of introducing welfare accounts. The first concerns the question of how sensitive public finances are in the account system to changes in unemployment and retirement age. The second concerns the effect of a reduction in marginal tax effects that an account system may induce. In order to do this, a simple forecasting model is used to assess likely effects of introducing universal welfare accounts in Sweden.

We consider a population of individuals represented by exogenous characteristics θ_t. We represent the level of claims for benefits for an individual by the function:

$$y_t = f(\bar{y}_t, y_{t-k}, \theta_t, X_t, P_t, t; \beta)$$

which depends on macroeconomic characteristics X_t, policy characteristics P_t, as well as other types of benefits $\bar{y}_t$ and lagged benefits. We estimate this relation by panel regression analysis from the LINDA sample.

---

[11] Many of these problems would arise also with an optimal private insurance.
[12] In that paper (Fölster, 2001) it is also carefully shown that the simulated panel of complete life cycles matches actual panel data well where they can be compared.

Our estimates $\hat{y}_t$ are then used to construct aggregate benefit expenditure by a weighted sum over the number of individuals with characteristics θ_j

$$\hat{y}_t = \sum_{j=1}^{N} w_j(\theta_j) \times f(\bar{y}_{j,t}, y_{j,t-k}, \theta_j, X_t, P_t, t; \hat{\beta}) \qquad (11.3)$$

where N is the number of individuals in the original sample.

The parameters of (11.3) are estimated in the form of two regressions using the LINDA panel data. The dependent variables are the market income ($I_{i,t}$) and the withdrawals ($Y_{i,t}$) as a function of the variables described above. Benefits include unemployment benefits, social assistance, sickness benefits, early retirement benefits and others. The following variables are used in the panel: Withdrawals from the individual welfare account ($Y_{t,i}$), Labour market income ($I_{t,i}$), Age ($AGE_{t,i}$), sex ($SEX_{t,i}$ $0 =$ man, $1 =$ woman), Level of unemployment in percent of the labour force ($UNEMP_t$). All variables are adjusted for inflation and GDP growth. The panel consists of 7,120 individuals over nineteen years. In detail the regression equations are:

$$W_{it} = CONSTANT + \beta W_{it-1} + \chi(SEX_{it}) + \alpha(AGE_{it})$$
$$+ \delta(UNEMP) + \varepsilon. \qquad (11.4)$$
$$I_{it} = CONSTANT + \beta I_{it-1} + \chi(SEX_{it}) + \alpha(AGE_{it})$$
$$+ \delta(UNEMP) + \varepsilon. \qquad (11.5)$$

where UNEMP is unemployment measured as total unemployment as percentage of the working force in period t, W is the withdrawal and Y is the market income. The results are as in the table 11.8 below.

In order to calculate projections moving forward, the estimates in Eq. 11.3 and assumed or calculated values of X_t and P_t and future demographics (which enter into θ_j) are substituted into the estimated relationship to calculate the next year's values. Eq. 11.3 is then applied with updated weights to reflect the different distribution of exogenous characteristics in the subsequent year.

We then use these results to simulate.[13] Note that in the panel we have 7,120 individuals in nineteen years who are between eighteen and sixty-four years. Therefore this regression should be a good base for a simulation of the withdrawals and payments into the account during an average working life. We simulate a period of forty-five years (between eighteen and sixty-four years of age).

[13] This exercise does not take account of the possibility that the switch to universal accounts may affect macroeconomic variables such as the unemployment rate. Such macroeconomic feedback effects are taken into account at the end of this section.

Table 11.8 *Results of the panel regression*

	Unstandardised coefficients		Standardised coefficients	
	B	Std. error	Beta	t
Dependent variable: aggregate withdrawals from accounts Y				
Constant	−9621.41	1135.90		−8.47
Y_{t-1}	0.47	0.00	0.52	210.53
SEX	6306.60	444.18	0.03	14.20
UNEMP	1175.09	66.29	0.05	17.73
AGE	406.47	27.93	0.04	14.55
R 0.53 Adi. F. Sa 0.28				
Dependent variable: market income I				
Constant	35113.3536	1034.120912		33.9547853
SEX	−9981.38	425.17	−0.03	−23.48
UNEMP	−622.27	58.53	−0.02	−10.63
AGE	−70.97	24.95	0.00	−2.84
II_{t-1}	0.89	0.00	0.88	615.92
R 0.89 Adi. R Sa 0.79				

We focus on the average person in the economy. If he or she has a surplus on the account, that is enough for a reasonable pension during the years of pension, at the end of the forty-five-year period – the system on the macro level is in balance. If the balance is not enough, or even negative, pensions will be lower. We also show the costs to the government in terms of percentage of GDP if the government wanted to guarantee the same average pension as the current system provides. One should keep in mind, however, that even the current system would probably be cut back or changed if life expectancy increased dramatically, or unemployment remained high over long periods of time.

We consider a policy reform in which the universal welfare account system incorporates redistribution, so that each person's pension level is at least as high as in the current system, in addition to ensuring that the account system is in fiscal balance. Thus the government has to pay money into the system when the average person's balance is not enough for the pension of the current system. In the empirical model above, we can test whether such government intervention is needed.

We find that the budgetary viability of the account system is very sensitive to swings in the unemployment rate. Consequently, it appears important that the switch from unemployment benefits to unemployment accounts be included in the adoption of welfare accounts. The reason is that this switch may be expected to improve significantly people's incentives to work. Under an unemployment benefit system, the workers are

Table 11.9 *Simulated increase in government costs for guarantees in the account system, and development of average pensions, as a function of changes in average unemployment, average age of persons in the working force, and reduced payments into the account*

Assumptions used in the simulations		Average annual pension, 1,000 kronor	Increase in government cost percentage of GDP
Unemployment	4%		
Average age	40	115	0
Unemployment	6%		
Average age	40	89	1.6
Unemployment	4%	99	0.96
Average age	45		
Lower payments into the account*		102	0.89
Unemployment	4%		
Average age	40		

* Payments into the account are assumed two percentage points of wages lower.

rewarded for losing their jobs (through the payment of the benefits) and penalised for gaining them (through the payment of income taxes).

Finally, we take macroeconomic behavioural feedbacks into account in several ways. For this purpose, we allow the level of payroll taxes to affect the employment rate.

We divide taxes into two notional categories: (i) the taxes necessary to finance the welfare benefits above, and (ii) the remainder, which we may classify as taxes that perform a redistributive function, in a broad sense of the term. We call these the 'benefit-financing taxes' and the 'redistributive taxes', respectively. In the guaranteed account system, the redistributive tax is reduced to 13.08 percentage points of payroll. In the current system, for example, the payroll tax is 33 per cent on top of income, but some 0–10 percentage points give rise to actuarially fair increases in expected benefits. The remaining 23–33 percentage points may be considered redistributive taxes. The exact figures vary with income levels. For example, people earning more than the maximum income compensated by social insurance face have no actuarial increase in benefits at the margin when they experience an income increase and pay higher payroll taxes. Currently about a third of all income earners earn more than the maximum compensated income in sickness benefits.

In our LINDA sample the average redistributive part of the payroll tax in 1996 was 27.4 per cent of payroll. A key question is then how

Table 11.10 *What could an account system imply for employment and payroll taxes?*

Elasticity of employment with respect to taxes	Increase in employment relative to current system	Payroll tax that balances public finances in the account system	Average redistributive share in current payroll tax
0	0	13.08	27.4
0.1	1.01	11.44	27.4
0.2	2.02	9.82	27.4

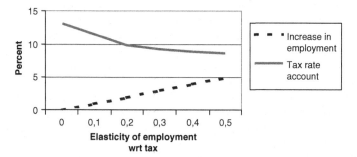

Figure 11.3 The consequences of introducing an account for the tax rate and employment with different elasticities of employment with respect to the total tax

this tax affects labour supply and demand. Since various studies come to somewhat different conclusions, we show the results for various values of the employment elasticity. In the following we define this elasticity as the percentage change in the rate of employment that results from a percentage change in total taxes on labour. The total tax on labour income is the sum of income taxes and the redistributive share of payroll taxes. Currently these average 52.1 per cent of gross labour income (before payroll taxes).

Finally, a key question is how a change in employment affects tax revenue and public expenditure. This is calculated using the same technique as described above to sensitivity of social insurance financing to unemployment. The results imply that in the current system an increase in employment by 1 per cent allows a reduction in the redistributive part of the payroll tax by 1.5 percentage points. Then table 11.10 describes how the move to an account system would affect employment and payroll taxes for different assumptions about the elasticity of employment with respect to taxes.

As the table indicates, even modest assumptions about the elasticity of employment with respect to the tax rate imply significant gains of moving to an account-based system in terms of increased employment and reduced taxation. These results are illustrated in figure 11.3.

11.5   Conclusions

This chapter has examined universal welfare accounts using Swedish data. We find that under fairly general assumptions, if accounts were introduced in Sweden, only a small number of individuals would have negative balances. Under the proposed reform, it is this small group that would be the beneficiary of the government's redistributive policy. Because accounts would allow redistribution based on wealth levels rather than period by period income, they would be cheaper to finance and hence the payroll tax burden on the economy would be lower.

We have developed a projection model to simulate the likely effect of accounts. If the unemployment rate remains the same as at present, then our results suggest that accounts would be associated with a considerably lowered tax burden.

Appendix A *Description of variables*

Variable	Acronym	Explanation
Taxable factor income	TBI	The sum of all income from employment, financial capital, real estate and firm ownership.
Taxable labour market income	MINK, AI	Income from employment and from taxed transfers.
Total tax	TSK	Total tax paid on taxable factor income and taxed tranfers.
Net income	Netink	Taxable factor income and taxed transfers minus total tax.
Disposable income	DISP	Netink plus non-taxed transfers.
Wealth	SF	All wealth that is subject to wealth tax.
Real estate tax	FSK	Tax on real estate.
Incomedecile	Inkdec	Individuals between 18 and 65 are divided into deciles according to their taxable factor income.
Incomecareer	$Inkdec_t -$ $Inkdec_{t-2}$	Calculated as the individual's income decile in year t minus her income decile in year $t - 2$.

References

Feldstein, M. and Altman, D., 1998, 'Unemployment insurance savings accounts', NBER working paper 6860.

Fölster, Stefan, 1997, 'Social insurance based on personal savings accounts: a possible reform strategy for overburdened welfare states?' *European Economy*, 4, 81–100.

—2001, 'An evaluation of social insurance savings accounts', *Public Finance and Management*, 1, 4.

Fölster, S. and Trofimov, G., 1999, 'Social insurance based on personal savings accounts: a theoretical analysis', working paper, the Swedish Research Institute of Trade, Stockholm.

Hussénius, J. and Selén, J., 1994, *Skatter och socialförsäkringar över livscykeln – en simuleringsmodell*. Expertgruppen för Studier i Offentlig Ekonomi, Stockholm, Ds 1994: 135.

Orszag, M. J., Orszag, P. R., Snower, D. J., and Stiglitz, J. E., 1999, 'The impact of individual accounts: piecemeal vs. comprehensive approaches', paper presented at the Annual Bank Conference on Development Economics. The World Bank.

Orszag, Michael, J. and Snower, Dennis, 1997, 'From unemployment benefits to unemployment accounts', Birckbeck College, London, mimeo, June 1997.

Sawyer, M., 1997, 'Income distribution in the OECD countries', *OECD Economic Outlook*.

12 Taxation in a global economy

Bernd Huber and Erik Norrman

12.1 Introduction

The intensifying economic integration among industrialised countries implies new terms for households, companies and governments. It is characterised by rapidly decreasing costs of information, integration of financial markets, lower costs for transportation and easier access to foreign markets by deregulation and abolishment of trade barriers. This increases the possibilities for individuals and firms to choose location of work, savings and investment. At the same time, national governments face restricted potentials to enforce taxation and raise enough revenue to finance increasing expenditure demands. Although the ambition to achieve free trade in a broad sense is advocated by most economists, the possibility of supplying public goods and of pursuing an egalitarian policy becomes more limited. In this setting, governments of small countries like Sweden, which may be characterised as having a tradition of high ambitions concerning the 'welfare state', must consider how to respond and adjust to the development. This chapter is intended to give some insight into the theoretical and empirical aspects of this debate.

12.2 Stylised facts on tax policy in Sweden and other countries

Since 1960, general government outlays have increased from 30 per cent of GDP to roughly 50 per cent on average in 1999 among OECD countries. In Sweden, this ratio has even more markedly increased from 32 per cent to 58.4 per cent. At least in the long run, the bulk of these expenditures has to be financed by taxes (and social security contributions which closely resemble taxes in many respects).

In most countries, the bulk of tax revenue comes from three sources: the taxation of consumption, labour income and capital income. Each type of taxation refers to a certain tax base. While there are considerable differences in tax rates and the overall structure of the tax system across countries, the pattern of tax bases is remarkably similar across countries

276

(see figure 12.1 and accompanying data). The consumption tax base accounts for roughly 45 per cent of the total tax base. Labour income is another 40 per cent, while the capital income tax base amounts to roughly 15 per cent of the total base. Figures 12.2–12.4 make clear that effective average tax rates on these tax bases vary considerably across countries, with Sweden, like the other Scandinavian countries, imposing above-average tax rates. In particular, Sweden has the highest effective tax rate on labour income.

However, this comparison provides a somewhat incomplete picture since taxes tend to interact. Most importantly, a tax on consumption also represents a tax on labour income since labour income is used to finance consumption expenditures. Calculating the total tax wedge on labour, i.e. the total tax burden on the average product of labour, the EU-wide average is roughly 48 per cent while, in Sweden, the tax wedge amounts to 62.5 per cent.[1] Thus, this more elaborate measure of the tax burden also identifies Sweden as a high tax country. However, one may also note that Sweden, like other Nordic countries, has undertaken radical tax reforms in the 1990s in which statutory tax rates have been considerably reduced.

One natural approach to understanding tax systems is to distinguish direct and indirect taxation. Roughly speaking, direct taxes, like income tax or corporate tax, are directly imposed, while indirect taxes, like VAT or specific commodity taxes are levied when goods and services are exchanged. In this chapter, for reasons of space we concentrate on the analysis of direct taxes. However, it should be clear that the system of indirect taxation also faces considerable challenges in the future. First, since taxes on goods and services represent to some extent (indirect) taxes on labour income, indirect taxes are subject to similar problems as labour income taxes. In addition, the common market within the EU poses particular difficulties for member countries to levy commodity taxes since consumers can exploit tax differences through cross-border shopping. The rise of the Internet will further aggravate these problems. EU countries like Sweden, which have traditionally imposed relatively high taxes, face particular pressures to reduce tax rates. It is illustrative that several Nordic countries have recently cut their alcohol taxes to reduce the extent of cross-border shopping.

12.3 Challenges for tax policy

The hybrid tax system

Historically, the income tax in most countries was built on the concept of comprehensive income taxation, which was pioneered by Schanz, Haig,

---

[1] European Commission (2000).

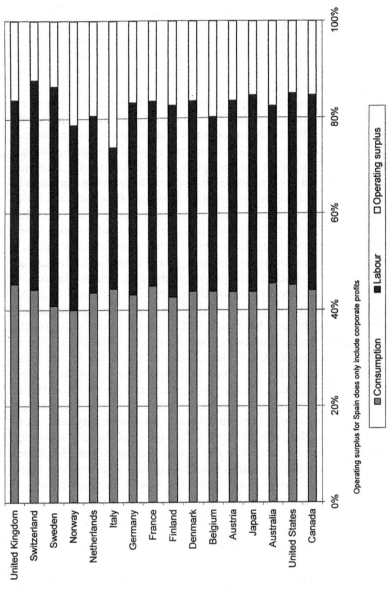

Figure 12.1 Tax bases in OECD countries (1996)
Source: OECD Revenue Statistics in Member Countries (1999).

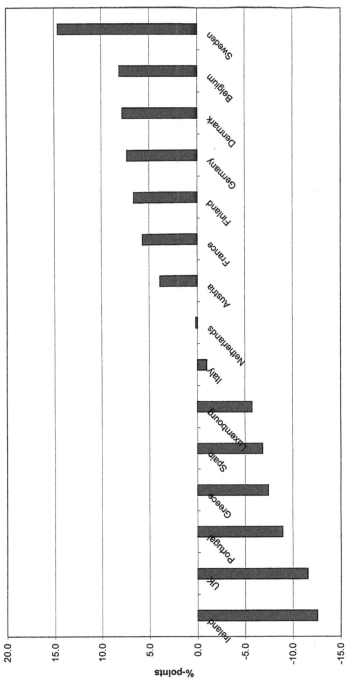

Figure 12.2 Deviation from average effective tax rate on labour (1999)
Source: European Economy EC Commission (2000).

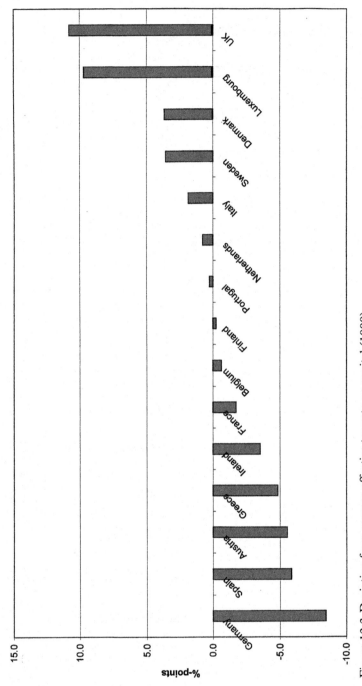

Figure 12.3 Deviation from average effective tax rate on capital (1999)
Source: European Economy EC Commission (2000).

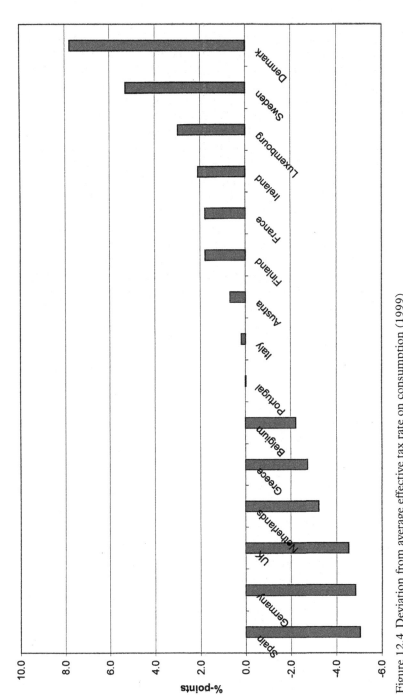

Figure 12.4 Deviation from average effective tax rate on consumption (1999)
Source: European Economy EC Commission (2000).

Simons and various other authors. Even today, the idea of a comprehensive income tax is still enormously influential and is often seen as an ideal for the design of income taxation.[2] The key principle of comprehensive taxation is that the total annual income of an individual, irrespective of whether it represents capital or labour income, is subject to the tax. In an idealised setting, total income is calculated on an accrual basis as the change in an individual's wealth, which comprises human and real capital. A comprehensive income tax is also often interpreted as taxation according to a taxpayer's ability to pay, which is measured by annual income.

In practice, most systems of income taxation differ in many respects from this ideal. In fact, the tax codes of most countries contain many elements of the alternative system of consumption taxation, which taxes the cash flows accruing to individuals and firms. It is, therefore, justified when current tax systems are sometimes denoted as hybrid.[3]

One of the key issues in tax policy in the future is that these hybrid tax systems face various challenges, which create pressures to reform. In what follows, we will first describe these challenges and then discuss how tax policy can respond to them.

Issues in tax policy

The current hybrid tax system is under pressure from various sides. To organise ideas, it is useful to distinguish three main types of challenges, which one may call

- tax distortions
- tax avoidance
- tax competition

Although our focus is on globalisation and tax competition issues, we start by discussing tax distortions and tax avoidance in brief.

Tax distortions

It is one of the key insights of public economics that taxes distort the behaviour and the economic decisions of the private sector and that these distortions may significantly reduce welfare and economic activity. The inefficiencies induced by a tax tend to increase in its tax rate.[4] However, the size of the welfare loss also depends on the extent to which the private sector changes its behaviour in response to taxation. If, for example, the

---

[2] See, e.g., Bradford (1986) and Gordon (2000) for a discussion of the concept of comprehensive income taxation.

[3] See Aaron, Galper and Pechman (1988).

[4] Using the simple approximation formula of the Harberger triangle, the welfare loss is proportional to the square of the tax rate.

interest elasticity of savings is high, it would imply that the taxation of savings induce relatively high welfare losses.

Unfortunately, there is often considerable disagreement about the size – and sometimes even the sign – of the elasticities of supply and demand. For example, estimates of the interest elasticity of savings range between 0 and 0.4.[5] Other studies, which estimate the intertemporal elasticity of substitution in consumption, also show considerable variation. Similarly, estimates of the compensated labour supply elasticity range from 0.1 up to 1.1 with the higher numbers for married women.[6]

Given these uncertainties, it is difficult to draw firm inferences about the effect of taxes on key economic variables like employment and capital formation. Therefore, it is also problematic to estimate the welfare losses induced by the tax system and, similarly, the potential welfare gains from tax reforms.

The distortionary impact of the tax system is not only relevant for the overall level of taxation, but also concerns the structure of the tax system. One particularly important issue is the tax treatment of capital income versus labour income.[7] Although it has attracted attention due to increasing capital flows between countries, the issue is important irrespective of globalisation.

A key principle of comprehensive income taxation is to tax capital income and labour income at the same rate. However, there has always been considerable controversy whether capital income should be taxed at all. For example, one well-known argument is that the taxation of capital income leads to a double taxation of labour income, since a wage earner who saves out of his after-tax labour income will then face an additional tax burden on these savings. A second argument for a zero capital income tax policy has been developed in a growth context.[8] The basic idea is that, in the long run, the capital income tax is effectively borne by other factors of production, for example by labour. Similarly, the theory of optimal income taxation also delivers strong arguments for a zero tax on capital income (at least in the long run).[9]

These results call for some kind of a consumption tax rather than a comprehensive tax.[10] The idea of consumption taxation has found many

---

[5] See Bernheim (1999) and Elmendorf (1996) for further details on the impact of taxes on savings behaviour.

[6] See Blomquist and Hansson Brusewitz (1990) for the assessment of labour supply elasticities on Swedish data.

[7] See Gordon (2000) and Keen (1997) for a recent survey on this debate.

[8] See Chamley (1986) and Judd (1985). Coleman (2000) provides a survey of this literature.

[9] See Mirrless (1971) and Stiglitz (1987) for further discussion.

[10] Even if one is not convinced by the arguments for a zero capital income tax, one should note that there is very little theoretical support for the view that, as under a comprehensive income tax, labour income and capital income should be taxed at the same rate.

supporters among economists and there exist various proposals of how consumption taxation can be implemented.[11] They all have in common that only labour income (and, possibly, initial wealth) is taxed while capital income is tax exempt, at the personal level. Such a tax system is effectively a tax on consumption since an individual's labour earnings over his lifetime equal his consumption in present value terms.[12] In addition, business income is taxed upon a cash flow basis. The key feature of a cash flow tax is that expenditures on investment can be deducted. The cash flow tax collects revenue on infra-marginal investment but does not distort the marginal investment decisions of firms.

Several studies have analysed the effects of a switch to a consumption tax.[13] While some authors find a considerably positive impact of consumption tax reform on investment and output, many of the results critically depend on assumptions about, for example, savings elasticities and the details of the reform like, for example, the tax treatment of old capital.

Tax avoidance

Tax avoidance represents another challenge for current and future tax policy. It can take several forms. First, there is the notorious problem of tax evasion. Estimates of the size of the shadow economy range between 10 per cent and 15 per cent of official GDP for many countries which implies a considerable reduction of tax bases. For a given amount of tax revenue, there are basically two alternatives to fight tax evasion.[14] First, tax authorities can try to step up their administrative efforts by increasing, for example, the probability of auditing.[15] In addition, governments may rely more strongly on those taxes which are less vulnerable to tax evasion. For example, the results in Gordon and Nielsen (1997) indicate that, in Denmark, the VAT dominates the labour income tax in terms of tax enforcement.

Other types of tax avoidance are the various legal and semi-legal forms of tax arbitrage. Tax arbitrage tries to take advantage of differences in the tax treatment of (i) different types of income or economic activities or

---

[11] An incomplete list would include, for example, Bradford (1986), Hall and Rabushka (1995) and Gentry and Hubbard (1998). In addition, there are several proposals to tax consumption directly (see, e.g., Kaldor, 1955 and Lodin, 1976).

[12] This simple argument ignores the initial wealth of individuals.

[13] See, e.g., Hubbard (1997) and Engen and Gale (1997) for a survey and further reference.

[14] In addition, the government can reduce tax rates (and its tax revenue) such that the marginal benefits from evading taxes decline.

[15] See Slemrod, Blumenthal and Christian (2001) for recent evidence on the effects of increased auditing.

of (ii) the entities through which income is received.[16] Many tax systems offer considerable opportunities for tax arbitrage. Some simple examples illustrate the scope of tax arbitrage possibilities. First, tax arbitrage can be used to reduce taxes on labour income. One strategy is to borrow and to buy low-taxed assets, for example, real estate. The interest on borrowing and depreciation allowances on the cost of the asset are then deducted from labour income such that highly taxed labour income is effectively transformed into lower taxed asset income. Another opportunity for reducing labour income taxes arises if the corporate tax rate is lower than the personal tax rate. Individuals may then try to reclassify their labour income as corporate income.[17] For example, owner-managers of closely held corporations would receive no or rather low salaries. Empirical evidence suggests that this type of tax arbitrage plays a significant role. For example, Agell and Persson (2000) report for Sweden that, in the 1980s, tax arbitrage has reduced the average tax rate on labour income by four percentage points. Gordon and Slemrod (1998) analyse the role of income shifting between personal and corporate tax bases and conclude that a 1 per cent reduction in the personal–corporate tax differential will raise reported labour income by about 3 per cent.

Capital income taxation is also affected by tax arbitrage. In this case, tax arbitrage exploits existing differences in the tax treatment of assets and differences in personal tax rates. According to Miller (1977), high tax investors will tend to hold lightly taxed assets while investors in low tax brackets will specialise in highly taxed investments such that each group maximises the benefits of its particular tax status. Further tax arbitrage opportunities open up if high tax investors borrow from low tax investors, such as pension funds, and invest these funds in tax-favoured assets.

Tax arbitrage of this sort seems to play an important role in many countries. In an influential paper, Gordon and Slemrod (1988) argue that, prior to the 1986 reform, the revenue from capital income taxation in the USA was approximately zero or even negative.[18] Sørensen (1988) reports similar results for Denmark. While the available data in Germany does not allow one to carry out a similar analysis as in Gordon and Slemrod (1988), the existing evidence tends to support their results for Germany as well. It turns out that, in 1992, the reported capital income (including income from rented real estate) in Germany amounted to

---

[16] See Scholes and Wolfson (1992) for a comprehensive discussion of the concept of tax arbitrage.

[17] See Gordon (1998). In order to reduce gains from income-shifting, Sweden has introduced special rules for closely held companies.

[18] Shoven (1991) confirms this result.

less than 1.2 per cent of GDP.[19] Similar results are found in Sweden (see below).

Tax competition

Tax competition represents a third challenge for tax policy. Much of the recent academic and political debate has concentrated on the consequences of tax competition for the taxation of capital income.[20] However, one may note that the openness of economies also affects the taxation of labour income and commodities.

In an open economy, the corporate tax essentially becomes a source-based tax on the return on domestic investment. It is one of the key insights of the tax competition literature that a small open economy should not levy source-based capital income taxes.[21] The intuition for this result is the following. From the perspective of a small open economy, capital is in perfectly elastic supply at the worldwide interest rate. If the country imposes a tax on the return of domestic investment, international investors will only supply funds if their after-tax return equals the world interest rate. This in turn implies that their effective tax burden is zero and that the burden of source-based capital income taxes must be borne by other factors of production, for example by labour through lower factor prices. However, the tax on domestic investment also involves an efficiency cost since it distorts the investment choices of firms. If the country does not levy this tax and instead only taxes labour income (assuming that labour is the only other input), it can avoid this efficiency cost without imposing any additional burden on labour. In favour of this thesis, it is often pointed out that statutory corporate tax rates have considerably declined over the last years (see table 12.1). However, this argument is somewhat inconclusive since reductions in statutory rates have been accompanied by a broadening of tax bases through, for example, less generous depreciation allowances.

How can one take into account the effects of a larger corporate tax base? The correct economic approach is to consider how the tax burden

---

[19] This number is calculated by using the German Income Tax Statistics (Einkommensteuerstatistik). One should also note that the results are distorted to some extent since they also reflect the impact of tax evasion and of the full imputation system of dividend taxation. Both factors tend to reduce reported capital income such that our measure overestimates the effects of tax arbitrage. On the other hand, one of the key channels of tax arbitrage in Germany is real estate investment of high-tax investors. Reported income from rented real estate was negative in 1992 and amounted to −0.5 per cent of GDP.

[20] See Wilson (1999) and Mintz (2001) for a recent survey. The literature on commodity tax competition is surveyed for example by Keen (1993).

[21] See Gordon (1986).

Table 12.1 *Taxes on corporate income as percentage of GDP and as percentage of total taxation 1970–97*

	Percentage of GDP			Percentage of total taxation		
	1980	1990	1997	1980	1990	1997
Australia	3.3	4.2	4.4	12.2	14.1	14.6
Austria	1.4	1.5	2.1	3.5	3.6	4.7
Belgium	2.5	2.4	3.4	5.7	5.4	7.5
Canada	3.7	2.5	3.8	11.6	7.0	10.3
Denmark	1.5	1.5	2.6	3.2	3.2	5.2
Finland	1.4	2.1	3.8	3.9	4.6	8.1
France	2.1	2.3	2.6	5.1	5.3	5.8
Germany	2.1	1.8	1.5	5.5	4.8	4.0
Ireland	1.5	1.7	3.3	4.5	5.0	10.0
Italy	2.4	3.9	4.2	7.8	10.0	9.5
Japan	5.5	6.7	4.3	21.8	21.6	15.0
Luxembourg	7.1	7.1	8.6	16.4	16.1	18.5
Netherlands	3.0	3.4	4.4	6.6	7.5	10.5
Norway	5.7	3.8	5.2	13.3	9.0	12.2
Spain	1.2	3.0	2.6	5.1	8.8	7.8
Sweden	1.2	1.7	3.2	2.5	3.1	6.1
Switzerland	1.7	2.1	2.0	5.8	6.7	5.9
United Kingdom	3.0	4.2	4.3	8.4	11.6	12.1
United States	3.0	2.1	2.8	10.8	7.7	9.4
OECD average	2.5	2.8	3.3	7.6	7.9	8.8
EU 15	2.2	2.7	3.5	5.9	6.8	8.5

Source: Revenue Statistics of OECD Member Countries 1965–99.

of marginal investment has changed over time. Recent studies (see, for example, Chennels and Griffith, 1997) report that, at the margin, taxes on corporate investment have only slightly declined. Intuitively, this result says that the positive effect of lower corporate tax rates on a firm's cost of capital has largely been compensated by the broadening of its tax base. This result is clearly inconsistent with the tax competition hypothesis according to which the marginal tax rate on corporate investment should have significantly declined.

A somewhat simpler way to capture the effects of base broadening is to consider the development of corporate tax revenue. Figure 12.5 shows how corporate tax revenue in OECD countries has evolved between 1980 and 1997. According to this figure, tax revenue has increased on average in the OECD as a percentage of GDP (which is also true as a percentage of total tax revenues). This phenomenon may reflect the fact that effective

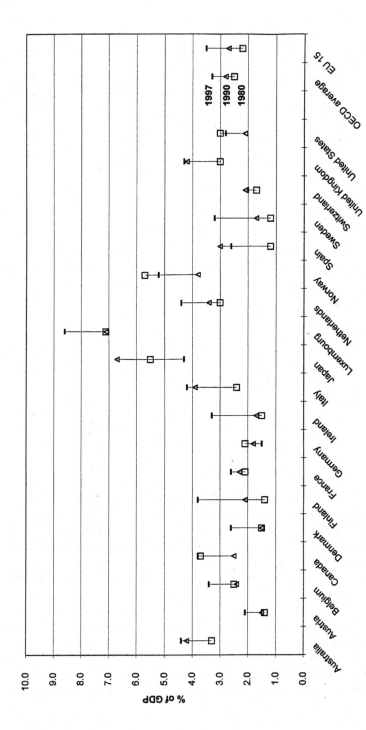

Figure 12.5 Corporate taxes as percent of GDP 1980–97
Source: Revenue Statistics of OECD Member Countries (1999).

tax rates have not declined to the same extent as statutory rates.[22] Again, this does not support the tax competition hypothesis.

These results indicate that the downward pressures on capital taxes have been less severe than the standard tax competition model would predict. There are several explanations why capital income taxes have not significantly declined.[23] For example, one reason may be the phenomenon of tax exportation. If foreign investors own domestic firms, the government has an incentive to shift tax burdens onto foreigners through higher corporate taxes.[24] Similarly, host countries of multinational firms have no incentive to cut their corporate tax if the home countries use the foreign tax credit method.

Can one thus conclude that tax competition is not an important challenge for tax policy? While some fears of a race-to-the-bottom may be exaggerated, there are nonetheless clear signs that the openness of economies exerts additional pressure on tax policy.

First, international capital mobility makes it more difficult to impose personal capital income taxes. In most countries, the personal capital income tax is organised as a residence-based tax on the return on domestic savings. Thus, the worldwide capital income of an individual is, in principle, subject to the income tax. The main problem is that individuals can easily evade taxes on the income from their foreign investments. This creates considerable incentives to invest abroad. Empirical evidence suggests that international tax evasion has substantially eroded the revenue from personal capital income taxation.[25]

Similarly, the degree of tax progression has declined in many countries. One explanation is the increased mobility of skilled high-wage earners whose taxes have consequently gone down while those of unskilled and less mobile workers have gone up. Although it is likely that it is the *average* tax on labour and not the marginal tax which is crucial for the decision to move from one country to another, the only way to reduce the average rate for high-wage earners without large losses in revenues is to cut the marginal rate.[26]

Table 12.2 summarises this development of marginal tax rates in the highest income level and for individuals with 66 per cent of the average

---

[22] The development may also to some extent be explained by an increasing profit share in the economy during the period.

[23] See Gordon (1998) for a discussion of the various arguments.

[24] If such policy is to be optimal, foreign-owned firms must earn infra-marginal rents. See Huizinga and Nielsen (1997).

[25] See, e.g., Shoven (1991). According to the Swedish Government, SEK 353 billion may be kept illegally by Swedes abroad.

[26] See Christiansen et al. (1994), p. 305.

Table 12.2 *Change in marginal tax rates (percentage points)*

	Marginal tax rate [1]		Top marginal rate of personal income tax
	66% of APW	100% of APW	
Australia	–	2.0	−10.0
Austria	–	–	−12.0
Belgium	36.3	5.3	−15.3
Canada	3.0	20.7	−2.7
Denmark	5.5	−8.9	−14.0
Finland	14.5	3.8	−13.0
France	10.9	1.1	−11.0
Germany	−18.6	4.2	–
Ireland	–	–	−10.0
Italy	14.5	9.0	−11.0
Japan	9.0	18.7	−20.0
Luxembourg	–	–	−7.0
Netherlands	8.9	−5.8	−12.0
Norway	4.2	−6.8	−16.5
Spain	3.4	2.4	−10.0
Sweden	−4.5	−22.5	−25.0
Switzerland	–	–	−1.5
United Kingdom	−4.5	−4.5	−20.0
United States	21.7	18.5	−10.4
Average	7.5	2.5	−12.4

[1] One-earner couple with two children. Includes personal incomes taxes, social security contributions by employees and 'universal' (not means-tested) cash benefits.
Source: OECD *Economic Outlook*, June 1998, Table IV.2 and Table IV.3.

production worker's income (APW) as well as for individuals with 100 per cent of APW.

Even if the potential gains for high-skilled wage earners may be quite high if they move to other countries, the mobility is still low. Does this mean that a country like Sweden can maintain high taxes on labour without problems? This may be a misinterpretation of facts. As chapter 2 in this volume points out, high taxes on labour may induce *firms* to be mobile even if labour itself is not. In the long run, this may also cause labour to become more mobile. Therefore, high labour taxation may still have significant negative welfare effects. A simple numerical example illustrates this point.

Suppose that the labour demand elasticity is −0.10. We approximate the welfare effects by the well-known Harberger formula, i.e.

$$\text{Excess burden} = \tfrac{1}{2} \times t^2 \times \eta^d \times wL$$

where η^d is the labour demand elasticity and t is the tax rate on labour income and wL is the total wage bill.[27] Figure 12.6 illustrates how the tax rate must be adjusted in order to keep excess burden constant, if the elasticity increases due to job mobility. The initial value of t is 60 per cent and η^d is 0.10. For example, the average tax rate on labour must be reduced from 60 percent to 50 percent, if labour demand elasticity increases from 0.10 to 0.15 in absolute terms.[28]

It is also interesting to analyse how an increased mobility of workers affects tax revenue. We can capture the effects of higher mobility by considering the development of the tax base of the local and the national income tax and social security contributions. Using data for 1999, our calculations are based on the following assumptions.[29]

The average growth rate between 1980 and 1999 in GDP was 1.88 per cent in Sweden. In case A, mobility is 1 per cent of high-income earners and constant during the period 2000–10.[30] Thus, under this scenario, 1 per cent of the high-wage earners leave Sweden each year. In case B, mobility slowly increases with 0.05 per cent per year, i.e. at the end of the period mobility is 1.71 per cent of high income earners. In case C, mobility increases more rapidly – the change is 0.15 per cent per year, such that 4.65 per cent of high-wage earners will leave Sweden in 2010.

Cases B and C simply show the direct effects on the tax base if high income earners move to other countries. However, if these individuals leave the country, indirect effects on the economy will also occur.[31] For each of the three levels of mobility, small and large indirect effects are considered.[32] Case D combines a small mobility with small indirect effects while case E assumes large indirect effects. Case F combines a higher mobility with small indirect effects. Finally, case G illustrates large mobility with large indirect effects.

Extrapolating the growth in tax bases according to the historic growth rate during the past twenty years, one obtains case A in figure 12.7.

[27] This formula assumes a perfectly elastic labour supply. This is a reasonable assumption if the unions follow a wage setting strategy which maintains a constant net wage of employees.

[28] We assume, for simplicity, no change in wL, when the excess burden is kept constant, which is of course a very special case.

[29] The calculations are based on Statistics Sweden *Inkomstfördelningsundersökningen 1999*.

[30] Statistics Sweden reports that 0.25 per cent of university-educated persons left Sweden during the 1980s and 0.80 per cent during the 1990s. Statistiska Centralbyrån (1997).

[31] A similar approach was used in Fölster and Lindström (1993).

[32] A small indirect effect assumes 0.5 of the direct effect on the local tax base and 0.75 of the direct effect on the national tax base. In the same manner, a large indirect effect assumes two times the direct effect on the local tax base and three times the direct effect on the national tax base. The base of social security fees is assumed to follow the base of local income taxes.

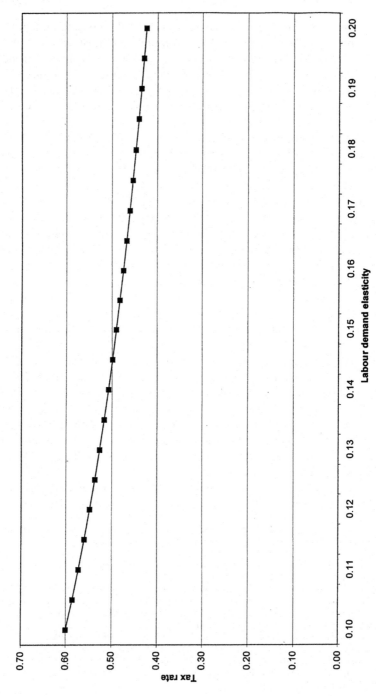

Figure 12.6 Tax rate given a certain excess burden

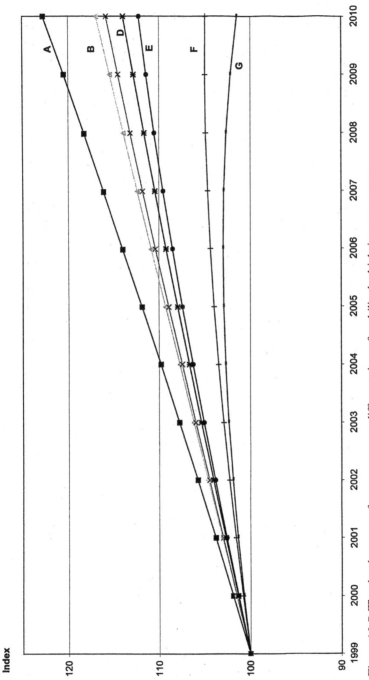

Figure 12.7 The development of tax revenues at different sizes of mobility by high-income earners
Source: Own calculations based on Statistics Sweden "Inkomstfördelningsundersökningen 1999."

Table 12.3 *Present value of future tax revenues during year 2000–2010*[1]

Case	Billions SEK	Deviation from case A	
		Billions SEK	%
A	7,109	0	0.0
B	6,957	−152	−2.1
C	6,933	−176	−2.5
D	6,878	−231	−3.2
E	6,842	−267	−3.8
F	6,644	−465	−6.5
G	6,571	−538	−7.6

[1] Calculated by a 3 per cent dicount factor. The calculations include the local income tax, national income tax and social security fees.

Tax revenue therefore increases by 23 per cent in real terms during this period.

Cases B and C illustrate how tax revenue would develop if mobility increases. In case B, they increase by 17 per cent instead of 23 per cent. In present value terms, total tax revenue increases by 2.1 per cent less, corresponding to SEK 152 billion during this period (see table 12.3).

In the extreme case G, total tax revenue drops by 7.6 per cent corresponding to SEK 538 billion in present value terms.

A conclusion, which may be drawn from the above simple exercise, is that the tax rate on labour may have to be cut in order not to induce welfare losses, if labour and jobs do become more mobile.

12.4   Options for tax policy

Tax coordination and tax harmonisation

Given these challenges, what are the options for tax policy in the future? Many authors have suggested that countries should try to overcome the problems of tax competition by coordinating and harmonising national tax policies.[33] At the international level, few attempts have yet been made to reach binding agreements on tax policy. One exception is the OECD, which is currently developing a set of rules to define the notion of 'harmful tax competition'. In the EU, member countries have – in line with the

[33] See, e.g., Sinn (1997).

current European treaties – largely retained their autonomy over direct taxation. There are, however, two exceptions. The member countries have agreed on measures to fight the above-mentioned evasion of personal taxes on *interest income*. According to the current plan, the EU will introduce a system of information exchanges between member countries. German tax authorities will then, for example, report the interest income of Swedish citizens to the Swedish tax authorities.

However, these coordination measures raise various issues. First, coordination only concerns the member countries rather than the whole world such that investors may shift their portfolios outside the EU.

Another problem of the current plans to coordinate direct taxation is that it is not only partial with respect to the region, but also with respect to the number of tax instruments covered by the coordination arrangement. This may allow member countries to substitute tax instruments whose use is restricted by EU agreements for non-restricted tax instruments. For example, one can show that a minimum withholding tax (which some member countries are allowed to impose during a transition period) can be completely neutralised by a change in depreciation allowances.[34] This is another reason to doubt whether the current tax coordination arrangements will turn out to be particularly effective.

Furthermore, it must be recognised that information acts like a withholding tax for a low tax country without giving any extra tax revenue to this country. It is, therefore, a matter of debate whether source countries have an interest to participate in information exchange.[35] Finally, pure administrative reasons complicate information exchange.

The main lesson to be drawn from these considerations is that successful tax coordination requires (i) the cooperation of other countries outside the EU, and (ii) that coordination arrangements cover all relevant tax policy instruments. Neither condition will probably be satisfied in the foreseeable future. As was mentioned above, the prospects for international tax coordination look rather dim. Similarly, it seems unlikely that member countries of the EU will agree on a wide-ranging coordination of direct taxes. One of the reasons is, of course, the objective of member countries to maintain national sovereignty over these taxes. In addition, the coordination of direct taxes raises complicated practical problems. For example, a coordination of corporate taxation within the EU requires a harmonisation of corporate tax bases which, however, vary considerably across member countries. One of many problems would be to define common rules or, at least, guidelines for the design of rules for depreciation

---

[34] See Fuest and Huber (1999).
[35] See for further discussion Bacchetta and Espinosa (2000).

allowances.[36] Another problem is that the potential benefits of tax coordination seem to be quite modest for many countries. Sørensen (2000) reports that global tax coordination will raise national welfare on average by 1.5 per cent of GDP.[37] Tax coordination within the EU, such as the introduction of a minimum withholding tax, will only yield less than 0.2 per cent for the EU. Thus, it seems very unlikely that much progress will be made in this respect in the near future.

Is moving to a consumption tax an option?

One other strategy is to transform the current hybrid tax system into a pure consumption tax. As was explained in section 12.3, the results of the literature on optimal taxation provide strong arguments in favour of consumption taxation. Furthermore, several specific proposals as to how to implement it, such as the flat tax, suggest that consumption taxation is simpler and more transparent than (a comprehensive or hybrid) income tax. In the presence of tax competition, the case for a consumption tax becomes even more compelling.

However, the transition from an income tax system to a consumption tax raises various problems. One issue is the treatment of the existing capital stock. Many authors have, therefore, argued that these problems of transition considerably reduce the attractiveness of consumption taxation.[38]

Furthermore, the cash flow tax may aggravate the problem of international transfer pricing since the generous depreciation rules of the cash flow imply a rather high tax rate which, in turn, makes it attractive for firms to shift profits abroad.[39] The cash flow tax is also vulnerable to domestic tax arbitrage. To understand this, recall the discussion in section 12.3 where we analysed the possibility to shift taxable income between the personal and the business tax base. To avoid such income shifting in a system of consumption taxation, several authors have argued that the top marginal tax rate on personal (labour) income should be equal to the tax rate of the (business) cash flow tax.[40] However, this measure eliminates any flexibility in the choice of tax rates on labour and business income. However, under this constraint it is not optimal to have a cash flow tax and/or a consumption tax.[41]

---

[36] See Commission for the EC (1992) (Ruding Report) for a proposal to harmonise company taxation in the EU. Mintz (1999) and McLure and Weiner (2000) discuss the idea of introducing formula apportionment.

[37] Welfare gains are somewhat higher if distributional effects are taken into account.

[38] See, e.g., Keen (1997).

[39] See Haufler and Schjelderup (2000).

[40] See, e.g., Bradford (1986).   [41] See Fuest and Huber (2001a).

One final argument against the cash flow tax is a purely pragmatic one. There are serious doubts whether a cash flow tax is consistent with international foreign tax credit arrangements.[42] For an individual country, this means that cash flow taxes paid by the domestic subsidiaries of foreign multinationals will not be credited in the home country of the multinational. This creates an incentive for an individual country not to adopt a cash flow tax.

Summing up, this shows that there are important arguments against the introduction of a pure consumption tax. This also helps to explain why most countries have decided against this tax. Given this, the switch to a pure consumption tax may not be a particularly attractive option for tax policy.

A pragmatic approach

If the international or EU-wide coordination of tax policies and the move to a consumption tax system are not viable options for tax policy, the key question is, of course, in which direction tax policy should develop in the future. This section briefly outlines the key elements of a pragmatic proposal for tax reform in a small open economy like Sweden. The approach is not a straightforward implication of an optimal tax model but instead represents a pragmatic solution, which tries to balance the various pressures on tax policy. Summing up, the key features of the proposal are the following:

- a cut in the personal income tax on interest income to 20 per cent;
- abolition of the wealth tax on listed shares;
- an increased actuarial relation between contributions and benefits in the social security system;
- a minor reduction of progression in the national income tax.

The basic idea of the proposal builds on the idea of the dual income tax (DIT), which was introduced in the Nordic countries a decade ago. Under this tax system, labour income is taxed at progressive rates, while capital income is subject to a relatively low tax rate. The DIT has several attractive features. As explained above, the crucial problems of personal capital income taxation are the incentives of taxpayers to avoid taxes by investing abroad. By reducing the capital income tax rate to a moderate rate, say 15–25 per cent, the gains from tax avoidance are considerably reduced. Individuals may then find it optimal to pay this moderate capital income tax instead of investing abroad, which is costly and, if taxes are evaded, illegal. The recent experience in countries like Austria with a positive but rather moderate tax on capital income suggests that this strategy

[42] See *Report of the Technical Committee on Business Taxation* (1997).

can yield considerable revenue gains. Lowering the tax rate in Sweden has some upside revenue potential since the current capital income tax base is close to zero or even negative when capital gains are subtracted. A cut in the capital income tax rate would also improve the incentives to save for retirement. Higher saving rates are often seen as one key element to solve the demographic problems of the social security system.

A second element in the proposal is to keep the corporate tax rate at a level which is roughly comparable to the level in other countries. This ensures that internationally operating firms have no incentive to reduce their tax base through transfer pricing such that profits are shifted from Sweden to low tax countries.[43] The revenue loss resulting from a reduction in the statutory corporate tax rate can be compensated by a broadening of the corporate tax base.

An important issue is the relationship between the corporate tax and the personal capital income tax. Consider first the tax treatment of dividends. We suggest that dividends paid out by firms quoted on the stock exchange are taxed at a higher rate than the personal capital income tax. This, of course, implies a double taxation of dividends earned by domestic residents. However, this need not necessarily increase the cost of equity financing for firms. If the marginal investor in large firms is a foreign investor, domestic dividend taxation does not affect the cost of equity financing at all.[44] Furthermore, one may note that there is an important legal reason why EU member countries probably have to fully tax dividends. Any double taxation relief granted for dividends of domestic firms, which does not also apply to dividends earned from foreign firms, may violate the principle of non-discrimination within the common market. This was one important rationale why countries like Germany and Great Britain have abolished their imputation systems.

In addition, the wealth tax should be altered in order not to include shares in listed companies. This will also prevent income shifting from the corporate tax base to the personal capital income tax base.[45] By keeping a wealth tax on interest-bearing securities, the tax burden on equity finance and borrowing is on the margin equivalent although double taxation applies on the former type.

Another feature of the proposal is that the tax wedge on corporate income in *small* firms should be equal to the personal capital income tax wedge (including the wealth tax). This removes the incentives to use corporations as savings vehicles or to pay out dividends, which are reinvested in corporate debt.

---

[43] See *Report of the Technical Committee on Business Taxation* (1997) on these issues in the context of Canada.
[44] See Fuest and Huber (2001b).
[45] For example, firm owners will lend fresh funds to their firms instead of buying equity.

If the corporate tax rate is 28 per cent and the tax rate on dividends is 30 per cent, the total tax burden on a firm's income distributed as dividend amounts to roughly 50 per cent. To ensure the neutrality of taxation with respect to organisational choices, this tax rate should apply to both corporations and unincorporated businesses.

One key critical aspect of the proposal is the relationship between this combined business tax rate and the (top marginal) tax rate on labour income. If these two tax rates diverge by too much, massive incentives for income shifting arise (see section 12.3). Sweden clearly faces this problem. While the total tax burden on distributed profits is 50 per cent in our proposal, the marginal labour income tax rate is well above 65 per cent including implicit taxation in the social security system.

High labour taxes also create incentives for high-wage earners to migrate to low-tax countries. As was discussed above, the mobility of high-income groups can considerably deteriorate the tax base. The role of high-income earners in the Swedish economy becomes clear from figure 12.8, which shows how the labour tax base is distributed between different income groups. Roughly 10 per cent of total labour income is earned by individuals with an income above SEK 280,000.

How should the tax policy respond to the problems raised by the mobility of high-income earners, job mobility and by income shifting? A realistic strategy is to reduce the marginal tax burdens faced by high-income individuals. This could be accomplished by a ceiling on social security contributions and a reduction in the top marginal income tax rate. If, for example, the ceiling is set at SEK 273,000 and the top rate is entirely abolished, the incentives for income shifting and for migration could be considerably reduced. The total cost of these tax reductions would amount to roughly 2 per cent of GDP.

Summing up, this reform concept implies the following tax wedges:

	Corporate tax rate (%)	Personal tax rate (%)	Wealth tax (%)	Total tax wedge (%)
Dividends big companies	28	30	0	50
Dividends small companies	28	30	0	50
Interest income	0	20	1.5	50[46]
Wage income[47]	0	50	0	50

[46] Evaluated at 5 per cent interest rate. For rates below this, the effective tax rate will be higher and vice versa.

[47] This is the highest rate. Note that social security fees will not be levied on amounts above SEK 273,000.

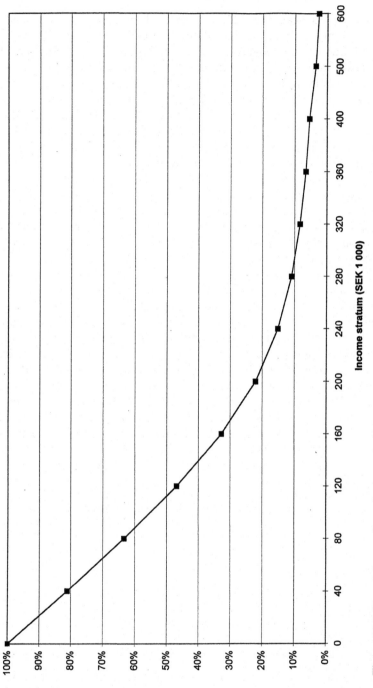

Figure 12.8 Remaining tax base above a certain income stratum in 1999
Source: Statistics Sweden "Inkomstfördelningsundersökningen 1999". Total population 20–64 years of age.

The total cost of this reform package in terms of tax revenue amounts to SEK 443 billion in present value terms over a ten-year period. One important potential source to finance this reform is the effects of the reform on mobility. If, for example, the reform could maintain mobility at the 1999 level, a large part of the reform would be self-financing through an increased tax base. For example, case F in section 12.3 predicts a revenue loss of SEK 466 billion through higher mobility. Thus, the net cost of the reform could be fairly low, if the reform succeeds in reducing mobility. Similarly, if the reform raises economic activity and growth, the net cost of the reform is also reduced.

One other route to finance the reform is to charge prices for government services. Many excludable public goods like schools, universities and child care can be financed by fees instead of taxes. Notice that this does not necessarily reduce the degree of redistribution since transfers to poor individuals who have to pay for these services can be increased.

On balance, this suggests that the pragmatic approach for tax policy outlined in this chapter can serve as a sustainable strategy for the future.

12.5   Conclusion

Small countries like Sweden, with high tax levels, must consider how to respond and adjust to the international development. We have analysed different models for taxation as a solution to the problems, which may follow by increased tax competition in the future. We do not regard pure consumption taxation as a realistic option. Instead, the dual income tax (DIT) introduced by the Nordic countries a decade ago is a powerful alternative to the present hybrid tax system, which is now in force in many countries. Although it solves many of the problems related to the hybrid tax system in an international economy, it has an inherent problem of income shifting in manager-owned firms. The DIT must therefore be carefully calibrated in order to cope with increased capital, labour and job mobility as well as income shifting problems. We propose a closer actuarial connection between contributions and benefits in the social security system and a minor reduction in the marginal tax rate of the national income tax system in order counteract labour and job mobility. Further, a cut in the tax rate on personal capital income seems to be necessary in order to work against capital flows to foreign countries.

References

Aaron, H. J., Galper, H. and Pechman, J. A. (eds.), 1988, *Uneasy Compromise: Problems of a Hybrid Income-Consumption Tax*, Washington: Brookings Institution.

Agell, J. and Persson, M., 2000, 'Tax arbitrage and labor supply', *Journal of Public Economics*, 78, 3–24.

Auerbach, A. J., 1991, 'Retrospective capital gains taxation', *American Economic Review*, 81, 167–78.

Bacchetta, P. and Espinosa, M. P., 2000, 'Exchange of information clauses in international tax treaties', *International Tax and Public Finance*, 7, 275–93.

Bernheim, B. D., 1999, 'Taxation and saving', NBER working paper, No. 7061.

Bond, S. R. and Devereux, M. P., 1995, 'On the design of a neutral business tax under uncertainty', *Journal of Public Economics*, 58, 57–71.

Bradford, D. F., 1986, *Untangling the Income Tax*, Cambridge, MA: Harvard University Press.

Chamley, C. P., 1986, 'Optimal taxation of capital income in general equilibrium with infinite lives', *Econometrica*, 54, 607–22.

Chennels, L. and Griffith, R., 1997, *Taxing Profits in a Changing World*, London: Institute for Fiscal Studies.

Coleman, W. J., 2000, 'Welfare and optimum dynamic taxation of consumption and income', *Journal of Public Economics*, 76, 1–40.

Eden, L., 1998, *Taxing Multinationals: Transfer Pricing and Corporate Income Taxation in North America*, Toronto: University of Toronto Press.

Elmendorf, D. W., 1996, 'The effect of interest rate changes on household saving and consumption: a survey', Federal Reserve Board, mimeo.

Engen, E. M. and Gale, W. G., 1997, 'Consumption taxes and saving: the role of uncertainty in tax reform', *American Economic Review*, 87, Papers and Proceedings, 114–19.

European Commission, 'European Economy 2000'.

Feldstein, M., 1993, 'The effects of marginal tax rates on taxable income', NBER working paper No. 4496.

—1995, 'Tax avoidance and the deadweight loss of the income tax', NBER working paper No. 5055.

Fölster, S. and Lindström, E., 1993, *Sveriges offentliga sektor i europeisk konkurrens, Bilaga 6 till EG-konsekvensutredningen*, Stockholm: Samhällsekonomi.

Fuest, C. and Huber, B., 1999, 'Can tax coordination work?', *Finanzarchiv*, 56, 443–58.

—2001a, Why don't countries introduce consumption taxation?, Munich.

—2001b, 'The optimal taxation of dividends under uncertainty', CESifo working paper.

Gentry, W. and Hubbard, R., 1998, 'Fundamental tax reform and corporate financial policy', in J. Poterba (ed.), *Tax Policy and the Economy*, 12, Cambridge, MA: MIT Press, 191–227.

Gordon, R. H., 1986, 'Taxation of investment and savings in a world economy', *American Economic Review*, 76, 1086–102.

—1998, 'Can high personal tax rates encourage entrepreneurial activity?', *IMF Staff Papers*, 45, 49–80.

—2000, 'Taxation of capital income vs. labor income: an overview', in S. Cnossen (ed.), *Taxing Capital Income in the European Union*, Oxford: Oxford University Press, 15–45.

Gordon, R. H. and Nielsen, S. B., 1997, 'Tax evasion in an open economy: value-added vs. income taxation', *Journal of Public Economics*, 66, 173–98.

Gordon, R. H. and Slemrod, J., 1988, 'Do we collect any revenue from taxing capital income?', in L. H. Summers (ed.), *Tax Policy and the Economy*, 2, Cambridge, MA: MIT Press.

—1998, 'Are "Real" responses to taxes simply income shifting between corporate and personal tax bases?', NBER working paper No. 6576.

Hall, R. E. and Rabushka, A., 1995, *The Flat Tax*, Stanford, CA: Hoover Institution Press.

Haufler, A. and Schjelderup, G., 2000, 'Corporate tax systems and cross country profit shifting', *Oxford Economic Papers*, 52, 306–25.

Hines, J. R., 1996, 'Tax policy and the activities of multinational corporations', NBER working paper No. 5589.

Hubbard, R. G., 1997, 'How different are income and consumption taxes?', *American Economic Review*, 87, Papers and Proceedings, 138–42.

Huizinga, H. and Nielsen, S. B., 1997, 'Capital income and profit taxation with foreign ownership of firms', *Journal of International Economics*, 42, 149–65.

Judd, K. L., 1985, 'Redistributive taxation in a simple perfect foresight model', *Journal of Public Economics*, 28, 59–83.

Kaldor, N., 1955, *An Expenditure Tax*, London: Unwin University Books.

Kaplow, L., 1996, 'On the divergence between "ideal" and conventional income-tax treatment of human capital', *American Economic Review*, Papers and Proceedings, 86, 347–52.

Keen, M., 1993, 'The welfare economics of tax co-ordination in the European Community: a survey', *Fiscal Studies*, 14, 15–36.

—1997, 'Peculiar institutions: a British perspective on tax policy in the United States', *Fiscal Studies*, 18, 371–400.

Krueger, A., 2000, 'From Bismarck to Maastricht: the march to European Union and the labor compact', NBER working paper No. W7456, January.

Leibfritz, W., Thornton, J. and Bibbee, A., 1997, 'Taxation and economic performance', OECD working paper 97/107.

Lodin, S. O., 1976, 'Utgiftsskatt – ett alternativ', SOU 1976: 62, Liberförlag.

McLure, C. E. and Weiner, J. M., 2000, 'Deciding whether the European Union should adopt formula apportionment of company income', in S. Cnossen (ed.), *Taxing Capital Income in the European Union*, Oxford: Oxford University Press, 243–92.

Mennel, A. and Förster, J., 2000, *Steuern in Europa, Amerika und Asien*, Herme/Berlin: Verlag neue Wirtschaftsbriefe.

Miller, M., 1997, 'Debt and taxes', *Journal of Finance*, 32, 261–75.

Mintz, J., 1999, 'Globalization of the corporate income tax: the role of allocation', *Finanzarchiv*, 56, 389–424.

—2001, *Taxation of Investment and Finance in an International Setting: Implications for Tax Competition*, University of Konstanz: Center for International Labor Economics.

Mirrlees, J., 1971, 'An exploration in the theory of optimum income taxation', *Review of Economic Studies*, 38, 175–208.

Musgrave, R., 1959, *The Theory of Public Finance: A Study in Political Economy*, New York: McGraw-Hill.

Report of the Technical Committee on Business Taxation, 1998, Ottawa.

Report of the Technical Committee on Business Taxation, 1997, Ottawa.

OECD, 1998, *Economic Outlook*, 63, June, Paris: OECD.

Scholes, M. S. and Wolfson, M. A., 1992, *Taxes and Business Strategy*, Englewood Cliffs, NJ: Prentice Hall.

Shoven, J., 1991, 'Using the corporate cash flow tax to integrate corporate and personal taxes', *Proceedings of the 83rd Annual Conference of the National Tax Association*, 19–26.

Sinn, H.-W., 1997, 'The selection principle and market failure in systems competition', *Journal of Public Economics*, 66, 247–74.

Slemrod, H., Blumenthal, M. and Christian, C., 2001, 'Taxpayer response to an increased probability of audit: evidence from a controlled experiment in Minnesota', *Journal of Public Economics*, 79, 455–83.

Sørensen, P. B., 1988, 'Wealth taxation, income taxation, and savings', University of Copenhagen, Institute of Economics, Blue Mimeo 163.

—2000, 'The case for international tax co-ordination reconsidered', *Economic Policy*, 31, 431–72.

Statistics Sweden, 1999, *Inkomstfördelningsundersökningen 1999*.

Statistiska Centralbyrån, 1997, 'Högutbildade I Sverige', *Faktablad*, no. 2, December.

Stern, N., 1987, 'The theory of optimal commodity and income taxation: an introduction', in D. Newberry and N. Stern (eds.), *The Theory of Taxation for Developing Countries*, Oxford: Oxford University Press for the World Bank, 22–59.

Stiglitz, J. E., 1987, 'Pareto efficient and optimal taxation and the new welfare economies', in A. J. Auerbach and M. Feldstein (eds.), *Handbook of Public Economics*, vol. 2, 991–1042.

Wilson, J. D., 1999, 'Theories of tax competition', *National Tax Journal*, 52, 264–304.

13 Taxation and education investment in the tertiary sector

Fredrik Andersson and Kai A. Konrad

13.1 Introduction

The public sector massively intervenes in the education sector in practically all OECD countries. Via free public provision of education, transfers to students, or high subsidies on education, the government strongly influences private education decisions. Education has elements of investment and consumption. For an analysis of public education policy the investment aspects are more relevant, and in what follows we will concentrate on these aspects.

Expenditures on education goods – from private and public sources – were 5.75 per cent of GDP on average in the OECD countries in 1998 (OECD, 2001a: 80). The variation in total expenditures across OECD countries was modest, ranging from 3.5 per cent of GDP in Turkey and 4.6 per cent in the Netherlands, to 7.0 per cent in Korea and 7.2 per cent in Denmark.

The public sector carries the lion's share of the costs of education in most OECD countries. In many countries primary and secondary education is financed almost exclusively by the public sector. An interesting fact is that the top group in terms of total expenditures includes countries with among the largest shares of public funding, like Sweden and Denmark, as well as countries with among the smallest public financing shares, like Korea and the USA (cf. OECD, 2001a: 93).

As has been illustrated in chapter 6, roughly a quarter of the education-goods expenditures are made on tertiary education; the OECD average is 1.59 per cent of GDP. It is important to note that the public-sector share seems to be larger in countries with higher income taxes. In fact, the correlation between the public-financing shares and the top marginal tax rates in 1998 is 0.42.[1] This positive correlation is in line with the hypothesis that public education spending is – at least to some extent – a

---

[1] Public-sector shares from OECD (2001a: 81); marginal tax rates from OECD (2001b: 38–9); countries for which either measure is unavailable are excluded.

second-best response to a problem of time-consistent over-taxation of the returns on human capital; we will discuss the hypothesis below.

There are several possible measures of the outcome of education expenditures. A measure of the overall use of education – both as a consumption good and as an investment good – is the average total amount of (tertiary) education acquired. The number of years is roughly in line with the resources spent; the correlation between total expenditures and expected number of years is 0.70.[2]

A related measure of the output of the education system, often argued to be particularly relevant for the broader economic performance of a country, is the extent to which an education system produces workers with high skills in science and technology. Figure 13.1 shows the number of science graduates (per 100,000) in a number of countries; the mean is 1,200. Notably, this statistic is very weakly related to total expenditures on tertiary education; the correlation is 0.04 (expenditures from OECD 2001a: 81).[3]

As surveyed by Temple (2001), empirical estimates of the private monetary return to schooling typically are in the range between 5 per cent and 15 per cent (depending on time and country), and the positive correlation between schooling and earnings is robust and uncontroversial.[4,5] A different way to measure the returns on education is to use macroeconomic variables. Temple (2001) also surveys this literature. According to these results, about 0.1 to 0.5 percentage points of annual growth can be attributed to improvements in labour quality.[6]

---

[2] Total expenditures from OECD (2001a: 81); expected number of years from OECD (2001a: 133); countries not reporting both are excluded.

[3] There are some cross-country comparisons of basic skills that may throw light on some aspect of the stock of human capital with particular reference to Sweden. It seems that the relatively large amount of resources spent on primary (and secondary) education in Sweden pays off in terms of literacy. In a comparison of twelve OECD countries 1994–5 (OECD, 1999: ch. 2) Sweden had uniformly the best literacy levels across age groups. Looking directly at scores obtained at a literacy test, Sweden ranked uniformly first across education levels. The record seems less unambiguously favourable as regards achievements in mathematics. In a test of eighth-grade students across all OECD countries, the average score among Swedish students was essentially equal to the mean; this is subject to some caution, however, since Swedish eighth-graders have one year less formal schooling than those in most other countries – this fact, on the other hand, seems noteworthy by itself. (There are findings indicating that mathematics is particularly important for labour-market success; see Björklund, 2000.)

[4] See also OECD (1997), Wright (1999) and Pereira and Silva Martins (2000).

[5] Björklund (2000) estimates simple log-linear wage equations for Sweden, finding that the return to an additional year of education was a 4.6 per cent wage increase; he also, however, discusses a number of limitations of simple estimates, and cites (scarce) evidence of education subsidies impacting measured private returns strongly.

[6] Strong effects are reported from Mankiw, Romer and Weil (1992), suggesting that doubling of investment in human capital yields an increase in output per worker by about 50 per cent. However, Temple (2001) also surveys the discussion that explains that these figures may strongly overestimate the effect.

Science graduates per 100 000

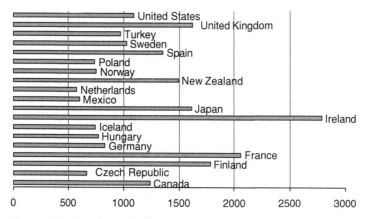

Figure 13.1 Number of science graduates per 100,000 persons in the
labour force 25–35 years of age
Source: OECD (2001a: 172).

13.2   Motivations for public education

As reported in the previous section, governments in all OECD countries
carry out an active education policy. In order to evaluate this policy, it is
important to understand why the government intervenes in this market
for investment goods. There are several reasons for this public intervention, some of which address efficiency aspects, while others relate to
distributional aspects.

Equal opportunities and redistribution

A point that is frequently made is the 'equal opportunities' argument,
according to which it is considered desirable to give access to education
investment to all children, regardless of the wealth, social status or education of their parents. The desirability of equal opportunities could be
justified by normative equity considerations as well as efficiency considerations. If there is heterogeneity among individuals with respect to their
ability to turn education investment into earnings or output, it would
imply a loss in efficiency if only the children of the rich have access to
human capital investment opportunities since the rents from investment
for children of poor parents with high returns on human capital investment would be lost.

Access to human capital investment is often restricted. First, children
of poor parents may be unable to finance their university education by

a private loan due to imperfections in the private credit markets. The government could open the access for this group of children by student loans, and by public provision of free university education. Second, and related to this, investment in human capital is a risky business. If there are no private markets for diversifying these risks, the government may step in and provide insurance by sharing in the investment cost as well as in the returns from the investment via labour income taxation. This second consideration has been the basis of much theoretical analysis (see, for example, Eaton and Rosen, 1980; Varian, 1980; Hamilton, 1987; and Anderberg and Andersson, 2001). Third, there may be an inefficient allocation of information about human capital investment opportunities, with children of parents with a superior educational background having superior access to information; this may cause some inefficiencies.

Empirically there is a strong link between parents' education and their children's education investment. This has been shown, for instance, for the UK by Ermisch and Francesconi (2001), for Sweden in Högskoleverket (1997: 45–7), and for Germany by Grüske (1994: 95n). Erikson and Jonsson (1996: ch. 1) scrutinise the evidence concerning the achievement of equal opportunity more broadly from a mainly sociological perspective, 'equal opportunity' meaning, essentially, that the educational distribution is independent of origin. Erikson and Jonsson conclude that while there are a number of factors that appear to promote equal opportunity (generally equitable living conditions being one such factor), there are only a few factors that have a clearly discernible favourable effect. The two most important such factors are the elimination of early decision points for students (contrary to some intuitions, students' choices are more sensitive to their background early on), and the elimination of 'dead ends' in the education system, i.e. elimination of lines of study that do not qualify for continuation.[7] Moreover, Erikson and Jonsson point out that a meritocratic system – i.e. a system which is selective with selection based purely on merit rather than involving subjective evaluations – on the whole tends to promote equal opportunity in the sense described. As to the effect of incentives on equal opportunity, this is a more controversial matter; Sjögren (2000) builds a model where a student's uncertainty about their ability in a particular occupation is larger the larger the 'distance' from parental occupation. She estimates the model on Swedish data, confirming the model prediction that students from poor backgrounds are more sensitive to economic incentives

---

[7] Recent work by Meghir and Palme (2001) – employing a rather rare instance of a natural experiment produced by the gradual introduction of the Swedish comprehensive school in the 1960s – corroborates this idea; the elimation of a 'dead end' in the old system changed significantly the distribution of education obtained.

for education. Erikson and Jonsson (1996) also consider the evidence concerning the effect of incentives, and conclude that there is evidence in both directions.

In order to assess these arguments as a basis for governmental intervention from an efficiency point of view, one needs to analyse the reasons for the constraints, and ask why the government could do better than the market.

A virtue of standard education policy is that it enables individuals who are credit constrained – i.e. individuals who are unable to finance their investments in the credit market – to make investments in human capital. This notion has received considerable attention in development economics (see, for example, Aghion and Bolton, 1997) and it is clear that credit markets are far from perfect due to asymmetric information and incentive problems. The government influences the market outcome by a number of regulations, in particular between borrowers and lenders. For instance, high minimum income guarantees and regulations that shift the burden of individual bankruptcy away from the borrower to the lender or to society are clearly beneficial from an *ex-post* view. High minimum income guarantees yield insurance, and bankruptcy regulations that waive individual debt after a short time period have nice incentive effects for starting to earn income again for those individuals who have become bankrupt and are locked in a poverty trap otherwise. From an *ex-ante* point of view, however, minimum income guarantees reduce the available collateral in lending relationships, and bankruptcy laws that make it easy to leave the state of bankruptcy generate moral hazard incentives and may reduce or eliminate the scope for private market arrangements. For these reasons, the scope for government action on credit market constraints and the non-existence of private insurance markets is limited.

The answer regarding whether the government can really improve upon a laissez-faire outcome, depends on what causes the market imperfections and credit constraints. If education activity and the use of subsidised education goods are unobservable, the general insights in Arnott and Stiglitz (1986) on moral hazard in insurance markets apply: in many cases the government can indeed improve upon the laissez-faire moral-hazard equilibrium by a mandatory scheme by which lump-sum financed education goods are subsidised or provided free to all individuals.[8]

---

[8] The intuition why the government can do what private insurance companies could not do in a competitive laissez-faire environment is as follows. Suppose an individual could purchase an education good that increases the probability of becoming highly productive, say, a book. Suppose that, from a welfare point of view, it would be beneficial if this book is purchased, because its cost is smaller than the expected human capital value it generates, but that this book is not purchased in the laissez-faire moral-hazard equilibrium

Credit market constraints and the information advantages of children with parents with above-average education may provide a clear basis for some education policy on redistributional grounds. Actual education policy, however, does not deliver the type of redistribution that is desirable from an 'equal opportunities' point of view. Given that the percentage of children who take up a university education is positively correlated with variables like parents' status or income, the present system is redistributive, but it redistributes on average more to families with rich or highly educated parents than to poor families.[9]

If education investment is a transfer from parents to children, then intergenerational aspects must be considered. Suppose the transfers are motivated by altruism. Given the strong correlation between parents' income and educational attainment and their children's educational attainment, public funding of university education is a redistribution from poor parents to rich parents. The redistributive impact is further increased if one takes into account the fact that in-kind transfers of education goods have to be used by rich parents to overcome a Samaritan's dilemma problem that is faced particularly by rich parents if they are altruistically linked with their children, as has been pointed out by Bruce and Waldman (1991).[10]

with competitive insurance markets. The government can charge a lump-sum tax from everyone and hand out the book for free to overcome this problem. An insurance company cannot do the same thing because nothing prevents the insuree from re-selling the book to someone who has purchased no or less insurance coverage from another insurance company that does not use a contract that includes the purchase of the book.

[9] Another aspect of this argument is the social Samaritan's dilemma problem (see Bruce and Waldman, 1991). If children have to finance their education investment and have to pay back a loan (whether this is a private loan or a public loan only makes a gradual difference with this problem), then it may be individually rational for the children to use up the loan and to stay below a critical income level at which repayments of the loan would start during their professional life, if such a critical income level exists (it exists in all welfare societies). One theoretical way to escape from this problem is to abolish or lower the critical income level. But this policy conflicts with the goals of a welfarist society. Alternatively, the educational grant could be made unconditional. This policy requires that there are other sources of government revenue that could be used for funding such a policy, but given the welfare losses that can be generated by the hold-up problem that is described by this Samaritan's dilemma, this cross-subsidisation may be worthwhile.

[10] If parents are altruistic and sufficiently rich, children may abstain from education investment in order to elicit an increase in transfers and bequests from their parents. This outcome is inefficient, and in-kind transfers to the children, like payment of tuition fees, can solve the dilemma. There is no strategic behaviour that could induce huge bequests from poor parents, and rich parents thus have an additional incentive to provide education to their children that poor parents do not have. A publicly provided university system can crowd out these private incentives. There is evidence that the relationship between social background and labour-market success gets weaker with higher education (Erikson and Jonsson, 1996: 45–6); such a relationship is in accordance with this argument.

If the aim of education policy is redistribution according to an equal opportunities argument,[11] one may reconsider its targeting. We will briefly discuss an education policy that could improve targeting. The policy is based on the idea of self-selection and has been outlined, for instance, by Besley and Coate (1991). A person can, at a given time, consume only one type or quality level of education. For instance, the consumption of an undergraduate programme in some discipline at a public university without tuition fees, and a similar programme at a private university with high tuition fees are mutually exclusive. Suppose that the government decides to provide free public education on the university level and chooses a low or intermediate quality level (for example, large classes, few teachers per student), and finances this programme by a per-capita tax. Then poor parents and rich parents both have to make a decision whether to send their child to the tuition-free school, or whether to spend high tuition fees for an outstanding programme. If university education for their children is a normal good, the population will be divided along income lines: the poor will prefer the tuition-free programme, whereas the rich will not make use of the tuition-free programme. Instead, they will send their children to the very top private schools, even though this implies paying high tuition fees. As a result, the poor and the rich jointly finance the tuition-free programmes, but only the poor use it. Accordingly, some equalising income redistribution can be achieved. Note that the government does not need to distinguish between poor and rich parents to make this work. It is the self-selection by which the rich decide to abstain from using the publicly provided programmes that brings about the desired income redistribution.

The returns to education and external effects

Empirical estimates of the returns to education were provided in section 13.1. For an assessment of education policy one needs to ask whether the total return to education is higher or lower than the private return. According to Temple (2001: 10), given the state of the art one cannot decide whether education investment generates these returns through productivity increases, or through signalling and information processing on existing productivity differences. Note also that both types of achievements have private and social benefits such that this question is not decisive for

---

[11] It is a legitimate question whether the existing types of education policy are designed to bring about redistribution from the rich to the poor, or to provide equal opportunities, or whether their distributional implications are on purpose. As is discussed in Epple and Romano (1996), the political economy outcome has a tendency for redistribution from the ends of the income distribution towards the middle.

whether the public returns of education exceed or fall short of the private returns. Elementary education, language skills, writing or reading skills, foreign language skills, and more recently computer skills are important for the functioning of communication, and they are therefore potentially associated with network externalities. Similar arguments may be used for skills stemming from advanced education, such as a common cultural or intellectual background.[12] The relevance of such network externalities is probably more pronounced for elementary education (reading, writing, basic mathematics), and also relevant for some intermediate (secondary) education. For tertiary education the relevance of network externalities is probably rather limited, and free university education should probably not build on this type of argument.[13]

An important external effect of education goods has been emphasised by the modern theory of endogenous growth (see, for example, Lucas, 1988). The cornerstone of this theory is that investment in capital generates returns, but only some of these returns can be appropriated by the owner of the investment. Some of the returns 'spill over' in a very dispersed way across the whole economy. But if only some fraction of the benefits of an investment is internalised in the decision of the investor, then under-investment results. Accordingly, the economy suffers from under-investment, and this is where governmental intervention may have its role.[14,15] The relevance of this argument depends on whether such macroeconomic spillovers of investment exist or not, and if they exist, how important they are. It is difficult to distinguish from a theoretical perspective whether such spillovers result primarily from human capital investment, from spending on research and development, or on other

[12] For a formal analysis of such network effects of, for instance, language skills, and the resulting inefficiencies, see, for instance, Konrad and Thum (1993).

[13] Gradstein and Justman (1999a, b) consider similar externalities, claiming that education has a 'socialising' function. If the education system is fully privatised, the outcome might be a less homogeneous society with fewer common norms and value judgements. They argue in line with the theory of network externalities in Gradstein and Justman (1999a) that education can integrate a society if the education system is appropriately designed, and that to achieve this requires government intervention. Parents do internalise only some part of the benefits of a higher degree of integration; that is, they take into account that integrating their own children benefits them, but they disregard that this also benefits the rest of the society. Accordingly, a fully privately designed education system may provide too little integration. While this is an interesting idea, it is mainly an argument for government intervention in the design of education, and not necessarily an argument that concerns the question whether education should be privately or publicly funded.

[14] See, for instance, Glomm and Ravikumar (1992) and Eckstein and Zilcha (1994).

[15] Further external effects occur with the education system. See, for example, Epple and Romano (1998).

investment activities, such as investing in physical assets, and empirical analyses do not reveal particularly unambiguous results.

Sectoral neutrality

Investment in human capital is only one of many alternative types of investment. In a laissez-faire economy, the various types of investment are used up to the point where they have the same marginal return. In a welfare state the various types of investment are typically distorted by taxes and regulations. These distortions of human capital investment may provide a second-best argument for public education policy.

Many Nordic countries (for example, Norway, Sweden, Finland and, with modifications, Denmark) tax the returns of different types of investment differently. Instead of following the principle of global income taxation that sums up all sources of income and subjects it to a uniform tax schedule, a dual system taxes capital income from ownership of physical assets at a lower rate than labour income; returns from human capital are part of labour income. Hence, the marginal tax rate on the returns of human capital exceeds the marginal tax rate on capital returns.

Nielsen and Sørensen (1997) argue that investment in human capital is not discriminated against, despite this fact. Whereas taxed earnings (savings) are typically the source of physical investment, a major share of human capital investment is generated from diverting leisure towards education effort. This leisure is an untaxed source of income. They conclude from this that there are tax advantages in human capital investment, and these tax advantages counteract the distortionary effect of higher marginal tax rates on the returns of human capital, compared with physical capital.

Exactly the opposite result is obtained in an analysis by Nerlove et al. (1993). They assume that the same (taxed) input is used to make investment in human capital and investment in physical capital. They conclude that human capital investment is discriminated against due to differences in depreciation allowances. Both physical assets and human capital depreciate. However, whereas depreciation of physical assets reduces taxable income, the depreciation of human capital is not (or very partially) accounted for in the tax laws.

Given these two countervailing effects, the question whether actual laws discriminate more strongly against investment in physical assets or investment in human capital cannot be decided easily. However, the analysis shows that there is some distortion between the inputs into human capital formation. We should expect that the input mix between time used for education, and (monetary) resources that are spent for education goods, is inefficient; a substitution of time by monetary effort is likely to improve welfare.[16] As it may be difficult for the government to measure and observe actual monetary or time effort, it must rely on second-best tools like co-financing goods that are complementary with education.

This insight has some implications. It suggests that an efficient education policy should change the private cost of different education inputs differently. Monetary inputs in education should be subsidised relatively more than time use. It could also be useful from this perspective to have requirements on maximum time periods for achieving certain education goals.

Government failure

Human capital investment returns are taxed heavily. The maximum marginal tax rate on labour income in OECD countries was 50.2 per cent on average in 1998. New Zealand had the lowest top marginal rate (33 per cent), and Belgium had the highest rate with 66 per cent (see OECD, 2001b). Boadway et al. (1996) apply the idea of time-consistent capital income taxation by a benevolent government that was formulated by Kydland and Prescott (1980) to human capital investment. Human capital investment is made when individuals are young. Its returns accrue ten to forty years later. Any investment made is sunk at the point when the taxes on human capital returns are decided. Individuals in their thirties, in the midst of their working life, cannot react to high marginal taxes by a reduction in their human capital investment. A government that aims at efficient taxation and that wants to minimise the welfare losses from tax-induced substitution effects knows that the tax rate on human capital returns does not distort human capital formation at the time when the actual tax is chosen, because human capital investment is already chosen and sunk at that point in time. Accordingly, the government chooses a high tax burden on the returns from the existing stock of human capital.

Individuals anticipate this type of tax policy already when they make their human capital investment decisions. The high *expected* tax burden is a disincentive for human capital investment at this time when this stock of investment is still endogenous. Time-consistent tax policy therefore yields high tax rates on the returns from human capital, too low education

---

[16] This point had been made already by Kaplow (1993). The inefficiency in the input mix does not imply that the absolute amount of time used in the production of human capital is too high. Given the various distortions at work, there may well be under-investment in the sense that more monetary inputs *and* more time should be used in the production of human capital.

investment, too small a stock of human capital, and possibly little tax revenue. Time-consistent tax policy results in a situation with excessive taxation and under-investment in human capital. The government would be better advised to follow a commitment strategy in which it commits to a tax policy for the next few decades. It would commit to lower tax rates than the ones that are *ex-post* optimal in a time-consistent framework. Human capital investment would be higher, and even the governmental tax revenue could possibly be higher than in the situation with anticipated time-consistent excessive tax policy.

The central question is how to achieve an appropriate degree of commitment that can avoid the welfare cost of discretionary time-consistent governmental behaviour. This commitment problem is particularly severe; it requires that the government credibly commits to tax rates for the next thirty to forty years, knowing that these desirable tax rates are much lower than the tax rates that the government would actually like to choose thirty or forty years later. It is doubtful whether that commitment is feasible for such a long time period.[17]

Boadway et al. (1996) offer a solution: they suggest mandatory education, or, perhaps more appropriate for tertiary education, subsidised public provision of education. Governmental intervention is caused here by another governmental intervention. Public subsidies are not a means for curing a market failure, but they cure a government failure.[18]

The same incentive problems appear for a Leviathan government that aims at maximising the tax surplus, net of public investment. If a dictator, or a small power group, extorts a country and maximises the surplus that can be extracted from extorting the country, any expenditure this group makes in terms of investment that enhances the country's output and prosperity in the future, is similar to the private investment by the owner of a company. This analogy has been pointed out by Olson (1993) and

---

[17] There is an intimate relation between the time-consistency issue regarding redistributive taxation, and the appropriate education policy. One may want to redistribute via the provision of education goods *ex-ante*, and generate an environment with equal opportunities at the education stage. But if the success of education investment is to some extent stochastic, there may be scope for redistribution even if, at some point in time, all individuals were in a situation with equal opportunities. We will not pursue this line of argument here, however.

[18] Several solutions to the government failure of excessive time-consistent taxation of human capital returns have been proposed in other contexts, but none of these solutions seems to be suitable for time periods of thirty years. Two types should be mentioned. Kehoe (1989) suggested that international mobility of tax bases and tax competition can substitute for the *ex-post* inelasticity of the tax base, limiting the scope for excessive taxation. We will come back to this when considering the issue of globalisation. Konrad (2001) discusses rents from asymmetric information on the actual productivity impact of individual human capital investments as a means to reduce the welfare effects of excessive time-consistent taxation.

McGuirre and Olson (1996) more generally. The dictator of a country who earns returns from governing the country today may consider how much to invest in the country. The investment increases the output and productivity of the country which he extorts, and he will be able to appropriate a share of the increase in output that is generated by the unit of investment. The dictator will invest up to the point where the sacrifices of the unit of investment which he gives up for investment equals the benefits from the share of the increased output which he can appropriate. Hence, his investment incentive is higher the higher the share of the marginal returns from investment which the dictator can appropriate. As long as the share of marginal returns which can be appropriated by the dictator is smaller than 100 per cent, the dictator will invest too little.[19]

Andersson and Konrad (2000b) show that an extortionary government and a benevolent government that would like to collect and redistribute taxes face very similar time-consistency problems of income taxation. A revenue-maximising dictator would then have similar incentives to use education subsidies as a second-best tool to cure this problem.

13.3   Globalisation

International mobility of production, inputs, consumption goods, information, knowledge, skills and individuals has increased recently. In this section we consider the impact of this trend for tertiary education. Two main aspects will be highlighted. First, increased mobility generates fiscal externalities. These fiscal externalities have incentive effects for the amount and type of public and private education and tax policy. Second, increased mobility changes individuals' exposure to risk and their risk management tools. But before we turn to these policy aspects we consider some empirical aspects of skill mobility; while this is not the only type of mobility with implications for tax and education policies, it is the one with most such direct implications.

On the significance of skill mobility

We would expect skill mobility to be increasing for a number of reasons. For instance, in Europe, the common market with free mobility of factors, goods and people has been advanced in 1992. Portability of

---

[19] Konrad (1995) follows a similar argument with respect to an economy with overlapping generations in which the old generation is in power and extorts the young generation by means of a pay-as-you-go financed social security system on the one hand, and provides output-enhancing public infrastructure and education investment on the other.

social insurance entitlements for workers who migrate between different European countries has also been improved.[20] In addition, the world has moved closer together by a number of developments. International trade has grown, and many consumption products – including music, movies and even television series – have been standardised worldwide and have become universally available.

To assess international skill mobility empirically turns out to be difficult, however. A comprehensive effort in this direction is the work on Nordic skill migration by Peder Pedersen, Marianne Røed and Lena Schröder in this volume. The reader is referred to their chapter (chapter 4) for a literature survey, discussion and new results, but we will nevertheless make some brief remarks.

It is often presumed that people with more education are more prone to migrate internationally. There are some obvious reasons for this presumption. It seems, clear, for example, that education directly or indirectly makes people acquainted with foreign countries and foreign culture; language skills, of course, are an obvious case in point. It also seems clear that the fact that a higher degree of specialisation coming with a higher education calls for searching a larger labour market; specialised skills in science, academia or engineering may be demanded only by a small number of employers in a country. There are, however, potentially countervailing forces; Röed (1996) points out that firm-specific skills may grow more rapidly for workers with more education, creating a stronger tie with the current employer. One can also argue that asymmetric information regarding skills is increasing in the skill level, and that it is therefore more expensive for high-skill workers to signal their skills to a foreign employer rather than a domestic one.

Empirically, the work of Pedersen et al. (this volume) shows for the countries considered – Denmark, Norway and Sweden – that migration is considerably higher for workers with more education. This may suggest that they are more mobile; also it seems clear that these are the workers most susceptible to wage incentives.

Concerning the magnitude of emigration from the countries considered, Pedersen et al. find that it is quite small, and that return migration moderates the likely impact of emigration of skilled workers. Nevertheless, they find, for example, that net emigration from Sweden of some key categories of workers has been significant recently (table 4.5). Thus, while it seems clear that migration is relatively small, this is subject to

[20] Of course, considerable obstacles remain and will remain given that social security systems in Europe differ along many dimensions (for example, size, links between contributions and benefits, redistributive elements, or types of funding). However, the progress that has been made in the EU already is remarkable.

a number of caveats.[21] First, the significance of even a small increase of emigration would be substantial if those emigrating were to return to a lesser extent than is historically the case, and the extent of return migration is not observable until some time after emigration has taken place. Second, equilibrium migration is not a good indicator of potential migration. The fact that migration of skilled labour within Europe is small may be due to intrinsically low mobility, or to relatively weak incentives. It is therefore very hard to predict the effects of stronger incentives and reduced institutional impediments to migration.

These caveats are important in light of the fact that a number of impediments to skill mobility are subject to attack by the EU. There are efforts, for instance, to facilitate portability of social benefits and to standardise university exams. Moreover, the dramatic increase in student exchange among EU countries may be significant. The combined effect of exam standardisation and student exchange is interesting: one potential problem for highly educated workers is the lack of information a foreign employer may have regarding the worker's qualifications; reducing this informational asymmetry may serve to remove a substantial impediment to international skill migration.[22] Such considerations open up the possibility that the combined effect of various aspects of globalisation and harmonisation may have sizeable consequences.[23]

In what follows we consider the implications of increased labour mobility, particularly the increased mobility of highly skilled workers, and the incentives this increase in mobility generates for private and public incentives for human capital investment.

Education and taxation

With high labour mobility, the public benefits of higher education do not always accrue where education is funded. Justman and Thisse (1997, 2000) point out that this may undermine existing frameworks for funding public higher education, reducing the local incentives for provision of public education. In their framework, they assume that education is publicly provided and funded by the owners of a factor that is complementary to skilled labour. If labour reacts to wage differentials, a region

---

[21] A discussion of empirical problems and a survey of some facts that support the hypothesis of increased mobility is given in Wildasin (2000a). He concludes that labour mobility has increased in Europe within the last decade, but that mobility is far from being perfect.

[22] A model analysing such information asymmetries can be found in Katz and Stark (1987).

[23] In addition, as pointed out by Pedersen et al., the growing pool of university graduates is manifest in the fact that emigration in the 1990s has grown, while propensities across levels of education have stayed relatively constant.

can attract skilled labour by reducing its own level of public investment in education. They conclude that in the uncoordinated Nash equilibrium there is public under-investment in education.[24] A related mechanism is explored in Poutvaara and Kanniainen (2000). Here the unskilled co-finance public education and are better off from this because skilled and unskilled labour are complements. Again, introducing international mobility of the highly skilled generates free-riding incentives: the financing share of the skilled cannot be sustained, and an inferior outcome results.

Human capital mobility has also been considered in the tax competition literature. The increase in international mobility of highly skilled workers is an additional constraint for national tax policy. This insight is well established and clearly illustrated by Cremer et al. (1996). These authors discuss how robust the effects of the additional constraint are, given different institutional assumptions, and survey the extensive literature that considers this effect. They find that the mobility of human capital (that is, mobility of the highly skilled workers) reduces the scope for redistributive taxation.[25]

Wildasin (2000b) has explored the interaction between the financing of human capital investments in an imperfect credit market and globalisation. The setting is one where education produces specialised skills. Unskilled workers are intersectorally mobile and geographically immobile; skilled workers are intersectorally immobile and globalisation makes them geographically mobile. Globalisation has the benefit of reducing the wage risk of high-skilled workers. Wildasin compares the case where the education investment can be financed privately with the case where it cannot. The key conclusion is that whereas globalisation is unambiguously beneficial in the former case, it leads to low-skilled workers carrying the entire cost of education in the latter case. While obviously extreme due to extreme mobility assumptions, the result is in line with a recurrent

---

[24] In Gradstein and Justman (1995) international mobility generates an incentive to over-invest. The idea here is similar to Keen and Marchand (1997) who consider infrastructure competition for foreign direct investment: if foreign direct investment is internationally mobile, regions can attract more foreign direct investment if they offer a skilful labour force. In an uncoordinated Nash equilibrium over-investment in infrastructure/local human capital occurs.

[25] Whether these effects are of practical relevance depends on whether the mechanisms that are described in the theory of tax competition are at work or not, and this question is closely related to the question of whether the highly skilled have become or will soon become highly mobile. Empirical analyses of tax competition problems exist with respect to a number of issues. However, the outcome of this empirical work is often ambiguous. While the outcome is typically in line with the predictions of tax competition theory, there are several other plausible and competing hypotheses that could explain the data similarly well. See, e.g., Brueckner (2000) for a survey.

observation in this context: the timing of education subsidies makes mobility of skilled labour very costly for immobile workers. Also, the trade-off concerning education investment when education is publicly financed is very harsh – education is productive but very costly due to the fact that its cost must be borne by low-skilled workers.

The result in Justman and Thisse (1997, 2000) rests on the assumption that education investment has to be publicly provided and funded for exogenous reasons. However, education could be the instrument that counteracts the government failure of time-consistent and excessive taxation. Suppose that international tax competition with respect to human capital income really takes place. If the highly skilled are perfectly mobile, the equilibrium tax rates in all countries are very low; in general terms, taxes reduce to pure equivalence taxation and redistribution ceases to be feasible.[26],[27] Accordingly, there is no excessive taxation in the equilibrium in the globalised economy, and therefore no need for an education policy compensating for excessive taxation.[28] For an extended analysis of the education-investment incentives of workers as well as governments in a scenario where education makes workers highly skilled and mobile, see Andersson and Konrad (2000a, b).[29]

Insurance aspects

Seen from the perspective of individuals who do not know yet whether their human capital investment will make them rich and successful or poor and unsuccessful, redistributive taxation has features of an insurance policy. Time-consistent taxation in a closed economy will provide too much insurance, however, and thereby provide too weak (second-best) incentives for human capital investment. If the public sector retreats from this insurance activity there will be a demand for private insurance. Whether

[26] Taxes used for public-good production might attract mobile factors if those factors benefit from the public goods in question. In fact, some empirical work on factor mobility indicates that infrastructure is more important than taxes for localisation decisions. The basic point is made by Wildasin (2000a); the latter point is made by James Markusen in a comment published in Wildasin (2000a).

[27] An important observation is that education subsidies, although not always redistributive, are likely to be subject to downward pressure from globalisation because of their timing properties: although a high-skilled worker considering the possibility of migrating internationally has probably benefited from education subsidies in his country of origin, this does not constitute a reason to stay.

[28] Kehoe (1989) was the first to notice that globalisation may resolve the time-consistency problem in taxation.

[29] The same forces may be induced if skilled labour is immobile, but capital complementary with skilled labour is internationally mobile. If net rents from the production utilising skilled labour and mobile capital are shared by workers and capital owners, the same logic applies.

and to what extent insurance markets will emerge is an interesting aspect of globalisation. The answer depends on the extent to which insurance provided by redistributive taxation has crowded out private insurance that would have existed in the absence of such taxation; the viability of such markets will obviously depend critically on the way informational problems in those markets are resolved.

In the setting considered by Andersson and Konrad (2000a) where the investment in human capital is risky, and where globalisation undermines redistributive taxation and leads to all education subsidies ultimately being borne by low-skilled workers, the welfare effects of globalisation depend critically on the possibility for workers to insure the outcome of their investment *ex ante*. If such income insurance is available, globalisation is unambiguously beneficial; if it is not available, welfare effects are ambiguous – there is over-insurance due to time-consistent taxation in the absence of globalisation, and there is no insurance in the presence of globalisation. It is clear, however, that unskilled workers fare badly under globalisation without private insurance, and that the policy trade-off when the only policy instrument is education subsidies borne by low-skilled workers is very harsh.

An aspect that has to be taken seriously in this context is the interim period. If globalisation was not anticipated by individuals who are now in their fifties, they did not anticipate that redistribution will cease to exist once they reach this age, and they will not have bought private insurance. Hence, for this generation, unanticipated globalisation will lead to a strong increase in inequality.[30]

Mobility differences

Different types of professions or individuals differ in their international mobility. Lawyers or tax consultants are typically less internationally mobile than are medical doctors, engineers, computer specialists or investment bankers. A government can choose whether to treat different professions differently, with respect to education investment subsidies and with respect to income taxes (see, for instance, Thum and Übelmesser, 2000), or whether to find a way to commit to treating mobile and immobile professions uniformly.

---

[30] The analysis in Andersson and Konrad (2000a) shows that risk spreading via redistributive taxation and private insurance markets are substitutes. Given the level of public risk sharing through redistributive taxation, the non-existence of private markets for such risks – such as private education loans that are paid back only in case of success – is not surprising. This non-existence does not prove that these markets would not exist if the government withdrew from this insurance activity.

With discriminatory tax rules, taxation and tax competition yield a situation in which immobile professions face high tax rates, and mobile professions pay little taxes. Accordingly, there is a hold-up problem with respect to investment in education for immobile professions, and no hold-up problem as regards education investment in professions that are perfectly mobile since the private investment incentives in these professions are high. According to the insights obtained from analysing the hold-up problem in the closed economy and from analysing globalisation, it is optimal to use public education subsidies as a second-best policy to counteract the problem of under-investment in the immobile professions, whereas no active education policy is needed in professions in which workers are perfectly mobile. The situation is more complex if discriminatory education subsidies are not feasible due to, for instance, education not being sufficiently specific, and specialisation for mobile or immobile professions occurring when some or all investment in education has already taken place. Similarly, discriminatory taxation is sometimes not feasible, for instance because it is ruled out as violating some basic egalitarian principles in taxation (for example, 'horizontal equity').[31]

A recurrent observation when considering mobility differences is that a net fiscal burden can be imposed only on low-income earners if discriminatory taxation is possible and if high-income earners are perfectly mobile and low-income earners are perfectly immobile. An implication of this is that an extortionary state would have to rely on immobile low-income earners as its main tax base. This fact generates an additional incentive for young persons to invest in human capital, and the relationship between productivity and mobility generates excess incentives for private human capital investment. An extortionary state that observes individuals trying to escape from taxation by investing in mobility-enhancing human capital has an incentive to make it more difficult for the citizens to acquire such human capital, for instance by taxing such activities. These issues have been analysed more closely in Andersson and Konrad (2000b).

13.4   Policy implications

We identified several important reasons for government intervention in the market for education.

[31] In a tax competition framework, if countries can choose *ex post* between uniform taxation and taxation that differentiates with respect to mobility, there is a tendency to differentiate tax rates with respect to mobility (Janeba and Peters, 1999). However, countries may coordinate on uniform taxation rules, and tax competition may then occur with respect to taxes obeying these rules. Keen (2000) has shown that whether tax revenue is higher with uniform taxation or with differentiated tax rates is surprisingly unclear; he presents the case where differentiated taxation generates more tax revenue.

First, concerns for redistribution and 'equal opportunity' arguments may call for education policies that overcome credit market constraints and inequities in the process through which people make educational choices. Current attempts to generate 'equal opportunities' are at best partially successful, and a whole battery of measures may be needed to counter the tendencies of a persistently skewed selection of students into higher education; as we have noted, there is evidence that private incentives and a strong emphasis on excellence may be beneficial rather than harmful in this regard. Moreover, free provision of education goods and education subsidies may reduce moral hazard problems in education goods markets and markets for student loans. A caveat in this context is that although perfectly well-functioning private insurance markets and perfect credit markets cannot be established, current governmental tax and education policy may partially be responsible for these market deficiencies and may have crowded out some of these markets. The government may be able to do a great deal to facilitate the emergence of such markets by changing the set of relevant constraints.

Second, it is unclear whether current education policy is an efficient means of redistributing from the rich to the poor. If this is the implicit aim of public education, one may want to choose an education system with several quality levels in which lower quality levels receive higher subsidies; in such a system redistribution occurs on a self-selection basis. Such alternative types of redistribution mechanisms may become more important in a globalised economy in which the scope for redistribution in general is reduced.

Third, we have compared the private and social benefits of education investment and identified a number of external effects of education. This analysis suggests that there are positive and negative externalities of education and the overall balance of external effects is unclear. The balance is more likely to be positive for primary and secondary education, however, suggesting that these types of education should be subsidised more strongly.

Fourth, we have considered the interplay between education investment and taxation, and several conclusions follow. The analysis suggests that there is a fundamental distortion of the 'input mix' in education; the costs of time inputs borne by students are deflated due to income taxation. An implication is that education policy should subsidise education goods other than the time input more strongly than the time input. This may justify strict requirements regarding the overall time (or the number of failed attempts in examinations), a student is allowed in obtaining a degree. It may also justify subsidies to physical assets that are used in education. Since students' time input is probably complementary to the other resources devoted to their education, this is a reason to emphasise quality rather than quantity in higher education. Further, we have argued that public education provision is partially motivated as a second-best tool for overcoming the hold-up problem that is generated by time-consistent excessive taxation of human capital returns. Globalisation eliminates the scope for excessive taxation and the need for this second-best tool.

Fifth, globalisation has a number of implications for a nation's optimal tax and education policy. In general, globalisation limits the scope for redistributive activities, and this may lead to lower taxes and less education subsidies. However, we may also expect a differentiation of taxes and education policy along the lines of differences in skill mobility for different types of education and different professions. Our overall conclusion is that globalisation will put pressure on government funding, including the public budget for expenditure on higher education, but that the simultaneous downward pressure on the taxes of the returns to human capital is a countervailing force in terms of sustaining the level of investment in human capital. The tightening of governments' budgets and the limits this imposes also on public expenditure on education, however, calls for governments to focus their effort on alternative instruments that help promote the goals of traditional education policy.

References

Aghion, P. and Bolton, P., 1997, 'A theory of trickle-down growth and development', *Review of Economic Studies*, 64, 151–72.
Anderberg, D. and Andersson, F., 2001, 'Investment in human capital, wage uncertainty, and public policy', *Journal of Public Economics*, forthcoming.
Andersson, F. and Konrad, K. A., 2000a, 'Human capital formation and globalization', forthcoming in *International Tax and Public Finance* 10, 211–28.
—2000b, 'Human capital investment and globalization in extortionary states', forthcoming in *Journal of Public Economics*.
Arnott, R. and Stiglitz, J. E., 1986, 'Moral hazard and optimal commodity taxation', *Journal of Public Economics*, 29, 1–24.
Besley, T. and Coate, S., 1991, 'Public provision of private goods and the redistribution of income', *American Economic Review*, 81, 979–84.
Björklund, A., 2000, 'Education policy and the returns to education', *Swedish Economic Policy Review*, 7, 71–105.
Boadway, R., Marceau, N. and Marchand, M., 1996, 'Investment in education and the time inconsistency of redistributive tax policy', *Economica*, 63, 171–89.
Bruce, N. and Waldman, M., 1991, 'Transfers in kind: why they can be efficient and nonpaternalistic', *American Economic Review*, 81, 1345–51.
Brueckner, J. K., 2000, 'Welfare reform and the race to the bottom: theory and evidence', *Southern Economic Journal*, 66, 505–25.

Cremer, H., Fourgeaud, V., Leite-Monteiro, M., Marchand, M. and Pestieau, P., 1996, 'Mobility and redistribution: a survey', *Public Finance*, 51, 325–52.

Eaton, J. and Rosen, H. S., 1980, 'Taxation, human capital, and uncertainty', *American Economic Review*, 70, 705–15.

Eckstein, Z. and Zilcha, I., 1994, 'The effects of compulsory schooling on growth, income distribution and welfare', *Journal of Public Economics*, 54, 339–59.

Epple, D. and Romano, R. E., 1996, 'Ends against the middle: determining public service provision when there are private alternatives', *Journal of Public Economics*, 62, 297–325.

—1998, 'Competition between private and public schools, vouchers, and peer-group effects', *American Economic Review*, 88, 33–63.

Erikson, R. and Jonsson, J. O., 1996, 'Can education be equalized? The Swedish case in comparative perspective', *Westview Press*, Oxford.

Ermisch, J. and Francesconi, M., 2001, 'Family matters: impacts of family background on educational attainment', *Economica*, 68, 137–56.

Glomm, G. and Ravikumar, B., 1992, 'Public versus private investment in human capital: endogenous growth and income inequality', *Journal of Political Economy*, 100, 818–34.

Gradstein, M. and Justman, M., 1995, 'Competitive investment in higher education: the need for policy coordination', *Economics Letters*, 47, 393–400.

—1999a, 'Education, social cohesion, and economic growth', *Discussion Paper No. 99–16*, Monaster Center, Ben-Gurion University.

—1999b, 'Human capital, social capital, and public schooling', paper presented at the EEA 1999 meetings.

Grüske, K.-D., 1994, 'Verteilungseffekte der öffentlichen Hochschulfinanzierung in der Bundesrepublik Deutschland – Personale Inzidenz im Querschnitt und Längsschnitt', in R. Lüdeke (ed.), *Bildung, Bildungsfinanzierung und Einkommensverteilung II*, Schriften des Vereins für Socialpolitik, N.F. Bd. 221/II, 71–147.

Hamilton, J. H., 1987, 'Optimal wage and income taxation with wage uncertainty', *International Economic Review*, 28, 373–88.

Högskoleverket (National Agency for Higher Education), 1997, 'Årsrapport för universitet & högskolor 1995/96' (yearly report for universities), Stockholm.

Janeba, E. and Peters, W., 1999, 'Tax evasion, tax competition and the gains from nondiscrimination: the case of interest taxation in Europe', *Economic Journal*, 109, 93–101.

Justman, M. and Thisse, J.-F., 1997, 'Implications of the mobility of skilled labor for local public funding of higher education', *Economics Letters*, 55, 409–12.

—2000, 'Local public funding of higher education when skilled labor is imperfectly mobile', *International Tax and Public Finance*, 7, 247–58.

Kaplow, L., 1993, 'Human capital and the income tax', National Bureau of Economic Research, working paper 4299.

Katz, E. and Stark, O., 1987, 'International migration under asymmetric information', *Economic Journal*, 97, 718–26.

Keen, M., 2000, 'Preferential regimes can make tax competition *less* harmful', mimeo.

Keen, M. and Marchand, M., 1997, 'Fiscal competition and the pattern of public spending', *Journal of Public Economics*, 66, 33–53.

Kehoe, P. J., 1989, 'Policy cooperation among benevolent governments may be undesirable', *Review of Economic Studies*, 56, 289–96.

Konrad, K. A., 1995, 'Social security and strategic inter-vivos transfers of social capital', *Journal of Population Economics*, 8, 315–26.

—2001, 'Privacy, time consistent optimal labor income taxation and education policy', *Journal of Public Economics*, 79, 503–19.

Konrad, K. A. and Thum, M., 1993, 'Fundamental standards and time consistency', *Kyklos*, 46, 545–68.

Kydland, F. E. and Prescott, E. C., 1980, 'Dynamic optimal taxation, rational expectations and optimal control', *Journal of Economic Dynamics and Control*, 2, 79–91.

Lucas, R. E. Jr., 1988, 'On the mechanics of economic development', *Journal of Monetary Economics*, 22, 3–42.

McGuire, M. C. and Olson, M., Jr., 1996, 'The economics of autocracy and majority rule', *Journal of Economic Literature*, 34, 72–96.

Mankiw, N. G., Romer, D. and Weil, D., 1992, 'A contribution to the empirics of economic growth', *Quarterly Journal of Economics*, 107, 407–37.

Meghir, C. and Palme, M., 2001, 'The effect of a social experiment in education', mimeo, UCL and Stockholm School of Economics.

Nerlove, M., Razin, A., Sadka, E. and von Weizsäcker, R. K., 1993, 'Comprehensive income taxation, investments in human and physical capital, and productivity', *Journal of Public Economics*, 50, 397–406.

Nielsen, S. B. and Sørensen, P. B., 1997, 'On the optimality of the Nordic system of dual income taxation', *Journal of Public Economics*, 63, 311–29.

OECD, 1997, 'Implementing the OECD jobs strategy: member countries' Experience', Paris: OECD.

—1999, 'Human capital investment: an international comparison', Paris: OECD.

—2000a, 'OECD in figures, statistics on the member countries', Paris: OECD.

—2000b, 'Education at a glance: OECD indicators', Paris: OECD.

—2001a, 'Education at a glance: OECD indicators', Paris: OECD.

—2001b, 'OECD in figures, statistics on the member countries', Paris: OECD.

Olson, M., 1993, 'Dictatorship, democracy, and development', *American Political Science Review*, 87, 567–76.

Pedersen, P., Röed, M. and Schröder, L., 2003, 'Emigration in the Nordic welfare states', this volume.

Pereira, P. and Silva Martins, P., 2000, 'Does education reduce wage inequality? Quantile regressions evidence from fifteen European countries', *IZA DP No. 120*, Bonn: IZA.

Poutvaara, P. and Kanniainen, V., 2000, 'Why invest in your neighbor? Social contract on educational investment', *International Tax and Public Finance*, 7, 547–62.

Röed, M., 1996, 'Education and international migration: theoretical aspects', in E. Wadensjö (ed.), *The Nordic Labour Markets in the 1990s*, part 2, Amsterdam: North-Holland.

Sjögren, A., 2000, 'Occupational choice and incentives: the role of family background', working paper 539, The Research Institute of Industrial Economics, Stockholm.

Temple, J., 2001, 'Growth effects of education and social capital in the OECD countries', mimeo, University of Bristol.

Thum, C. and Übelmesser, S., 2000, 'Mobility and the role of education as a commitment device', mimeo.

Varian, H., 1980, 'Redistributive taxation as social insurance', *Journal of Public Economics*, 14, 49–68.

Wildasin, D., 2000a, 'Factor mobility and fiscal policy in the EU: policy issues and analytical approaches', *Economic Policy*, 31, 337–78.

—2000b, 'Labor-market integration, investment in risky human capital, and fiscal competition', *American Economic Review*, 90, 73–95.

Wright, R. E., 1999, 'The rate of return to private schooling', *IZA Discussion Paper No. 92*, Bonn.

14   Debt strategies for Sweden and Europe

Martin Flodén

14.1   Introduction

During the final decades of the twentieth century, most European countries accumulated large, and in peacetime unprecedented, public debts.
Interest payments on the debts now constitute an important fiscal burden.
Today these countries also face another challenge to the public budget.
In the coming thirty to forty years, the share of people of working age is
predicted to fall significantly. Considering this reduction in the relative
size of the labour force, it may be wise to start adjusting public policy
now. In particular, fiscal constraints may become less tight in the future
if public debts are reduced today. This chapter explores what paths for
the public debt and the budget surplus are optimal in the face of ageing
populations.

Twelve European countries are included in the study. For all these
countries, the optimal policy is to start reducing public debt immediately
and continuously until some time between the years 2030 and 2045.
The optimal average budget surplus varies between 1 and 4 per cent of
output annually for these countries. The calculations show that for most
countries the welfare loss of pursuing a balanced-budget policy instead
of the optimal debt policy would be modest but not negligible.

The demographic change

Figures 14.1–14.3 show the historical and predicted demographic development in the countries considered.[1,2] Figure 14.1 clearly displays
that the share of workers in the population will fall during the coming
thirty years. In Sweden, for example, this share is predicted to fall from
59 per cent in 2001 to 52 per cent in 2035. The figure also shows that

---

[1] People aged twenty to sixty-four are assumed to be of working age, while people under
twenty are 'young' and people above sixty-four are 'old' or 'retired'. Data are from the
United Nations, 1998.

[2] Lindh (this volume) provides a thorough discussion of the demographic development.

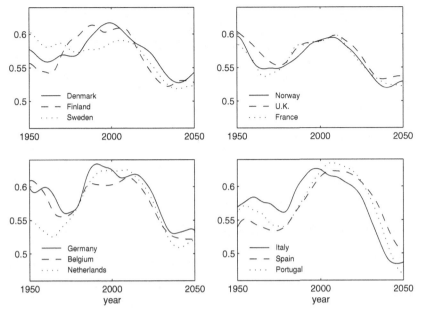

Figure 14.1 Share of people in working age (20–64)

the population ageing is predicted to be similar in all countries, but that the demographic impact will be largest in Southern Europe.

Figure 14.2 shows that the share of old people in the population has increased and is predicted to continue to increase. The pattern is again similar for all countries, but most remarkable in Southern Europe. In Sweden, the fraction of retirees is predicted to increase from 19 per cent today to 29 per cent in 2035. Figure 14.3 shows that the increased dependency burden from population ageing will be offset by a reduced fraction of children in the population. The fraction of children will fall from 24 to 21 per cent in Sweden. Calculations in Domeij and Floden (2001) show that, at least for Sweden, increased life expectancy and falling birth rates contribute to population ageing approximately to the same extent.

Impact on public budget, saving and production

Population ageing can influence the overall economy and, in particular, the public budget in several important ways. Before developing these issues further, let us consider a simple experiment conducted to demonstrate that the changing age structure is likely to be quantitatively important. The experiment is based on the demographic forecasts for Sweden.

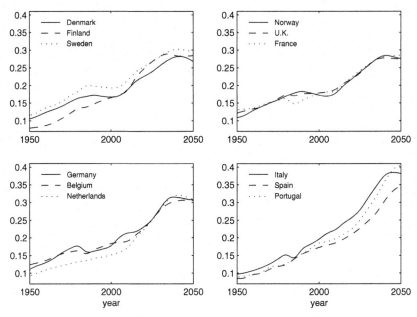

Figure 14.2 Share of old (65+) in population

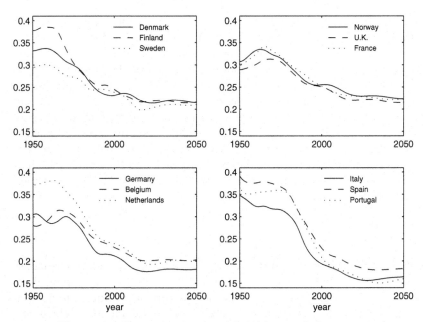

Figure 14.3 Share of young (aged 0–19) in population

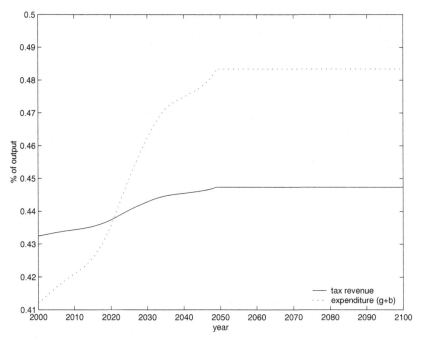

Figure 14.4 Direct impact of demographic change on public budget (Sweden)

Assume that future government policy will be identical to the average policy in the recent past, and that everyone of working age supplies one unit of labour. Further, assume that public transfers and public consumption per capita is constant and equally divided between different age groups. Figure 14.4 shows the resulting development of tax revenues and public spending (not including interest payments) over time. The experiment predicts that the primary surplus will deteriorate by five percentage points in the coming forty years. Calculations by the OECD (1998: 33) result in a quantitatively similar effect on the public budget.[3]

The real response to the demographic change will be more complicated than is indicated by the experiment above. First, individuals may change their behaviour in response to changing demographic structures. For example, Bohn (1999) and Domeij and Floden (2001) show that if people live longer, incentives to save and work when young may be strengthened

[3] The OECD calculations also include some (not explicit) predictions of changes in policy and behaviour. The OECD calculations for Belgium, Canada, France, Germany and the Netherlands are quantitatively similar. The demographic impact is predicted to be slightly smaller in the USA, negligible in the UK and most severe in Japan.

since people then want to accumulate more reserves for their old age. Moreover, if the population ageing implies that future pension benefits will be less generous, people will save more when young to compensate for that reduction. Since people save more, the capital stock may increase and productivity per worker will increase. The increase in savings can therefore mitigate the demographic impact on production. Domeij and Floden demonstrate that these offsetting effects are most likely to occur in countries with little distortive taxation. Consequently, countries with a large public sector are least likely to be helped by the individual response to population ageing.

Second, the interest rate and wage rate are likely to change during the demographic transition. As the number of workers falls, capital will become less productive and the interest rate will fall. Cutler et al. (1990) and Elmendorf and Scheiner (2000a, 2000b) therefore argue that the optimal response to an increased dependency burden is to reduce the national savings rate.

Third, as the experiment above indicates, maintaining an unaltered public policy will not be sustainable, and possibly not desirable. Expenses must be cut or revenue increased. The model used below is developed to examine how revenue should vary if expenses are held fixed at the current level. To some extent, the tax increases can equivalently be interpreted as expenditure cuts. However, Domeij and Floden (2001) show that savings responses to tax increases and benefit cuts can be very different, at least if individuals are not altruistic to other household members. For example, people will increase savings today if they expect future pension benefits to be low, while an increase in future social security taxes does not directly affect today's workers.

Fourth, the experiment ignores that worker productivity (wages and labour-market participation) and consumption needs may vary with age and time. In the model spelled out below, effective labour supply is adjusted for age-specific productivity and participation rates. Throughout the study, public spending and public transfers per capita are assumed to be held constant at the present level.[4] Inferring the present level from the data is, however, not unproblematic. As the benchmark, all public outlays are assumed to be uniformly divided between age groups. An alternative parameterisation of the model attempts to assign age-specific values to public outlays.

Health care costs account for a substantial part of public outlays. Since the elderly consume more health care than other groups, one could expect these costs to increase as the population grows older. But, as life

---

[4] There is no explicit productivity growth in the model, so 'constant' should be interpreted as 'constant relative to productivity'.

expectancy increases, people of a certain age will become healthier and thus demand less care. Several studies indeed indicate that health care costs are more closely related to the remaining lifetime than to age.[5] The model specification with age-specific public expenses may therefore exaggerate the future increase in public outlays.

14.2   The model

This section presents a formal model framework for analysing how the demographic development will affect the economy when households, firms and governments adjust their behaviour to these changes, and when interest rates and wages adapt to restore equilibrium in factor markets. The reader not interested in the technical details of the model can jump to the end of this section, where the main mechanisms of the model are summarised.

Consider an economy populated by a large number of identical and infinitely lived households. A fraction η of household members are active in the labour market and have one unit of time to dispose of. Members of the household maximise their joint utility.

A large number of competitive firms maximise profits,

$$\max F(k, \eta v h) - w\eta v h - \lfloor (1 + \tau^k)r + \delta \rfloor k$$

where F is the production function, k is the capital stock, h is labour supply per worker, v is the efficiency of the labour force, w is the wage per efficiency unit of labour, τ^k is the tax on capital returns, and δ is the depreciation rate of capital.[6,7] Competition ensures that the interest rate and wage rate equal the marginal product of capital and labour,

$$(1 + \tau^k)r_t = F_{1t} - \delta \tag{1}$$

$$w_t = F_{2t} \tag{2}$$

where t denotes time and F_1 and F_2 are the marginal products of capital and (efficiency) labour.

Let β denote the time discount factor, U the instantaneous utility, let c^a and c^i denote consumption per active and inactive household member, respectively, and let g denote public consumption. Household preferences are then described by

$$\sum_{t=0}^{\infty} \beta^t U\left(c_t^a, c_t^i, h_t, g_t, \eta_t\right).$$

---

[5] See, for example, the discussion in chapter 4 in Batljan and Lagergren (2000).
[6] The efficiency term, v, depends on the age structure of the labour force.
[7] The tax on capital returns is source-based so that it also applies to foreigners investing in the country.

The household budget constraint is

$$a_{t+1} = R_t a_t + \left(1 - \tau_t^h\right) w_t H_t + b_t - (1 + \tau^c) C_t \tag{3}$$

where a_{t+1} is savings from period t to period $t + 1$, $R = 1 + r$ is the gross interest rate, τ^h is the income tax rate, $H = \eta v h$ is the aggregate labour supply in efficiency units, b is a lump sum transfer from the government, $C = \eta c^a + (1 - \eta) c^i$ is aggregate private consumption, and τ^c is the consumption tax. The budget constraint can be rewritten as a lifetime constraint,

$$\sum p_t \left[(1 + \tau^c) C_t - \left(1 - \tau_t^h\right) H_t - b_t \right] = R_0 a_0$$

where $P_t / P_{t-1} = 1/R_t$. The household's first order conditions are then

$$\frac{U_{1t}}{\eta_t} = \frac{U_{2t}}{1 - \eta_t} \tag{4}$$

$$\frac{U_{3t}}{U_{1t}} = \frac{-\left(1 - \tau_t^h\right) v_t w_t}{1 + \tau^c} \tag{5}$$

$$\beta^t U_{1t} = \lambda p_t \eta_t (1 + \tau^c) \tag{6}$$

where λ is the Lagrange multiplier on the budget constraint. If p_0 is normalised to unity, the household's budget constraint reduces to

$$\sum \beta^t \left[U_{1t} \left(c_t^a - \frac{b}{\eta_t (1 + \tau^c)} \right) + U_{2t} c_t^i + U_{3t} h_t \right] = \frac{U_{10} R_0 a_0}{\eta_0 (1 + \tau^c)}. \tag{7}$$

Let d denote the public debt. The government's budget constraint is then

$$d_{t+1} = R_t d_t + g_t + b_t - \tau_t^h w_t H_t - \tau^k r_t k_t - \tau^c C_t \tag{8}$$

By substituting the household budget constraint (3) into (8), the government's budget constraint can be rewritten as

$$\sum p_t (g_t + C_t - \tau^k r_t k_t - w_t H_t) = R_0 (a_0 - d_0). \tag{9}$$

The world economy

A small open economy takes factor prices for given. These prices are determined on the world market, and it is assumed that policy in the world economy balances the public budget in each period.[8]

---

[8] This assumption is arbitrary and will not be consistent with the implications of optimal public policy. As an alternative, the implications of assuming that future factor prices will be constant at the present levels are also considered.

The world economy is thus characterised by a sequence of tax rates, $\{\hat{\tau}_t^h\}$, that fulfils the budget constraint

$$0 = r_t d + g_t + b_t - \hat{\tau}_t^h w_t H_t - \tau^k r_t k_t - \tau^c C_t \tag{10}$$

for all periods t. In this budget constraint, the levels of debt, d, public expenditure, g, and transfers, b, are exogenous, as is the demographic development and the tax rates on capital and consumption. Total household asset holdings must equal the sum of the capital stock and total government debt in a closed economy,

$$a_t = k_t + d.$$

The interest rate, wage rate, and capital stock are determined by this restriction in combination with (1) and (2). Household decisions for a_{t+1}, h_t, c_t^a, and c_t^i are determined by the first order conditions (4)–(6) in combination with the household budget constraint (3). The initial capital stock, k_0, and initial household assets, a_0, are given.

Optimal debt policy in a small economy

The interest rate path is exogenous to the small open economy. Capital can move freely between countries but labour is immobile. Competition still ensures that interest rates and wages equal the marginal products of capital and labour. Equations (1) and (2) must therefore hold also in the small open economy.

A feasible government policy is a sequence of tax rates, $\{\tau_t^h\}$, fulfilling the budget constraint and a transversality condition. To find the optimal policy, it is convenient to reformulate the government's optimisation problem as a Ramsey allocation problem where the government chooses sequences of consumption and labour supply under the additional constraint that these sequences are consistent with household optimisation. For more on the Ramsey allocation problem, see Chari and Kehoe (1999) and Atkeson, Chari, and Kehoe (1999).[9]

The Ramsey allocation problem is thus

$$\max_{\{c_t^a, c_t^i, h_t\}} \sum \beta^t U\left(c_t^a, c_t^i, h_t, g_t, \eta_t\right)$$

subject to the household and government budget constraints, (7) and (9), and household optimisation, (4) and (6). The first order conditions to this problem are reported in Floden (2001). Note that one of the household optimisation equations, (5), is used to solve for tax rates as a function of allocations.

---

[9] Their sections on open economy models are particularly relevant.

Model interpretation and model implications

The main mechanism implied by the model is that households want the consumption stream per household member to be smooth. Further, households prefer to supply labour in periods when the wage is high and when the labour-income tax is small, but they also have a preference for leisure being smooth over time. Savings behaviour is thus to a large extent affected by households' desire to smooth consumption and leisure.

The government's choice of tax policy affects households' ability to smooth consumption and leisure. If taxes are volatile, households face conflicting interests of smoothing leisure and supplying labour when the after-tax wage is high. As Barro (1979) has demonstrated, holding taxes constant and letting debt fluctuate will therefore be close to the optimal policy.[10]

Two parameters are central in the specification of the model. The fraction of workers in the population, η, will fall as populations grow older. This parameter is directly inversely related to the dependency ratio – the number of non-workers per worker.[11] The average efficiency of the labour force, ν, will change as the age structure of the labour force changes. Efficiency will be high when a large fraction of the workers are middle-aged, since these workers are productive (have high wages) and have high participation in the labour force. This efficiency parameter also captures productivity differences between countries, but the model abstracts from technological development. The model is, however, equivalent to a model with constant and exogenous technological development where public expenditure grows at the same rate as technology.

Questions regarding intergenerational implications of the demographic change cannot be addressed in this framework since households are infinitely lived. Furthermore, since the non-working population consists of both children and retirees, the model does not explicitly distinguish between increased life expectancy and reduced birth rates. However, since individuals are altruistic to other household members, separating the life expectancy and population growth rate effects is less important than in the standard overlapping-generations models used by, for example, Domeij and Floden (2001).

14.3   Data, specification and solution strategy

The previous section described the equilibrium conditions for the world economy and for small open economies taking prices as given. The

---

[10] If wages were constant over time, perfect tax smoothing would indeed be optimal.
[11] The dependency ratio is $1/\eta - 1$.

strategy now is to solve for the interest rate path that is consistent with world market equilibrium. The path for pre-tax wages can then be solved as a function of these interest rates. The world market prices are then used when solving for the optimal policy in each of the twelve countries. Before solving the model and searching for optimal debt policies we must specify the utility and production functions in more detail, provide initial values for public debt and household wealth, determine exogenous characteristics of public policy in different countries, and provide data on the demographic development in these countries.

The utility function is assumed to be

$$U(c^a, c^i, h, g, \eta) = \eta \frac{(c^a)^{1-\mu} \exp[-\zeta(1-\mu)h^{1+1/\gamma}]}{1-\mu}$$
$$+ (1-\eta)\frac{(c^i)^{1-\mu}}{1-\mu} + v(g)$$

where v is some increasing function. Risk aversion, μ, is set to 2 for the baseline calibration. Estimates of the intertemporal labour supply elasticity, γ, typically range between 0 and 0.5 – see for example Altonji (1986), Flood and MaCurdy (1992) and Aronsson and Palme (1998).[12] As the benchmark the elasticity is set to 0.3 but a lower ($\gamma = 0.1$) and a higher ($\gamma = 0.5$) elasticity are also considered.

The effective potential labour supply depends on the size of the labour force (captured by η) and by its efficiency (captured by v). The fraction of individuals that is active in the labour market, η, is shown in Figure 14.1. People aged twenty to sixty-four are assumed to be workers.[13]

Worker efficiency is affected by the age structure of the labour force. Middle-aged workers appear to be both more productive (reflected by a higher wage rate) and to participate in the labour market to a higher extent than young and old workers. The variable v captures these effects.[14]

The consumption tax rate, τ^c, and the initial tax rate on labour income, τ_0^h, were taken from table 14.4 in Carey and Tchilinguirian (2000). They

---

[12] The intertemporal labour supply elasticity is equal to γ when $\mu = 1$, and approximately equal to γ otherwise. In practice, estimates of the elasticity are often estimates of γ rather than the elasticity.

[13] The demographic forecasts are based on the United Nations' estimates from 1998. Thomas Lindh kindly provided this data.

[14] Age-specific productivity is based on estimates for the United States reported in Hansen (1993). Participation rates are estimated by Fullerton (1999) and are also based on US data. See Floden (2001) for a more detailed description of how v is calculated. Note that the same adjustment factor v was used for all countries. In reality, age-specific participation rates may be quite different in different countries because of different education or retirement patterns. However, the quantitative importance of v is small, so such differences are likely to be negligible.

Table 14.1 *Country-specific parameters*

	τ_0^h	τ^c	$\bar{d}$	$\bar{b}$	$\bar{g}$	w (%)
Belgium	0.397	0.187	1.110	0.163	0.192	1.53
Denmark	0.428	0.257	0.516	0.144	0.269	0.79
Finland	0.445	0.227	0.406	0.167	0.250	0.78
France	0.402	0.180	0.646	0.179	0.190	8.87
Germany	0.359	0.158	0.617	0.154	0.178	12.34
Italy	0.363	0.160	1.152	0.150	0.171	8.60
Netherlands	0.410	0.187	0.606	0.137	0.234	2.37
Norway	0.355	0.269	0.332	0.115	0.264	0.67
Portugal	0.227	0.205	0.554	0.108	0.170	1.48
Spain	0.304	0.137	0.706	0.129	0.156	5.95
Sweden	0.485	0.187	0.644	0.147	0.265	1.34
UK	0.210	0.169	0.492	0.147	0.112	8.83
Canada	0.287	0.131	0.825	0.070	0.192	4.68
USA	0.226	0.061	0.571	0.071	0.126	41.78
World	0.291	0.122	0.653	0.114	0.156	100.00

Note: w is the country's population weight.

calculate effective average tax rates for OECD countries using an improved version of the method suggested by Mendoza et al. (1995). The first two columns in table 14.1 summarise these country-specific tax rates.

Production is given by the Cobb–Douglas function

$$y = F(k, H) = k^\theta H^{1-\theta}. \tag{11}$$

Initial steady state

All economies are assumed to be in a steady state in year 2000. These steady states are calibrated to be similar to the actual economies in the recent past. The initial net position of households against the rest of the world is assumed to be zero in each economy (see Nordin et al., 1992: 30–32, for Swedish evidence), hence $a/y = d/y + k/y$. The tax rate on capital returns, τ^k, is assumed to be 40 per cent in all countries.[15]

The time discount rate, β, is calibrated so that the capital-output ratio equals 2.5. The capital share in production, θ, is set to 0.36, and the depreciation rate of capital, δ, is set to 10 per cent per year. Consequently $(1 + \tau^k)r = 0.044$.

---

[15] Estimates of tax rates on capital income vary between studies and appear unreliable. Estimates around 40 per cent are common; see, for example, Carey and Tchilinguirian (2000).

Table 14.2 *Parameter values and initial steady state*

Risk aversion	μ	2.000
Labour-supply elasticity	γ	0.300
Time discount rate	β	0.969
Capital-output ratio	$\overline{k}$	2.500
Capital share	θ	0.360
Interest rate	r	0.031
Hours worked, percentage of available time	h	0.330
Tax on capital returns	τ^k	0.400

Public transfers, b, are based on OECD's Social Expenditure Data Base. Transfers per capita for the initial steady state are calculated as the sum of public spending on old-age cash benefits, disability cash benefits, occupational injury and disease, sickness benefits, survivors, pensions, family cash benefits, unemployment benefits and housing benefits. The values are from 1995 or 1996 depending on availability, and all values are relative to GDP per capita.[16] Public debt is gross government debt in year 2000 from OECD's Economic Outlook, relative to GDP from the same data set. Table 14.1 reports the country-specific parameter values used in the initial steady-state.[17]

Initial public debt and public policy in the world economy are assumed to be the population weighted average of debt and policy in the USA, Canada and the twelve examined European countries. The population weights and resulting world averages are also reported in table 14.1.

It is assumed that labour supply is 33 per cent of available time in the initial steady state for the world economy, and that $\beta R = 1$ (otherwise no steady state would exist under optimal policy). Seven variables then remain to solve for in the steady state, c^a, c^i, ζ, w, y, g and r. The seven equations used to solve for these variables are the household budget constraint; the government budget constraint; the production function; the first order conditions for factor prices (two equations); and the first order conditions for c^i and h.[18] Table 14.2 summarises the parameter values that are common to all economies.

[16] The transfers reported by OECD are gross and may be subject to taxation in some countries. The adjustment factors reported in Adema's (1999) table 3, row 1, have therefore been used to adjust the OECD figures. Adema does not report adjustment factors for France, Spain and Portugal. The German adjustment factor was used for France, while the Italian factor was used for Spain and Portugal.

[17] The levels of public consumption reported in the table are solved from the equilibrium conditions as described below.

[18] These equations are reported in detail in Floden (2001).

The seven equations used to solve the world economy are also used to find the initial steady states for each small economy. In these economies, however, the preference parameter ζ is set to the same value as in the world economy, and initial labour supply is not calibrated.

Future development of public expenditure

Two alternative approaches are used for choosing the future paths of transfers and public consumption. Both approaches attempt to predict what happens if there are no changes in policies. The first approach assumes that these variables remain constant at the level from the initial steady state. The implicit assumptions are then that costs grow proportionally with technological development (recall that there is no such development in the model), and that costs are independent of the age structure in the population.

The alternative approach tries to predict how the demographic development will affect public expenditure. Per capita levels of public expenditure in the initial steady state are then calculated separately for the young, for workers, and for the old. These per capita levels are then assumed to remain constant, but total expenditure will be affected by the demographic composition of the population. When calculating the group-specific transfer levels, it is assumed that disability cash benefits, survivors, pensions and housing benefits are evenly divided in the full population, that family cash benefits are evenly divided among the young and the workers, that old-age cash benefits only accrue to the old, and that occupational injury and disease benefits, sickness benefits and unemployment benefits only accrue to the workers. Many items in public consumption are (implicitly) assumed to be independent of the age structure (for example, police and defence). Health care costs education costs and spending on day care and long-term care are allocated to the different age groups.[19,20]

---

[19] Health care costs are assumed to be four times higher per capita for old persons (aged 65+) than for others (see Batljan and Lagergren, 2000: section 3.2). Further, it is assumed that only the old consume long-term care, only the young consume day care and primary and secondary education, and only workers consume tertiary education. The data sources are OECD (1998: table VI.3.) for health care and long-term care, and OECD (2001: table B2) for education costs. Public spending on long-term care was estimated to be 50 per cent of total spending in Italy, Spain and Portugal, and 80 per cent in Denmark.

[20] The resulting age structure of transfers and public consumption is reported in Floden (2001). The age structure of public consumption in Sweden is similar to that reported in Olsson and Nordén (1999). The calculations for transfers, however, appear to assign considerably smaller values to children than Olsson and Nordén did.

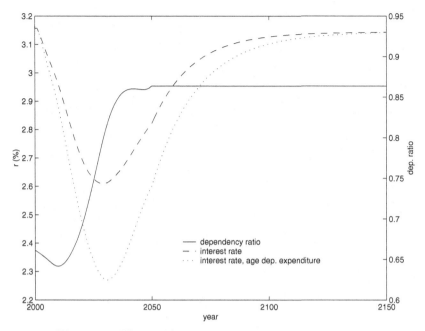

Figure 14.5 The world economy

14.4   Findings

Figure 14.5 shows the interest rate path that solves the system of equations (10). As expected, interest rates fall during the transition to a new steady state with an older population. The capital stock must shrink in this transition since there are fewer workers in the new steady state. Because population ageing *per se* calls for more savings, the return to savings must be low in the transition to reduce incentives to save and thus allow for a shrinking capital stock. In the long run, however, interest rates return to the equilibrium level.

Figure 14.6 shows the optimal paths for debt and taxes in Sweden, and resulting effects on the Swedish economy.[21,22] The top right panel in the figure shows that the optimal policy is to reduce debt during the initial years, before the demographic situation deteriorates. The dashed lines in figure 14.6 show the implications of optimal policy when world market prices are assumed to be constant. Note first that the implied

---

[21] The figure also reports the results of a balanced-budget experiment that is described below.

[22] Corresponding figures for the other countries display the same general pattern for taxes, debt, hours worked and output.

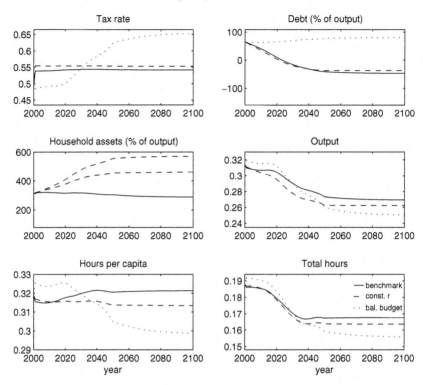

Figure 14.6 Implications of policy choices (Sweden)

optimal policy is almost identical to the optimal policy in the benchmark scenario when the interest rate responds to the demographic change. The model was also solved with different values of the risk-aversion and labour-supply elasticity, but the optimal policy is consistently similar to the one shown in figure 14.6. With the alternative assumption for the development of public expenditures, the implied policy is an even sharper reduction in debt, accompanied by a higher initial tax raise.

Note also that although the middle-left panel in the figure shows that private savings would be higher if the interest rate did not respond to the population ageing, this effect on savings is not reflected in production levels. Except for the very first years, output is higher in the benchmark economy. Two factors cause this result. First, interest rates are low during the population ageing episode because the number of workers is falling, implying a higher capital-output ratio and thus making workers more productive. Second, lower interest rates reduce interest payments on public debt so that less taxation is required in the benchmark economy.

Table 14.3 *Implications of optimal policy: initial tax effect*

	$\Delta\tau_{2001}$		
	$\{g,b\}$	$\{g_t,b_t\}$	constant r
Belgium	5.4	11.7	6.9
Denmark	6.9	14.0	8.4
Finland	8.3	17.2	9.7
France	4.6	13.0	5.9
Germany	4.4	16.2	5.4
Italy	6.8	20.6	8.0
Netherlands	8.1	20.5	9.2
Norway	5.2	11.0	6.3
Portugal	2.3	7.2	3.0
Spain	4.1	13.6	4.8
Sweden	5.4	12.4	7.0
UK	2.1	6.3	2.9

The table shows the tax increase (in percentage points) the first year with optimal policy.
Note: $\{g,b\}$ denotes the benchmark specification, $\{g_t,b_t\}$ denotes the specification where public expenditure depends on the population's age structure, 'constant r' denotes the specification with constant world market prices.

The optimal policy in terms of tax rates is to increase taxes in the first year and then let them remain approximately unchanged. This result is not surprising and is in line with the tax smoothing argument put forward in Barro (1979).

Tables 14.3–14.5 report the implications of optimal policy for the respective countries. Results are reported for the benchmark specification of the economy, for the alternative assumption about the path of public expenditure, and for the assumption of constant world market prices. We see that the implied optimal policies are similar for most countries. Table 14.3 shows that the optimal, immediate, tax increase varies from 2.1 per cent for the UK to 8.3 per cent for Finland. Table 14.4 shows that average annual budget surpluses should be between 1.3 per cent for the UK and 4.1 per cent for the Netherlands during the first ten years and similar during the following decades. Finally, table 14.5 shows the implied reductions in debt levels.

The differences between the extreme countries – the UK, which appears least affected by the demographic change, and Finland, Italy and the Netherlands, which appear most affected – are explained by several factors. First, the size of the public sector matters for the effectiveness and

Table 14.4 *Implications of optimal policy: necessary budget surplus*

	first 10 years		first 30 years	
	$\{g,b\}$	$\{g_t,b_t\}$	$\{g,b\}$	$\{g_t,b_t\}$
Belgium	3.1	6.6	3.0	6.1
Denmark	2.8	6.0	2.1	4.5
Finland	3.4	7.2	2.3	4.7
France	2.5	7.0	2.3	6.0
Germany	2.7	7.8	2.7	7.2
Italy	4.0	10.7	4.2	10.6
Netherlands	4.1	10.1	3.7	8.4
Norway	2.5	5.9	2.1	4.8
Portugal	2.0	5.2	2.6	6.1
Spain	3.4	9.2	4.2	10.2
Sweden	2.5	5.7	2.7	5.0
UK	1.3	4.1	1.4	3.7

The table shows the average annual budget supplus (in percentage points) implied by optimal policy.
Note: $\{g,b\}$ denotes the benchmark specification, $\{g_t,b_t\}$ denotes the specification where public expenditure depends on the population's age structue.

Table 14.5 *Implications of optimal policy: change in public debt*

	until 2010		until 2030	
	$\{g,b\}$	$\{g_t,b_t\}$	$\{g,b\}$	$\{g_t,b_t\}$
Belgium	−30.0	−60.9	−86.8	−182.7
Denmark	−26.5	−56.6	−65.2	−135.7
Finland	−32.8	−69.2	−71.3	−144.8
France	−24.1	−65.1	−68.0	−179.1
Germany	−26.2	−73.4	−81.4	−222.9
Italy	−38.7	−97.2	−124.6	−324.8
Netherlands	−40.0	−94.7	−116.1	−264.6
Norway	−24.0	−56.8	−64.1	−147.6
Portugal	−20.5	−50.6	−81.0	−184.6
Spain	−35.5	−88.2	−131.1	−319.3
Sweden	−23.7	−52.6	−80.1	−150.9
UK	−13.1	−39.6	−40.2	−120.9

The table shows the increase in debt (in percentage points) implied by optimal policy.
Note: $\{g,b\}$ denotes the benchmark specification. $\{g_t,b_t\}$ denotes the specification where public expenditure depends on the population's age structure.

distortions of taxation. The excess burden of taxation increases with the size of the government sector; thus taxes are more distortive in countries with a large government sector, such as Finland, and the effect on tax revenue of a 1 per cent increase in tax rates is smaller. Second, population ageing has a larger impact on the public budget in countries with high public expenditure. Third, in countries with a large initial public debt, such as Italy, the optimal policy is to reduce this debt significantly (see table 14.5) in order to lessen the future fiscal burden. Fourth, figure 14.1 showed that the demographic change will be somewhat less severe in the UK than in many other countries. Finally, some countries (most notably the Netherlands and Belgium) are predicted to have a particularly unfavourable development of the age-structure within the group of workers.[23]

Alternative policies and welfare effects

How important is it that the government tries to follow the optimal debt strategy? Would welfare be significantly reduced if mistakes were made or if the government pursued other objectives? To answer these questions, the optimal policy was compared to a policy balancing the public budget in each period.[24] The alternative policy is thus a sequence of tax rates, $\{\hat{\tau}_t^h\}$, that fulfils equation (10) for each t when the sequences for interest rates and wages are exogenous.

The dotted line in the top-left panel of figure 14.6 shows the sequence of tax rates that balances the Swedish budget. While tax rates can be held down initially, substantial increases are required between 2020 and 2050 when the number of retirees increases. Consequently, hours worked and output are lower in the long run with the balanced-budget policy. Again, the corresponding figures for all other countries are similar.

Although the balanced-budget policy is quite different from the optimal policy, the difference in households' welfare turns out to be modest. Table 14.6 shows welfare losses for different specifications of the model. As expected, tax smoothing is more important when labour supply is elastic. Still, a welfare loss of 0.5 per cent of annual consumption amounts to less than US$ 100 per person and year. With labour-supply elasticities like those typically used by macroeconomists, the welfare losses of deviations from the optimal policy would be sizeable.

The results reported in table 14.6 also indicate that under the alternative assumption of age-dependent public expenditure, pursuing a

---

[23] Portugal, Spain and Denmark are predicted to have the most favourable development. The negative impact on long-run productivity is 1.9 per cent in Portugal and 5.3 per cent in the Netherlands according to the authors' calculations of v.

[24] Note that the study ignores business-cycle fluctuations. A balanced-budget policy in the model economy is therefore less drastic than a balanced-budget policy in the real world.

Table 14.6 *Welfare loss with balanced-budget policy*

	benchmark	$\gamma = 0.1$	$\gamma = 0.5$	$\{g_t, b_t\}$
Belgium	0.24	0.05	0.75	n.s.
Denmark	0.21	0.05	0.67	n.s.
Finland	0.35	0.07	n.s.	n.s.
France	0.13	0.03	0.31	n.s.
Germany	0.12	0.03	0.28	n.s.
Italy	0.44	0.10	n.s.	n.s.
Netherlands	0.60	0.11	n.s.	n.s.
Norway	0.09	0.03	0.19	0.78
Portugal	0.06	0.02	0.10	0.43
Spain	0.25	0.07	0.56	n.s.
Sweden	0.50	0.08	n.s.	n.s.
UK	0.01	0.00	0.02	0.10

Note: Welfare loss in percent of annual consumption. N.s. = 'no solution'. $\{g, b\}$ denotes the benchmark specification. $\{g_t, b_t\}$ denotes the specification where public expenditure depends on the population's age structure.

balanced-budget policy will be unfeasible in most countries. This is due to a Laffer-curve effect. To balance the budget, year-to-year fluctuations in public expenditure and in the tax base may require sharp fluctuations in the tax rate. But if taxes are already high, further tax increase may induce households to substitute labour supply into periods with lower taxes. Thus only the countries with low public expenditure (the UK and Portugal) or a small initial debt (Norway) appear able to balance the budget in that scenario.

Cutler et al. (1990) argue that although the optimal policy for the US government probably is to reduce the public debt in the years before the dependency ratio deteriorates, the welfare gains of such a policy are likely to be small since taxes are not particularly distortionary. The present study supports their story (the welfare gains for the USA would be smaller than those found for the UK), but also indicates that their arguments are not valid for the typical European countries, where the public sector is larger and where the demographic development is somewhat more problematic.

14.5   Concluding remarks

The above analysis ignores several factors that can have important effects on public finances in the future. Most of these factors are discussed in other chapters in this volume. The contributions by Andersen,

Huber and Norrman, and Pedersen et al. show that the process of increased internationalisation, tax competition between EU countries, and a more mobile labour force can make the collection of taxes more difficult. Such changes would be similar to an increased labour-supply elasticity, making taxes more distortive over time. Taking such factors into account would therefore make the case for reducing the debt today even stronger.

Implicitly, the study has also assumed that the generosity and structure of welfare and pension systems and public services are unaffected by the demographic change. The internationalisation and population ageing may imply that the generosity of welfare systems must be reduced or that welfare systems must be reformed. Households may then respond by increasing savings and labour supply, and thus reduce the importance of debt reduction today.

Furthermore, maintaining an unaltered level of public services may be difficult when the demographic structure changes. For example, even if consumption needs for children and old people are identical and do not change over time, population ageing requires investments in the infrastructure (schools cannot easily be transformed into hospitals). Evidence reported in Bucht et al. (2000) shows that, at least in the short run, school expenditure does not seem to vary directly with the number of students.

There is little doubt that most developed countries will see an ageing of their populations in the coming thirty to forty years. Still, forecasting the long-term future is difficult and associated with many sources of uncertainty. Lindh (this volume) reports that previous forecasts of survival probabilities have been biased downwards, and that nativity is volatile but difficult to predict. Nativity may also be influenced by policy, something which has been neglected here. Migration is another factor that is difficult to forecast (for example, migration flows may be influenced by war episodes or changes in immigration policies) but that can influence demographic structures.

Considering the above caveats, the implications of the model and experiments conducted should be interpreted cautiously. The following conclusions, however, do not appear daring. First, population ageing will put pressure on future public finances. In the long run taxes must be raised or public spending cut. Second, at least if intergenerational issues are ignored, welfare is enhanced if public debts are reduced during the next two or three decades. Finally, the welfare benefits of such policies compared to policies that hold debts constant are likely to be small or modest, except in countries with a large public sector and/or a large public debt.

References

Adema, Willem, 1999, 'Net social expenditure', OECD Labour Market and Social Policy Occasional Papers, No. 39.

Altonji, Joseph G., 1986, 'Intertemporal substitution in labor supply: evidence from micro data', *Journal of Political Economy*, 94, S176–S215.

Aronsson, Thomas and Palme, Mårten, 1998, 'A decade of tax and benefit reforms in Sweden: effects on labour supply, welfare and inequality', *Economica*, 65, 39–67.

Atkeson, Andrew, Chari, V. V. and Kehoe, Patrick J., 1999, 'Taxing capital income: a bad idea', *Federal Reserve Bank of Minneapolis Quarterly Review*, Summer.

Barro, Robert J., 1979, 'On the determination of the public debt', *Journal of Political Economy*, 87, 940–71.

Batljan, Ilija and Lagergren, Mårten, 2000, 'Kommer det att finnas en hjälpande hand?' (in Swedish), Bilaga 8 till Långtidsutredningen 1999/2000.

Bohn, Henning, 1999, 'Will social security and medicare remain viable as the US population is aging?', *Carnegie-Rochester Conference Series on Public Policy*, 50, 1–53.

Bucht, Charlotte, Bylund, Jessica and Norlin, Jonas, 2000, 'En åldrande befolkning – konsekvenser för svensk ekonomi' (in Swedish), Bilaga 9 till Långtidsutredningen 1999/2000.

Carey, David and Tchilinguirian, Harry, 2000, 'Average effective tax rates on capital, labour and consumption', OECD Economics Department working paper No. 258.

Chari, V. V. and Kehoe, Patrick, J., 1999, 'Optimal fiscal and monetary policy', in J. B. Taylor and M. Woodford (eds.), *Handbook of Macroeconomics*, 1C, Amsterdam: Elsevier Science.

Cutler, David M., Poterba, James M., Sheiner, Louise M. and Summers, Lawrence H., 1990, 'An aging society: opportunity or challenge?', *Brookings Papers on Economic Activity*, 1, 1–73.

Domeij, David and Floden, Martin, 2001, 'Macroeconomic adjustment to demographic change', manuscript, Stockholm School of Economics.

Elmendorf, Douglas W. and Scheiner, Louise M., 2000a, 'Should America save for its old age? Population aging, national saving, and fiscal policy', manuscript, Federal Reserve Board.

—2000b, 'Should America save for its old age? Fiscal policy, population aging, and national saving', *Journal of Economic Perspectives*, 14: 57–74.

Flodén, Martin, 2001, 'Aging populations and strategies for public debt in Europe', manuscript, Stockholm School of Economics.

Flood, Lennart and MaCurdy, Thomas E., 1992, 'Work disincentive effects of taxes: an empirical analysis of Swedish men', *Carnegie-Rochester Conference Series on Public Policy*, 37, 239–78.

Fullerton, Howard N., Jr., 1999, 'Labor force participation: 75 years of change, 1950–98 and 1998–2025', *Monthly Labor Review*, 122, 3–12.

Hansen, Gary D., 1993, 'The cyclical and secular behaviour of the labour input: comparing efficiency units and hours worked', *Journal of Applied Econometrics*, 8, 71–80.

Mendoza, Enrique G., Razin, Assaf and Tesar, Linda L., 1995, 'Effective tax rates in macroeconomics: cross-country estimates of tax rates on factor incomes and consumption', *Journal of Monetary Economics*, 34, 297–324.

Nordin, Maj, Olsson, Hans, Wickman-Parak, Barbro and Tengblad, Åke, 1992, 'Nationalförmögenheten', SOU 1992: 19, Appendix 11 to Långtidsutredningen 1992 (in Swedish).

OECD, 1998, 'Maintaining prosperity in an ageing society', Paris: OECD.

—2001, 'Education at a glance', Paris: OECD.

Olsson, Hans and Nordén, Carl J., 1999, 'Befolkningsutvecklingen och framtida välfärden' (in Swedish), mimeo, TCO.

15 Policy options for reforming the welfare state

Torben M. Andersen and Per Molander

15.1 Time for policy reform

The unifying theme of this volume is whether basic objectives of the extended welfare state found in the Scandinavian countries can be met in a more efficient way at the same time as it is adapted to address important challenges including internationalisation and demographic shifts. A satisfactory discussion of this question requires both a detailed account of the changes in the environment as well as a careful consideration of both the expenditure and revenue sides of the public sector. The chapters in this volume have addressed various important items on this agenda. Without claiming a fully exhaustive coverage of all topics, it is worthwhile to take stock of the various analyses in an attempt to identify possible reform options. In our view the welfare state is not in an immediate crisis requiring sudden abrupt policy reforms, but we find that the problems and challenges are important enough to call for serious consideration of policy changes. The main reasons are that some of the changes needed will attain their full effect only after a considerable timespan, and that some changes also need to be announced well in advance to have the desired effects. To be specific, we think in terms of a time perspective of about three decades. Still, this implies that the timespan for initiation of policy reforms is short, if policies are to address the problems in an appropriate way that also ensures that the future policy path is transparent and stable.

The background of the following discussion is the extended welfare states as developed in particular in the Scandinavian countries relying on a large public sector and universal principles for fulfilment of central welfare state objectives. We refer in this concluding chapter more specifically to Sweden as a case example of the Scandinavian welfare model, as it has been covered in most chapters in the book; by relating the discussion to a specific country it can be more precise.

A prominent argument in the debate is that welfare regimes are particularly persistent and mainly derived from political considerations (see, for example, Scharpf, 2000). Public support for welfare state arrangements remains strong (see, for example, Boeri et al., 2001; Svallfors, 1999), but the value of such opinion polls is seriously limited by methodological difficulties (for a discussion of the Swedish literature, see Molander, 1999a). If the persistence thesis were generally true, major changes in welfare regimes or policies should not be expected. Although we share the view that convergence of welfare regimes at a global level should not be expected, we find that purely political explanations are insufficient. First, they overlook the fact that actual welfare arrangements are often hybrids of the pure theoretical models, and that the precise organisation often reflects historic developments. Within the broad frames of what is understood by the welfare model there is substantial scope for discussing the specific way by which to achieve the major objectives of the welfare state. This is not an either-or issue, or a simple question of welfare state retrenchment, but a question of adaptation of the welfare model to the problems and challenges it is facing. Second, policies will eventually have to take account of changes in fundamentals, and as we summarise below, there is overwhelming evidence supporting the view that fundamentals are changing and calling for policy adaptation. As we have argued in chapter 1, one rationale for many welfare arrangements and the very reason why they allow countries with extended welfare state to remain among the richest countries in the world is that they are motivated by market failures and that they may have beneficial efficiency effects. It follows that if market fundamentals change, it is necessary to consider whether welfare state policies should be modified accordingly.

It is sometimes argued that the Scandinavian welfare model faces less pressure than other welfare models. One argument is that the Scandinavian countries have been leading in various dimensions (female emancipation, changing family structures, etc.), something that would explain the growth of the public sector (Kautto et al., 2001). Other countries are perceived to be lagging in this development, but will eventually go through the same process and have to expand their public sector. We find the empirical support for this convergence view questionable. Although some trends are universal, the response to them need not be. So far it has not been; over the last decades the relative ranking of countries in terms of the relative size of the public sector has remained very stable. A related argument is that the Scandinavian welfare model is better suited to cope with challenges like internationalisation, either because of more swift policy adjustments or because a relatively smaller tax burden falls on low-income groups due to progressive elements in taxation (Scharpf, 2000). In comparative perspective it seems to be an open question whether policy adaptation has been quicker or more adequate in the Scandinavian countries. If anything, the development in Sweden during the late 1980s and the early 1990s does not look like a model example, and policy reforms were launched in an atmosphere of crisis. On the specific issue of taxation, one should not overlook the fact that although the relative burden might be lower for some low-income groups, the absolute burden is still higher than in most other countries, and the latter is the most relevant for the terms at which workers compete across borders. Moreover, internationalisation is not only confined to changes in the labour market for low skill groups. In addition, it may be argued that the universal welfare model is more vulnerable than other welfare models to migration, since migration breaks the solidarity over the life cycle on which extended social insurance arrangements build (see below).

Given that neither the persistence nor the convergence argument is very compelling, the Scandinavian model is neither resistant to nor necessarily particularly well suited to address the important challenges induced by changes in economic fundamentals. The following discussion raises a number of issues to be addressed by such policy reforms.

15.2   Changes in the environment: taking stock

An important fundamental change is the ongoing process of *international integration*, which has widespread implications and may change economic structures in significant ways. While it has been proceeding over decades it has been intensified in recent times due to both technological changes and policy decisions. Moreover, the integration process is changing its nature, implying that previous experience of small and open economies may be an inappropriate yardstick for the changes to come. Internationalisation is a process that makes it more difficult to sustain a classical, tax-financed welfare state of the Scandinavian type. The revenue side is threatened both by mobility of tax bases and potential increases in the distortions caused by taxation. At the same time, the economy is exposed to new risks, which may generate a demand for additional insurance (see chapter 2). This creates the policy dilemma that the need for welfare state arrangements may increase at the same time as their financing via general taxation becomes more difficult. The simple solution of retrenchment of the welfare state does not solve the problem. The question is more complicated – how to change and reform welfare state arrangements such that basic objectives can be met taking into account the changes in the environment.

The Scandinavian welfare model is particularly vulnerable to *migration*, since it relies on risk pooling across agents in a lifetime perspective. If 'better' risks opt out and 'worse' risks are attracted, the implicit insurance model threatens to break down, as would private insurance markets offering undifferentiated insurance in the presence of adverse selection problems. Migration among the highly educated is currently not at a level that represents a major threat (see chapter 4). This may change, however, and past experience may be a bad indicator of how younger generations will behave in the future, given the increasing globalisation of information flows and cultural influences. Economic crises may also change this pattern and increase the net outflow. Even taking into account that a majority of the emigrants return within, say, ten years, it may become a financial problem that some of the highly educated spend a significant period of their working life abroad when they are normally net contributors to the public sector. Johansson (2001) estimates the fiscal loss from even current limited migration flows to between 0.5 and 1 per cent of GDP.

Demographic changes leading to an ageing population affect public finances in several ways. Expenditure on health care and care for the elderly will increase. There is relatively wide consensus that the effect on health care is limited, perhaps 10–15 per cent in real terms up to 2030, because the demand tends to be concentrated to the last few years in life. The cost increase in care for the elderly is expected to be relatively larger (Batljan and Lagergren, 2000). The effect on income transfers (pensions) is potentially larger in relative terms. The major pension reform launched in Sweden in 2000 aimed at reducing the risk of future serious imbalances in the pension system. The system is in principle autonomous, but the state guarantees a basic level – a commitment that may become a heavy burden under unfavourable circumstances. Even if such scenarios do not materialise, ageing will affect public finances indirectly. Demographic shifts in the working population also affect productivity, saving and other important macro variables (chapter 3). By consequence, there will be indirect effects on the public-sector balance. Summing up the net effect on public finances is largely positive over the next decade, but then the sign shifts and becomes negative towards the middle of the century.

A pivotal factor in these circumstances is the labour market. Technological developments tend to be skill-biased, shifting labour demand towards skilled groups. International integration will reinforce the 'competition' across countries in human capital and skills, and therefore add to the effects of the skill bias. It is important that this effect arises even in the absence of labour mobility through channels like trade and foreign direct investments, etc. While Scandinavian countries have been successful in preventing the increase in unemployment during the 1970s and 1980s from having serious detrimental effects on inequality, it has come at the consequence of an increase in the transfer burdens resting on the public sector. This is hardly an objective; nor is it necessarily a viable policy to maintain a large fraction of the working age population on public transfers. Adding the additional transfer burden due to ageing and the skill-biased development in labour markets, a serious challenge for welfare policies remains.

The most visible effect of the challenges discussed above is the pressure on public finances. Losses in tax revenues due to increased tax base mobility or other changes are difficult to estimate precisely, but the figure suggested by Huber and Norrman (chapter 12) is at least 1 per cent of GDP, perhaps as large as 3.5 per cent under unfavourable circumstances. The policy changes suggested by the authors would reduce tax revenues by about 2 per cent of GDP, but given that they are expected to reduce or eliminate some of the problems associated with tax base mobility, the net cost is much smaller.

The combined direct and indirect effects of demographic change are estimated to worsen the public-sector balance by 5–6 per cent of GDP (chapter 3). This is in agreement with previous estimates by the OECD (1998) and the EU Economic Policy Committee (2001). The combined negative effects on the public-sector balance of the environmental changes discussed appear to lie in the interval 6–10 per cent of GDP. To this should be added the requirements on a sustainable debt policy. As is shown by Flodén (chapter 14), the requirements differ vastly between countries depending on current debt levels and other factors, but in any case the general message is that current debt levels should be lowered if anything.

Finding an appropriate programme to deal with the problems listed cannot be reduced to closing a financing gap, however. Equally important are measures that aim at improving incentives, reducing information deficits, or changing professional practices, thereby contributing indirectly to more efficient policies.

15.3   Choice of welfare strategy

Is it possible to reform the welfare state without jeopardising key objectives? A voluminous literature on the choice of welfare-political strategies (Esping-Andersen, 1990, 1999; Pierson, 1998; Korpi and Palme, 1998) claims to have established links between the choice of strategy and policy outcomes in important respects. The standard categorisation is between liberal, corporatist and general (or universal) welfare policies. Because there is a correlation between the design chosen and political traditions in industrialised countries, they are sometimes referred to as Anglo-Saxon, Central European and Scandinavian, respectively.

This line of reasoning is based on two major claims. First, the size of the public sector (or the welfare budget) is claimed to be strongly correlated with the degree of equalisation accomplished. Countries with a large public sector allegedly tend to have less dispersion in the distribution of income. Second, the causal explanation proposed for this is that a general welfare policy comprises the whole population, which creates ties of solidarity between the middle and lower income strata; churning favours the economically weak.

These claims have played an important role in the welfare policy debate in Scandinavian countries in particular. As a basis for policy conclusions, they are seriously inadequate. As pointed out already in the introductory chapter, gross measures of public expenditure are seriously misleading (Adema 2001). Actual outlays differ much less than simple statistics show, and the difference is systematic in the sense that countries with high expenditure levels tend to have larger gross levels of expenditure, and vice versa. The debate should not focus on such aggregate measures but rather on the important distinction between the roles of organising, providing and financing welfare activities.

Comparisons of inequality across countries cannot be used directly to infer the relative success of welfare policies. If the population is small and homogeneous, inequality may be low even if welfare policies are not very successful in meeting egalitarian objectives and vice versa. Detailed comparisons of welfare arrangements related to specific social events do not yield clear conclusions on how well Scandinavian welfare models perform, although there is a tendency that they are more favourable to groups with no or weak attachment to the labour market (Hansen, 2000). It is also interesting that measures often perceived to be important for redistribution may not be very effective or in some cases even counterproductive when policies are evaluated in terms of their implications for life income (Danish Economic Council, 2001). Detailed studies of support to the elderly (Forssell et al., 1999) also show that there is no correlation between public outlays and equality, whether measured as the relation of pensioners' disposable income to that of the average workers', or within the group of pensioners.

The second argument for the Scandinavian type of welfare policy – that targeting will reduce the political support for welfare arrangements – can also be questioned. What determines the equalising effect of transfer programmes on disposable income are net transfers. Basically, this boils down to transfers from the high-income strata to the low-income strata, whereas the system is largely neutral with respect to middle-income groups. The strategic argument claims that integrating middle-income groups among the beneficiaries creates a stable coalition between low- and middle-income groups. But if the latter are largely unaffected, any such coalition must be based on a misunderstanding – hardly a legitimate basis for normative welfare policy, nor a stable foundation for real-life policy-making.

We are thus not convinced that welfare policies at the extended level in the Scandinavian countries have developed and remained because the population has been unable to see through the veil of the public budget. Many problems of the welfare state can be understood in the perspective of the difference between individual and collective rationality, and does not require reference to electorate illusion. Moreover, attitude polls, to the extent that they can be relied upon, indicate no difference in attitude to the weakest groups between Anglo-Saxon and Nordic countries (Kangas, 1997).

In summary, the idea that the overall design of welfare polices more or less uniquely determines policy outcomes does not seem to stand up to an empirical test. The freedom of choice among policy instruments is therefore substantial; there is scope for reforms reducing the overall expenditure and tax level without jeopardising egalitarian objectives.

15.4   Towards sustainable public policies: an overview

Public policies include a rich variety of instruments. Some aim at affecting the incentive structure generally by lowering distortions arising from public intervention or disincentive arising from the way social insurance is organised; others aim at changing organisation, provision or financing in specific areas to achieve more cost-effectiveness, flexibility and adaptation to demands from the population. Usually there are complementarities between reform proposals affecting different areas, which implies that they cannot be evaluated separately but have to be considered as a package. This also implies that there are often synergetic gains to be made from different types of reform. In some instances, it may be difficult to reap the benefits from system redesign unless the institutional framework is changed simultaneously. In the following sections, nonetheless for practical reasons we separate the reform alternatives into three different categories – institutional reform, public service rationalisation and social insurance redesign.

Preferably, any policy package designed to redress the balance between revenues and expenditures should be analysed within a general-equilibrium framework. For several reasons, we do not believe this to be an accessible route. The complexity of the issues raised cannot be handled within one single manageable model, a problem that is reinforced by the fact that changes in institutional arrangements are also involved. In addition, problems of projecting, for example, the growth rate over the horizon being considered here is in itself an obstacle for a precise quantitative assessment. The numbers given are thus meant to be indicative of the order of magnitudes we expect to be at stake, and not a precise forecast or estimate of the consequences of policy changes.

The political economy of welfare reforms will not be discussed in any depth here. A necessary first step in any reform process is to work out the problems and challenges and consider possible policy responses. The next step would then be questions of implementation. But even if this second step is carried to a successful end, there is no guarantee of success. Gains and losses associated with policy changes are always uncertain, and persuading interest groups to accept uncertain gains rather than clinging to the status quo may be difficult. Second, even if an economic analysis shows that all stakeholder groups can benefit in absolute terms from a certain change of policy, relative figures are important in politics, at all income levels. Third, institutional change – which we believe to be a necessary component of any successful reform package – nearly always affects some parties negatively, and an *a priori* requirement on consensus may simply be impossible to satisfy. To overcome such difficulties, rational argumentation on the basis of socio-economic analysis seems to be the only accessible route to reform.

15.5   Total withdrawal

The most common argument for public action is some kind of market failure, such as public goods aspects or failures deriving from asymmetric information. In the public goods case, orthodox theory (Lindahl, 1919/1958) prescribes that the willingness to pay among the citizens should be monitored and used as a basis for charging the citizens once the optimal level of production has been determined. As is well known, this solution fails for both strategic and administrative reasons. Nonetheless, willingness-to-pay investigations have been carried out in a number of areas, for instance environment and culture, and sometimes give an indication of whether the willingness to pay is concentrated to a minority or spread across the whole population. In case the willingness-to-pay is concentrated, the argument for public intervention is weak, given that the group of interested citizens is likely to solve its transaction problems without assistance from the state. In the area of environmental policy, for instance, there are indications that the demand for clean air is spread across the population, whereas the demand for localised goods such as recreational areas or interesting biotopes is much more concentrated. These results are difficult to generalise, however (for an overview, see Herzing, 1999).

Empirical results of this kind open up the possibility of retreat from public commitments coupled to welfare gains. It appears that such gains are mainly to be found in limited policy areas, however. Neither environmental policy nor cultural policy is important from a public finance point of view; total state expenditures in Sweden on habitat protection and what can be labelled as elite culture purposes are well below 0.5 per cent of GDP. Further, the scope for total retreat in the welfare policy area that is the focus of the analysis seems very limited. For this reason, this policy alternative will not be explored further.

15.6   Institutional reform

Constitutional measures

A voluminous literature has analysed how the macro-political framework affects policy outcomes, in particular in the public finance area. Persson et al. (2000) report empirical findings, based on data from a large number of democracies, suggesting that presidential rule yields public expenditure levels that on the average lie about 10 per cent of GDP lower than parliamentary systems. Such policy proposals lie beyond the scope of the present discussion, and we will not pursue that line further.

Decentralisation, or fiscal federalism, is sometimes suggested as a means to limit government (Brennan and Buchanan, 1980). The empirical support for this idea is weak, however. The Nordic states have among the most autonomous local governments to be found anywhere, and simultaneously distinguish themselves by unusually large public sectors. Decentralisation of public power and the authority to tax may be justified for many reasons but appears to be an uncertain road to lowering public expenditures.

Institutional measures

At a lower level in the regulatory hierarchy, budgetary rules have proved to be important to fiscal policy outcomes across the world (von Hagen and Harden, 1994; Poterba, 1994; Stein et al., 1999; Lao-Araya, 1997). These results have led to more or less fundamental overhauls of the central government budget systems in Sweden (Molander, 1999b) and more recently in Norway. The basic aim has been to ensure a better decision structure to control the overall level of public expenditures via better managed (top-down) decision structures. Rattsø's results (chapter 5) indicate that similar gains can be made at the municipal level, possibly in conjunction with a judicious choice of tax base at the local level. The potential saving is of the order of 1–2 per cent of GDP.

The insurance offices responsible for the administration of social security are another candidate for institutional reform. In some countries these insurance systems are not managed by agencies but by autonomous legal entities, although publicly financed more or less completely (at least at the margin). The model originated in Belgium (whence the term 'Ghent model'), but has spread for instance to Sweden. Labour market insurance is managed by the trade unions whether the insured person is a member or not. The total resource flow is 15–20 per cent of GDP in Sweden.

The origin of the Ghent system is that the insurance started as a private initiative, which was eventually certified by the state and became subsidised. The level of subsidisation has risen over time, reaching about 90 per cent for unemployment insurance; the general social insurance system (sickness insurance etc.) relies on public resources altogether. As an argument for this unorthodox system of management, the historic origin is long since obsolete. The drawbacks of the system have become all the more evident over the years – unequal treatment of persons with identical characteristics, problems of auditing, and inadequate cost control. Equally important, the financing structure implies that the common-pool problem arising via public budgets is worsened. The problems of the sickness insurance system (see below) seem difficult to relieve without some sort of institutional reform.

Contracting out, vouchers etc.

At an even lower level of the institutional hierarchy we find experiments with contracting out, school vouchers, etc. As shown in chapter 5, the general experience from contracting out is on the whole positive, although the picture is somewhat mixed, in particular when quality dimensions are taken into account. It appears that problems of asymmetric information and the existence of alternatives play a central role in determining the outcome of these experiments. More specifically, services whose output can be easily measured in quantitative terms – refuse collection is a case in point – lend themselves to contracting fairly easily. In other services, such as education or care for the elderly, there are important dimensions that seem difficult or impossible to quantify. In such cases, it seems necessary to give citizens the choice of supplier, using some sort of vouchers. On the other hand, it must be underlined that voucher systems work best in the case of mandatory systems such as basic education. For insurance-type services such as care for the elderly, there remains the need for a gate-keeper and, by consequence, some sort of bureaucratic control.

In some areas, such as health care, where problems of information and distribution are numerous and difficult, a relatively straightforward way to increase pressure on producers is to publish reliable data on performance. This sort of yardstick competition can be efficient, although great care must of course be exercised when deciding precisely what indicators are relevant to form a representative picture of the service in question.

Monopoly situations, whether private or public, are not conducive to efficient management or consumer power. Contracting out and voucher systems are definitely important as instruments to challenge classical monopolies. But the design of such solutions must be carefully adapted to the situation at hand. Further, the purchasing power associated with a voucher is an open question; whereas voucher systems can be expected to increase competition and quality given the price level, they do not necessarily reduce the overall expenditure level.

15.7   Public services

A number of measures aiming at reduced public expenditure are based on increased private involvement in the public sector – in financing, supply or at the consumption stage. The general aim is to attain a better balance between costs and benefits of activities that are organised by the public sector. When user fees are introduced, part of the financing role is shifted to the user. This will improve resource allocation and force producers to adapt to the preferences of the population. Another alternative is to substitute private provision for public, in order to reduce costs. This can be implemented either by contracting out or by letting private produc-ers compete within a publicly managed system, with or without public producers. Increased private influence on consumption finally refers to systems where the users are given some freedom of choice, based on vouchers or, in the limit, a cash transfer such as child allowance. In this case the public sector retains the role of financing and possibly of provi-sion, but the possibility to choose can make supply better adapted to user preferences, and public entities more cost-efficient.

Education

Education is a key building block of the welfare state. Public involvement is justified by the objective of providing equal opportunities in education for all. In addition, it is well documented that the social return to edu-cation is high and that it is a main contributor to productivity growth.

No doubt this policy has had its impact, but international integration and mobility in particular raise issues on how to arrange education in the future. International integration makes education even more important. The base of production and trade is to a decreasing degree depending on natural resources, and increasingly relying on human capital. Empirical evidence also confirms that availability of well-educated labour is a strong factor when firms choose their locations (Midelfart-Knarvik et al., 2000). It is also well established empirically that the social return to research and development exceeds the private return (Salter and Martin, 1999), although opinions differ about the magnitude of the difference. Both of these facts give an argument for further public involvement in education and research. At the same time, however, international mobility is increasing which is particularly problematic for countries having a primarily public-financed education and training system. The most successful individuals in this system also tend to have the best opportunities to exploit the possibilities offered by migration, and to the extent this happens the public sector loses its investment in education and training. This gives an argument for less public involvement in the financing of education and training, especially higher education (see chapter 13).

These opposing forces create a policy dilemma. International integration increases the importance of human capital investments, but also the difficulties for society in reaping the benefit from such investments. As shown by Emmerson and Reed (chapter 6), the mix between private and public financing varies substantially across the OECD countries. European countries tend to have free higher education, whereas the USA belongs to the group where a more important part of the financing has private sources, and scholarships are used to compensate for part of the social bias in recruitment of students that would otherwise prevail. Nonetheless, the correlation between the salaries of fathers and sons is significantly higher in the USA than in Sweden (0.4 versus 0.25; Björklund and Jäntti, 1993), which indicates that this compensation is not sufficient to generate a comparable equalisation of opportunities. Introducing fees in the mandatory or near-mandatory parts of the educational system is not a relevant policy option; one may as well reduce child allowances or other subsidies to child families. A relevant option may be a fee for higher education. If user fees are payable only for the final (two or three) years of study for higher education, the risk of the human capital investment for the individual would be small. Moreover, recent analysis shows that public subsidies to higher education are actually negative from a distributional point of view, since subsidies are granted to individuals who tend to end up in the higher end of the income distribution (Danish Economic Council, 2001). Also the analysis by Emmerson and Reed (chapter 6) illustrates that the effects of subsidies are not always as expected; the transition from subsidies to loans in higher education have an equalising effect on the income distribution.

Private schools exist alongside public to a varying extent in many OECD countries (OECD, 1995), but fully-fledged voucher systems where both production and consumption are subject to private choice are less common. In any case, the experience from countries where voucher systems have been tested, such as the USA, is that such systems may be efficient in promoting quality (Chubb and Moe, 1990; Schneider et al., 2000) but have little to do with the problem of curbing expenditure.

Health care

Health care can be both publicly and privately supplied. It is worth stressing that private production can be in the form of non-profit institutions (for example, as in the USA), which addresses the argument often made that 'health should be beyond profit'. It is worth keeping in mind that health care has an obvious insurance dimension; the demand varies drastically between individuals and to a large extent for reasons not controlled by the individual. Individuals suffering from more serious health problems also tend to end up in the lower end of the income distribution because their opportunities in the labour markets are affected. This is not to say that there are no alternatives to tax financing; privately supplied insurance for primary health care is an alternative to be considered. Since serious adverse selection problems are present, it is important that such schemes be mandatory and negotiated collectively, for instance by trade unions (see the section on social insurance below). Such a scheme may reduce the common resource problem, while maintaining solidarity and a sufficient risk diversification across the population. Hence, the gains in incentives are obvious; much can be gained by prophylactic services of various kinds. The costs of primary care correspond to about 1 per cent of GDP.

A full-scale transfer to a Health Maintenance Organisation system is a more complicated operation, but even a limited privatisation such as the one indicated requires a careful design of the interface between the private and the public parts of the system. As the US example shows, the overall costs of the health care system may increase substantially if the wrong incentives are generated by the rules of the game.

The health care service is special in the sense that problems of asymmetric and incomplete information are numerous, implying that the patient is very imperfectly informed. Simple services, such as choosing the location where one's baby is to be born, can easily be left to individual choice, but such simple cases are exceptions. In most cases guidance from a physician, for example, is required to help the patient find her way to the appropriate service.

Child care

Child care is a heterogeneous service. Care of small children is a natural candidate for private production and consumer choice. The service is relatively simple, parents are competent consumers, and the threshold to entry is low. For somewhat older children, child care is close to primary schooling, and the arguments for and against private alternatives coincide with those advanced in the school debate.

Financing is a more complicated matter. Given that working parents contribute to the tax revenues, there is a collective interest in child care. Moreover, the tax-wedge tends to make 'out of family' solutions less attractive. Therefore a second-best case can be made for subsidies. Finding the appropriate level of the subsidy is more difficult. Until recently, fees accounted for between 15 and 20 per cent of the financing in Sweden. Charging full cost would make the service inaccessible to large groups, even if the cost were made deductible from income taxes. By contrast, the recent cap on day-care fees in Sweden has increased the subsidy level even further. The justification given has been to reduce marginal effects stemming from income-dependent fees, but given the substantial dead-weight losses – subsidies are given to households that would use the service anyway – current subsidy levels are almost certainly above optimum (see the discussion in chapter 6). In any case, at most 1 per cent of GDP is recoverable through fees, and such a system would have significant distribution effects.

Care for the elderly

The problems in supplying care for the elderly is in many respects similar to that of child care. Production is relatively easy to privatise, and there is a strong case for letting the clients choose. The choice should include mandatory elements in order to rule out moral hazard and time-inconsistency problems, and in some cases the individual may also prefer to enter binding contracts before getting too old. Financing, by contrast, is difficult. There is both a saving and an insurance element involved, since an individual is unable to predict in advance what kind of services he or she will need, and for how long. Fees have to be income- and asset-dependent if they are not to be detrimental to egalitarian objectives. Such a dependency would most likely have negative effects on saving behaviour.

The latter depends, critically, however on the expectations held by individuals concerning who has the main responsibility of insuring income. As the previously cited study by Forssell et al. (1999) indicates, individuals and households adapt their private saving to the rules defined by the state they are established in. This is precisely why reform initiatives have to be announced well in advance to affect retirement and pension plans.

Current total costs lie between 3 and 4 per cent of GDP, and 1 per cent at most seems to be the limit of the contribution from fees. At that level, there would most certainly be significant effects on saving, reported assets, etc., and it is questionable whether such a fee level is socio-economically efficient.

A mandatory public insurance – equivalent to an earmarked tax – is a solution that has been introduced in Germany and Japan. Even in the presence of such an insurance scheme, there is a need for a gatekeeper that decides on what services should be supplied in the individual case. The potential for expenditure cuts (leaving out for a moment the ageing-population problem) seems on the whole to be limited. Still a reform in that direction is worthwhile considering, as it may contribute to reducing the tax-wedge.

15.8   Social insurance

In the area of social insurance, the burden on the public budget can be eased either by reducing the extent to which the benefits are actually exploited or by transferring part of the responsibility for financing and providing the insurance to other agents.

Reducing social insurance expenditure

There are several ways to reduce the extent to which insurance programmes are used, including both general and specific measures. The general method is to change the rules defining the system in question. The soft way is to *open up new possibilities*. Recently, the Swedish parliament has legislated the right to continue working between sixty-five and sixty-seven years of age for those who want to do so. This is a first step towards increasing the actual retirement age. *Information* can be a way to change behaviour, for instance by altering physicians' practices in using the sickness insurance, or by stimulating more active job search in the case of unemployment.

The next step is to *change incentives* in order to make the non-use alternative more attractive compared to the use alternative. Recent empirical evidence shows that retirement can be delayed by making continued work more attractive compared to retiring (Gruber and Wise, 1999), and that lower remuneration rates in the labour market insurance lead to more active job search (Carling et al., 1999), etc.

When changing incentives is not enough, *basic restrictions* can be altered. Increasing the retirement age by a year or two is way to improve the public financial balance, even if there is some choice involved via early-retirement schemes (Palme and Svensson, 1999). A move in this direction seems logical in light of the fact that life-length is increasing.

The decision to retire

Turning to the more specific discussion, the *pension system* obviously plays a key role in the future of public expenditure. There has been a fairly rapid decrease of actual (as opposed to the official) retirement age in OECD countries, although more so in some countries than in others. As indicated above, rules and incentives are central to the behaviour. The analysis by Palme and Svensson (chapter 9) shows that the Swedish pension has not accomplished the strong improvement in incentives that was originally envisaged. The financial stability of the new system is better, in particular with respect to unfavourable macroeconomic scenarios, but the desire to equalise material wellbeing reduces incentives to further effort substantially. The conclusion therefore seems to be that raising the formal retirement age is the only possibility to improve the financial balance significantly. For other OECD countries, notably Belgium, France, Italy and the Netherlands, the picture is different; here, improving incentives to continued work appears both a possible and necessary means of improving the situation.

Increasing the retirement age by one year by deferring the whole system of benefits improves tax revenues somewhat but not much, because the labour supply in the age group between sixty and sixty-four is already limited. The gain is mainly on the expenditure side, and the total net improvement equals about 0.5 per cent of GDP.

Sickness insurance

The load on the *sickness insurance* system as measured by the average number of sick-days has swung violently in Sweden during the last ten years. The figure fell drastically during the first half of the 1990s, both because of lower absence and because employers took over responsibility for the first two weeks of absence. In recent years, public expenditure has doubled and now corresponds to about 2.5 per cent of GDP, excluding employers' sick-leave payment. There is obviously no single physiological factor that accounts for this drastic increase, and countermeasures must be sought over a wide area. Sickness insurance is a medical treatment, and like other treatments it can have side-effects – in this case loss of social networks, competence and self-confidence. It is a well-documented fact that prescription practices among physicians differ widely, and can be altered without jeopardising patients' health (Englund et al., 2000; Arrelöv et al., 2001). Also economic incentives, such as introducing more waiting days, can be considered; these should not be accumulated at the beginning of the period of absence but appear at regular intervals, for instance every two weeks.

A conscious and systematic effort to bring down the expenditure level could reasonably yield between 0.5 and 1 per cent of GDP. Privatisation of traffic-related absenteeism can yield a small contribution (see below).

Unemployment insurance

Unemployment insurance, including supplementary education programmes, consumes about 2 per cent of GDP in Sweden. Recently, this insurance has been subject to reform. The ceiling of the remuneration has been raised, but simultaneously the requirement on accepting job offers has been sharpened. A trade-off between efficiency of the insurance and income security is involved here. The incentive structure can be strengthened by reducing benefit levels, eligibility, etc., but such proposals are sometimes detrimental also to individuals who are doing their best to return to the labour market. Requirements on active job-search or supplementary work, for instance for the municipality, reduce the attractiveness of exploiting the unemployment insurance system (Nichols and Zeckhauser, 1982; Besley and Coate, 1992), and this may often be more acceptable than affecting incentives via reduced benefit levels. In order to ensure legitimacy, activation programmes have to be meaningful. Obviously, measures that at the same time improve the level of competence are to be preferred. A risk is that such a scheme develops into a *de facto* expansion of public employment or other ways of reclassifying unemployed.

The most pressing reforms here seem to be institutional and financial. The insurance system is managed by the trade unions, whose main interest, given the member stock, is to limit the labour supply. At the same time, unemployment has no financial implications at the margin, given that wage earners' contributions are independent of unemployment figures and account for only about 10 per cent of total expenditure. Persons who have not been genuinely interested in full-time employment have abused so-called part-time unemployment. The insurance scheme has also been used jointly by employers and trade unions to bring about early *de facto* retirement. There have also been formal complaints about the way in which the insurance cases are handled; equal cases have been treated unequally, and the right to appeal has been crippled because of administrative errors (LO, 1999).

Basic principles imply that the smallest distortions of the unemployment insurance scheme for wage determination are achieved when the insurance scheme has the same level of centralisation (decentralisation) as wage setting itself. This has to be weighed against the fact that a centralised scheme achieves the most in respect to risk diversification. In a process where wage formation is becoming more decentralised (Calmfors et al., 2001) it is thus natural to question whether the unemployment insurance scheme is still organised in the best way possible.

A transfer of the responsibility for managing the insurance to an agency such as the National Labour Market Administration would seem natural. Raising the financial contribution of the wage earners to the insurance – at least at the margin – would improve incentives to responsible behaviour in the labour market. Differentiating the premium across sectors can also be considered; the present distribution of the economic burden subsidises sectors with high unemployment and leads to higher unemployment. About 1 per cent of GDP would seem recoverable via an institutional reform and increased co-financing from the insured.

Welfare accounts

Welfare accounts (chapter 11) exploit the fact that a large fraction of the redistribution in current social security systems concerns redistribution over the life cycle rather than between individuals. By tying flows to individuals and focusing on lifetime rather than annual redistribution, incentives at the individual level can be improved. Social security comprises elements of insurance, redistribution and saving. The idea of welfare accounts works best when the element of saving dominates. In the insurance context, the improvement comes at the price of increased co-insurance premia.

As shown by Fölster et al. in chapter 11, there is scope for considerable improvement of incentives while largely – although not fully – maintaining the Pareto restriction at the aggregate level. In other words, most but not all citizens could benefit in absolute terms from the changes proposed. Nonetheless, there may be problems both of legitimacy and incentives in a welfare account system. Even in a society consisting of individuals with identical risk panoramas, different persons will experience different outcomes for purely random reasons. Over the life cycle, some will, for instance, be ill more frequently than others. Because of differences in genetic endowments and other factors beyond the individual's own control, outcomes will differ even more. The legitimacy of an account system with no insurance element above a minimum pension level might be called into question.

A second problem, acknowledged by the authors, is that the cost to the individual of some contingency would depend on how much has been accumulated in the account. Someone who falls ill early in life would benefit from the floor in the insurance, whereas someone to whom this happens later in life is expected to carry a larger part of the burden herself.

An incentive problem arises for those who for various reasons find themselves with large negative account positions during their active period. A low-income earner in this category may have small possibilities to affect her pension, in which case the account discourages effort rather than stimulating it.

The effect on the public expenditure level is indirect and depends on incentive effects. The calculus in chapter 11 indicates potentially large gains, but more research into the incentive effects as well as a more precise description of the regulatory framework of the accounts is necessary before more precise estimates can be made.

Welfare accounts represent a highly interesting innovation in the area of welfare policy, which is likely to find a place in the overall design of welfare policy in the future. In areas where the saving element dominates, such as education, a reform would seem relatively unproblematic, and is in fact already on the political agenda. In other areas, more research and elaboration are needed before they can be given a prominent role. The effect on expenditure and tax levels would depend on how widely accounts would be applied, but is potentially significant.

Transferring responsibilities

As shown by Söderström and Rikner (chapter 7), privatisation to the *individual* level is on the whole a cumbersome operation in the area of social insurance, the main obstacle being large variations in risk and adverse selection. Privatisation leads to differentiation of premia, which is justified in terms of improving the incentive structure but comes at the potential cost of less risk diversification. Work injury insurance is perhaps the best example of an insurance for which privatisation would work and be beneficial, and privatisation of this insurance has also occurred in several Nordic countries in recent years. Insurance covering hospital care and sickness absence related to traffic accident is another candidate, the costs corresponding to about 0.2 to 0.3 per cent of GDP. The total privatisation potential would thus amount to between 0.5 and 1 per cent of GDP.

Becoming old is not a stochastic event like becoming ill; ageing can be expected from the time of birth. The welfare society has a strong interest in ensuring that old people have a decent standard of living. This can be achieved via a public pension scheme of the pay-as-you-go type, but as is well known, such schemes are very vulnerable to demographic shifts. Leaving saving for pensions to individuals' discretion would not be a viable solution in a welfare society for the obvious time-inconsistency problem – those who choose not to save will be bailed out in a society with strong egalitarian preferences. Therefore such a system has to be mandatory to ensure that all are covered, and to prevent adverse selection problems from undermining the functioning of private markets. This will lower tax distortions (see Belan and Pestieau, 1999). But also premium reserve systems are vulnerable; demographic and economic shocks are liable to create undesired swings in outcomes. Hybrid systems resting on the three pillars of public commitments, collective pension programs and private saving therefore seem to be the solution to which pension structures should converge. As shown by Pestieau (chapter 10), hybrid systems emerge naturally as efficient solutions when redistributive goals are taken into account.

One way to relieve the state of part of its financial burden is through *negotiated insurance schemes* at the trade union level (chapter 8). Most problems of adverse selection are solved if the insurance is collective. A negotiated insurance scheme has the attraction that decisions about benefits are made at the same level as wage determination, eliminating important incentive problems arising when insurance is centralised and wage formation decentralised (Andersen, 2001). The potential is large, several per cent of GDP, depending on where the ceiling of the public insurance scheme is set. As a reference point, in the Netherlands negotiated insurance schemes correspond to about 5 per cent of GDP. There are some adverse effects on distribution (chapter 8), but the joint effect of public and negotiated insurance must be taken into account when judging whether the overall solution is acceptable. The risk of such a system is that it will project differences in labour market performance into pension status, but such differences are already present, stemming directly from the design principles of Scandinavian welfare policy. The critical point is the treatment of people whose attachment to the labour market through life is weak or absent, a group for whom an obligation still rests on the welfare state.

15.9   Public debt policy

Financing increasing expenditures and decreasing revenues by borrowing is not a viable policy option. Flodén's analysis (chapter 14) shows clearly that there are no arguments for relaxing fiscal policy in the medium term to allow for a higher public debt. If anything, the public debt should be reduced currently in order to make room for accommodation later on, but the cost associated with a non-optimal policy is not very high as long as the public debt is not too large. For highly indebted countries such as Italy, there are strong arguments for strengthening fiscal discipline already in the short- and medium-term perspective.

15.10   Synthesis

Table 15.1 attempts to summarise the previous results as a basis for the policy discussion. The contributions from various measures are not necessarily additive, but the figures presented nonetheless give an indication of the orders of magnitude involved. It can be concluded that the public-financial gap arising from internationalisation, demographic change and the requirements of an optimal debt policy amount to between 6 and 10 per cent of GDP, with 8 per cent as a best guess. It appears that the gap can be closed by a suitable combination of measures available, but none of these countermeasures is easy, and some may come at the price of a limited increase in inequality. Some measures imply genuine cost reductions, such as reduced slack in public service production, whereas others imply that costs are transferred from the state to other agents. In the latter case, the justification is that incentives are improved at the same time as the burden on the public sector is eased.

It is natural to ask what happens if there is no change in current policies. Is it possible to live with a tax ratio that is about eight percentage points higher than today's, or around 60 per cent in the average? As we pointed out in the introductory chapter, it is difficult to prove a significant relationship between tax ratios and growth rates, but there are nonetheless numerous micro studies that illustrate the importance of incentives for the willingness to work. The socio-economic losses may thus be important even though the effect on growth rates is difficult to identify. What then do we know about the connection between expenditure or tax ratios and employment? Within the OECD area, the correlation between public expenditures and the employment ratio is weakly negative (see Scharpf and Schmidt, 2000). One reason why the correlation is weak is that the employment ratio is defined as the ratio of the population between twenty and sixty-five years in the labour force, consequently not

Table 15.1 *Pressure on the public balance and measures to counter them*

Pressure on the public balance	Estimated pressure (% of GDP)	Comments
Revenue losses from increased mobility	1–3.5	Some costs incurred even in the absence of mobility
Demographic change	5–6	
Optimal debt policy	>0	Costs of non-optimal policy limited
Total	6–10	

Countermeasures	Estimated contribution (% GDP)	Comments
Institutional change		
Municipal level (strengthened budget process, property tax base)	1–2	
State-managed social insurance	1	Unified application of regulatory framework
Services		
Reduced subsidies in higher education (loans)	<1	Reduces income spread
Fees in health care	small	
Fees in child care	<1	Distributional or marginal effects
Fees in care for the elderly	<1	Possible effects on saving
Social insurance		
Pensions (increasing retirement age by 1 year)	0.5	2 years yield 1 per cent
Unemployment insurance (increased co-financing)	1	Improved incentives
Privatisation of insurance against work injuries and traffic-related injuries	0.5–1	Improved incentives
Mandatory primary care insurance	1	
Negotiated insurance in all areas	several	Depending on the ceiling of the public insurance

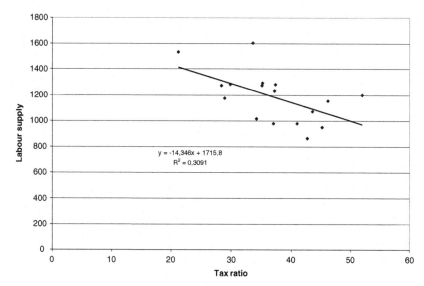

Figure 15.1 The relationship between tax ratio (percentage of GDP) and labour supply (average number of hours per year per person in working age)
Source: Own calculations based on OECD (2001), Statistical Annex.

compensating for part-time labour. A better alternative is to compare the actual number of hours worked, as they are reported in the labour force surveys (OECD, 2001). There are differences in the way these surveys are performed that can make the results not fully comparable, but there is no reason to assume that the comparison is systematically biased by such differences.

The relationship that emerges is illustrated in figure 15.1. As can be seen from the diagram, there is a fairly clear relationship; a higher tax ratio yields a lower average employment figure, and the R^2 value is just above 0.3. At the same time it should be noted that single countries can deviate from the average relationship. Sweden has a higher labour intensity than expected given its tax ratio, depending on a relatively coherent policy of tying welfare benefits to labour force participation; a substantial fraction of public expenditures – maternal leave, subsidised child care etc. – are used precisely to stimulate that participation. On the other hand, this relatively favourable position makes it more difficult to mobilise labour further, when the public sector becomes subject to external financial pressure. It is also important to stress that the diagram is based on historical experience. If, for instance, mobility increases, problems will increase as well.

On the basis of the relationship estimated in figure 15.1 it is possible to calculate roughly the consequences of raising the tax ratio by six to eight percentage points. The expected average labour supply would decrease by about 100 hours per year. In fact, tax revenues reach their maximum in absolute figures around a tax ratio of about 60 per cent; if the tax ratio were increased, as might happen inadvertently during an economic downturn, tax revenues would decrease. By consequence, even if a tax ratio of 60 per cent can be implemented, the price in the form of reduced private consumption would be rather high. How this would be perceived would of course depend on the general economic development during the coming decades. As chapter 3 has shown, the picture is not altogether free of problems.

Summarising, a no-change policy, leading to an increase in tax ratio by about eight percentage points, can be expected to reduce labour supply in a situation where the main requirement is rather that labour supply be increased. Such a development is of course to be avoided.

We repeat that the time for action is limited. Policy change is a slow process, and some of the measures to be considered are such that households must be given ample time to adapt. Great flexibility is required in the choice of policy instruments, and governments must be prepared to learn from other countries unhampered by their welfare-political heritage.

References

Adema, W., 2001, *Net social expenditure* (2nd edition), DEELSA/ELSA/WD(2001)5, Paris: OECD.

Andersen, T. M., 2001, 'Welfare policies, labour markets, and international integration', *International Tax and Public Finance* (forthcoming).

Arrelöv, B., Borgquist, L., Ljungberg, D. and Svärdsudd, K., 2001, 'Do GPs sicklist patients to a lesser extent than other physician categories? A population-based study', *Family Practice*, 18, 4, 393–8.

Batljan, I. and Lagergren, M., 2000, *Kommer det att finnas en hjälpande hand?* (Will there be a helping hand?), background report no. 8 to the Long Term Survey, Ministry of Finance, Stockholm.

Belan, P. and Pestieau. P., 1999, 'Privatizing social security: a critical assessment', *Geneva Papers on Risk and Insurance*, 24, 114–30.

Besley, T. and Coate, S., 1992, 'Workfare versus welfare: incentive arguments for work requirements in poverty-alleviation programmes', *American Economic Review*, 82, 249–61.

Björklund, A. and Jäntti, M., 1993, *Intergenerational mobility in Sweden compared to the United States*, working paper 4, Institute for Social Research, Stockholm University.

Boeri, T., Börsch-Supan, A. and Tabellini, G., 2001, 'Would you like to shrink the welfare state? The opinions of European citizens', *Economic Policy*, 32, 7–50.

Brennan, G. and Buchanan, J. M., 1980, *The Power to Tax: Analytical Foundations of a Fiscal Constitution*, Cambridge: Cambridge University Press.

Calmfors, L., Booth, A., Burda, M., Checci, D., Naylor, R. and Visser, J., 2001, 'The future of collective bargaining in Europe', in T. Boeri, A. Brugiavini and L. Calmfors (eds.), *The Role of Unions in the Twenty-First Century*, Oxford: Oxford University Press.

Carling, K., Holmlund, B. and Vejsiu, A., 1999, *Do Benefit Cuts Boost Job Findings?* IFAU working paper 8, Institute for Labour Market Policy Evaluation, Uppsala (forthcoming in the *Economic Journal*).

Chubb, J. E. and Moe, T. M., 1990, *Politics, Markets and America's Schools*, Washington DC: Brookings Institution.

Danish Economic Council, 2001, *The Danish Economy*, Autumn.

Englund, L., Tibblin, G. and Svärdsudd, K., 2000, 'Variations in sick-listing practice', *Scandinavian Journal of Primary Health Care*, 18, 48–52.

Esping-Andersen, G., 1990, *The Three Worlds of Welfare Capitalism*, Princeton: Princeton University Press.

—1999, *Social Foundations of Postindustrial Economies*, Oxford: Oxford University Press.

EU Economic Policy Committee, 2001, *Budgetary Changes Posed by Ageing Populations*, EPC/ECFIN/655/01-EN final, October.

Forssell, Å., Medelberg, M. and Ståhlberg, A.-C., 1999, 'Unequal transfers to the elderly in different countries – equal disposable incomes', *European Journal of Social Security*, 1, 63–89.

Gruber, J. and Wise, D. A. (eds.), 1999, *Social Security and Retirement around the World*, Chicago: University of Chicago Press.

Hagen, J. von and Harden, I., 1994, 'National budget processes and fiscal performance', *European Economy, Reports and Studies*, 3, 311–418.

Hansen, H., 2000, *Elements of Social Security*, The Danish National Institute of Social Research Report, 00: 07.

Herzing, M., 1999, 'The willingness to pay for public goods', mimeo, Centre for Business and Policy Studies, Stockholm.

Johansson, L., 2001, 'Fiscal implications of migration' (work in progress), Department of Economics, University of Stockholm.

Kangas, O., 1997, 'Self-interest and the common good...', *Journal of Socio-Economics*, 26, 5, 475–94.

Kautto, M., Bjorn Hvinden, J. F., Kvist, J. and Uusitalo, H., 2001, *Nordic Welfare States in a European Context*, London: Routledge.

Korpi, W. and Palme, J., 1998, 'The paradox of redistribution and strategies of equality', *American Sociological Review*, 65, 661–87.

Lao-Araya, K., 1997, 'The fiscal constitution of a developing country: the case of Thailand', PhD thesis, Indiana University, Bloomington.

Lindahl, E., 1919/1958, 'Die Gerechtigkeit der Besteurung', English translation: 'Just taxation – a positive solution', in R. A. Musgrave and A. T. Peacock, 1958, *Classics in the Theory of Public Finance*, London: Macmillan.

LO, 1999, *Arbetslösheten i praktiken* (Unemployment in Practice), mimeo by S. M. Andersson, Swedish Trade Union Corporation, Stockholm.

Midelfart-Knarvik, K., Overman, H. G., Redding, S. J. and Venables, A. I., 2000, *The Location of European Industry, Report prepared for the Directorate General for Economic and Financial Affairs*, European Commission, Brussels, working paper 142.

Molander, P., 1999a, *En effektivare välfärdspolitik* (Towards a more efficient welfare policy), Stockholm: SNS Förlag.

—1999b, 'Reforming budgetary institutions: Swedish experiences', in R. Strauch and J. von Hagen (eds.), *Institutions, Politics, and Fiscal Policy*, Boston: Kluwer.

Nichols, A. L. and Zeckhauser, R. J., 1982, 'Targeting transfers through restrictions on recipients', *American Economic Review*, Papers and Proceedings, 72, 372–81.

OECD, 1995, *Education at a Glance*, Paris: OECD.

—1998, *Maintaining Prosperity in an Ageing Society*, Paris: OECD.

—2001, *OECD Employment Outlook*, June, Paris: OECD.

Palme, M. and Svensson, I., 1999, 'Social security, occupational pensions, and retirement in Sweden', in J. Gruber and D. A. Wise (eds.), *Social Security and Retirement around the World*, Chicago: Chicago University Press.

Persson, T., Roland, G. and Tabellini, G., 2000, 'Comparative politics and public finance', *Journal of Political Economy*, 108, 6, 1121–61.

Pierson, C., 1998, *Beyond the Welfare State: The New Political Economy of Welfare*, London: Polity Press (2nd ed.).

Poterba, J., 1994, 'State responses to fiscal crises: the effects of budgetary institutions and policies', *Journal of Political Economy*, 102, 799–821.

Salter, A. J. and Martin, B. R., 1999, 'The economic benefits of publicly funded basic research: a critical review', SPRU, electronic working paper series no. 34 (www.sussex.ac.uk/spru).

Scharpf, F. W., 2000, 'Economic changes, vulnerabilities and institutional capabilities', ch. 1 in F. W. Scharpf and V. A. Schmidt (eds.), *Welfare and Work in the Open Economy, Vol. I: From Vulnerability to Competitiveness*, Oxford: Oxford University Press.

Scharpf, F. W. and V. A. Schmidt (eds.), 2000, *Welfare and Work in the Open Economy, Vol. I: From Vulnerability to Competitiveness*, Oxford: Oxford University Press.

Schneider, M., Teske, P. and Marschall, M., 2000, *Choosing Schools: Consumer Choice and the Quality of American Schools*, Princeton: Princeton University Press.

Stein, E. et al., 1999, 'Institutional arrangements and fiscal performance: the Latin American experience', in J. Poterba and J. von Hagen (eds.), *Fiscal Institutions and Fiscal Performance*, Chicago: Chicago University Press.

Svallfors, S., 1999, *Mellan risk och tilltro* (Between risk and trust), Umeå: Umeå Studies in Sociology.

Index